TWO MEDITERRANEAN WORLDS

Other volumes in the Globalization and Autonomy series:

Global Ordering: Institutions and Autonomy in a Changing World
Edited by Louis W. Pauly and William D. Coleman

Renegotiating Community: Interdisciplinary Perspectives, Global Contexts
Edited by Diana Brydon and William D. Coleman

Empires and Autonomy: Moments in the History of Globalization
Edited by Stephen M. Streeter, John C. Weaver, and William D. Coleman

*Unsettled Legitimacy: Political Community, Power, and Authority
in a Global Era*
Edited by Steven Bernstein and William D. Coleman

Cultural Autonomy: Frictions and Connections
Edited by Petra Rethmann, Imre Szeman, and William D. Coleman

Indigenous Peoples and Autonomy: Insights for a Global Age
Edited by Mario Blaser, Ravi de Costa, Deborah McGregor,
and William D. Coleman

Property, Territory, Globalization: Struggles over Autonomy
Edited by William D. Coleman

Globalization and Autonomy: Conversing across Disciplines
Diana Brydon, William D. Coleman, and Louis W. Pauly

See also the *Globalization and Autonomy Online Compendium* at
www.globalautonomy.ca

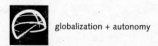 globalization + autonomy

TWO MEDITERRANEAN

Diverging Paths of Globalization and Autonomy

WORLDS

Edited by Yassine Essid and William D. Coleman
Translated by Käthe Roth

UBCPress · Vancouver · Toronto

20 19 18 17 16 15 14 13 12   5 4 3 2 1

Printed in Canada on ancient-forest-free paper (100% post-consumer recycled) that is processed chlorine- and acid-free.

Library and Archives Canada Cataloguing in Publication

Two Mediterranean worlds: diverging paths of globalization and autonomy / edited by Yassine Essid and William D. Coleman; translated by Käthe Roth.

(Globalization and autonomy, 1913-7494)
Translation of: Deux Méditerranées: les voies de la mondialisation et de l'autonomie.
Includes bibliographical references and index.
Issued also in electronic formats.
ISBN 978-0-7748-2318-0

1. Globalization – Mediterranean Region. 2. Autonomy – Mediterranean Region. 3. Mediterranean Region – Politics and government – 1945-. 4. Mediterranean Region – Social conditions – 1945-. 5. Mediterranean Region – Economic conditions–1945-. 6. Mediterranean Region – Intellectual life. I. Essid, Yassine II. Coleman, William D. (William Donald). III. Series: Globalization and autonomy

DE100.D4813 2012   909'.09822   C2012-900555-X

Canadä

UBC Press gratefully acknowledges the financial support for our publishing program of the Government of Canada through the Book Publishing Industry Development Program (BPIDP), and of the Canada Council for the Arts, and the British Columbia Arts Council.

UBC Press
The University of British Columbia
2029 West Mall
Vancouver, BC V6T 1Z2
www.ubcpress.ca

Contents

The Globalization and Autonomy Series: Dialectical Relationships in the Contemporary World

THE VOLUMES IN THE Globalization and Autonomy series offer the results from an interdisciplinary Major Collaborative Research Initiative (MCRI) funded by the Social Sciences and Humanities Research Council of Canada (SSHRC). SSHRC set up the MCRI program to provide a vehicle to support larger projects with research objectives requiring collaboration among researchers from different universities and across a range of disciplines. The MCRI on Globalization and Autonomy began in April 2002. The research team involved forty co-investigators from twelve universities across Canada and another twenty academic contributors from outside Canada, including scholars from Australia, Brazil, China, Denmark, France, Germany, Slovenia, Taiwan, the United Kingdom, and the United States. Drawing on additional funding from the International Development Research Centre (IDRC), the project became affiliated with a separate interdisciplinary research team of twenty-eight scholars, the Groupe d'Études et de Recherches Interdisciplinaires sur la Méditerranée (GERIM). GERIM is based in Tunisia and includes members from France, Spain, Jordan, and Lebanon as well. Scholars from the following disciplines participated in the project: anthropology, comparative literature, cultural studies, economics, English literature, geography, history, music, philosophy, political science, and sociology.

The project was conceived, designed, and implemented to carry out interdisciplinary research. We endeavoured to put disciplinary-based theories and conceptual frameworks into dialogue with one another, with a view to developing new theories and understandings of human societies. Four conditions needed to be met if research was to be done in this way. First, we brought humanities and social science disciplines into a relationship of mutual influence, where perspectives were integrated without subordinating one to another. To achieve this integration, the team agreed on a set of core research objectives informed by existing writings on globalization and autonomy. Members developed a number of research questions designed to address these objectives and a research plan that would permit them to address these questions in a focused, systematic way. Second, team members individually were encouraged to think inside disciplines other than their own and to respect differences across disciplines in terms of how the object of knowledge is constructed. Third, team members were selected to ensure that the research was carried out using multiple methodologies. Finally, faced with researching the complex relationships involved in globalization, an interdisciplinary approach meant that our work would be necessarily pluritheoretical. We held to the view that theories would be most effective when, in addition to applying ideas rigorously, their proponents acknowledged the limitations of any particular theoretical perspective and consciously set out to cross boundaries and use other, sometimes seemingly incommensurable, perspectives.

To ensure intellectual integration from the start, team members agreed on this approach at the first full meeting of the project and committed to the following core objective: *to investigate the relationship between globalization and the processes of securing and building autonomy.* To this end, we sought to refine understanding of these concepts and of the historical evolution of the processes inherent in both of them, given the contested character of their content, meaning, and symbolic status. Given that *globalization* is the term currently employed to describe the contemporary moment, we attempted to:

- determine the opportunities globalization might create and the constraints globalization might place on individuals and communities seeking to secure and build autonomy
- evaluate the extent to which individuals and communities might be able to exploit these opportunities and to overcome these constraints
- assess the opportunities for empowerment that globalization might create for individuals and communities seeking to secure and to build autonomy

- determine how the autonomy available to individuals and communities might permit them to contest, reshape, or engage globalization.

In seeking to address the core objectives for the project, we moved our research in three interrelated directions. First, we accepted that globalization and autonomy have deep historical roots. What is happening today in the world is in many ways continuous with what has taken place in the past. Thus, the burden of a contemporary examination of globalization and autonomy is to assess what is new and what has changed. Second, the dynamics of the relationship between globalization and autonomy are related to a series of important changes in the locations of power and authority. Finally, the globalization-autonomy dynamic plays out in the construction and reconstruction of identities, the nature and value of community, and the articulation of autonomy in and through cultures and discrete institutions. In each of these three areas, the team developed and agreed to answer core questions to provide clear direction for the research. The full text of the questions is available at http://globalization.mcmaster.ca/ga/ga81.htm.

Over successive annual meetings of the team, our research coalesced around the following themes: institutions and global ordering; democracy and legitimacy; continuity and rupture in the history of globalization and autonomy; history, property rights, and capitalism; community; culture; the situation and struggles of indigenous peoples; and the Mediterranean region as a microcosm of North-South relations. The researchers addressing these themes tended to be drawn from several disciplines, leading to interdisciplinary dialogue within each thematic group. The themes then crystallized into separate research problems, which came to be addressed by the volumes in the series. While these volumes were taking form, the project team also developed an online publication, the *Globalization and Autonomy Online Compendium* (see next page), which makes our findings available to the general public through research summaries; a glossary of key concepts, organizations, people, events, and places; and a comprehensive bibliography. The ultimate objective of all of these publications is to produce an integrated corpus of outstanding research that provides an in-depth study of the varying relationships between globalization and autonomy.

Globalization and Autonomy Online Compendium

Readers of this volume may also be interested in the *Globalization and Autonomy Online Compendium* (available at www.globalautonomy.ca). The *Compendium* is a collective publication by the team of Canadian and international scholars who have been part of the SSHRC Major Collaborative Research Initiative that gave rise to the volumes in the Globalization and Autonomy series. Through the *Compendium,* the team is making the results of their research available to a wide public audience. Team members have prepared a glossary of hundreds of short articles on relevant persons, places, organizations, events, and key concepts and have compiled an extensive searchable bibliographical database. Short summaries of the chapters in other volumes of the Globalization and Autonomy series can also be found in the *Compendium,* along with position papers and peer-reviewed research articles on globalization and autonomy issues.

Preface to the English Edition

THIS BOOK WAS COMPLETED before the events of the so-called Arab Spring began in December 2010 in the country of Tunisia, the home of the large majority of the scholars in this book. The revolutions for change that broke out in Tunisia, Egypt, and Libya, on the south shore of the Mediterranean Sea, reflect both the effects of globalization processes discussed in this book and the desire for collective autonomy and individual autonomy. In surveying the differences between the wealthier European Union states and the poorer states on the southern shore, this volume reveals the underlying causes of demands for change: the lack of responsible, democratic governance; economic stagnation; cultural insecurity and loss; religious differences and a growing "global Islam"; problems in the education system; and a growing number of educated but unemployed young adults. This book is, therefore, a useful source of analysis and data for understanding why populations living on the southern shore of the Mediterranean might demand profound change. By tracing the growing influence of a form of "global Islam," this volume also points to the kinds of conflicts that the Arab Spring precipitated between those who want religion to have more influence in the governance of society and those who look towards more secular forms of government.

William Coleman

Acknowledgments

THE VOLUME EDITORS WOULD like to express their deep gratitude to Kristina Maud Bergeron for her editorial assistance in preparing the final manuscript for the French-language edition. William Coleman would like to thank the Canada Research Chairs program, which supported his contributions to this volume. He would also like to thank Emily Andrew, senior editor, and Peter Milroy, director, of UBC Press for their continued support and enthusiasm for the Globalization and Autonomy Series. He appreciates their willingness to move ahead with the translation of this book from its original French edition. The Press engaged an outstanding translator for this task, Kathe Roth. Her professionalism, her immense translating skills, and her ability to capture the essence of this book are appreciated. Finally, William Coleman would like to express his gratitude to Holly Keller and her colleagues for their usual high standards and advice when it came to the process of publishing this book.

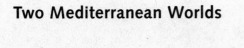

Two Mediterranean Worlds

Introduction

Yassine Essid and
William D. Coleman

BECAUSE OUR GROUP ENCOURAGES openness to all fields of knowledge — as the name Groupe d'études et de recherches interdisciplinaires sur la Méditerranée (GERIM; Interdisciplinary Research Group on the Mediterranean) indicates — the members of the team that wrote this book work in a wide range of disciplines. This heterogeneity enabled us to place the social and human sciences in an interactive relationship in which perspectives are integrated without one being subordinated to any other. At the methodological level, the team members agreed on this fundamental project requirement. We then had to ensure members' intellectual engagement and that we could reach consensus on our research subjects and objectives. Although everyone concurred on the significance of the phenomenon called globalization — a historically unprecedented phenomenon, since the entire world has never before been subjected to a single economic, political, and cultural system — how it interacts with autonomy seemed unclear, if not completely opaque.

With regard to the Mediterranean, the idea was to form a team that was as representative as possible of the region, including both the north shore and the south shore of the geographic basin. Colleagues from Tunisia, France, Spain, Lebanon, and Jordan were recruited and brought into the project. A pluridisciplinary team of twenty-two researchers was built comprising economists, historians, anthropologists, a philosopher, an Islamologist, a specialist in Judaic studies, a musicologist, and a psychiatrist. We learned to collaborate and have discussions without regard for our respective statuses of professor, associate professor, assistant professor, or doctoral student.

We also had to make sure that our team was consistent, united, and capable of envisaging the research subject without a particular political or emotional attitude. We had to gradually convince our colleagues to reconstruct reality without prejudices or preconceptions. This was a difficult task, since the subject, globalization, tended to resonate in the minds of our researchers, especially the younger ones, with Americanization, neo-imperialism, Westernization, and similar terms. They were asked to read the numerous studies made available by the project designers in order to orient themselves in relation to the work of their transatlantic colleagues, notably on the concepts of globalization and autonomy.

Finally, we had to consider how this volume would contribute to the existing books in this series, for it would be justified only if it offered a different perspective and point of view to the project. The notion of point of view should be thought of here as the *place from which one speaks,* the *place at which one situates oneself to speak.* This place is the Mediterranean region.

Why the Mediterranean region? Because we all saw it as a privileged ground for investigation on both the cultural and geo-strategic levels in a project that, by definition, was intended to be all-encompassing. Moreover, studying ongoing globalization, insofar as it is taking place beyond our control, would be both rich and edifying in the Mediterranean context. For these reasons, we decided to devote ourselves entirely to this space, to make it the exclusive subject of an economic, cultural, and historical investigation. A good number of questions that are now vital for the future of the world have their original point of focus in the Mediterranean. Even if it is not on the leading edge of the globalization movement, the Mediterranean is at the centre of the world's concerns.

Dealing with globalization — economic, political, and cultural — and autonomy in the Mediterranean first means distancing ourselves somewhat from the globalist or universal-focused discourse that presumes that all of humanity can be integrated by doing away with the economic, political, and cultural conditions specific to each country or region. Whereas in Northern countries we can easily credit agents with a capacity for rational economic behaviour, in Southern countries economic transactions are still largely commanded by the state or dictated by social or familial obligations. Between the universal capacity that constitutes the norm in Western democracies in the North and the particular realities of each Southern country are interposed institutions whose actions are based on the assumptions of neoclassic economics; these assumptions have been more or less imposed on the entire world, and we know what the results have been. We deduce from this observation that the attitude towards globalization cannot be identical in every state.

Taking the Mediterranean as a reference, we can make the following remarks. First, there are states that have achieved modernization but not modernity: they are characterized by an absence of civil society, an attachment to national interests, entrenched ideas about sovereignty and borders, and a government that holds a persistent monopoly on legitimized violence. Second, there are postmodern states, Western-type democracies, that have rejected the use of force to settle their disputes; in these states, security is based in large part on transparency of foreign policy and interdependent economies.

There are, therefore, many differences between countries on the north shore of the Mediterranean and countries on the south shore, and these are the main focus of this book. A number of peoples live around the Mediterranean. Plato would have said that they are like frogs around a pond: they share a common past, but historical circumstances — invasions, religion, colonization, and economic and technological progress — have created deep divisions among them. Thus, countries in the North are prosperous and developed, while those in the South have difficulty, given past experiences, catching up with the developed nations. This is the context within which globalization is taking place. A discussion of globalization and autonomy in the Mediterranean requires, first, that we overcome these differentiations. In the North, the social state, by offering a predictable existence (Bourdieu 2000) through the welfare state, has provided the social supports that allow individuals to establish themselves as autonomous subjects. There is nothing like this in the South, where, socially and politically, individuality is diluted in community, tribe and clan, family, or neighbourhood. Furthermore, by depriving individuals of the tools for exercising citizenship, governments have deprived them of all autonomy.

Governments that act this way remind us that the concept of autonomy can also be defined as collective in nature. This notion refers to the capacity of communities — states, cultural minorities, and Aboriginal peoples — to devise their own laws, or, in other words, to exercise their right to organize themselves. In democratic theory, the two concepts of autonomy — individual and collective — are mutually reinforcing. As the philosopher Jürgen Habermas (1996, 120, emphasis in original) explains, "The idea of self-legislation *by citizens,* that is, requires that those subject to law as its addressees can at the same time understand themselves as authors of law." Although this is often true in Northern countries, the essays in this book show that the exercise of collective autonomy by Southern states often leads to repression of individual autonomy, and this becomes more common as globalization accelerates.

What are the historical roots of globalization in the Mediterranean? The following four aspects seem to us to be the most important:

- *Historically,* the Mediterranean has been the site of hegemony, imperialism, and colonialism.
- *Culturally,* it was the cradle of monotheistic religions and the source of their impetus to take over Rome, then the North; it also gave rise to great and prestigious societies. Today, it is at the centre of East-West confrontation.
- *Economically,* it is a region of great contrasts: industrialized and underdeveloped countries, North-South, Europe-MENA (Middle East and North Africa), and so on.
- *Strategically,* it is a region of open or incipient political and military conflicts.

Given this perspective, studying the North-South reality of the Mediterranean has its specificities in terms of the following:

- the pace of economic integration with globalization
- the desire to democratize political life
- the desire to adhere to the values of good governance
- the desire to review concepts of family, the liberalization of women's status, secularism, and so on
- the capacity to have access to elementary, secondary, and higher education; reduction in economic disparities; and the closing of the digital divide.

For the first time in history, there have been attempts at Mediterranean integration that are not hegemonic, imperialistic, or colonialist, including the Barcelona Declaration, the Euro-Mediterranean partnership agreements, and the 5 + 5 Group. Because the economic development gap between the north and south shores remains so wide, however, these attempts have failed; today, integration is reduced to security cooperation and common management of migratory flows.

And so, what is the relationship today between globalization and autonomy? This question is addressed in a region where there are two types of societies, geographically united but socially, culturally, and economically unequal. The Mediterranean offers a good case study of North-South opposition:

- In one type of society, individuals' roles and choices are subjected to customs and often-implicit rules — a restrictive system that nevertheless provides support and sustenance. In Southern societies, people's relationships with the spheres of daily life and existence fit within what Cornelius Castoriadis (1975, 138-43) terms *heteronomy* — that is, the rules governing behaviour are produced beyond the control of individuals, who apply these rules, often unknowingly, through the transmission mechanism that forms the culture.
- In another type of society, this heteronomy has long been challenged by *autonomy,* which is the rule supposedly produced and applied by individuals at the end of a decision-making process that expresses collective autonomy. In Northern societies, in which the rise of individualism took place over the twentieth century, this change underlies, feeds into, and is fed by collective autonomy.

Individuals in the Mediterranean also have divergent relationships with practices of everyday life. For those in the North, these practices are the sum of individual, more or less enlightened or rational choices (individual autonomy); for those in the South, they are inscribed within a network of material constraints and embedded in a tight fabric of representations, functions, and social and symbolic statuses (collective and individual heteronomy). Globalizing processes have the effect of placing these two cultural realities in a relationship of opposition rather than convergence: they arbitrate between the heteronomy of the one, by eroding it, and the autonomy of the other, by reducing it. This dynamic is where the focus of our work lies.

Adapting and Integrating: Governing in Globalization

One fundamental aspect of globalization is governance, the subject of the contribution by Abdeljabbar Bsaies, whose essay leads off this book

(Chapter 1). In fact, the efforts of almost all countries today, and particularly Southern countries, to open up to international trade and foreign investment and to form markets that go beyond national boundaries reduce national economic and political influence. The autonomous exercise of national sovereignty is thus tending to fade. In this context, the International Monetary Fund (IMF) and the World Bank (WB), the international community's tools for monetary and financial regulation, have been transformed into intermediaries for the hegemony of Western powers. Faced with these bodies' policies, a series of resistance fronts — a sort of global civil society — is taking shape to demand an alternative globalization that includes democratic institutions and the right to life, global citizenship, and dignity for all human beings. Moreover, the convergence of technological and political changes has made the world both smaller and less tolerant of social and political injustices. Nongovernmental organizations (NGOs) pursue interventionist activities throughout the world more quickly and effectively than previously. Oppressed peoples and individuals now have powerful allies for consolidating their autonomy, either individual or collective, and therefore enjoy greater voice on the international scene and more political weight in their own countries. As Bsaies emphasizes, this is the essence of adaptive governance: as it evolves, it is characterized by new relations between the state and citizen, and between the state and groups.

The question of governance is even more pointed in Southern countries, which are subjected to the dictates of international organizations that require them to review their methods of government and management. After Structural Adjustment Programs (SAPs) failed in a number of Southern countries typified by a strong state presence and ineffective institutions, resulting in what may be termed public governance, these countries were pressed by international financial institutions to show "better governance." The notion of better governance involves the characteristic features of market governance with a particular emphasis on the state's respect for the law and accountability by the holders of power.

Bsaies distinguishes between two types of governance. The first, which he calls effective governance, is an abstraction based on the neoliberal theoretical model, which defines the contours of good governance as giving primacy to law and the laws of the market in the citizen-state relationship. It would be the most appropriate for the effective operation of a market economy. Faced with this type of governance, states react to preserve aspects of individual and societal autonomy through appropriate institutions forming specific governances.

Bsaies refines the notion of governance of reference and discusses two cases of specific governance. In the North, France functions based on principles closer to the model of governance of reference, but with a renewed attempt by the state to maintain autonomy regarding social arbitration. In Morocco, in the South, governance departs from the reference model and is still conditioned by interpersonal relationships; in contrast, civil society is increasingly taking over from the old authoritarian state relationships, pushing the country closer to the reference model. The author's objective is to see if these models of specific governance make it possible for the two countries to preserve their respective economic margins of manoeuvre and political autonomy following their integration into globalizing markets and related processes.

The author then describes how the countries on the south shore of the Mediterranean have reacted to the good governance proposals that have penetrated on the economic level. They take up these proposals, to varying degrees, because almost all Southern countries, because of their economic difficulties, have been forced to implement SAPs and liberalize their trade. However, these countries' social, historical, and political structures, combined with the weakness of their civil societies, have enabled them to preserve their authoritarian — and sometimes quasimonarchical — exercise of political power. Thus, when globalization is sufficiently constraining, and when there is a civil society tradition, the state, and then the government, should theoretically weaken, which is translated into a loss of autonomy. Conversely, civil society becomes stronger, and men and women who had previously been subjects are able to accede to citizenship.

Bsaies illustrates another form of governance that is taking shape in Morocco as the state reduces its intervention in various fields of economic and social activity under the constraints imposed by implementation of an SAP and by the country's integration into globalizing markets. The evolution of this process has gradually led to the creation of a civil society that, unlike those of Morocco's neighbours, has become so important that the government is forced to deal with it. Those forming this associative fabric have sought autonomy vis-à-vis political parties and have strived for a separate identity by adopting, among other things, a national human rights charter in 1990. This step towards increased autonomy offers a possible path to institutional change initiated by its own momentum through the effects of globalization. In the end, it may lead Morocco, by its own path, towards democracy and, consequently, towards a stronger role on the global stage.

Whereas good governance raises the first challenge arising from neo-liberal globalization, integration of the region (or regionalization) raises a second. A book on the Mediterranean could not ignore the issue of the relationship between what is commonly called the Euro-Mediterranean Process (EMP), launched in Barcelona in 1995, and globalization. This is the subject of the essay by Faika Charfi and Sameh Zouari (Chapter 2).

Let us take a brief look at the historical background of the inception of this process in order to get a sense of its full scope. It started with the Euro-Arab Dialogue, which was instigated in 1973 and formally institutionalized in 1974. In 1979, the revolution in Iran and the invasion of Afghanistan by Soviet troops signalled the weakening of Arab nationalism and the concurrent rise of the Islamist movement (Chevallier 1997). Taken together, the signing of the Camp David Accords, the first Gulf War, the collapse of the Soviet empire, and US supremacy in a unipolar world saddled the European Community with new responsibilities. The Arab states also sensed the need to rethink their own responsibilities, after long having split their alliances between a hegemonic United States and an expanding Europe. The US offensive to occupy economic positions in the region after the Gulf War (notably through the different economic reform programs imposed by its secular branches, the WB and the IMF), the aggravation of regional conflicts, the rise of religious fundamentalism, successive failed attempts at economic reform in Southern countries and these countries' persistent underdevelopment, and the difficulty of stemming uncontrolled migratory flows stimulated by the deterioration of social conditions in these countries made it urgent for Europe to find an answer to the following question: How can development be encouraged in the countries on the south shore of the Mediterranean in a rapidly changing global and regional context?

States responded via economic, political, and cultural interventions in the Mediterranean:

- *Economically,* they installed a free trade zone that lasted from 1995 to 2010 and opened a large market to all Mediterranean products. At the same time, to make products from the Southern countries competitive, Europe agreed to support the economic transition of

Southern countries with financial aid to encourage the development of social and urban infrastructure.

- *Politically,* the conviction was upheld that economic liberalization would ineluctably lead to political liberalization.
- *Culturally,* the myth of the Mediterranean Sea as the cradle of civilization was reformulated to justify this sudden economic and geopolitical interest.[1]

Out of these changes came the organization in 1995 of the Barcelona Conference and the inauguration of the "partnership" process. Given the meagre results obtained, however, hopes faded that the region would climb to the rank of regional power. The partnership did not lead to a marked increase in private investment, and the economic reforms did not lead to political reform and democratization — to the contrary (Hibou 2003). More than ever, Europe needed the authoritarian regimes on the south shore of the Mediterranean to form a first line of defence against would-be immigrants and to contain Islamism. As for the free trade zone, the cornerstone of the mechanism, it excluded agricultural products, the only comparative advantage held by the Southern countries, and was simply a "mechanism that was inserted into the global dynamic of liberalization undertaken in Europe. Yet liberalization alone, in a context of deep inequality, could guarantee neither economic development nor integration of profoundly destructured societies, especially because these were free trade zones under European conditions" (Naïr 2003, 297, our translation). Despite its stated desire to participate, massively and decisively, in the future of the countries on the south shore of the Mediterranean, the European Union (EU) seemed to be exclusively interested in and supportive of cooperation programs dealing with terrorism, clandestine immigration, personal mobility, information, and other specific issues. In other words, Europe's Mediterranean policy was more and more structured according to the threats that the Southern countries were reputed to pose and in response to the presence in the North of large immigrant communities from the South.

It remains unclear whether this ambition to construct a Euro-Mediterranean space is a desire for autonomy on the part of a Europe threatened by globalization, a revolt against the US foothold in the region, or an attempt to build a reserved domain by creating a large market in the Mediterranean. Another possibility is that the EMP is an extension of a regionalization policy, begun with the construction of Europe, and thus an attempt to engage Southern countries on a partnership basis — a hybrid status midway between association and membership. Making this choice involves:

- forgetting that Europe's new political will is based on the liberalism prevalent in the context of the Treaty of Maastricht. By proposing an opening and liberalization of Southern economies, Europe is simply continuing with an ideology that it has always promoted. Well before the Barcelona Process, European countries had subscribed to the economic globalization rationale that has dominated and fuelled the region, if only via outsourcing of some activities to Southern countries[2]
- forgetting that free trade, which is the basis for the entire Euro-Mediterranean partnership approach, "in fact falls within the dynamic of the imperial market world-system. A subregion of the world-system, Europe proposes that the Mediterranean countries be, in their turn, a sub-subregion" (Naïr 2003, 298, our translation) for which the partnership would be nothing but a rapid and painful transition to the liberalized market
- finally, forgetting that this "partnership" undeniably reflects a very liberal ideology: supporting this point is the centrality, in institutional terms, of free trade zones between each partner in the South and the EU, the adoption of Structural Adjustment Programs, the primacy of economic and trade strategies over social and development strategies, [and] the conviction ... that economic liberalization will lead to political liberalization" (Hibou 2003, 119, our translation).

In short, the EMP is perfectly integrated with Europe, as a response to globalization — in ways not to thwart it but to make it more acceptable and less noxious.

Globalization and History: Great Texts and Religion

The examination of globalization and autonomy in the Mediterranean space also takes us deep into the history of the region. These depths are explored in two case studies: Ibn Khaldūn's analysis of society (Chapter 3) and translation of the Bible from Hebrew to Castilian in the fifteenth century (Chapter 4). This translation was commissioned by a Muslim ruler who called upon a Jewish scholar to produce the first-ever edition of the Bible in the vernacular in Spain.

History is also central to understanding the relationship between globalization and religion. Religion is first discussed by Yassine Essid in his study of Islamism at a time when the deregulation of Islam is giving free rein to multiple Islams (Chapter 5). Just as globalization sets out to standardize the human being in the name of universal reason, Islamization sets out to standardize good and evil in the name of God; these approaches are interdependent. The mechanisms of authority framing Islam — family, social traditions, and local customs — as well as the great historical religious institutions with concrete jurisdiction over the truth are increasingly discredited by globalization. There has been a vast liberalization of the market for symbolic goods, over which the great institutional bodies no longer have control; this development has induced a trend towards homogenization of autonomous belief systems that are able, in a context of general cultural globalization, to find a place in world-scale networks.

In different Mediterranean cultures, women are linked to important aspects of culture that they have transmitted through the ages: language, religious beliefs, oral literature, and ecological and artistic knowledge. More recently, with growing access to education and training, women have brought a new dynamic to the spheres of business, politics, education, and culture. Nevertheless, the status of women varies widely between the northern and southern Mediterranean countries, among women living in different Southern countries, and among women living in rural and urban environments. Changes in the status of Muslim women in Mediterranean countries — with a few exceptions, such as Tunisia and Turkey — have evolved very slowly. In the Arab Mediterranean countries, women of working age constitute only one-third of the job-seeking population and less than one quarter of the employed population. Although women now have greater access to education, their job prospects are not improving to the same extent. Could this be the consequence of deeply rooted cultural, religious, or legal discrimination?

Taking a look at various historical contexts, both colonial and postcolonial, and their impact on the evolution of Arab Muslim women, Latifa Lakhdhar examines the side effects of socio-economic policies linked to globalization and their repercussions on women's autonomy (Chapter 6). Has globalization been good for women in the Arab Mediterranean?

Whereas in the countries on the north shore the question is essentially a political one, in the countries on the south shore the social and religious remain inextricably entwined. For example, there are two primary sources of jobs in the region, especially in the Maghreb countries and Turkey: the public sector and the manufacturing sector, particularly the textile and clothing industry. Both are currently undergoing a contraction: the former has seen a reduction in public expenditures, and the latter has suffered a loss of competitiveness on European markets because of the elimination of the Multifibre Arrangement on 1 January 2005. The current trends in economic policy thus do not favour the integration of women into the official economy and, consequently, there are not many opportunities for financial autonomy through paid work. Globalization, already strongly prejudicial to women's material situation, also affects their legal and cultural status. Lakhdhar underlines that globalized Islam, "incapable of evolving towards an egalitarian ideology or a more secularized vision of social relations," has brought back into fashion "all of the archaic norms governing relations between the sexes — relations thought to have been left in the past. The 'Islamic veil' is its most obvious expression."

Before reaching this conclusion, however, Lakhdhar takes us through the various historical stages that led women into a situation that may point to regression rather than progress in their quest for autonomy. For example, although the end of colonialism and access to political independence helped to emancipate Arab women in the Mediterranean through education and jobs, it nevertheless did not accord them greater autonomy. Moreover, women, as the most vulnerable group in society, were the first to feel the effects of the development crisis, which resulted in greater pauperization and a drop in their status as the rise of Islamism accelerated. This issue is even more relevant in the context of globalization. The preservation of cultures requires the social and intellectual development of all social actors, men and women, and the taking into account of the opinions of both sexes. When they are absent from this dialogue, women become victims of cultural relativism and Islamism, which tend to reduce their rights and worsen their condition.

Cultural Autonomy: Music and Food

The field of culture draws, more than other fields, on new technologies. In the past, family, school, places of worship, the daily press, clubs, parties, and associations both provided essential links between individuals and the outside world and served the purpose of sorting, prioritizing, evaluating, and transmitting information and cultural content carried by the media. This is no longer the case. Individuals, confronted with waves of various kinds of cultural content over multiple channels, are no longer able to partake of this beneficial filtering. It has become clear that what is at stake in cultural hegemony and private control of cultural industries is the capacity of communities to produce their own culture and resist the selective invasion of cultural goods. Accordingly, no political party, state, or local community can remain indifferent to the industrialization of culture. Thus, the question of cultural policies is posed at each level of political community and on the world scale. How can unique cultures — traditional and local ones — react to such waves? What are the consequences for the cultural autonomy of communities and individuals?

Prominent among the themes that call for reflection in relation to globalization and autonomy are music and food. Music is the expression of deep human feelings anchored in culture and traditions, as embodied in the intonations of people's voices and the playing of instruments, as rudimentary or sophisticated as they may be, as well as the emotional reactions of listeners. As planet-wide distribution and mass production take hold, music is not only increasingly overflowing geographic and cultural boundaries but also sometimes escaping its creators, becoming what is now known as world music. Food is imbued with strong gustatory, ritual, and collective dimensions; ever since cooking was discovered, men and women have constantly transformed, accommodated, and ameliorated it through conquests. Various inventions, notably of techniques for conservation and distribution, have led to what is called, analogously, world cuisine.

For these reasons, we have devoted much space to these two aspects. The first chapter on the subject is by Myriem Lakhoua, a musicologist well aware of the stakes of globalization and of the autonomy of music in the Arab Mediterranean world and in the Maghreb diaspora in Europe (Chapter 7). Following her work are several chapters written by a team of anthropologists interested in the changes affecting regional eating habits in the Mediterranean and the capacity of populations in this region to preserve their culinary culture and resist the hegemony of the globalized market.

Opening the series of contributions on food, Amado Millán Fuertes (Chapter 8) reminds us that the theme of food is at the confluence of all of the other themes addressed in this volume: trade, culture, forms of government, economics, religion, agricultural policy, and the right to have regular, permanent, and free access to nutrition that is qualitatively and quantitatively adequate and sufficient and that corresponds to the cultural conditions of the peoples who consume it. This right has even been enshrined in the constitutions of countries such as South Africa.

Fuentes de Ebro, a mainly agricultural village in Spain, is Rulof Kerkhoff's subject of study (Chapter 9). In the 1960s, the residents were able to combine a small local industry with mechanized farming of wheat, corn, and alfalfa destined for the market. The village also possesses a rich market-gardening production zone, irrigated by a tributary of the Ebro River and by the Ginel stream, which is reputed to confer exceptional qualities upon vegetables. One of these is the famous Fuentes de Ebro sweet onion *(Allium cepa)* — a vegetable whose fate serves as an example of resistance by the local to the global. In general, however, the well-known saying "Tell me what you eat, and I will tell you who you are" is belied in the era of globalization. Modern food no longer possesses authenticity, is no longer identifiable, and therefore creates a problem of identity for consumers of the product, who, not knowing what they are eating, no longer know who they are. The revolution of far-reaching distribution, which has led to an extreme variety of products put on the market, with origins that are difficult to trace, is a direct consequence of globalization and trade liberalization. It becomes a source of anxiety for consumers, and producers lose control over their product.

According to Almudena Hasan Bosque, the author of the third essay on food (Chapter 10), socio-cultural practices and representations associated with food are starting to change, on both the local and global levels, at the same time as norms and values are changing. Bosque uses the case of Amman, Jordan. Until recently, much of the daily food supply in the city was produced locally. A limited number of products were imported, and they were often highly valued, either because they were consumed on rare occasions or because they enhanced the taste of everyday dishes. Individuals' nutritional environments were thus relatively stable throughout their lives. This situation no longer holds. The development of wide distribution in the North, and then its expansion to the southern Mediterranean countries over the last decade, has inaugurated the era of mass consumption for the novelty-seeking consumers of these countries.

Finally, Paula Durán Monfort (Chapter 11) analyzes the effects of globalization as a phenomenon of the acculturation of local food models.

She is particularly interested in the changes observed in food-distribution spaces in Tunisia around a particular product: meat. She has also observed the strategies that social actors develop in relation to this food and its local or globalized availability.

Cultural Autonomy: Languages and Education

Globalization is not reducible to liberalized market integration, new technologies, or the emergence of global thought; it is also the source of an intermingling of cultures. How can cultural autonomy be preserved? All of the Arab countries of the Mediterranean have, at one time or another, been confronted with the question of language, a fundamental element of identity, along with territory and, today, religion. How can I express my identity and culture in my own language? Is it still my own? And do I still have a choice?

Envisaging the relationship that writers have with their readers in a context of globalization is the theme of the essay by François Zabbal (Chapter 12). Zabbal sees literary texts as inscribed in a local history that is heavily marked by form, style, and content. This old territorial order of literature, however, now seems submerged in the imperatives of the world market. The national origin of works is blurred without disproportionately affecting their content. Their provenance is of little consequence, provided that the language used permits them to be sold. The result is literature without a particular social space and identity. Well before the advent of globalization, however, Arabic authors glorified deterritorialization of the literary work not only in order to gain freedom of expression but also, especially, because the local market for Arabic-language books lacked both readers and recognition.

What makes a creative work such as a book cross national borders? It is a question that involves how fields of cultural production and transnational trade (in other words, globalization) function. The economic approach — identifying the translated book as a good that is produced and consumed according to the law of supply and demand, and that circulates according to the laws of national and international trade — is not pertinent here. It conceals the specificity of cultural goods and of the terms of their distribution and valuing. Thus, in retracing the paths taken by Arabic-language books to exist elsewhere than their country of origin, Zabbal's analysis leads inevitably to the problem of relations of force among languages, national cultures, and global powers.

We must consider here the relationship between an Arab context of production, suffering from a lack of readers, and a Western receiving context, in which Arabic literature occupies a modest rank. It is a case of cultural transfer that is ruled not by the logic of the market (as is the case for American literature, for example), but by the intervention of certain institutions or a particularly motivated publisher or distributor that is interested in a small country's literary production or a non-Western literature. For dissemination of such literary works not belonging to central languages to occur, and for this product to become globalized — in other words, for the market to take account of cultural diversities — two steps must be taken. The first step is *partial autonomy,* provided by translation, which enables the work to cross the threshold beyond the source language but remain attached to a territory and a nationality. The importing of Arabic-language books depends, at this stage, on a strategy of limited production based on limited selection criteria: low print runs, quality of translation, small readership, grants, relationship between the countries, and other factors. This is a market, but the market for creativity, which responds above all to cultural criteria. The second step is *total autonomy,* in which the creative work responds above all to economic criteria, and in which publication is no longer embedded in relations of force among countries and their languages. Authors write directly in the global language in order to free their work both from the structure of the hierarchical transnational space, with its modes of domination, and from all individual or institutional intermediaries, to become global and autonomous.

Once they achieved independence, the three Maghreb states faced this problem. The unanimously repeated slogan was that no cultural identity would be possible without an Arabic language that it was high time to reclaim. Morocco and Tunisia, as protectorates, and Algeria, as a colony, had become bilingual, with French as the predominant language. The education system, largely in French, involved teaching neither Arabic nor national history, and very little Islamic culture.

Tunisia, the subject of Mongi Bahloul's essay (Chapter 13), was established as bilingual (Arabic-French) when it became independent. The first educational reform in 1958 was to eliminate French in the first and second years of primary school, but it was reinstated in the third year as the language of arithmetic and common knowledge. "This reform," writes Chedly Fitouri (1983, 68, our translation), "maintained the options of unbalanced and conflictual biculturalism" throughout the protectorate period. Programs were then designed with large sections devoted to national history, Arabic, and Islamic culture, leaving the teaching of scientific subjects to French "as the sole means of guaranteeing an opening to the modern world and providing the country with the effective means of battling underdevelopment" (ibid.).

Arabic is not only the language of independence, of national history, of religious identity, of integration with the Maghreb but also of the Arab world. A political and ideological language, Arabic left neither choice nor autonomy to the collectivity. As an expression of the state's political orientation, it was imposed and planned throughout the Tunisian educational system. In an independent but underdeveloped country, French had been considered an instrument for catching up — for access to modernity and economic development. Although seen as being in the domain of scientific education, French left behind it, in an era of exacerbated nationalisms, a lingering sense of alienation and cultural dependence. As the focus of a political and ideological debate, it was imposed on the population in spite of everything, under the leadership of the planned state. Nevertheless, whatever one might say about it, French is not an imperialist language; the Algerian author Kateb Yassine has even called it the "spoils of war." A language of coexistence and human rights, French is recognized as a means of facilitating access to other languages. In addition, it is spoken by the sizeable Maghreb diaspora in France. Thus, different roles are attributed to Arabic and French, and "this balancing, between the quest for identity and the aspiration to modernity, is perhaps what best characterizes biculturalism in the three countries of the Maghreb" (Fitouri 1983, 73, our translation).

In contrast, English, the language of globalization and economic exchange, a utilitarian language, reputed to be ideologically neutral but culturally invasive, has been left to the free choice of individuals without interference by the state. In Tunisia, for example, English has no specific status; it has not supplanted French, nor has an equivalent status been claimed for it. Although it is treated as a foreign language taught as an option, like German and Spanish, English has been strongly promoted, since the early 1960s, by the culture departments of the US and British embassies. It was said that French was the language of integration into modernity, but while French required a state policy, English was swept in by globalization, bringing its cultural baggage with it. It thus became the mode of transmission for a culture that was de-materialized, not reduced to patrimony or objectives, and posed no problem to the political system. This lack of connection between cultural identity and language is another strength of English, which has the status of a language of communication — and this is not the case for Arabic or, incidentally, French. Unlike French, suspected of association with neocolonialism, English did not provoke cultural conflict by forcing initiation to a second culture or having pre-existing roots in an indigenous cultural tradition — in other words, English respected autonomy. In fact, it was the language par excellence for autonomy, especially of individuals (Naïr 2003, 24; Rabenoro and Rajaonarivo 1997).

Beyond this historical overview, Bahloul's discussion shows that, at first, the linguistic question was the prerogative of the state, which it managed according to its domestic and foreign constraints. The Tunisian government's official attitude towards English did not result, as it did for Arabic and French, in friction between Arabic, the language of authenticity (ineffective), and French, the language of opening (charged with history and resentment). English was imposed on people without provoking soul searching. It was an even more deliberate choice given that Arabic was unable to serve as a universal language.

We have seen how the commodification of music, through communications technology and mass reproduction of cultural goods, threatens artistic creation and the very future of creators. Education faces a similar phenomenon, and it is not by chance that we speak today about the formation of *human capital,* an expression that is reorienting all educational programs, and perhaps even the very spirit of education. Houda Ben Hassen, in her essay, discusses a field that is still beyond the market sector to a great extent: higher education (Chapter 14). Using two examples, France, north of the Mediterranean, and Tunisia, on the sea's south shore, Ben Hassen shows how globalization is resulting in the convergence of higher education systems. In both countries, this standardization process started because of the need to cut costs and improve the employability of graduates — both concerns reflecting the market laws that underlie globalization. The three main actors in higher education — teachers, students, and advisers — are seen, in these two examples, to be gradually losing their autonomy.

Globalization and Autonomy: The Economic Question

Throughout history, the Mediterranean has been the object of a number of attempts at economic integration. The current plan to form a regional free trade zone is nominally a voluntary project, and its economic dimension is highlighted. Its central axis is the creation of a large free trade zone around the Mediterranean Basin, which will be tied to the European Union. This project, in parallel with that of globalization, was advanced considerably with the signing of trade-liberalization agreements among Mediterranean countries. From the point of view of the region as a whole, they serve as the foundation for a regional coalition progressing towards globalization of trade and production. From the point of view of each country, Mediterranean integration raises the need to redefine national economic autonomy, which is at risk of being eroded by economic opening and its implications, and involves a questioning of the actors' socio-economic positioning.

The GERIM working group on economics has sought to analyze the possible outcomes of movements towards greater integration and their social and economic implications at the regional and domestic levels. The authors report on the Mediterranean integration project and its progress, as well as the motivations of the concerned parties, the means that they are implementing, and the new socio-economic configuration that could result around the Mediterranean.

In his essay, Lotfi Bouzaïane (Chapter 15) exposes the dilemma in the region, which is torn between integration with the global market and the need to preserve some autonomy. He observes that the current form of globalization is the result of a long process in which the countries in the region have been engaged since the 1940s. This process took a new turn at the end of the twentieth century, with trade liberalization. However, paradoxes continue to hinder the progress of globalization and lay bare the weaknesses of autonomy in relation to insertion into the global economy, and even into the regional zone. Persistent gaps in standards of living are key to these paradoxes. As a consequence, two issues will continue to be prominent on the road to the region's economic integration: mobility of individuals and management of natural resources. In an exploration of the region's future between autonomy and globalization, Bouzaïane observes that opposing models of society, currently covered heavily in the media, are an outcome of other, more influential economic and geopolitical variables.

Passing from the general to the specific, a series of studies illustrate Bouzaïane's premises. Rim Mouelhi uses the sociology of organizations to analyze the Mediterranean in relation to how the stakes of globalization might weaken or strengthen the projects of the main actors in the region (Chapter 16). She discusses possible alliances and conflicts among these actors in their efforts to safeguard their autonomy and push their plans forward and shows that, in general, there is a convergence of interests in favour of globalization. But whereas actors in the northern Mediterranean countries are in a position of strength and join the process without fearing for their autonomy, countries in the South are ready, in Mouelhi's view, to sacrifice part of their autonomy to take advantage of more of the economic development promised by globalization.

Samouel Béji deals with the challenges of autonomy linked to financial liberalization for developing countries in the Mediterranean South (Chapter 17). All of these countries have been engaged in SAPs or similar policies to various degrees since the 1980s. Béji shows how all of the countries on the south shore, except for Libya and Syria, now have partially or completely modernized financial systems. The region as a whole has remained cautious, however, about integration into the international financial system, and domestic investments and savings remain more strongly embedded than in the rest of the world. The countries of the South continue to fear the implications of greater financial opening on their collective autonomy, for both monetary and fiscal policy. Added to this fear is the new risk, not yet defined clearly, of deterritoralization of currency.

Jihen Malek compares industrial policies in the Mediterranean countries before and after globalization (Chapter 18). She attempts to establish that under the effects of international free trade agreements — and the mitigated results of these policies — these countries are shifting from a policy of direct support, using a wide range of instruments, to one of support almost exclusively for research and development and attracting foreign direct investment. States are trying, through this change, to influence the nature of industrial activities, which will develop and provide access to the targeted objectives. Malek adds, based on the cases of France, Italy, and Tunisia, that states in the North have much more institutional capacity to implement such an industrial policy successfully.

Nizard Jouini discusses the economic implications of the integration of southern Mediterranean countries into the global economy by showing that this integration translates into more interdependence with the rest of the world (Chapter 19). Jouini also observes that greater economic opening by countries in the region, theoretically the source of more growth, will lead to the convergence of income per inhabitant with the European average for a limited number of countries, such as Cyprus and Israel. Turkey, Tunisia, and Egypt will retain the same gap with this average. For the other countries, the gap will grow. Finally, Jouini observes that integration into the global economy is being conveyed by the development of civil society. He indicates that the greater opportunities for financing the activities of NGOs and the larger sphere of activity now open to these organizations because of contraction of the state's role are the most decisive driving forces in this evolution. In this regard, Jouini concurs with Bsaies' analysis of the situation in Morocco.

In her essay (Chapter 20), Fatma Sarraj shows that globalization results in the development of outsourcing activities that contribute to the fragmentation of production processes among different firms and world regions. According to Sarraj, the Mediterranean is only beginning to develop outsourcing. Within the Mediterranean space, the redeployment of Northern firms' activities to Southern countries may strengthen the economic integration of the region and be a source of greater regional autonomy. The future of potential investments will depend on greater involvement by the region in outsourcing activities. At the moment, however, the region is not as attractive as are other world regions. In Sarraj's view, more competitiveness must be developed in the business environment to draw more outsourcing activity. Competitive costs, which once encouraged subcontracting (a primary form of outsourcing), are no longer sufficient for access to greater integration into the globalized production process.

The book ends with an interview by one of the volume editors, Yassine Essid, with a psychiatrist, Dr. Hashmi Dhaoui (Chapter 21). As a psychiatrist and psychoanalyst practising in a country on the south shore of the Mediterranean, Dr. Dhaoui discusses with Essid a very specific character of the Maghreb and the East Mediterranean: the Arab individual. By *individual,* he does not mean someone who comes to see him for treatment, but an individual representative of a community, or a society, who today is prey to a complex malaise provoked by an increasingly globalized world. Psychoanalysis serves here as a tool for interpretation of the current state of affairs in this region, and that is why this interview comes at the end of the book.

Conclusion

There was a time when the Mediterranean was the centre of the world. An impressive range of historical civilizations vied to take possession of it: Babylonians, Akkadians, Hittites, Phrygians, Assyrians, Achaeans,

Mycenians, Phoenicians, Dorians, and even peoples from neighbouring shores — Himyarites, Sabians, and Anatolians. Each rival wanted sole power and supremacy. All of these attempts were halted at the threshold of success — all except one, perhaps: the Roman Empire. For about three centuries, the Pax Romana managed to unify what Romans called the *mare nostrum*. Government by men, pacification of the territory, administration by the state, respect for the cultural diversities of subject peoples, and fluidity of trade and communications were ensured under the vigilant eye of a capital that saw itself as eternal because of the Pax Romana.

The miracle, certainly unique in ancient history, was the maintenance of the *limes* citadels protecting the empire from what came to be called the barbarian invasions. The chaos that followed these destructive incursions divided the empire until the advent of Islam. The new energy that came with the Islamic Arabic thrust, much more cultural than simply religious, as is commonly believed, sought to emulate the Roman success in commanding everything within the Mediterranean perimeter and beyond. The plans were aborted for many reasons, some of them analyzed in this book, and for a long time Islam was confined to the southern half of Iberia and, of course, the southern shores of the Mediterranean.

After the beginning of the Reconquista and especially with the discovery of the Americas, Islamic energy in effect withdrew definitively to focus on the southern part of the Mediterranean. Ibn Khaldūn was the first to intuit a resurgence in creativity by the people of the south shore towards the north shore, accompanied by a desire for power, hegemony, and subjugation.

Eventually, the most definitive outcome was the dividing up of a South utterly stripped of all of its resources and reduced to an indigenous status at the Congress of Berlin in 1878. It was an arrangement that was far from satisfactory for the peoples in the region, and their desire for freedom was finally expressed in their regaining at least their political autonomy in the aftermath of the Second World War and the advent of the United Nations. The resulting nation-states, whose independence was earned through a deceptive process that some called neocolonialism, have been unable to make progress. It has been necessary to redress the delays accumulated under the fiat of globalization that was unfurling beyond their control, through which the entire field of human existence was being standardized relative to a world scale, leaving no room for political initiative.

Today, two Mediterranean worlds confront each other, irremediably irreconcilable despite timid and tactical attempts at formulating unifying projects. In the face of Europe, which is tending to move its centre of gravity farther eastward, and which sees globalization as inevitable and necessary, is a second Mediterranean. Often shaken by stormy agitation, vulnerable, this second Mediterranean forms a political economy in thought alone; not only will it not have any major effect on major economic and financial issues, but it will remain increasingly shut out from the decision-making processes that affect it.

It is the ambition of this book and its contributors to determine whether the paths to globalization and autonomy for these two Mediterranean worlds will remain forever divergent. Facing the constraints of forced integration, followed by the extreme interdependence of economic, social, political, religious, and cultural spaces, or the effects of international organizations' prescriptive programs, is there still room for these developing countries on the southern shore to negotiate their fate and perhaps ward off the inevitability of exclusion?

PART 1   Adapting and Integrating: Governing in Globalization

The first two chapters of this book discuss two dominant aspects of contemporary globalization: neoliberalism and regionalization. In Chapter 1, Abdeljabbar Bsaies methodically describes the implications of neoliberal globalization on the governance of states. He defines what he calls the reference governance model and the concomitant idea of good governance, and he explores the applicability of this model to democratic states on the north shore of the Mediterranean and autocratic states on the south shore. Taking the examples of France and Morocco, he observes that the autonomy of both states is clearly negatively affected by globalization, the effects of which are felt particularly strongly in Southern countries.

In Chapter 2, Faika Charfi and Sameh Zouari reflect on the current regionalization processes that flow from globalization. Over the past forty years, the states on the Mediterranean south shore have witnessed the unfolding of an extensive and intensive process of regionalization in western Europe, which was then extended to eastern Europe. Both the European Union and the countries of the Maghreb have been interested in a more thorough integration of the south shore into this process. Charfi and Zouari describe the ins and outs of this attempt at integration, which the Barcelona Process, initiated in 1995, attempted to translate into action. The process was intended to prepare the ground for integration of the European Union, which had fifteen member states at the time and twelve Mediterranean countries, with a view to establishing a common strategy for a security structure and economic prosperity in the Euro-Mediterranean region. After analyzing this policy and the initiatives adopted on either side, the authors conclude that the Euro-Mediterranean zone is still a largely fragmented region, with one dominant developed pole, concerned mainly with the success of its expansions east and south, and a constellation of small economies with delayed development whose integration is either minimal or *nonexistant*.

chapter 1   **Globalization, Governance, and Autonomy**

Abdeljabbar Bsaies

TODAY, THERE IS MUCH talk about globalization; countless works discuss the phenomenon and present its many characteristics and its effects on the course of activities throughout the world. Some authors, such as Zaki Laïdi (see, in particular, Laïdi 2002), wonder if globalization, beyond its obvious economic aspect, is in fact a social theory. Such a reflection is no doubt legitimate given the evolution of societies that have been integrated into globalization in recent decades. The essential objective of globalization is to liberalize trade by transcending borders (Scholte 1997); in a neoliberal perspective, it tends to see the market as the institution that coordinates economic activity. This liberal vision of society is hinted at by Adam Smith (1976 [1776]) and described by F. August Hayek (2007), who feels that globalization should be extended to almost all countries in order to create a planetary market.

To achieve this goal, globalization requires an appropriate institutional infrastructure that allows free, unfettered markets and a compatible mode of governance, based on the values of political, institutional, and economic freedom. International organizations (the International Monetary Fund [IMF], World Bank [WB], and the World Trade Organization [WTO]) and multinational firms seek to legitimize this ideal form of governance either by institutional paths (membership in the WTO, for example) or through the play of market forces and the strategies of economic operators. Once implemented, neoliberal governance, which I call the reference governance model or market governance, inevitably proves restrictive both for states and individuals. Those who wish to preserve what they have gained react, predictably, by manifesting their desire for autonomy.

Before developing this argument, I briefly present the essential characteristics of the reference governance model or market governance, which, when it forms the basis of globalization, is called good governance. Because the goal of globalization is extension over as much of the planet as possible, in both developed and developing countries, implicit in good governance is a vocation of universality. However, distinctions must be made with regard to its possible application, depending on the structural characteristics of the countries involved. Northern developed countries have democratic regimes, while the majority of Southern countries have developing status and lag behind in imposing the law as the instrument of choice to regulate political and social organization.

The two Mediterranean regions, my field of investigation, illustrate precisely this political and institutional contrast between Northern and Southern countries. Thus, to begin with, I explore the form of governance that enables Northern countries to preserve their autonomy in the face of globalization, at both the state level and the level of individuals or groups of individuals; the effects of this governance; and the institutional transformations that it requires. I use France as an example. Second, I look at the countries of the South Mediterranean. As we know, these countries, heavily indebted during the 1980s, had to implement a group of measures set out in Structural Adjustment Programs (SAPs) inspired by the Washington Consensus, itself of neoliberal inspiration. The SAPs were designed not only to improve these countries' economic situation but also to integrate them into globalization. For most of them, the SAPs were a failure that has been attributed to their poor institutional situation. The notion of good governance, a form of governance derived from market governance, was designed to force a remodelling of their institutional landscape in order to adapt it to the practices of globalized activities. The countries that have adopted good governance have had to obey economic and trade injunctions. They have also managed to preserve the authoritarian nature of their political regimes, exercising control over their societies and individual citizens with a mode of government based on interpersonal relationships, because civil society is dominated by the government and seen as unimportant. In a country with a tradition of civil society, globalization may be so restrictive that the state and, subsequently, the government weaken, leading to a loss of state autonomy. In contrast, it is also possible that civil society will be strengthened, and that men and women who had been subjects will be able to accede to citizenship. In the Moroccan example, I present a model of another type of governance of this sort that is taking shape, which, in the end, may lead the country towards democracy by a different path.

Globalization, Market Governance, and Reactions in the Northern Mediterranean: The French Example

In the introduction, I noted that globalization requires institutions that advance its progress; these institutions combine to form market governance. This type of neoliberal governance is based on values, established in the eighteenth century, that advocate individual freedom as well as corporate freedom on unfettered markets. Thus, the state is excluded from the economic sphere, since its role, beyond its royal prerogative, is limited to guaranteeing economic contracts and making sure that the rules of competition are respected so that markets can function efficiently. Once barriers to free trade are lifted, nations can be integrated into a market that forms a single economic community, and laissez-faire and free trade become the principles behind all economic and social progress.

The general premise of this arrangement, with market regulation, prevailed throughout the nineteenth century (Boyer 1978). After the troubled interwar period, the neoliberal order was established in 1944 by the signature of the Bretton Woods Agreements, designed to ensure as much international monetary stability as possible, which led to the setting up of the WB, the IMF, and, later, the General Agreement on Tariffs and Trade (GATT). This new order was imposed at the cost of concessions made to certain forms of interventionism via state regulatory action, resulting in the welfare-state system that was to ensure strong growth during the "thirty glorious years" between 1945 and 1975. Since the crisis in the 1970s, the interventionist state has been strongly challenged and held responsible for the failure of the system. The advent of globalization brought with it new production structures, new players — particularly multinational firms (MNFs) — and a new institutional structure designed to enhance market operations. The dominant idea today is that the state, through its interventions, creates obstacles to the normal course of business, reduces market efficiency, impedes the establishment of social justice, and hinders economic growth. Thus, reducing interventionism will free up the circulation of capital, goods, and services, ensuring that markets function well. Market governance therefore seeks to weaken the state by strengthening civil society and private firms, as both a counterweight to government and to represent neoliberal theses.

These are the general characteristics of the reference governance model, which establishes market rule with, inevitably, restrictions on both states and individuals. How have countries north of the Mediterranean reacted to these restrictions? Have they managed to retain their autonomy?

Effective Governance: The Case of France

Because it would be difficult to discuss all of the northern Mediterranean countries, I first give an overview of the characteristics of most of the countries in the region. Then I look more closely at France — although it is impossible to say that it is representative of the forms of governance that prevail in each of these countries, because their respective histories and cultures are so different.

Most of these countries (those in the Iberian Peninsula, France, Italy, the Balkans, Greece, Bulgaria) are modern, if we define modernity as a group of values based on the idea of the individual as an autonomous subject and on the exercise of freedoms and democratic practices. As we have seen, these are elements of the reference governance model. On the economic level, some countries, such as France, Italy, and Spain, are fully developed, while others are less so, but all are involved in the process of globalization and must deal with constraints that push them to adopt institutions appropriate to the efficient functioning of free markets.

All of these countries are considered democratic and hew to the basic elements of market governance. However, the appropriate institutions — in other words, the design of governance — cannot be uniform from country to country, as each has a specific history, culture, and institutions. If it were applied uniformly, market governance would likely be in opposition to these national diversities. One must, rather, expect both states and individuals to want to adapt to globalization, although the former try to preserve some attributes of sovereignty under threat of the effects of globalization, and the latter try to preserve their basic assets — in a word, a degree of autonomy. The case of France will illustrate this approach to governance. Although the French state has lost much of its margin for manoeuvre, it has managed to integrate into the global-ized economy by undertaking competitive integration. The French state has maintained its position at the centre of the social process, whereas individuals, singly and in groups, have found ways to resist the new constraints imposed by globalization.

Governance in France: The Search for Compatibility between the Welfare State and Neoliberal Management

The origins of contemporary France lie in the Third Republic, which established the Jacobin tradition of territorial centralization of power and the all-powerful state. The founders were interested in creating republican spirit. This conception of society is based on the idea of citizenship defined as belonging to the nation. It presumes that citizens have equal rights and prescribes the elimination of particular identities to the profit of a national identity acquired, among other things, by cultural homogenization of the public space (Dieckoff 2000).

The republicans realized that this conception of citizenship might be seen as abstract, and local support would help to create a stronger attachment to the national community. Valorizing the local was a concrete way to shape the idea of the nation and, beyond that, to create national unity. In this context, the state was designed to be the guarantor of the general interest. In effect, in opposition to the liberal conception of the state as confined to the role of arbiter, the republican view proposed active state intervention in economic and social life.

After the Second World War, in line with the republican tradition, the state was called upon to regulate economic and social functions. This pressure gave rise to the welfare state, which ensured the continuation of sustained growth with full employment and guaranteed a gradual rise in purchasing power for the greatest number of citizens, thanks to a policy of redistribution and social protection for all of the population — or almost all. However, this interventionism became more and more difficult to manage as growth slowed, and, at the same time, social demands from larger and larger groups were expanding, leading to costs that the state was no longer capable of assuming. At the same time, and here we must see the source of the current French governance, the new global economic order was gaining strength, causing profound economic, social, and financial changes. Under globalization and its attendant restrictions, the state, firms, communities, and individuals were forced to adopt new institutional norms and envisage a different form of social management. These norms, in their optimal forms in the view of globalization, are the basis of market governance and supported by neoliberalism, as discussed above. Implemented in a country with a state tradition such as France, which is invested in social benefits obtained following compromises negotiated under the aegis of the state, such governance might easily provoke a social upheaval with unpredictable consequences. Faced with the strain of neoliberalism that was developing in right-wing circles such as the Club de l'Horloge — which envisaged it as social Darwinism in which the laws of natural selection would be combined with the laws of the market — the proponents of managerial neoliberalism sought, through new compromises, to reconcile the welfare state with such neoliberal perspectives. This current was not suddenly imposed on the French economic and social spheres, but was gradually adopted by a leadership elite concerned with preserving its influence by anticipating the changes underway, which it proposed to regulate by reinterpreting the role of the welfare state.

However, even with a weakened state, this elite, aware of the French people's attachment to certain social benefits, set out to design a form of governance that would solidify the pre-eminence of the economic sphere, with the support of the state and in partnership with other groups, while setting up new mechanisms for the social safety net. It was thus through state action that adaptation to the neoliberal prescriptions proved possible. The state instituted a governance of adaptation that, over the course of its evolution, was to be characterized by new relationships between the state and citizens and between the state and groups.

By the State

For a better understanding of how this governance was deployed, I first describe the status and role of the state in the globalized framework. The state still plays a predominant role in French society — no arrangements can be made without its participation — and this seems to contradict the neoliberal conception of the state. In fact, many liberal authors have posited that under the effect of globalization and over time, the state will be minimized — reduced to tasks that, in the context of market governance, will make it a "servant" of the market.

The French state has a status that is quite different from the one that proponents of globalization seek to confer upon it. Of course, the constraints of globalization have challenged some of the public-policy practices and objectives that prevailed in the times of the welfare state, but the state has proved adaptable; it has subscribed to free trade both by its membership in the WTO and by complying with the new global economic order dominated by international finance and the influence of MNFs. France has liberalized its capital market, opened its borders to global trade, and, as a member of the EU, applied the European directives, most of them of neoliberal inspiration, that have reduced governments' margin of manoeuvre — which some authors squarely term a loss of state autonomy. Indeed, given the speculative behaviour of capital, no government would take the risk of impeding its movement and incurring the penalty of seeing it travel elsewhere; the consequence is the restriction of autonomous monetary policies. Furthermore, the rules that the EU imposes upon member states include rigorous budgetary discipline (3 percent of GDP) and a narrow range for inflation rates. Thus, under globalization and the increasingly liberal orientation of the EU, states are forced to adopt many policies that go against the perceived interests of segments of their populations.

On the economic level, the opening of borders and market liberalization have made it possible for foreign firms to move into France and establish partnerships with national firms, acting in their own interest without the state being able to intervene, notably with regard to layoffs.[1] Similarly, when MNFs and local firms decide to move production offshore, in whole or in part, the state cannot step in, even though such moves obviously result in job losses and increased insecurity.

In the light of these observations and many others, has the state become powerless or, at best, is it confined to tasks designed to serve the market in compliance with neoliberal prescriptions? In fact, states are attempting to orient themselves towards insertion into the global economy through competitiveness: we then speak of competitive integration and a competitive state (Deblock 2002). In this context, and this is one of the features of adaptive governance, industrial activities are reorganized in networks related to the global market (the Airbus 380 jumbo jet and the European Eureka space launch vehicle are examples). Moreover, under market integration, firms make decisions, notably with regard to investment, no longer in the perspective of a national market but with a view to regional and global markets. Specifically, competitive integration is understood as integration into MNF networks, in order to attract foreign investment and take over markets.[2] Integration also leads to competition among nations that is conceived as being based as much on the national interest as on trade policies, policies to attract foreign investment, and support given to "national champions" (Reich 1991).

33

Thus, the state adapts by engaging in what some call "profiteering adapted to market opportunities,"[3] a practice that shows that there has been less a retreat by the state than a new form of intervention. These adaptations are made with a concern for efficient interstate competition, to take better advantage of the internationalization of markets. There are repercussions on the social level: new protection measures and an aggravation of insecurity following the inevitable job losses caused by corporate restructurings. Groups and individuals react by creating new configurations of relations among the state, society, and themselves.

State and Society: Functional Democracy

One major component of society is the group of firms and workers that influence socio-political regulation by institutionalizing collective action. What has been called corporatism and, later, neocorporatism (Jobert and Theret 1994) dates from the era of large firms and public utilities within which privileged status was granted to certain groups of workers, such as miners, railway workers, and postal workers, in exchange for certain conditions, such as ensuring the continuity of public services.

Essentially, corporatism is seen as the collective incorporation of firms and workers into social regulation, through either co-management or job-regulation mechanisms, in order to reach a social compromise. There are different forms of corporatism. The first is trade corporatism involving groups such as workers at the Régie autonome des transports parisiens, the Société nationale des chemins de fer, and Air France. Such corporations act as partners with the state in codifying activities and preferential situations and do not hesitate to engage in protests or trigger conflicts (strikes, occupations of premises, and other actions) to obtain concessions of all sorts through state regulation. A second contrasting type of corporatism proceeds through agreements and results in co-administration, in particular regarding the domestic job market, as shown by workers and employers at Électricité de France. Finally, there are micro-corporatist factors in some large private firms.

That there are several forms of corporatism makes it difficult to establish a general social compromise. Thus, a corporatist social compromise is established in large firms and public utilities, industries, and services in which all interested parties, management and non-management, seek to legitimize their privileges. In the agricultural sector, the farmers' unions, and particularly the Fédération nationale des syndicats d'exploitants agricoles, representing a highly rural group, aim to co-manage agricultural policy, going as far as directly managing some public programs.

In this multi-faceted system involving broad but partial social compromises, the state establishes agreements and ensures that they are coherent. This is possible because many leaders of large firms, through their connections with the senior civil service, to which the majority of them once belonged, have had input into reorienting the state's decisions. In most cases, however, the state still plays an essential role in establishing social compromises with all of the corporations.

With slower growth, the pressure exerted by globalization, and trends towards individualization, the state's margin of manoeuvre has been reduced, leading, among other things, to restructurings and reforms in concert with the social partners. It is only as a last resort that market norms are envisaged for public management. In effect, whereas a vertical model of the civil service once prevailed, driven and directed by a powerful administration with expert elites, the weakening of the state has given rise to a horizontal approach in which cooperation and negotiation with a number of actors has become necessary.

These multiple and diverse stakeholders — citizens' movements, networks, associations, national and international NGOs (such as Greenpeace) — act interdependently with the government with a view to collective action. These relationships have changed the balance between the state and civil society, as the latter is strengthened by organizations in the associative sector (or third sector) that are developing the social economy. These organizations, which respond to needs previously met by the state, are able to influence government decisions. All groups seek to occupy the space in an organizational perspective (Thuot 1994) that characterizes functional democracy, which is taking over from representative democracy. Although it is formally represented by the legislature and by state unity, democracy is declining as the crisis in the welfare state swells, diminishing the state's capacity to promote social regulation centrally. The state has noted the differentiation between society and its many private interests, solidarities, and specific identities. It has therefore engaged in partnerships with social actors, inaugurating a new model of political organization, functional democracy, the mechanisms of which are based on cooperation; public policy results from compromises negotiated among different agents. Thus, participation in functional democracy, unlike participation in representative democracy (equal rights for each citizen regardless of social condition), has to do with membership in organized bodies or having a specific socio-economic status. Organizational space thus becomes meaningful in this way: groups, associations, and corporate-type organizations promote their interests, seeking to occupy the space available in order to obtain negotiated compromises. In total, the state remains present in the social articulation in France as manager and guarantor of social compromises. At the same time, even in a situation of slow growth, social groups in different sectors have been able to preserve their basic gains by negotiating and cooperating with the state.

In other situations, particularly when there are budget deficits, the state has envisaged partial privatization of enterprises such as Air France, Gaz de France, and the Société des Autoroutes, although these proposals have provoked protests by employees and fairly widespread public disapproval of the civil service (and the social safety net). Thus, the state is in retreat in neither the economic sphere nor social management, even though it is suffering the restrictions of globalization. It is pursuing a path other than the one leading to its elimination.

Moreover, social groups, through resistance — a form of preserving autonomy to defend their interests — do not hesitate to react to the state's attempts to reorganize its activities in the light of new financial and economic data imposed by neoliberal globalization. The state is engaged in retracting the social safety net because of the size of the public deficit caused by expenditures allocated to this sector. The reforms being proposed, oriented towards efficiency in compliance with neoliberal prescriptions, are provoking violent protests that lead to new relationships between the state and individuals.

The Social Aspect: The State and Individuals

The state was able to adapt to neoliberal globalization, through competitive integration, only at a high cost. Given the constraints of competitive markets, it had to give priority to the economy, supporting firms whose competitiveness-seeking strategies inevitably led to layoffs because of the job flexibility dictated by neoliberal logic. Similarly, technological developments made it possible for capital to escape union pressure, and collective agreements and institutional arrangements dating from the

Fordist era increasingly gave way to individual contracts with downward pressure on salaries (Mishra 1999). In addition, fiscal policy, a major instrument of social policy in the time of the welfare state, became more restrictive and generally benefitted firms and capital, to the detriment of other categories of the population — employees and the middle class.

In this context, the state was forced to deal with social problems in ways other than it had in the time of the welfare state. Now, social benefits were based on an organizing principle not of reducing inequalities but of eliminating poverty. Public intervention was reserved for the most disadvantaged, and the wealthier classes were left to find social protection through insurance and private services.

In this perspective, an in-depth reform of social security was planned, in order to redress a large budget deficit that had previously been covered by the state. A reform bill was drafted to substantially reduce social protection benefits that had been provided to almost the entire population. The bill was drafted by experts in administration, most of whom subscribed to neoliberal theses according to which state expenditures had to correspond to the management methods governing private enterprise.

The reform bill encountered strong resistance from the vast majority of the population; not only were the French attached to the social safety net system, but they also were determined to defend it in the streets. Tens of thousands of people gathered for demonstrations in France's large urban centres, and the prime minister of the time, Alain Juppé, was forced to withdraw the bill. Another bill, designed to reorganize the trucking industry, also had to be withdrawn after a long strike by truckers.

The government therefore had to institute a benefits system that distinguished vocational solidarity, represented by social security, from national solidarity. Social security was focused more on the working population, for whom solidarity was meant to provide insurance for the social partners. National solidarity policies were addressed to those excluded from the job market and to a struggle against poverty: allowances for handicapped persons and single parents; income support through a solidarity tax on wealth; benefits for housing; and an urban solidarity fund through which inhabitants of wealthy neighbourhoods contributed to the social development of disadvantaged neighbourhoods. There was thus a stratified system that had the excluded on the one side and the privileged, benefitting from public social insurance plus private insurance, on the other. How the state dealt with the excluded confirmed its role of offering targeted social protection, giving rise to a differentiated citizenship. Such policies departed from the past, when citizens were considered equal members of the community that formed the nation.

As the state withdrew and social cleavages appeared (Jacques Chirac ran his 1995 electoral campaign for the presidency on the theme of the "social fracture"), the perception of citizenship weakened, and individuals suddenly acquired more autonomy. These cleavages were accentuated by the re-emergence of regions, territorially delimited spaces within the national boundaries to which people were feeling a growing attachment, to the point of provoking "regional patriotism" (Dieckoff 2000, 16, our translation). The state was not opposed to this kind of identity on the face of it, but it sought to control it institutionally by organizing regions into autonomous territories (the Pasqua Acts of 1995 and, especially, the Raffarin Act of 2004), culturally (recognition of local dialects, among other things), and economically and socially (separate budgets to fund local projects approved by regional assemblies).

By taking these steps and even more pronounced action for certain territories, such as Corsica and New Caledonia, the state was in fact managing diversity while trying to preserve the unity of the republic. With decentralization, communities could promote their local interests through negotiations with the government and in partnership with the state. The assertion of local autonomy was an indication of greater institutional autonomy and a new form of citizenship that was not incompatible with the sense of belonging to a national entity.

Meanwhile, individuals, and especially groups of individuals, were defending their own interests. The writer Max Gallo stated, "There is no longer a state or a national community, but a juxtaposition of groups of individuals, communities defending their legitimate interests" (quoted in Pécheul 1999, 183, our translation). Along the same lines, Armel Pécheul observed, "There is no longer common interest or common legitimacy, but undeniably a return to a certain form of tribalism; there is no longer any reason to force groups, more and more concerned with themselves, to live together" (ibid., 184, our translation).

The individualization of groups strengthened their autonomy and was expressed by their penchant for negotiating or cooperating with the state to arrive at social compromises guaranteeing their benefits. Some groups contested the state's engagement with neoliberal globalization and being subjected to directives, generally considered of neoliberal inspiration, from Brussels. The most spectacular of these was the Bolkestein Directive, calling for liberalization of the European services market. It provoked a general outcry by the sectors concerned and was quickly withdrawn.[4] Even more significant was the rejection by a clear majority in France of the planned European Constitutional Treaty, which was criticized for a liberal orientation that, according to its detractors, did little for the social safety net or the defence of jobs.

In the light of these developments, the state, individuals, and groups found ways to react to globalization and its effects; not only did they strengthen their autonomy, but they also were able to preserve their basic benefits. In the context of national solidarity, even those left out by the economic upturn (labelled "lame ducks" by the neoliberals) were able to receive some protection provided by the state, which considered this protection to be a social debt (Jobert and Theret 1994) to be paid to the part of the population that was victimized by globalization. Thus, as France integrated into globalization, it was able to negotiate the constraints imposed by globalization and take advantage of the expansion of markets to increase the volume of its exports.[5] Meanwhile, individuals reacted in different ways to the transformations that society was undergoing. Some withdrew in favour of their regional identity to benefit from a form of autonomy, as the regions had administrative structures (regional councils, assemblies, and other bodies) in which the principle of election was the rule, ensuring a more effective democratic function, because of the advantages of proximity, than existed at the national level. Others belonged to groups that promoted their interests by establishing social compromises with the state. Both alliances did not hesitate to contest proposals or bills that they felt went counter to their interests with strikes, demonstrations, and sometimes violence. Often, these movements were so vigorous that they caused the bill that they targeted to be rejected, or at least revised. This form of autonomy was expressed either directly, through a popular vote (referendum) or a rejected bill, or indirectly, by a bill being voted down.

Thus, governance was manifested as a partial contestation of certain presumptions deduced from analyses of neoliberal market governance. As we have seen, the state is not simply one agent among others. On the financial front, faced with the assaults of neoliberalism, its margin of manoeuvre has been substantially reduced, since it can no longer unilaterally determine monetary exchange policies or oppose movements of capital. Regulation of the employment market is slipping beyond its grasp and being replaced by labour flexibility, which causes unemployment and insecurity. On the economic level, the state continues to negotiate social compromises with different groups. It has also adopted a satisfactory way to provide a social safety net for the most disadvantaged in the context of national solidarity.

For individuals, globalization is a daily constraint that affects both those who are employed and those excluded from the job market, and it is experienced as the source of job insecurity or loss. However, through withdrawals to identifying with the regions, social compromises made with the state, or struggles in the streets, individuals and groups have been able to preserve some of globalization's major benefits.

Good Governance and Reactions South of the Mediterranean

The expression *good governance* was coined by the World Bank following the failure of SAPs in a number of Southern countries. As noted in the introduction to this book, the World Bank explained this failure as a result of too much state intervention and ineffective institutions. This type of governance, which may be called public governance, is distinguished by an absence of transparency and by waste generated by poor allocation of resources, since markets do not function freely to reveal relative scarcities. Good governance basically takes up the main features of market governance by accentuating respect for freedom, a state of law, access by all citizens to the *res publica,* and accountability for those who exercise power.

Economically, neoliberal-inspired good governance favours the market and assigns the state a reduced role. The state is called upon to leave production to the private sector and confine itself to ensuring that the rules of competitiveness are respected. The state must undertake macro-economic reforms in order to create a climate propitious to private-sector business. In foreign trade, customs tariffs must in the long run be abolished, creating free trade and thus inserting local markets into more globalized, competitive markets. In this general framework, the state is effectively at the service of markets (as is already the case with market governance), which means that it must withdraw from most of its prerogatives. To weaken the state further, good governance seeks to strengthen civil society.

Good governance has become pervasive, to varying degrees, in almost all Southern countries, which, because of their economic difficulties, have been forced to implement SAPs and liberalize trade. However, these countries' social, historical, and political structures, combined with their weak civil societies, have enabled them to preserve their authoritarian — and sometimes hereditary — political arrangements. I turn now to discussing how the regimes in these countries have reacted by enacting forms of governance that enable them to preserve their economic margin of manoeuvre and political autonomy following their insertion into globalization. I then look more closely at Morocco, which, through experience tempered by its own strengths and by the effects of globalization, offers a possible path for institutional change.

Governance in Countries South of the Mediterranean

Essentially, the countries under consideration here are those of the Middle East and North Africa (MENA) region, which are very different from countries in the North. In the North, there are states bound by the rule of law. In the South, the states are authoritarian regimes, except for Israel and Turkey, which are considered democratic, although not very respectful of human rights — the former with regard to the Palestinians, the latter when it comes to its Kurdish minority.[6]

These states have common historical and social roots. They were tribal societies, and power was exercised by the most powerful clan in the tribe, which remained in power until another, more powerful, clan supplanted it.[7] Social life was organized based on allegiance to those in power and the subjection of individuals to the general will of the group, embodied in the chief, who guaranteed their protection, ordered group life, decided what tasks were to be accomplished, and ensured that each family had access to resources.

These countries underwent colonization (by the French in North Africa, Syria, and Lebanon, by the English in Egypt, and by the Italians in Libya) and were determined to recover their sovereignty through national liberation movements. During this period, they were swept up in the imperative of national liberation, represented by a leader with the support of a nationalist party. The leader was endowed with historic stature and charisma, with the result that governance was characterized by an omnipresent state dominated by the figure of the holder of power. In most countries (with the notable exception of Algeria), the state had existed for a long time but was in some form of reconstruction after the colonial period. This reconstruction was built on the heritage of a form of organization of state power based on a powerful public administration

41

with a mode of governance characterized by a dominant state and a large public sector.

Following the advent of political independence, the elites surrounding the leader were concerned with construction of the nation-state, which they achieved by creating a state with powers sufficient to eliminate the colonial economy and build a foundation for a national economy. Because there were few influential actors and a lack of means and know-how, the state undertook this project practically alone. It was launched under the impetus of the chief/leader/Rais/Zaim, who, wearing the halo bestowed by the struggle for national liberation, stood out as guide and point of reference. Such leaders were often surrounded by a single, completely loyal party, and many of their backers were appointed to high positions in the administration. This structure tended to strengthen as the leader's power, with overwhelming support, was consolidated. Typically, institutions and public life were strictly controlled by the central government. Thus, the legislature, which contained representatives from a single party, became simply an appendage of the government and ratified decisions made by the executive. Similarly, members of the judiciary, who were chosen for their loyalty to the regime, had no independence and meted out justice according to the instructions they were given. There was almost no institutional opposition or civil society available to contest the state's decisions. In effect, in order to preserve its power, the government suppressed all opposition, and the few recognized political parties existed within the limitations imposed upon them by the government. Organizations were controlled in different ways: union leaders were handpicked, and association presidents came from the single party or had proved their allegiance to the government.

Through the public sector and government departments and agencies, the state controlled most economic activities, decided on the orientation of investments, provided funding, and left only minor sectors to private firms. Interventionism, combined with a planned economy, made its mark everywhere: the currency-issuing authority was at the beck and call of the government, state banks usually granted credit without feasibility studies, agencies managed various activities, and so on.

Under such circumstances, the sense of belonging to a nation becomes abstract and emotional, making it difficult to achieve national identification with a state.[8] The sense of belonging remains with the family first and foremost, creating traditional relationships and forms of solidarity in

Southern countries,[9] whereas in the North this solidarity is institutional (Ben Abdelkader and Labaronne 2006). In the South, solidarity is material in nature: the family and the clan provide assistance and protection to their members. Furthermore, nepotism favours members of a particular family or region. More important are the institutional and political aspects of this unified society, which is more concerned with the immediate interests of its members and relegates demands involving personal or civil liberties or political rights to second rank. The personal nature of power, combined with the characteristics of an intermeshed society, determines the political functioning of the government, articulated around the binomial of allegiance and loyalty, on the one hand, and privileges and advantages (Michalet and Sereni 2005), which enable power to endure, on the other. The main beneficiaries are those in the circles of power, who draw various benefits and thus become the main supporters of crony capitalism (ibid., 11). This form of governance prevailed until it ran into major economic difficulties manifested through domestic and, especially, foreign deficits. Under these conditions, in the 1980s, most countries on the south shore of the Mediterranean had to seek aid from international organizations, which resulted in the implementation of SAPs to integrate them into globalization.

The primary focus of the SAPs was economic, but their effects induced economic and social consequences that resulted in a remodelling of society into one group that could profit from the new situation and another group that was penalized by it. In compliance with the SAP recommendations, the Southern countries had to start by re-establishing economic equilibrium both domestically, by reducing public expenditures, and, in foreign trade, by devaluing their currency in order to develop exports and restrain imports, with the goal of narrowing the trade deficit. After this stage, structural reforms were undertaken in order to liberalize economies and open them to global trade, on the one hand, and to encourage a market economy by strengthening the private sector, on the other hand. A number of trade-liberalization measures were adopted, resulting in the elimination, usually gradual, of customs barriers and trade restrictions. Domestically, the market and prices were deregulated. At the same time, the private sector grew and invested in tourism and in manufacturing industries for export, including textiles, agriculture, and fishing. To reduce the budget deficit, the state acted to slow the pace of development of health care, education, and the social safety net and cut back on public investments. It also sought to encourage private-sector investments through statutory incentives and tax breaks and by assuming responsibility for the infrastructure costs of attracting enterprises.

From this situation, a new economic and social configuration emerged. On the one side were those who were oriented towards foreign trade and were able to take advantage of the favourable exchange rate, supported the measures taken in the SAPs, and seemed to be the main backers of the government. On the other side were small businesses producing for the local market, a population that was unemployed or job-insecure due to work flexibility, and people of modest means leading a difficult life, for whom a minimum social safety net had to be envisaged. In terms of results, with few exceptions, investments stagnated, economic growth slowed, and the social climate worsened, a situation exacerbated by a new form of organized opposition manifested in the rise of radical Islam. Drawing a lesson from this relative failure, international organizations blamed the states, declaring their public governance a failure and suggesting that they adopt good governance.

Did countries subjected to SAPs react to globalization by implementing the appropriate measures to conform to good governance? How did these states, and their citizens, manage to adapt to globalization and yet preserve their autonomy?

Good governance had both an economic and an institutional side. For most countries, the economic side consisted of implementing measures advocated by international organizations (the IMF and the World Bank); the results differed from one country to another. On the institutional level, a distinction was made between democratic countries and those with an authoritarian regime. The latter resisted the institutional changes that they were asked to make. Their degree of resistance depended on the potential reaction of civil society. In countries in which civil society seemed embryonic or tightly controlled, the state was able to preserve its essential attributes, thus maintaining tight political and social hegemony. In countries with deep-rooted associative traditions, on the other hand, civil society could become an interlocutor for the government. In these countries, globalization, through the constraints that it imposed on states, would help to strengthen civil society and establish new relations between the public and private spheres, giving rise to a new form of governance.

In most countries south of the Mediterranean, such a scheme was quite uncommon, and Morocco, to which we shall return, was a rare exception. Whereas in the North, globalization was perceived as an intrusion, and the state and civil society joined together to attenuate its effects, in the South it weakened states while strengthening civil society, enabling the latter to assert its autonomy. Moreover, in the North, where democracy dominated, individuals gained freedom and autonomy, opening the path to modernity and citizenship; in most Southern countries, however, individuals remained subjects. The broadening of the space occupied by civil society, it is reasonable to think, would encourage a transformation in the individual's status from subject to citizen. If this were the case, globalization would have the merit of giving rise to societal autonomy; it would permit the emergence of individuals through citizenship. In the North, the notion of the individual preceded or was contemporaneous with that of citizenship; in the South, however, individuality, as opposed to subjectivity, came into existence as a realizable idea only with the emergence of civil society.

Such a path was an alternative to the process that gave rise to "Western-style" democracy and would offer countries south of the Mediterranean and others, especially in sub-Saharan Africa, a possible avenue to social change. In fact, such a path is implicit in good governance, which accentuates the role that civil society can play in countries with a strong centralized government. Although it is concerned with ending the poor management by governments in these countries, good governance helps to strengthen civil society to create a counterweight to the all-powerful state. Such a change is inevitably made over time and under specific conditions. In the meantime, most governments installed in Southern countries continued to resist institutional changes, contenting themselves with implementing, as economic necessity dictated, the economic measures imposed by globalization — measures oriented towards liberalization of both foreign and domestic trade, as the international organizations wished. Thus, freedom of trade was strengthened as customs tariffs were reduced and domestic economic spaces were opened to foreign enterprises, which could move in by purchasing privatized companies or acquiring shares. To attract business, special free trade zones were created. Similarly, incentives were offered for foreign direct investment. Domestically, markets were gradually liberalized with the abandonment of price controls.[10] A major effort was also undertaken to strengthen the private sector through measures such as a favourable tax regime, discounted interest rates, development of special zones, legislation on more flexible work, and an exchange rate favourable to exporting firms.

Such good governance measures had different results from country to country. However, on the institutional level, states also pushed back against the good governance model. Whereas it was expected that the state would shrink and confine itself to tasks likely to strengthen the market, practically all of the countries concerned remained strong states, and some countries took personal power almost as far as monarchy. An executive leader dominated the entire political scene, making the decisions that affected the country and seeking to extend his power by rewriting the constitution and, in some cases, transforming the government into a hereditary authority.[11] This crushing monopoly over the exercise of power conditioned the country's political and social life. In general, the government also created a powerful public sector with a strongly bureaucratized administration composed of offices, agencies, and public enterprises acting in various sectors and with standards of public management that were often ineffective. These practices were denounced by international organizations, which saw the solution in good governance.

In short, the actions and accomplishments of institutions in Southern countries were opposed to the principles of good governance. The governments of these countries were pressured to adopt more liberal policies, but this pressure was never followed up with action. Nevertheless, in some countries, such as Morocco, the situation evolved, and elections eventually took place under conditions of transparency; in the 1990s, an opposition party won the election, and its leader was charged with forming a government. Morocco was undergoing a series of domestic and foreign transformations. On the one hand, civil society in the country was quite consistent and played an appreciable role in various fields, tending to introduce more freedom into political life. On the other hand, Morocco, which was seeking membership in the EU, wanted to offer a reassuring image (Denoeux 2004, 69). Similarly, in Algeria, serious economic and social upheavals from 1989 to 1992 (riots in 1988, followed by violent repression) forced the government to open up to the world by authorizing the existence of a number of political parties, including one religious party, the FIS (Islamic Salvation Front). Thus, governments made concessions only under pressure, but these concessions did not challenge the fundaments of the regime in place.

The importance of civil society in each country was a function of its respective political and social structures. Civil society was supposed to act as a counterweight to the state, as a good governance advocate, but the realities of power in Southern countries conditioned the activities of their respective civil societies. Thus, the first cleavage appeared between countries with effective democracies and those with formal democracies.

One example of civil-society behaviour in a country with a formal democracy is offered by Egypt. In a book that deals almost exclusively with Arab NGOs — essential components of civil society — Sarah Ben Néfissa (2004) observes that there are two types of NGOs: advocacy NGOs and service and assistance NGOs. The latter are qualified as para-administrative organizations. The former have as a base, in Egypt and in other countries with a similar political regime, the small well-to-do segment of the middle classes. Their activities are aimed essentially at establishing fundamental freedoms, having human rights respected, and encouraging a democratic regime. These NGOs have little interest in the problems of populations, generally of a material nature, which explains the low level of support that they receive from poorer people with daily life needs. In the government's view, once difficulties with authorization had been overcome, the NGOs were considered subversive, and they were therefore subjected to much harassment, both administrative and police-related, and some were even banned. Nevertheless, these organizations constantly fought abuses of power, and they successfully placed human rights on the agenda in the Arab world (ibid.).

Similar demands arising from the requirements of globalization were placed on the agenda of good governance. Thus, states with a formal democracy were able to preserve the essence of their power, and the question was whether, by acting this way, these countries were showing autonomy. Accused by both international organizations (Kaufmann 2002) and the UN's Human Rights Commission of infringements on fundamental rights, these countries pointed out that, as sovereign nations, they intended to make their own choices with regard to institutional matters, in keeping with their history, civilization, culture, and traditions and in step with the progress of their economy. They pushed their claim to a political identity by stating that democracy, understood as Western, could not be imported but must be the result of a lengthy endogenous process proper to each country. The argument was apt, since it had taken at least two centuries for democracy to take root in the West! It was also said that this was another attempt by the West, representing itself as the exclusive

47

model in this area (Mappa 2000, 122-36), to impose its values and exclude those of others. Thus, proposing the democratic model (and at worst seeking to impose it, as was the case with the US plan for the Greater Middle East) was an ideological issue. This anti-West discourse was used by authoritarian regimes to justify their refusal to change their power structures, thus asserting their political autonomy.

The establishment of democracy in the West had its own genesis and paralleled the inception of the concepts of individuality and modernity. This was the basis of the transition to a society in which the individual was autonomous, Montesquieu's "singular being." Such individuals were part of a society in which they subjected themselves to an institution that they had created, and to which they belonged through reason — that is, the law, which itself is founded on reason. The principle of alterity followed, conveyed on the one hand by respect for the freedom of others and assertion of the universality of human rights and on the other hand by the acceptance, through consent, of a social contract by the separation of individual freedom from contractual freedom. The birth of democracy resulted from a deep and long rupture with an old order characterized by the primacy of divine transcendence and the weight of tradition. This transformation took place in Europe, which then sought to transpose its principles wholesale into social and historical contexts in which traditional societal forms have endured, such as allegiance and loyalty to a clan or a chief. It was therefore no surprise that the legitimacy of these principles was questioned in these countries.

Such arguments would seem to support the point of view of authoritarian regimes, which used them whenever necessary. But if one addresses the question of democracy as it is envisaged by authoritarian regimes that see it as depending on the country's economic development, implementing such development would involve the participation of the greatest number. Such an undertaking must involve a national community, in which decisions are shared among representatives of the state and of the citizens. In this context, the state would be called upon to arbitrate among demands made by different groups by seeking to reconcile the interests of both. Thus, individuals, as citizens and no longer subjects, would become social actors who could influence the nation's general progress (Enriquez 2000, 113) by referring to their traditions and inventing new paths. This thinking supposes that institutions permit all individuals to express themselves so that power is seen as something to be shared. The result would be decentralization of decision making; as

Enriquez (ibid., 114, our translation) concludes, "Development becomes plural and decentralized."

It was hoped that civil societies would be produced in these countries through "bottom-up" democracy, which is different from the "Western-style" democracy so strongly denounced by authoritarian regimes as an intrusion into their domestic politics. The democratic principle of conducting peaceful struggles for values and ideas, while remaining incontestable, makes the argument of authoritarian regimes ineffective. It does not lead them, however, to modify the nature of their power, even though cases of economic success under authoritarianism are quite rare (the case of South Korea under the dictatorship of Park being the exception). Usually, interest groups gravitate to the government in order to benefit from its largesse.

But whereas these regimes show resistance on the institutional level, the constraints that they undergo because of their integration into globalization reduce their potential for intervention, thus opening the field to action by civil society, particularly the service NGOs. These organizations' actions represent a form of bottom-up social participation and could constitute the seed of participatory democracy. In the short term, service NGOs play the role of a palliative for the state's economic and social action, as the government has more and more trouble satisfying social demands. Thus, they offer a way to attenuate the stresses of globalization — an important difference in the form of economic and social management used to contend with globalization. In France, the state not only negotiates its integration into globalization but also mediates between the interests of different groups by formulating different social compromises with them. Thus, it acts as both economic agent adapting to globalization and manager of diverse, increasingly autonomous groups by intervening to preserve their benefits. In the South, by contrast, the state is no longer able to cope with poverty and different forms of insecurity, and civil society is more and more called upon to step in. Will civil society therefore become the interlocutor with the state, or better, a stakeholder in the making of decisions, inaugurating a new form of governance?

With few exceptions, in countries with a formal democracy, NGOs and other organizations have been able to play some role in the economic and social field because they have placed themselves, as Ben Néfissa (2004, 21, our translation) emphasizes, in the "bosom of the state." In fact, most of these NGOs are para-public in nature and maintain a client relationship with the state. The state tolerates them as a supplementary instrument for its interventions or as a means of communication between those in power and the society, or a resource for social and political VIPs, and, if necessary, as a source of recruitment of political personnel (ibid., 19).

Most Arab NGOs that are recognized and authorized by governments maintain such relationships. This part of Arab civil society is the official part. The other associations and NGOs, forming what Ben Néfissa calls "virtual civil society," must be authorized by the government — authorization that is given parsimoniously so as to impede the emergence of a civil society that might become a counterweight to it and fertile soil for a democratic process. In fact, the efforts that are made by NGOs to act on behalf of disadvantaged populations have not permitted society to express itself from the bottom up and thus to trigger significant institutional changes. In reality, these associations' activities are tolerated only when they are confined to the economic and social fields. Thus, all social progress, in the broader sense of the term, is conditioned by the authoritarian leader's desire to tighten his hold on the political and social spheres in general, and on civil society in particular.

This conclusion drawn by international organizations is in contrast to their earlier contention that the assertion of civil society in these countries would provoke institutional transformations. Having seen the limits on civil society's margin of freedom to act, these organizations are now deploying their efforts to reform the state, with a view to expanding the "supply" of democracy. Denoeux (2004, 92, our translation) notes, "As vigorous as it might be, civil society cannot preserve its role as an engine of democratization and better manager of public affairs unless it operates in a favourable environment, one essential component of which is the presence of effective state institutions." There is thus a relationship between institutional infrastructure and the development of civil society in certain countries with a formal democracy. Envisaging the problem in this way might imply that there is no civil society in these countries. Yet, according to Ben Néfissa (2004, 19, our translation), "This administrative reality of Arab NGOs does not mean, however, that Arab societies are controlled by and subjected to the state. They still have an exceptional capacity for self-organization and survival within an economic reality that includes poverty, unemployment, misery and, sometimes, civil war or war of liberation, as in Palestine." This statement fits well with changes in Morocco.

Effective Governance in Morocco: "Bottom-Up" Democracy

In Morocco, the associative movement expanded as the government tightened its grip on society, and today there are almost thirty thousand associations (Roque 2004, 34, 37). The origin of this movement goes back to the very foundation of Moroccan tribal society, in which family and community culture were the dominant features and mutual assistance behaviours within the group were very strong. Because this tradition has endured, Moroccan society is quite cohesive today. It was only in 1958, however, that freedom of association was sanctioned by a royal *dahir* decree. During the 1960s and 1970s, the associative movement, firmly controlled by the monarch, remained discreet. Only in the early 1990s, when some political liberalization was initiated by King Hassan II, who was concerned about the international context and wanted Morocco to join the EU, did the associative phenomenon become an important part of the country's social and political life (ibid., 61). This reality was reinforced as the state reduced its intervention in different areas of economic and social activity under the constraints imposed by implementation of the SAP and integration into globalization. The state increasingly liberalized its economy and handed over more management to the private sector, as advocated by good governance. As the state withdrew, civil society broadened its base, diversified into different fields, and gradually took on greater importance within society. These changes highlight one of the consequences of globalization: with the state's margin of manoeuvre reduced, civil society can gain strength, through its contact with the populations concerned, to become the expression of bottom-up democracy. This process differs from the strategy that prevails in the North, where the state mediates among civil society's actions and is able to adapt to globalization through governance that engages with the relevant organizations.

In Morocco, civil society substituted for the state by performing tasks that were usually the state's responsibility, thus attenuating the harshest effects of globalization. On the political and social level, the state's difficulties, the international pressure exerted on the government, and the enterprising activity of different components of civil society led to a realignment of public and private action, prefiguring a new form of governance. In fact, the public space was reconstructed with the increasingly pronounced assertion of civil society. This bottom-up adaptive governance was formulated patiently following a long process during which the power of the monarchy (with, successively, the reigns of Hassan II and Mohamed VI) came to terms with the associative and protest movements represented by human rights groups, the feminist movement, and Berber cultural associations.

The process took place in two stages. During the first stage, King Hassan II dominated political life in an absolute monarchy and tolerated no challenges to his rule. The only associations authorized were charities and welfare organizations, many of them run by religious movements. All other forms of expression were repressed severely.[12] During the second stage, in the 1980s, a series of events led to the emergence of human rights movements and the beginning of an active political dynamic and associative scene. The context of globalization, whose credo includes the opening of spaces to the exercise of freedoms, made it possible to protest human rights violations. Moroccan lawyers initiated this movement locally; they courageously defended political prisoners and were supported by the families of victims of repression, who formed their own organizations to challenge the monarchy. The breakthrough broadened with the formation of associations supporting human rights, a social movement that became a "political force for change and a new form of action" (Mouaqit 2004, 88, our translation). Among these associations were the Organisation marocaine des droits de l'homme (created in 1988), the Comité de défense des droits de l'homme (1992), and the Centre marocain de coopération et des droits de l'homme (1989). On the whole, these associations sought to be independent from political parties and worked to create an identity by adopting a national human rights charter in 1990. With this political vocation, the human rights movement chose a path of action consisting of maintaining a permanent state of tension with the government. As expected, the government resisted, and obstacles to the exercise of freedoms were maintained. Nevertheless, the strength of the associative movement, and external pressure by organizations and media from around the world, led the government to soften its position on human rights in the early 1990s. From this détente came reforms to the legal detention system in 1991, the ratification by Morocco of the convention against torture in 1993, the creation in the same year of a human rights department in the government, the abrogation of the dahir of 1935 regarding repression of demonstrations, and the release of political prisoners in 1989, 1991, and 1993.

This relative political détente became manifest late in Hassan II's reign by the rise to power of an opposition party at the head of what was called an interim government. After the coronation of young Mohamed VI, civil society gained more strength. In addition to human rights organizations, which spearheaded the movement that brought political life out of its stasis (Mouaqit 2004, 85), other categories of associations and groups, each in its own area, helped to bolster civil society and extend the private sphere's occupation of the public space. Certainly, despite the presence of new actors, the existing political system continued to prevail. But as economic conditions worsened in Morocco, especially starting in the 2000s — stagnation of production, the effects of drought, domestic and foreign deficits — a window opened, giving civil society an opportunity to expand and bringing to the economic and political scene a new actor, the entrepreneur, whose objectives based on neoliberal thinking were to induce new public-private partnerships. Because of the kingdom's economic difficulties, the government was forced to liberalize the economy and accelerate the privatization process. As a result, private entrepreneurs were solicited by both international organizations and the Moroccan government. Furthermore, given the state's effort to build infrastructure and its limitations in this sector (and in others), civil society, through multiple associations, became a stakeholder in the country's economic and social modernization. Entrepreneurs' associations and social groups were the vectors of the reconfiguration of the interdependence between the economic and political sectors and contributed to restructuring the public space. They created an opening for democracy in the process. The line between public and private interest was moved, permitting the emergence of a new type of governance in which civil society was very influential.

Behind this process was private entrepreneurs' desire to succeed in business, especially as privatization took hold. They also used their financial skills for social and political ends. In fact, they converted their human capital of expertise into the potential for political demands (Catusse 2004). Whatever paths these actors took — the traditional path of privilege, the neo-corporatist path represented by the Confédération générale des entrepreneurs marocains (CGEM), or more individual paths — they sought economic and social recognition. For instance, they not only created wealth and jobs in various sectors, but they also took charge of community projects in both urban and rural settings and funded charity and sports activities. In 1995-96, the CGEM became a power broker in a new socio-political relationship, negotiating directly with local actors such as unions and with international partners (ibid., 176), instituting forms of cooperation with a view to social compromises. Through their economic and social action, they had opportunities to exert some influence on politics. Entrepreneurs participated in and won local and legislative elections and pushed their point of view in alliances of groups; they were instrumental in reforming and modernizing the political system, although they did not challenge the consensus around the formal political system. This social and political change was possible because the state, suffering economic and political constraints, was seeking "links with and paths to social and political intermediation" (ibid., 165, our translation).

Other components of civil society (political parties, unions, economic modernization and local development associations, feminist associations, Berber associations, and NGOs of all sorts) contributed to forging a new type of relationship between the public and private spheres. Like human rights associations, these groups, acting together, formed an endogenous phenomenon, which was reinforced by globalization. In fact, political parties and unions had been present in Morocco for a long time. By 2002, there were twenty-two political parties (Yata 2004, 179), most of them in the opposition, making various demands, although these demands did not challenge the institution of the monarchy. This real multi-party system was in itself the expression of a transformative society; whatever the ideological and political orientations of the respective parties, their common objective was to change the authoritarian nature of the monarchy (Roque 2004, 22). These parties became stronger in the 1990s, in the wake of the political freedoms agreed to by Hassan II and maintained by his successor. During this period, a political cleavage opened. On one side was a political trend towards modernism and openness to a democratic transition and, on the other side, a conservative trend represented by Islamist parties. However, all parties were characterized by rigid management and a degree of passivity, and a number of associations, particularly those promoting human rights, sought to separate themselves from the parties to preserve their autonomy.

The associations' actions for economic and social modernization best reflected civil society's importance in society at large. Quickly, these associations became substitutes for the inadequate Moroccan state, performing tasks that it could no longer assume and launching projects in different sectors: rural electrification, supplying potable water, irrigation, and infrastructure. Small and medium-sized enterprises were assisted by the creation, among other things, of a micro-credit and management-assistance system. Associations also attempted to reduce poverty by helping to create small, local job-creation projects in order to attenuate the unemployment that affected various classes. On the social level, a number of associations fought illiteracy by organizing classes, mainly in the countryside. Similarly, given the state's inaction in the health care field, associations mobilized doctors and nurses in rural neighbourhood clinics.

Other associations had more specific objectives. The first feminist associations were formed in the 1940s to promote a new status for women to replace the status defined by Islamic laws and principles, which stripped women almost completely of autonomy. Women's activism found support following the gradual integration of Morocco into the world market, which pushed the country to adopt institutional reforms to make its laws comply with the international conventions that it had ratified. Some of these reforms dealt with the status of women (Sghir Janjar 2004, 111), and women sought to influence the legislative process to obtain greater freedom. Politically, feminist associations assailed the conservatism of the traditional fringe that was opposed to the desire of the government and progressive organizations to emancipate women (ibid., 117). In addition to this strictly feminist activity, the associations were involved with disadvantaged classes: they conducted literacy campaigns, provided vocational training (particularly sewing classes), and supported charity works. Because these activities had immediate effects on the population, their position within Moroccan society was consolidated, and they became an important component of civil society. Their undertaking, particularly with regard to women's emancipation, was in line with attempts at change to which all of civil society subscribed, on the political and social levels as well as in public opinion.

The objective of associations promoting the Berber culture and identity was to see Berber peoples gain a rightful place in Moroccan society. This demand was completely legitimate, since Berbers formed the majority of the country's population. However, their identity and culture had long been marginalized, if not completely ignored. Only recently, under pressure from the associations, had the government begun to take account of Berbers' economic and commercial dynamism and their aspirations. For instance, Moroccan television, in addition to broadcasting in Arabic, the country's official language, began to broadcast programs in the three main dialects of the Amazigh language. In the schools, classes in Amazigh were planned, although the associations did not succeed in making them compulsory. In addition to this search to recover their identity, the Berber associations, like other economic and social development associations, were active in the fields of education, micro-projects, and community infrastructure. The Sous region in southern Morocco offers an instructive example of the Berber associative phenomenon (Roque 2004, 247). Here, an associative movement formed in a local communitarian culture showed that it could serve as the basis for modern associations. Its management method was based on the notion of lineage, according to which decisions were made at village meetings attended by either heads of families or leaders of the community's main lineages. The implementation of a democratic principle based on representation and participation stood in opposition to the principle of authoritarian decision making by a central government. Thus, the "base" expressed its point of view and participated, even if indirectly, in the making of decisions. The underlying hope was that Moroccan society would persuade the government to allow it to participate in the decision-making process.

In light of these various changes, it is possible to sketch out the contours of this nascent form of governance, the joint result of the consolidation of civil society and the reorientation of royal power to be open towards working with these groups. Globalization encouraged both movements. On the one side, civil society, in addition to its inherent dynamism, benefitted from a climate of greater freedom offered by globalization to solidify its base. On the other side, globalization weakened the power of the monarchy as it ceded power to engage in global markets and in pursuit of relations with the EU. Thus, this new form of governance tended towards a dualist structure, leading to relations between the government and private agents either as individuals, in which the status of the individual was to be defined, or as agents acting in organized groups that formed civil society.

The structure of the government remained unaltered, at least formally. In fact, the monarch still made the ultimate decisions regarding affairs of state. However, long-standing opposition political parties were consolidated, and the monarchy, now under the reign of Hassan II, respected the majority will of the population, expressed by the election of representatives to the legislature, and entrusted management of government business to the majority party or the coalition in power (in fact,

Youssoufi's government [1998] and then Tetou's belonged to the opposition party). This was not parliamentarianism as practised in the West, in which a prime minister governs with the support of a majority in the legislature, but a consensual relationship between the king and the head of government with regard to the exercise of power, with all parties agreeing that the nature of the regime would not be challenged.

Although such an agreement was slow in coming, it was more and more accepted by the monarchy, which also had to deal with the rise of Islamism, either in the context of legal parties (Yata 2004, 63-66) or because of violence in the streets. The government and the opposition (Mouaqit 2004, 86) found common cause in confronting political Islamist forces. This formal aspect of the exercise of power was oriented by the presence of other components of civil society. Some, in particular human rights associations, although they attempted to stay in the background, were political participants during the reign of King Hassan II and were used by different means to exert pressure on the government. Many other associations invaded the economic and social fields either by replacing the state, which was less and less able to play this role, or by partnering with it. Because they worked closely with the populations concerned, they acquired some legitimacy and were recognized as being directly or indirectly involved in making decisions.

In this model, it seems that the monarchy is no longer the absolute power that it once was. Although globalization reduced the state's margin of manoeuvre, it was, in fact, a multi-faceted civil society, acting in various ways, that first brought the system out of its stasis by taking on the role of interlocutor with the government in the management of society. There was a period of real transformation in Moroccan economic and social structures, through a process that was mainly endogenous, although it also benefitted greatly from an international situation dominated by globalization. Unlike other civil societies in the South, which were still dominated by their governments, civil society in Morocco not only succeeded in achieving autonomy but was also on the path to developing bottom-up democracy. This civil society asserted itself day by day, its actors increasingly becoming intermediaries between the population and the government. This way of doing things differed from the operations of traditional political parties, with which the public was quite disillusioned; it also explains the relative distance maintained between associations and parties.

Although tribal influence, especially in rural areas, persisted, modern forms of organization were possible. This was the case for a number of associations in the Berber Sous region (Roque 2004), where organizations were formed in both rural and urban environments, by modern paths, without colliding with the organizational structure of populations. This approach is significant for the future of Moroccan society. In effect, the associative movement, through its actions, is in the process of transforming people's status from subject to citizen. The presence of various associations and organizations has made possible forms of social participation, critique, and control (Claret 2004) that have strengthened aspirations towards greater freedom, created new values, and modified traditional structures. As civil society develops, citizenship is strengthened in different ways.

These trends, together, point to an innovative role for social actors that, through an increasingly dense social fabric, are forging citizenship and therefore participating in social change. Certain reforms have already been ratified by the state. That the associative movement is at the origin of a certain democratic evolution in Morocco is borne out by several facts. First, an active civil society is becoming more and more predominant and presenting itself as an interlocutor with the government. Second, and more important, the associations and organizations act in relation to, and for the benefit of, the populations concerned. Although this civil dynamic is necessary for the emergence of democracy, it does not produce democracy in itself. Such a change will require deeper changes within Moroccan society (see Roque et al. 2004). What is original about the Moroccan experience, however, is that it presents an alternative to the installation of an imported democratic process, which has little chance of success even when it is not disparaged. It is evident that the influence of civil society in Morocco has become sufficiently significant that, in comparison with the form of government that prevailed under an authoritarian monarchy, governance provides a completely different image of that society. First, there is a growing intermingling of public and private spheres that allows society to be represented and express its aspirations. Second, freedoms are expanding now that human rights are better respected and freedom of the press has been guaranteed. Finally, and most significantly, citizenship has emerged. In this transformation, globalization has played a supporting role in an essentially endogenous phenomenon. It has had the effect of broadening the spaces in which associations and local organizations are active and of strengthening civil society, the engine of this transformation.

When it comes to autonomy, it is the state that has been subjected to the most pressure by globalization; it has lost some of its prerogatives, and these losses have reduced its spheres of intervention. In contrast, globalization has benefitted civil society and individuals. The former has taken advantage of the withdrawal of the state to occupy the spaces that it has abandoned. The latter, because of the change in the international environment, have been able, through human rights associations, to obtain more guarantees with regard to exercising freedoms. Finally, the activities of associations offered the means for raising subjected populations to an awareness of the possibilities of citizenship through participation. They came to perceive that their situations were not simply being taken into consideration but were receiving sufficient attention to improve their lot in life. As people find that they are less and less marginalized, thanks to the efforts of associations, they find an identity and move from being subjects to becoming citizens.

This outcome is one of the most important aspects of the implementation of this form of governance. By enabling local concerns to emerge through the presence of civil society, it allows people to become citizens without having to cut the ties linking them to family and clan. Citizens, by this definition, become so in their civic activities and not in any universal sense (Catusse 2002, 175). The evolution towards citizenship and a civic sense is further encouraged by the private sector's expanding role in economic development. The private sector, guided by economic rationality, has the potential to instill new behaviours in economic agents and support novel, increasingly urban ways of life that generate new social arrangements.

chapter 2

Globalization, Autonomy, and the Euro-Mediterranean Space: The Issues of Regional Cooperation and the Challenges of Sovereignty

Faika Charfi and Sameh Zouari

THE BARCELONA PROCESS, LAUNCHED in 1995, legitimized long-established relationships between Europe and the countries on the south shore of the Mediterranean. Historical and cultural links and, especially, geographic proximity contributed to the assertion of the European Union (EU) as a main trading partner for these countries. Attempts at regional integration, stimulated by early partnership agreements between Europe and its ex-colonies in Africa and Asia, confirmed the EU's role as a regional leader. The main purpose of the Barcelona Process was to define a workable integration framework for the Mediterranean region. It was intended to constitute Europe's response to globalization processes because, beyond strategic interests, the EU was seeing its autonomy and sovereignty shrinking, its natural zone of influence crumbling, and its importance in the Mediterranean space waning. The countries on the south shore hoped to reap economic advantages from regionalization in the form of having their structural reforms financed and benefitting from technological transfers that would generate productivity gains. Regionalization was thus perceived as an alternative that would permit not only more advanced development but also an opportunity to avoid the undesirable effects of globalization.

Looked at more closely, regional integration is a phenomenon with two facets and two speeds. On the one hand, by becoming EU members, eastern European countries mark a new stage in their relations with Europe, based on the recapture of communitarian gains. On the other hand, at the same time as Europe is extending eastward, it is building a Euro-Mediterranean free trade zone that may pose a major economic and political challenge to countries in the region in coming years. This challenge is true in particular for Mediterranean countries, which, apart from Israel, are clearly behind Europe in terms of overall development. Economic prosperity and a political-strategic union, two objectives of the Barcelona Process, remain out of reach for these countries.

In this chapter, we discuss the economic and political aspects of Euro-Mediterranean integration. First, we situate the phenomenon of regionalism in the overall context of globalization and review certain key concepts, such as integration, autonomy, cooperation, and governance. Then, we analyze the issues involved in regional cooperation and how sovereignty is being put to the test in relation to the Euro-Mediterranean space as it is being constructed. Finalization of the Euro-Med project, as we shall call it, is likely to end states' decision-making autonomy; they will be forced to act within prescribed limits bounded by the rules of regional behaviour, on the one side, and the interests of national communities, on the other. After outlining a brief history of Euro-Mediterranean relations, we present a typology of countries in the zone according to their level of development in order to identify the form of integration (deep or shallow) implemented and its implications for development trajectories. We discuss intraregional asymmetries in the Euro-Mediterranean space — those within the broader community and between this community and the rest of the Mediterranean partner countries; we must also not lose sight of the need for the entire Mediterranean Basin to actively participate in and cooperate on the international scene. This typology confirms the idea of a schism between the countries of eastern Europe, which have been promoted to the rank of full members, and countries on the south shore of the Mediterranean, whose status is limited to their quality as partners. In addition, these Southern countries have apparently become caught in a rivalry between the EU and the United States that subjects them to many and varied pressures.

Regional Trade Agreements: Reflections of and Responses to Economic Globalization

As an economic process, globalization is defined by models based on foreign trade and deregulated markets. It is an evolving and diffuse process (McGrew 1997) that challenges individuals' autonomy and states' sovereignty. If a picture of how globalization will evolve in terms of freedom and equality seems difficult to anticipate, the vision of a successful project for "self-government by collectivities" (Nassaux 2005, 112, our translation) or the construction of an ideal of human rights (Castillo 2001) is just as elusive.

Faced with the challenges of globalization, many countries have opted for regional integration. Integration movements, when they are presented as hybrids such as the binomial "North-South," have been a factor in highlighting the gap between developed and developing countries, and this is also the case in the Mediterranean region. In these models, Southern countries are often marginalized and forced by large countries into commitments that they are not always able to honour. The example of the tripartite coalition of India, Brazil, and South Africa led those gathered at Cancún to believe that developing countries could have a say in multilateral negotiations.[1] However, most developing countries were not very vocal, because they lacked the means to promote their interests. Some attempts at South-South integration have come to fruition, such as MERCOSUR (the Southern Common Market in Latin America) — despite the diverging motivations of each partner in this "confederal" integration model (Siroën 2004). In Asia, another example of integration has encouraged intraregional trade over the last fifteen years. Although the dynamic has been weakened at times, the success of the Asian model is no longer in doubt. As Siroën (ibid., 15, our translation) notes, "Many see a liberal reasoning, an aspect of the globalization process, in this spread of regional accords. Others, on the contrary, perceive the strengthening of regional ties if not as an alternative to globalization, then at least as the lesser evil." The debate over these questions is based on the conception of the corresponding type of integration, the degree of autonomy, and the form of governance.

Regional Integration, Sovereignty, and Governance: Some Flashes of Clarity in Almost Total Confusion

It is difficult to judge how integration, sovereignty, and governance should be understood. To define these concepts, we must first distinguish the economic sphere from the political and geopolitical spheres.[2] It is necessary to see the connections between the economic and geopolitical spheres in order to understand the integration schemes implemented all over the world.

Integration, as a reflection of economic globalization, is generally defined as a movement of opening within a bilateral or regional framework. By inducing stronger competition, this movement stimulates the autonomy of the market, while pushing states to regulate that market. An integration project would seem problematic, at this stage, for both firms and states. As a result of the new strategy of controlling their production space, firms have become "nomads," going in search of sites that are most propitious to investment and low-cost production. Under integration, achievement of these objectives must not limit firms' decision-making autonomy but must encourage them to expand and to join markets.[3] Greater demand for performance and profitability, however, combined with sometimes-uncontrolled development of markets and uncertainty in the decision-making environment, makes firms more vulnerable and affects their autonomy.

Regional integration, or simply the choice to open to free trade unilaterally, leads to erosion of national governments' power and a shrinking role for the welfare state. Circumscribed within regulation of market behaviours, this erosion results in a clear loss of political, economic, and, sometimes, social autonomy, complicating the exercise of "public governance." Nevertheless, although multilateral commitments impose greater constraints on states, regional integration is presented as a coherent framework that would preserve, or strengthen, state sovereignty. International and intergovernmental organizations, which have the mission of defining a normative framework for the overall rules of conduct, have become instruments for representing the dominant power of their member states. Whether directed towards unipolarity or tripolarity, globalization has forged a system of unbalanced relations that international institutions have often reinforced.

Looked at from a different angle, regional integration presumes an adequate degree of cooperation. The cooperative game, however, often limits states' decision-making autonomy by forcing them to respect common rules. Although the substance of regional integration agreements preserves state autonomy, these texts define the limits of good conduct and require a certain form of self-discipline. Regional cooperation often refers to an essentially institutional aspect, described in the

World Bank reports as "good governance," which appears to be the missing link in development models (Pouillaude 1999; see also Chapter 1).

Integration in the Mediterranean Region: Cooperation or Confrontation?

The Mediterranean region is often described as a space of profound asymmetries at two levels: the first among countries within the community, the second in relations between countries within the community and those outside it. When divergences between countries north and south of the Mediterranean Sea are amplified, the two kinds of shock produced, general and specific, are even more painful because the countries are asymmetrical in structure and/or behaviours. First, we discuss the impact of these asymmetries on the success of a regional integration model by exploring the degree of regional disparity created and the adjustment mechanisms implemented to absorb or cushion shocks caused by regional integration. Second, we look at whether the loss of national autonomy resulting from the imperatives of cooperation is compensated for by greater regional autonomy. The answer to these questions is to be found in the degree of integration into the Euro-Mediterranean zone. We begin by describing the main aspects of the Barcelona Process.

The Barcelona Process: An Ambitious Project

A historical approach to the Euro-Mediterranean region reveals the difficulties inherent in any account of relations among countries in the region (Brasseul 2004). Despite a long and fundamentally conflictual history (Regnault 2004), Mediterranean relations are now presented in terms of "partnership" or the newly coined "neighbourhood policy." Launched in 1995, the Barcelona Process laid the foundation for a project of integration among the member states of the European Union (fifteen at the time) and the twelve Mediterranean third countries (MTC).[4] The goal was to arrive at a view to a common strategy for the institution of security mechanisms and achievement of economic prosperity in the Euro-Mediterranean region. This project was part of a partnership strategy that recognized the virtues of the free market while preserving a certain amount of national autonomy. In our view, however, any analysis of Euro-Mediterranean relations must take account of the simultaneous evolution of economic, political, and cultural components. This was the case for the Euro-Mediterranean dialogue, which was not confined to

North-South economic questions but also took into consideration the other two components.

In its economic component, the Barcelona Process called for the construction, by 2010, of a Euro-Mediterranean free trade zone, essentially for industrial products. Economic cooperation was financed by credits from the Mediterranean Economic Development Area (MEDA) fund, formed to help partner countries with their sector-based and general Structural Adjustment Programs, based, after 2001, on advances made on conclusion of association agreements with the EU. Beyond the negotiations on liberalization of certain economic sectors in bilateral partnership projects with the EU, the Mediterranean partners were asked to harmonize their laws with regard to competition rules and to make conditions more favourable for the circulation of capital in the region.

In its political component, the project was intended to establish a regular political dialogue among partner countries to define a common security strategy for the region. The countries of the south shore were still seeking an appropriate solution to the profound Israel-Arab antagonism in order to ease the pressure of the conflicts in the Middle East. The "5 + 5" dialogue started in 1990 was a subregional forum aimed at creating a space for dialogue on peace and stability in the Mediterranean. Other meetings, focusing on essentially military issues or, in a broader perspective, on political visions of crisis management, have since been organized with the participation of some NATO member states.[5]

The third component, society and culture, is designed to promote a social dimension in the Euro-Med project and further the cultural and societal dialogue in the region. During the 2002 Euro-Mediterranean Conference in Valencia, the decision was made to create the Anna Lindh Euro-Mediterranean Foundation for the Dialogue between Cultures, the vocation of which is to strengthen dialogue among cultures through a program of well-defined activities involving youth, education, and the media.

The inclusion of these three components made the project launched in Barcelona both seductive and ambitious. However, the striking heterogeneity of the countries in the region raised doubts about its successful outcome, since the interests of the different actors were not necessarily convergent. The EU was concerned about migratory flows, about repercussions that the political situation in some partner countries in the South might have on its stability, and about deficits observed in the South with regard not only to development but also to human rights and democracy, which it saw as essential elements in the partnership (Scalambrieri 2004). For the Southern countries, the goal of regional cooperation was implementation of regional transversal programs facilitating macroeconomic and sector-based reforms that these countries were likely to pursue. This goal indicates that the economic, and particularly financial, aspect of the partnership remained a priority for countries in the South.

The Heterogeneity of the Mediterranean Partners: Strength or Weakness for the Region?

One of the main characteristics of the Mediterranean region is its heterogeneity, which leaves observers skeptical about the feasibility of the integration project. Based on studies and statistical data on the region, it is possible to gain a more realistic picture.

When it comes to the evolution of Euro-Mediterranean populations, the demographic indicators leave no doubt about the divergence between the Northern and Southern countries. The United Nations Development Programme's (UNDP) *Human Development Report 2005* projects a demographic growth rate for the period 2003–15 seven to ten times higher for the Mediterranean partners[6] than for the fifteen original EU countries, while the rate is negative (the lowest level being -0.5) for the ten New Member States of the Union (NMS-10), all in eastern Europe. The report notes that the size of the population aged sixty-five years and over is of greater concern for the fifteen original EU countries and also, to a lesser extent, for the NMS-10. In contrast, the populations in the Mediterranean partner countries are much younger. Thus, a demographically fragmented Euro-Mediterranean space is still searching for its identity, which is apparently submerged in its "demographic paradox" and diversities.

With regard to territorial dynamics, the countries on the two shores have fairly similar problems — the exception to the heterogeneity observed in other areas. The region, overall, is characterized by a growing wave of littoralization and urbanization that threatens potential and natural economic rents. In the South, urbanization is generated by migratory waves moving towards the shoreline and large cities, a development that is due essentially to industrialization and the expansion of tourism; this migration both accentuates the imbalance in regional development and impedes sustainable and controlled urban development. Migratory flows from South to North feed European anxiety, because this influx of illegal labour is occupying the urban employment market more or less anarchically, making European cities fragile and particularly sensitive to inequality, poverty, and exclusion.

From an economic standpoint, the figures show a major gap in wealth among the countries in the zone. The EU contributes to 83 percent of the region's wealth and 20 percent of global wealth, compared to 17 percent and 5 percent, respectively, for the southern and eastern mediterranean countries.[7] In 2003, the average GDP per inhabitant, in current dollars, was US$30,536 within the EU, US$8,609 in the ten eastern European candidate countries, and US$3,832 in the Mediterranean partner countries. In terms of trade, the EU is the privileged economic partner of the Mediterranean South, but the reverse is not true. The EU is the source of more than half of all imports to the Mediterranean partner countries and the destination for 46 percent of their exports. This bias is most accentuated for countries such as Turkey and the Maghreb countries, particularly Tunisia. The EU is both the main supplier to, and the main client of, the Maghreb, for both goods and services. It plays the same role, to a lesser degree, for the countries of the Machrek.[8] Thus different parts of the southern region demonstrate different levels of commitment towards the EU. For the EU, in contrast, the Mediterranean partner countries are only marginal trade partners, involving a negligible share of European trade — just over 6 percent in 2003, below its 1995 level (Femise 2005). Even in 1994, Coulomb and Jacquet (22, our translation) observed that "economically, outside of oil perhaps, the European Economic Community could do without the Maghreb, while the opposite is not true." They wondered, in fact, if, "from this point of view alone, the Maghreb exists ... for the Community." This asymmetry in volume of trade, accompanied by chronic trade deficits, provoked the Mediterranean partner countries, particularly those of the Machrek, to reorient their trade flow towards the rest of the world, diversifying the provenance and destination of their goods and services to somewhat improve their trade position. In 2004, their exports to other parts of the world grew by 27 percent and their imports by 36 percent compared to the previous year (Femise 2006).

To create a group typology of countries in the zone (other studies have developed similar typologies), we used the human development indicators (HDIs)[9] of 2003, published in the United Nations Development Programme Report (2005), and the observed values of GDP/inhabitant in that year. This process yielded the following categories:

- A wealthy North — an HDI above 0.900 and a GDP/inhabitant of more than $25,000 — composed of Austria, Belgium, Denmark, Finland, France, Germany, Ireland, Italy, Luxembourg, the Netherlands, Sweden, and the United Kingdom.
- A developed Euro-Med — an HDI above 0.900 (with the exception of Cyprus and Malta) and a GDP/inhabitant of between US$12,000 and US$21,000 overall — composed of Cyprus, Greece, Israel, Malta Portugal, Slovenia (considered a "good student" by the EU, which admitted it as the thirteenth member country of the Eurozone on 1 January 2007), and Spain.
- A peripheral East — an HDI of between 0.800 and 0.900 and a GDP/inhabitant of between US$4,000 and US$9,000 — composed exclusively of NMS countries: the Czech Republic, Estonia (although its HDI indicator is above 0.900), Hungary, Latvia, Lithuania, Poland, and Slovakia.
- A weak South — an HDI of between 0.600 and 0.800 and a GDP/inhabitant of below US$4,000 — composed of Algeria, Egypt, Jordan, Lebanon (where, however, the GDP/inhabitant is US$4,224), Libya, Morocco, the Occupied Palestinian Territory, Syria, Tunisia, and Turkey.

This statistical summary of the region and its main characteristics is provided to show that, economically, the Barcelona Process complements and supports a scheme of trade integration in which the EU forms the pivot. It constitutes an "ad hoc regulatory framework" (Yvars 2006, 1, our translation) for the weakly developed economies of the region. The trade tradition that has been forged over time between Europe and the Maghreb, mainly, but also between Europe and the Machrek, makes the project look like a naturally integrated trade zone. A gnawing question remains, however: how can the Barcelona Process succeed despite the obvious heterogeneity of the partners? Because the geostrategic component is fundamental to this type of project, the success of the process depends not solely on greater economic cooperation but also on the willingness of the partners to subscribe together to a dynamic that may cost them some of their political autonomy. Without talking of neocolonialism, we must nevertheless recognize that a new form of implicit domination can be glimpsed in North–South alliances. It is a complex and fundamental point with many repercussions, and we shall return to it.

Constraints, Autonomy, and Cooperation: Their Place in the Barcelona Process

The European Union project owes its success to the desire of the founding countries to go beyond the reconstruction phase to development and progress. The countries that joined the EU in successive waves, although behind in development, took advantage of major structural funds to catch up, both economically and institutionally. The sharing of a common history, religion, and culture and being part of a geographic continuum were factors in overcoming the difficulties and constraints of expansion.

The situation is different for the countries on the south shore of the Mediterranean, since they are limited to a partnership supported by funds (MEDA) that are immeasurably smaller than the structural funds. Other issues include the rejection of all institutional integration and divergent economic systems (weaker economic structures, major social pressures, age pyramids that are wider at the base, difficulties with integration into the job market, and so on).

Theoretically, the Barcelona treaty did nothing to restrict the autonomy of the Southern states; they retained the freedom to choose macroeconomic and social policies. Countries in the EU, in contrast, are subjected to strict control by European institutions, which limits their autonomy. However, because they are so dependent on the European market and have so little influence in negotiations, the Southern states' autonomy is more theoretical than real. Because of the great heterogeneity of the different partners, the Barcelona Process cannot replicate the European model. The clearer the divergence among the partners, the more variable the "degree of constraint" (Yvars 2006, 13, our translation) imposed on them: greater for the weaker states and less so for the stronger ones. Furthermore, although it partially overcomes the challenges of heterogeneity, North–South integration does not exclude the persistence and aggravation of confrontation strategies in the region: the intrusion of new actors, such as the United States and, less forcefully, Asian countries, threatens to upset, or even break, its fragile equilibrium.

European Projects with American Ideals: The Leaders' Race

Recently, regional integration experiments have resulted in a multiplication of agreements with one or another of the great poles of the Triad. The diversity of these agreements raises questions about the nature of the relations established among the different partners. Does the centre treat its various peripheries uniformly or asymmetrically? Regional integration movements have traditionally involved zones in geographic proximity. Sometimes, however, this integration overflows natural zones of influence to extend to other centres, thus minimizing the importance of geographic proximity. It would be interesting to see if such a situation exists in the Mediterranean in the context of a competition between the European Union and the United States. To find out, we must assess the geostrategic relations between the European pole and each of its two peripheries.

The South Mediterranean: Economically Turned towards Europe, Politically Turned towards Asia

First, it must be kept in mind that, economically, the European market is the main supplier and outlet for South Mediterranean countries. In addition, the EU supplies 36 percent of all foreign direct investment contributions and €3 billion in the form of loans and donations, making it the principal source of investments. The EU is also a favourite destination for immigrants and a major source of tourist flows. Politically, however, the Maghreb is more turned towards an Arabian East that is deeply concerned with the Israel-Arab conflict. Second, the peoples of these two groups, together, are attempting to revive an Arab and Muslim entity that is geographically, linguistically, and culturally unified. The Iraq War and the perception of a Europe increasingly detached from its southern neighbours have tended to breathe new life into this movement.

The rise of globalization has made countries aware of the need to strengthen their Mediterranean identity, although this identity may have a variety of origins and purposes. For Europe, the partnership with the South is mainly political in nature: it aims to preserve good relations with Arab countries despite the Israeli fact, while keeping an eye on the energy stakes. Strategically, the south shore of the Mediterranean forms a reserved domain; during the Cold War, it had to be kept sheltered from the covetousness of the two great powers, and today it must be preserved from the growing interest of the United States. This is a sort of one-upmanship: the EU is managing to reconcile "family" and "neighbour" relations.

Integration of the NMS-10 with the EU: Conditions and Advantages of Membership

In January 2005, the ten countries identified as comprising the NMS-10 group officially joined the European Union, bringing EU membership to twenty-five nations. The EU's offer to these countries was conditional on their meeting a number of basic social, economic, and political criteria. For instance, a rise in their socio-economic indicators would imply that they were converging towards the level of the EU-15. For some, these conditions meant adhering to Western models of governance and, consequently, an acceleration in the steps towards privatization that would allow them to partake of the logic of market competition. A second economic condition was the need for the NMS-10 countries to harmonize their fiscal and regulatory systems with those of the EU. Socio-economic convergence had to be accompanied by political conditions. The pre-membership agreements were based on the principles of respect for human rights, establishment of a state based on the rule of law, and democracy as prerequisites for membership. The states of eastern and central Europe were also invited to match democratic states in these areas. In 1993, the European Council of Copenhagen set out guidelines by which candidate countries could meet these conditions: institutionalized separation of powers, free elections, and respect for an active political opposition and for minorities.

Nevertheless, the effect of expansion on the NMS-10 countries was positive, due to the major growth in rates of foreign direct investment (FDI) flows into these territories in the mid-1990s, and beyond their pre-membership period (Commission européenne 2005). The eastern European countries were successfully integrated into the EU in two stages: a transitional pre-membership period involving the reconversion of these countries to a market economy, and full membership, which demanded not only the dismantling of tariffs on trade in goods and services but also the free circulation of production factors between NMS-10 and EU countries. During both stages, an increase in FDI was encouraged, although it was due mainly to outsourcing by European producers. As the EU was the main investor in the NMS-10,[10] far ahead of the United States, the growth in EU investment flows slowed in some cases, although the flows were not redirected or displaced to the advantage of the NMS-10. A slow-down in industrial growth is forecast, but services should remain strong. All of this evidence shows that European investments in the Southern countries are very low compared to those in the NMS-10 countries.

The Rivalry between the European Union and the United States

In their race to world leadership, the EU and the United States are en-croaching more and more on territories that are not part of their respect-ive traditional geographic areas. This competition can be analyzed at two levels. On one level, the EU and the United States are following the same plan, first multiplying bilateral agreements with partners situated on their periphery that have comparable levels of development (United States–Canada, early European Economic Community [EEC] expan-sions), and then reaching out to developing countries. This recent form of North-South vertical integration (as opposed to North-North hori-zontal integration) gives incontestable superiority to the leader, at least when it comes to negotiations. On the other level are signatures of inte-gration agreements between, for example, the United States and a trad-itional EU partner, or the reverse. The economic rationales, justified or not, do not conceal the importance of the geopolitical and geostrategic stakes in the establishment of such transcontinental agreements, which include those concluded between the EU and Mexico in 2000, the EU and Chile in 2002, the United States and Jordan in 2000, and the United States and Morocco in 2004.

It is therefore increasingly obvious that regional integration, which is defined as a process of association among partners of equal or unequal levels of development, no longer necessarily involves geographic prox-imity, even when such partnerships encroach on competitors' terrain. In fact, many other integration movements have replaced the concept of geographic neighbourhood with that of "economic and political neigh-bourhood," such as the free trade agreements between the EU and South Africa in 1999 and between the United States and Singapore in 2003.[11]

Absence of a True Transnational and Multilateral Vision in the Mediterranean

In the light of preceding developments and although Euro-Mediterranean integration is high on the economic and political agenda of countries on the south shore, there are no signs that these countries are successfully attaching themselves to the EU. The countries of eastern Europe seem better placed to draw full profit from their membership and their re-classification in the hierarchy of European states. The process of regional integration initiated by the Barcelona Conference was not sufficient to create an economically prosperous and politically integrated space. The existing inequalities among the countries of the region have made the integration strategy an initiative imposed unilaterally by the EU on its Mediterranean partners. Because it is not based on transnational cooper-ation or on a multilateral (or "plurilateral" [Regnault 2004]) vision, the logic of integration proposed by the EU to its southern periphery amounts to exercising a right of inspection in its zone of influence. All the while, the EU acts without regard for the consequences of this policy on the economic or geostrategic position of its partners.

Forms of Integration and Cooperation Practices

The form of integration in the Mediterranean zone follows the centre-periphery model, the EU being the centre and the NMS and southern Mediterranean countries forming the periphery. These two groups are not homogeneous, especially since Europe has expanded to encompass twenty-seven countries. There are now two peripheries dealing with two widely divergent integration proposals.

In scholarly debates, integration is seen as part of the phenomenon of regionalism. Kébabdjian (2004) differentiates new regionalism from old regionalism. The former involves a fascination with adopting extroverted trade strategies and a form of "deep integration" that underlies institu-tional harmonization — that is, the "pooling of the regulatory system" or "shared regulation ... associated with centralized administration" (Siroën 2004, 45, our translation). In contrast, Kébabdjian explains, the regionalization of the 1960s was based more on strategies of substitution for imports on the regional level, which became a sort of self-centred regionalism. In a dichotomous typology, regionalism may be termed as *deep* or *shallow* integration (Regnault 2004).[12] This distinction in effect describes the differences between North-South Mediterranean integra-tion and the extension of the EU eastward. As targets of shallow integra-tion, as Kébabdjian (2004, 160, our translation) observes, the countries on the south shore constitute "satellites of the European bloc; they form a micro-constellation without economic consistency or international negotiating power." Deep integration applies to the EU as a whole and to the successive waves of expansion, including those involving the NMS countries.

Regional integration of the two Mediterranean shores is being built on a bilateral, rather than a multilateral, basis, even though multilateralism was strongly mediatized in the first conception of the Barcelona Process. In fact, each country in the zone has negotiated a partnership agreement with the EU to form, by superimposition, a framework agreement for all Euro-Mediterranean partners. Thus, the partnership has been created through a series of bilateral agreements between the EU, on the one hand, and the respective countries of the southern Mediterranean and eastern Europe, on the other hand. Because the status of the eastern European countries was changed by recent expansions, the partnership, in its multilateral form, no longer constituted a plurilateral agreement through which a form of association would be established between the European states, on the one hand, and all other Mediterranean countries, on the other. There was thus a power asymmetry favouring the EU in the negotiations, and the Southern partners missed an opportunity to form a pressure group that might have gained more out of the talks.

Thus Euro-Mediterranean integration appears, at first glance, to be North-South; the agreements shaping it ostensibly evoke the need to promote South-South trade and cooperation. This emphasis is based on the obviously weak level of trade within the Maghreb, which represents only 3 percent of foreign trade in the region (Femise 2005). Research on and development of a more complementary relationship among these countries' economies would raise the potential for positive trade. It is difficult for the necessary regional integration among the Mediterranean partners to be translated into action, despite the existence of cooperation agreements such as the Marrakech Agreement of 1995. This agreement led to the formation of the Union du Maghreb arabe (UMA), comprising Algeria, Libya, Mauritania, Morocco, and Tunisia, and the Agadir agreement, signed in 2004 with a view to establishing a free trade zone among Egypt, Jordan, Morocco, and Tunisia. In fact, the UMA has often been called "stillborn."

The "membership offer" that the EU made to the eastern European countries differed from the "neighbourhood dialogue" that it opened with the countries in the South. In the latter instance, EU policy called for the project to be a *discriminatory plan* leading to an unbalanced form of

Table 2.1   Forms of integration in the Euro-Med Zone

	Mediterranean partners	NMS-10/NMS-12
Type of integration*	Shallow integration	Deep integration
Centre-periphery structure	Accentuated	Moderate
Policy	Neighbourhood	Belonging

* Regnault (2003); Hugon (2003, 2005).

association. The new European Neighbourhood Policy, which concerns not only the Mediterranean countries but also Azerbaijan, Belarus, Georgia, Moldavia, Russia, and Ukraine, is based on multi-dimensional cooperation involving various action plans. It envisages concluding new strategic agreements, neighbourhood agreements, that do not stress tariff dismantlement (Femise 2005). Its goal is to give neighbouring countries the potential to participate in various EU activities promoting greater political, security, economic, and cultural cooperation. According to priorities set jointly with the partner countries, action plans were to be adopted "privileging political dialogue and reforms, trade, and measures gradually preparing the partners for participation in the fair domestic market and domestic affairs, energy, transportation, the information society, the environment, research and innovation, social policy, and contacts among communities" (ibid., 8–9, our translation).

Table 2.1 recapitulates all of the considerations regarding forms of integration into the Euro-Med zone. The table shows that an accentuated centre-periphery strategy with the proposed neighbourhood policy is associated with shallow integration for the Mediterranean countries, while the NMS countries slated for deep integration gain membership status in a moderate centre-periphery strategy.

Integration into the Euro-Mediterranean Zone and Governance

In the late 1980s, most of the developing countries in the Mediterranean region made a commitment to structural economic reforms. These reforms, liberal in nature, have led to a stabilization of macroeconomic imbalances and a growth strategy focused on exports and regional integration.

Subjected to the directives of international institutions, the Southern countries have not made significant efficiency gains or caught up to the average levels of income per inhabitant in Northern economies.

We have observed in this chapter that there seems to be definite asymmetry among countries in the Mediterranean region. The integration process implemented in the Euro-Mediterranean partnership policy could further aggravate intraregional asymmetries rather than attenuating them, thus strengthening divergences among the development trajectories of countries in the zone. Three effects might explain this divergence:

- *The proximity effect:* this is the more or less positive linkage effect for a country depending on its proximity or distance from the "centre." The imperative of development and economic catching-up may explain the positive effect that developed centres have on the nearest peripheral regions. We have attempted to apply this conception to countries in the Euro-Mediterranean zone in order to assess the proximity effect for each group of countries identified by the typology described in the preceding section. We chose the six founding countries of the Treaty of Rome as the most representative of the idea of "centre."
- *The structural effect:* this refers to an economic convergence on the "centre," representing the scope and degree of integration. It may combine a number of effects: specialization effect (index of concentration of exports, index of specialization); competitiveness effect (index of industrial performance); technological effect (linked to the capacity for innovation and technological dissemination, which may be measured by expenditures on technological research and development); and competition effect (reallocation effect measured by market penetration rate, mobility of factors, qualified labour force per sector). Since there is no exhaustive database covering all of the countries in the sample, we assess this effect mainly in light of the numerical data defined in the present research and borrowed from other studies.
- *The institutional effect:* this refers to a country's policy choices and quality of governance. It is measured by a range of governance indicators (drawn from recent analyses by the World Bank in this area).

Table 2.2 offers one way to assess these various effects by reference to the typology of states around the Mediterranean.

Table 2.2 Effects leading to different levels of development

	Proximity effect	Structural effect	Institutional effect
Wealthy North	+++	+++	+++
Developed Euro-MeD	+++	++	++
Peripheral East	++	+	+
Weak South	+	–	– –

Positive effect: +++ strong; ++ moderate; + weak.
Negative effect: – – relatively strong; – weak.

The "wealthy North" group — a group of developed northern countries, including the founding countries of the EU — shows a strong proximity effect, which is explained by cultural similarities, and a largely positive geographic effect. Because these countries form the reference group, structural and institutional effects are at the same intensity.

There is a similar proximity effect in the "developed Euro-Med" group. In this group, as well as Israel, geographic distance is largely compensated for by cultural affinities and economic convergence. While remaining significantly positive, the structural and institutional effects are more moderate, because of this group's attachment to the countries of southern Europe (essentially, Greece) and to the presence of Cyprus and Malta, two small island economies. The "peripheral East," with an identity still marked by its having belonged to the Soviet bloc and just emerging from a transition phase, is developing a moderate proximity effect, and structural and institutional effects are weakly positive.

In contrast, the "weak South" shows a weak proximity effect, mainly due to the influence of the Machrek, which forms, in a way, the "last periphery" of the Euro-Med. In spite of aspirations to deeper integration, the Southern countries do not manifest a real desire to elevate structural and institutional reforms to satisfactory levels, especially because the EEC funds allocated for this purpose are limited.

The Euro-Mediterranean Region: Completed or Still under Negotiation?

The Barcelona Process, initiated in 1995, was a step forward on the path to liberalization of industrial trade. The next step, set out in the negotiations, will involve the liberalization of services and investments. At the moment, only agricultural trade is still controversial. This issue, however, is not specific to the Euro-Mediterranean landscape. The agricultural dossier negotiated at the World Trade Organization meeting at Marrakech (1994) has proved to be the most contentious in the subsequent group of proposed reforms designed to ensure greater opening to world markets.

Although there have been economic advances, a number of observers feel that Barcelona has limitations for both the countries of Europe and its Southern partners; the latter feel that too many reforms are being asked of them, that their interests are not being sufficiently taken into account, that they are not benefitting from the same advantages as the NMS-10 (and, more recently, NMS-12) countries, and that the efforts made do not seem to be commensurate with the support programs chosen. We should remember here the discriminatory effect of MEDA assistance allocated to the Mediterranean countries, which is clearly inferior to the structural funds to which the NMS countries have access. For its part, the EU is questioning the lack of institutional reforms. To this must be added the fear that growth in overall trade among countries in the region will lead, in the end, to a form of unequal integration, in which the advantages bestowed through a two-speed process are diverted to the broadened centre, the EU, to the detriment of the periphery.

Regionalism in the Mediterranean poses the essential question of whether construction of a Euro-Mediterranean region would push the EU beyond its introverted vision to encourage the emergence of institutional structures with broadened jurisdiction covering the entire Euro-Mediterranean zone. It is premature to answer such a question, especially because the integration zone is far from being constructed but remains, in many views, under negotiation. Proof of this conclusion was the initiation of the neighbourhood policy in 2003, which, unlike the Barcelona vision of a Euro–Med zone of 15 + 12, involves 27 + 1 candidate countries to which are added six potential candidates and sixteen neighbours (the nine Mediterranean countries, Armenia, Azerbaijan, Belarus, Georgia, Moldavia, Russia, and Ukraine). No one can predict the effect of the neighbourhood policy on the final Euro-Mediterranean configuration or what will happen after the neighbourhood policy expires.

Conclusion

Despite discourses that trumpet the ambitions of harmonization and the imminent common future of all partners, the Euro–Mediterranean zone is still a largely fragmented region with one major developed pole, concerned mainly with the success of its own expansion initiatives, and a constellation of small economies with delayed development that are not economically integrated. The construction of a Euro-Mediterranean space must certainly start with the EU taking an "a-centric" position and not promoting a quasi-unilateral vision. Although the South has partially overcome the shock of the old conflicts with Europe, it must also subscribe to a strategic vision of a stable zone extending to the borders of Europe. The common future must result from the sharing of prosperity among all shoreline countries and the rest of the EC countries. Diversity must not be based on the inequality of partners. The successful construction of a Euro-Mediterranean space would, however, be a great advantage given the emerging challenges to the great economic poles on the world scene (North American Free Trade Agreement, Association of Southeast Asian Nations) and rapidly growing powers such as China and India.

In spite of the ambition underlying construction of the Euro-Mediterranean zone, notably for the Southern countries, this project must be positively envisaged in the context of globalization and autonomy. Although it presents difficulties, regionalization would be, for the shoreline countries, a chance to set their own rules and make real choices about autonomy.

PART 2 Globalization in the Great Texts

Globalization has a history, and a number of studies have shown that it is not confined to the past thirty years. In the dynamic of human interactions, striking similarities come to mind between past thought and protest movements and some of the issues and events that today's globalization raises. It is in this spirit that the studies in the two following chapters are presented.

The first case study is by Olivia Orozco de la Torre, who draws interesting analogies between categories and concepts in the history of civilizations contained in Ibn Khaldūn's *Muqaddimah (Prolegomena)* and the tensions regarding the process of globalization observed today in Arab Mediterranean countries. In Ibn Khaldūn's conception of history, civilization expands at the expense of *'asabīyya,* or group solidarity, which is gradually weakened; similarly, globalization is currently perceived as a phenomenon that affects the structure and threatens the autonomy of local communities. Those analyzing the future of Arab societies in the southern Mediterranean could find relevance in Ibn Khaldūn's description of three phases of the evolution of societies as a constant duel between the state and the market.

In the second study, Sonia Fellous addresses the question of the relationship between knowledge and power — more particularly, knowledge as a factor in national unification in the service of power. Fellous describes the unique undertaking of translation of the *Alba Bible.* This humanist enterprise took place in the Iberian Peninsula at a time when it was the last region of Europe where three monotheistic religions, Christianity, Islam, and Judaism, cohabited.

'Asabīyya, Market, and Society: The Contemporary Relevance of Ibn Khaldūn's Vision of Social Change

Olivia Orozco de la Torre

AT THE END OF the Second World War, Karl Polanyi (1957, 3) began his book *The Great Transformation* by stating, "Nineteenth-century civilization has collapsed." He then analyzed the changes that had led to this outcome through an examination of the eighteenth- and nineteenth-century processes that had shaken British society, then the remaining European societies, transforming their economies from premodern to market-based. In Polanyi's view, premodern economies were characterized by the fact that the market institution was *embedded* within society, in the sense that a particular group of institutions, norms, and customs defined and limited the role that economic activities and markets could play in the social system as a whole. However, these institutions and social entities, which regulated premodern markets, began to erode in the early eighteenth century. The Industrial Revolution and the expansion of international financial markets introduced new models of social and economic organization. These factors led to the creation of societies based on contractual relations and dominated by the economic principles of maximization of profit and utilitarianism, which threatened old forms of social organization by reducing human relations to simple market relations (ibid., 41-42). The consequences, Polanyi explained — the rise of socialism, nationalism, and Nazism, as well as the world wars that were their extension — were reactions by societies and individuals to processes that had alienated human beings and destroyed their basic social safety net (ibid., 237-48).

An analogy can be made between the picture that Polanyi paints of the years of the Great War and the last stage in the historical cycle, the collapse of civilization, described by Ibn Khaldūn in the introduction to his universal history, the *Muqaddimah,* written in 1377. He gives an account of the dynamic that led to the decline of civilization through the weakening of *'asabīyya,* a connection or feeling that ensures the maintenance of the social group as a whole, and the emergence of competing forms of 'asabīyya — what some nineteenth-century authors saw as a form of social cohesion that could lead to nationalism.[1] It was only much later, in 1981, that Ernest Gellner used the concept of 'asabīyya to explain nationalism in the Arab world.[2] Like Polanyi, Gellner saw the rise of nationalism as the result of social distortions generated by economic development in the region. In his view, nationalism became more attractive in Arab societies that were newly independent and beginning the development process, because it was seen as a substitute for the kinship relations that were being challenged by the new economic and social context.

Gellner compares Ibn Khaldūn to Durkheim, whom he calls a "theoretician of social cohesion," and he highlights the similarity between Khaldūn's concept of 'asabīyya and Durkheim's "mechanical solidarity," a form of social cohesion based on likeness (Gellner 1981, 86). However, Gellner concludes that Ibn Khaldūn lacked a concept to explain social cohesion in more complex societies, a role filled in Durkheim's system by the concept of organic solidarity, a form of social cohesion based on complementary relations or mutual support (ibid., 88). Thus, in Ibn Khaldūn's view, the expansion or growth of civilization seems to lead inevitably to social disintegration and the fall of the dynasty, which is succeeded by a new dynasty, capable of stimulating a new and strong sense of group solidarity. It is always possible to postulate, as some authors have, that for Ibn Khaldūn, religion is the source of the social cohesion required when the social group expands. Setting aside the religious aspect, Gellner defines the emergence of nationalism, which was promoted in the Maghreb after independence, as the feeling or element of cohesion called upon to fill the void left by the weakening of 'asabīyya following the expansion of the social group.

The situation of industrialization and rising nationalism analyzed by Gellner has changed considerably since he wrote his book, in the early 1980s. As a result of the inevitable expansionist dynamic of capitalism, as structuralist Marxists assert, or simply as an item on the neoliberal agenda summarized in the "Washington consensus," as Susan George posits, the last two decades of the twentieth century became a new stage in Polanyi's *The Great Transformation* (George 1999). In effect, some see globalization as a *second* "great transformation."[3] The process, described by Polanyi, of a market that tends to invade all aspects of social life and push out other forms of social relations seems to have climbed to completely new levels because of globalization. Not only have markets been released from any constraints, but they also have escaped the confines of the nation-state. At the same time, consumerism is becoming a new model of human organization in different world regions. Mediterranean societies have not been exempt from the effects of globalization and consumerism during the last two decades. Whereas Gellner observed the consequences of the expansion of industrialization and national construction in the Arab world, the first stage of the great transformation, the current situation seems to constitute the next stage in this process. If we extend Polanyi's logic, globalization can lead only to new conflicts, as mistrust and opposition build within communities that see their existence threatened by the advent of the new context of globalization.[4]

Ibn Khaldūn offers some concepts and categories that are quite relevant to an analysis of the social, political, and economic tensions that are arising today in the societies on the Mediterranean south shore. His concept of 'asabīyya, the role of this concept in the history of civilizations, and, in particular, his vision of recurrent tensions between small communities and the larger society are of interest to those who wish to examine the dynamic of contemporary societies at the crossroads of globalizing currents and the local alternatives of societies' economic and political autonomy.

Ibn Khaldūn was writing in the context of the decline of a particular form of empire — what Robert Simon calls the "patrimonial imperial system" — which is why G. Bouthoul ([1930], quoted in Simon 2002, 40) dubbed him the "philosopher of decline." This period of disintegration was characterized by the eruption of local struggles to preserve or establish community autonomy in opposition to centralized or broadened policies that were no longer sustainable (ibid., 16). While recognizing the importance of the political context, in this chapter I emphasize the economic and social aspects of Ibn Khaldūn's thought, drawing analogies that it may have with contemporary developments.

The Reception of Ibn Khaldūn by European Thinkers

Gellner was not the first to compare Ibn Khaldūn to other exceptional philosophers and thinkers. For Durkheim and French sociology, more generally, the Tunisian thinker was, to paraphrase Simon, the patron saint of a variety of disciplines, from economics to anthropology and history, and his theories were likened to those of Machiavelli, Montesquieu, Adam Smith, Comte, Marx, Pareto, and many others.[5] Ibn Khaldūn's terminology, in turn, led to a vast literature, long debates, and numerous reinterpretations of its different meanings, dimensions, and applications to contemporary controversies and critiques.[6] In sociology, Ibn Khaldūn was considered one of the initiators of the *verstehende methode* because of his use of ideal types, such as "tribal" and "impersonal solidarity," and dichotomies, such as urban-rural, sedentary-urbanized–Bedouin (Gellner 1981, 88; see also Anderson 1984, 118). His categories have been compared to the ideal types used by Weber and Ferdinand de Tönnies, and to the Hegelian dialectic.[7] In effect, the dichotomy that Tönnies established between the social types of *Gemeinschaft* (the communal, elementary group founded on neighbourhood connections) and *Gesellschaft* (society or the larger group sustained by instrumental objectives) bears traces of the Khaldūnian division between Bedouin society and sedentary-urban society described in the *Muqaddimah*.

Part of the attraction of Ibn Khaldūn's work, which might explain the profusion of writings devoted to it and the versatile use of its concepts, arises from the heuristic power of the "conceptual and paradigmatic frameworks" on which he constructed his philosophy of history (Talib 2005, 70, our translation). However, the heuristic power in Ibn Khaldūn's world is likely the result of how his texts were first received and read in Europe, how they affected European imaginaries, and how, as a consequence, they shaped contemporary conceptions of social change.[8]

A detailed analysis of how the different translations of the *Muqaddimah* were received, similar to the analysis that Hannoum conducted for *L'histoire des Berbères,* is, as far as I know, still to be done. In their studies of the reception of the *Muqaddimah,* however, Simon (2002) and Hannoum (2003) put their fingers on an aspect that is essential to my analysis: the interwoven history of the reception of *Muqaddimah* and the construction of knowledge in the modern social sciences in Europe. In 1887, Tönnies published *Gemeinschaft und Gesellschaft,* only six years before Durkheim's book came out but twenty-four years after the first translation of the

Muqaddimah (by Slane, 1863-68) appeared, and almost a century after European "Orientalist" thinkers began to become familiar with Ibn Khaldūn's work.[9] Obviously, it is difficult to know whether Tönnies had read the *Muqaddimah (Introduction to Universal History)* in French or through German historiography, or if the book had an influence on Durkheim and on French sociological research.[10] As Simon and Hannoum have noted, sociology in France developed in parallel with the study of the Berbers in Algeria, which was being conducted at the same time as Ibn Khaldūn's work was being discovered, along with the vision of history depicted in the *Muqaddimah* (Simon 2002, 23). Nevertheless, as Simon suggests and Hannoum illustrates textually, this early reading of Ibn Khaldūn's categories — in particular, the hypothetical opposition between Berbers and Arabs, which later research negated — was profoundly affected by colonial discourse.[11] After the French conquest of Algeria in 1830, this discourse claimed to see a "civilized" character in the Berber allies, as opposed to a supposed inherent incapacity of Islam to develop because of its attachment to nomadic characteristics.[12] As a consequence, Ibn Khaldūn's categories not only resemble or predate those of European anthropology and sociology but also are part of the imaginary within which the European concepts took shape.

Ibn Khaldūn's Vision of Social Change

Among the aspects of Ibn Khaldūn's vision of history that are relevant to the analysis of the current context of globalization in the Mediterranean, two deserve particular attention: his definition of 'asabīyya, and the role that it plays in social change and in the transition from one stage to another in the history of civilization. With regard to the first aspect, it is important to clarify the nature of the "social connection" and the types of social groups to which 'asabīyya refers. This will enable us to verify whether it is related to the type of solidarity or cohesion that unifies certain communities in their demands for more autonomy or independence from the global trends and models of economic and social organization that globalization seems to impose. With regard to the second aspect, it is essential to reconsider the roles played by 'asabīyya in genealogy and the evolution of dynasties from the *badāwah* stage (Bedouin society) to the *hadârah* stage (civilization). The objective here is to examine how expansion of civilization — and, incidentally, the grandeur and decadence of the dynasty, according to Ibn Khaldūn — is related to the process of globalization. This involves, first, ascertaining that the expansion of civilization and the elevation of dynasty created a process of economic and social integration that weakened other forms of social organization; second, examining whether this expansion process destabilized the dynasty's political structures, thus creating tensions and reactions within local communities.

Ibn Khaldūn's Concept of 'Asabīyya and Its Different Interpretations

The first definition in the dictionary for the term 'asabīyya is tribal solidarity or group spirit (Wehr 1994, 720). In a contemporary context, it is defined as a form of national awareness or patriotism. The adjective asabī may be translated as "nervous" or perhaps even "neurotic," accounting for its possible neurological nature in the order of human passions. The word 'asabīyya is derived from the root word 'asaba, conveying the idea of attachment or connection. In this sense, it functions well as a link or social cement that ensures the preservation of a human community and could be translated as "social cohesion," an interpretation shared by all of those who approach Ibn Khaldūn from a sociological point of view. The word 'asaba also applies to the group (any association or solidarity of family relationships), which links it to the concept that Ibn Khaldūn uses to define lineage, which Hannoum (2003) translates as "generation," jīl (pl. ajyāl), a designation in which 'asabīyya is also manifested.[13]

Ibn Khaldūn first used the term in the introduction to the Muqaddimah, in which he explains that Al-Mahdī succeeded in his undertaking not only because he was descended from the Fatimid Caliphate but also because the people of his tribe, the Harghah-Masmūdah, supported him in the name of their shared 'asabīyya, his status, and the fact that his genealogical tree was rooted among them (Ibn Khaldūn 2004, 38).[14] As a consequence, Ibn Khaldūn is clearly referring here to the concept as a sort of tribal connection or sense of belonging to the group. He presents the concept of 'asabīyya more explicitly in the second chapter, in which he discusses the Bedouin form of social organization. 'Asabīyya is presented as the factor that ensures the survival of the tribe in the desert, giving the group the strength necessary to defend itself from possible attacks by rival groups. It is thus fundamentally a survival strategy, based on the deepest feelings of family ties, if not co-ancestry, that emerges among the members of a clan or tribe. Ibn Khaldūn then extends the use of the term to a more political connection.[15] It is a vision of the origins of human society that can be found in Aristotle: the most natural form of human organization is the extension of the family and those "suckled with the same milk" (Aristotle 1999). Also according to Aristotle (ibid., 4-5), blood ties define the earliest forms of human society that emerged as family relations and lineage. Reminiscent of Aristotle's view of the loyalty that the barbarians owed to the king, Ibn Khaldūn's notion of 'asabīyya not only covers the idea of the need to be concerned with the closest relatives and solidarity among members of a single tribe but also involves the loyalty that the members of the tribe or clan owe to the political leader, the one who commands all the others in battle.[16]

From Ibn Khaldūn's initial uses of the term, 'asabīyya may be translated as group feeling or solidarity in the context of the tribe, the clan, or the small human community. For a group of people who form an independent or relatively autonomous social entity that is isolated and in competition with other groups in a hostile or difficult environment, 'asabīyya is considered both a source of group cohesion, based on blood relations and family ties, and a guarantor of political legitimacy and command. In other interpretations, this type of legitimacy may also take the form of adherence to revealed religion (Saadé 1966, 166).[17]

Later on in his text, Ibn Khaldūn extends the meaning of the term to his explanation of social and historical change. Other than in tribes or during political uprisings, he examines how 'asabīyya may appear, to various degrees, among *mawali* clients and even in an urban environment (Ibn Khaldūn 1958, vol. 1, 269, 276, 284, 328, 332, 336, 381; vol. 2, 87, 119). The weakening of 'asabīyya is seen as a crucial aspect in the fall of dynasties, whereas the strengthening of 'asabīyya among competing groups or lineages that were marginalized during the expansion phase of civilization becomes the decisive factor in their taking power. This is how Ibn Khaldūn explains the succession of dynasties in the history of the Islamic world and the emergence of local dynasties emancipated from the centre (Gabrieli 1930, 488).

Different readings of the literature show the multiple and ambiguous uses of this term in Ibn Khaldūn's discourse. De Slane's mid-nineteenth-century translation left the door open to a wide range of interpretations and contexts, from family to partisan and national groups.[18] The nineteenth-century readings of Ibn Khaldūn interpreted (or modernized) the term in relation to European references — for example, to Machiavelli's notion of virtue — and several important studies in the 1930s tied it to the emergence of race consciousness or nationalism

(Simon 2002, 33, 40). Erwin I.J. Rosenthal's 1932 translation underlined the importance that Ibn Khaldūn accorded to the human group as a fundamental aspect of socialization, as an intermediary concept of group solidarity between the individual and the full Muslim community, the *ummah* (ibid., 45). Later, Kamil Ayad and Francesco Gabrieli contributed to a better comprehension of the concept by returning it to its context and restoring its complexity. Ayad noted that 'asabīyya is not an invariable form but a multiple one, because it is applicable not only to the tribe but also to the state or the empire, which explains the different types of "natural cohesion" (ibid., 42-43). Gabrieli also conceived of it as a "flexible and changing category" that enabled Ibn Khaldūn to break with preceding orthodox religious discourses and reconcile Islam with tribal solidarity.[19]

Following the analyses of Ayad and Gabrieli, Muhsin Mahdi (in 1957) and then Franz Rosenthal (in his 1958 translation of the *Muqaddimah*) emphasized the more sociological nature of the term. Rosenthal discussed the positive and generally abstract meaning that Ibn Khaldūn gave 'asabīyya as a factor in dynamic mobilization within the group, an argument that lent itself to a more sociological reading of the term.[20] From there, the notion of 'asabīyya was extended to mean "group feeling," which was interpreted as "social cohesion" by the proponents of a "sociologist" Ibn Khaldūn, and as "social solidarity" by Mahdi and, after him, by Simon and Katsiaficas.[21]

For the purposes of this analysis, I define *'asabīyya* as a multi-faceted category that encompasses different types of "natural cohesion" and social mobilization. We shall see some of its facets more clearly in the analysis of Ibn Khaldūn's historical dynamic.

'Asabīyya: Historical Development and Models of Exclusion

Ibn Khaldūn begins the *Muqaddimah* by presenting individuals as products of the natural and environmental conditions in which they are situated and have been raised. He then discusses the features that distinguish a prophet from other people and introduces his theory of prophecy. Only then does he turn to analysis of different types of social groups, from Bedouins and Arabs to sedentary peoples. The Bedouins seem to have the simplest form of social association because of certain material conditions. Through the nature and energy of this form of social organization, which is transformed by both religion and political propaganda, 'asabīyya becomes a decisive factor in the emergence of political structures, as discussed in Chapter 3 of the book. In Chapter 4, Ibn Khaldūn turns towards the economic relationship between the Bedouins' rural environment and the "civilization" of urban dwellers.[22] In the expansion phase of civilization, a dynasty or lineage, which began as nomadic and with 'asabīyya rooted in the Bedouin way of life, becomes sedentary and develops until it finally loses its nomadic or Bedouin nature and the related values. The transition from al-'umrān 'al-badawī to al-'umrān al-hadārī, from nomadic civilization to sedentary civilization, determines the entire dynamic of growth and decline of the civilization.

Nevertheless, in the *Muqaddimah,* the Bedouins coexist and interact with forms of sedentary social organization. Ibn Khaldūn mentions, for instance, the existence of trade and economic relations between the two societies, although these relations cost the Bedouins some of their original character. When a sedentarized form of social organization trades or comes into contact (coexists) with a nomadic form of social organization for a relatively long period, the former "corrupts" the latter by instilling the values and social norms of a sedentary way of life. This "corruption" is spread by trade and consumption. Groups of rural dwellers or Bedouins trade basic raw materials, such as farm goods and cattle, for processed or luxury goods made by the urban social group. In this way, the Bedouins become habituated to abundance and superfluity and acclimated to more comfortable ways of life. As a consequence, their 'asabīyya is dulled, and they end up being completely assimilated into the sedentary form of social organization, otherwise known as civilization. In fact, according to Ibn Khaldūn, the Bedouins began to use money solely because of their trade with sedentary groups (Ibn Khaldūn 1967, 236).

In Ibn Khaldūn's vision, consumption is the corrupting agent that leads to the collapse of all civilizations or empires. He explains how, in ensuing generations, the dynasty ceases to follow the spirit of struggle — the spirit of 'asabīyya. Over time, sovereigns become more genteel and lose "the secret of the Bedouins."[23] The representatives of the dynasty and the dignitaries in power adopt pedantic manners and become habituated to luxury and comfort. Given the needs generated by elite consumption models, populations are more and more burdened with taxes, which consequently restrict the society's capacity to develop (economically, in terms of revenues from land and manufacturing; spiritually and psychically, in terms of loss of courage, clan spirit, and motivation to progress), leading finally to the decline of the civilization. The reference to elites' consumption of material goods is clear, since Ibn Khaldūn speaks of their accumulation of everyday objects *(hawā 'ijuhum)* rather than basic necessities *(hājāt)*.[24] There is an obvious contrast between this situation and the idealized portrait that Ibn Khaldūn paints of the Bedouins, characterized by magnanimity, tolerance, nobility, modesty, and lack of interest in the wealth of others (1967, 434). This discourse draws on a tradition that can also be found among earlier authors, such as Ibn Rushd.[25] Corrupted by luxury and comfort, society is weakened, and 'asabīyya is dulled because of the expansion of markets and consumption (of luxury goods) by elites and leaders. In Ibn Khaldūn's view, spiritual decline accompanies material growth in the final stage of the expansion of civilization (Saadé 1966, 170).

There is a second aspect of 'asabīyya that is particularly appropriate to the contemporary context. As we have seen, sociological interpretations of the term have accentuated its essentially sociological nature and the positive dynamic that it presents for community cohesion and growth (in a progressive sense). However, the stationary, and sometimes even reactionary, nature of the concept must also be taken into account. As Simon explains, this form of social cohesion or solidarity defines not only the beneficiaries of the system but also those who are excluded from it. On the basis of Gabrieli's analysis, Simon compares 'asabīyya to the redistribution mechanism, which defines the "victims and beneficiaries" in a group according to their position in the changing social stratification.[26] By defining the beneficiaries of the social system, 'asabīyya becomes the main factor in maintenance of the system, the civilization, and the power structure that it helps to define and reproduce. In effect, whereas Ibn Khaldūn describes 'asabīyya as the feeling born of the need to protect the members of one's own family or clan, he attributes the same type of connection or complicity to relations established with clients or allies.[27] As a consequence, 'asabīyya also appears as the social connection that rules reciprocity and redistribution relations defining economic interactions in premodern societies (Polanyi 1957, 47).

Ibn Khaldūn's Vision and Contemporary Mediterranean Globalization

Five analogies may be drawn between Ibn Khaldūn's vision of social change, in particular his concept of 'asabīyya in the history of civilization, and the perceptions and tensions that have been observed in the current process of globalization.

First, according to Ibn Khaldūn, the expansion of civilization is related to a process of economic and social integration in which local communities (Bedouin tribes) are inserted into a larger structure (created by a particular dynasty) that weakens the local community's way of life and social cohesion. This is how the globalization process acts as the market economy expands. By imposing global economic forms of interaction, globalization disrupts local forms of economic organization and breaks up traditional or pre-existing sources of "natural cohesion" and order in local communities. Thus, the economic element present both in Ibn Khaldūn's social model and in the current globalization process is the role played by markets as distorting agents. In Ibn Khaldūn's view, the Bedouins' spirit and way of life, their 'asabīyya, were ruined because they let themselves be swayed by contact with the attitudes and consumption models of sedentary groups through trade and money. In the current context of globalization, the new consumption and economic interaction models are perceived as distorting instruments that alienate and corrupt local social and cultural forms.

Second, as expansion and unfettered markets threaten old redistributive and identitary mechanisms, local movements form ties in reaction to globalizing currents in an attempt to escape the dominant lifestyles and trade seen as being imposed upon them by globalization.[28] These communities, living on the edges of this process, articulated around what Castells (1998, 30-31, our translation) calls "resistance identity," seem to emerge and coexist in the face of the expansionist tendency of globalization. Tribal groups acted similarly when sedentary groups expanded.

A third analogy is related to the weakening of the dynasty's 'asabīyya during its expansion phase, the very process of which erodes its social base and thus destabilizes its political structure. Here, a comparison may be made with the nation-state in the current process of globalization and the "legitimizing identities" on which this entity was built.[29] Whether nation-states are on the path to disappearance in the South Mediterranean region (which is debatable, given the strength of some of their structures and political alliances, particularly in rentier states), national sentiment, which surged in the postcolonial period and which Gellner has analyzed in detail, has clearly diminished. Most people seem to be withdrawing from such national projects because of the negative effects of globalization, the welfare state's abandonment of its social commitments, or unpopular policies generated by structural reform programs. Markets and consumption play an analogous role. In Ibn Khaldūn's view, society, corrupted by luxury and comfort, is weakened, and 'asabīyya is ruined because of the expansion of markets and the consumption of luxury goods by elites and members of the government during the period of dynastic development. Some current critiques of globalization take a similar tone. The expansion of consumer society is considered to offer to the masses what Ibn Khaldūn's urban civilization offered the elites: material comfort or the hope for such comfort.[30] This objective is attained, however, only at the price of spiritual and cultural decline. Spiritual decline, which Ibn Khaldūn considers to be an element that must ineluctably accompany material growth during the final stage of civilization, becomes a crucial issue for all religious groups and movements reacting against the expansion of consumption and globalization (Saadé 1966, 170). These movements draw on Qur'anic precepts about trade and on works by medieval Muslim theologians and jurists, who felt that the market had to be regulated according to Islamic principles and values, to design their ideal model of economic organization in opposition to the current model imposed by globalization (Orozco de la Torre 2006, 140 and 143; Torrey [1892], cited in Bonner 2005, 405).[31]

A fourth analogy is that the forms of 'asabīyya, which have been weakened by the initial expansion of civilization, may serve as alternative sources of cohesion and mobilization when the dynasty itself collapses or when the social system is destabilized. In Ibn Khaldūn's view, one of these forms may emerge to impel the creation of a new dynasty to succeed the previous collapsed dynasty. Similarly, in the context of globalization, local communities may become alternative sources of social cohesion through implementation of new forms of organization; in the Mediterranean region, these local communities seem to be based on faith. In this sense, as Castells predicted in the 1990s, these resistance identities, based on Islamic fundamentalism, have given rise in the region to a movement of identities of purpose, in which Islamic movements offer new models of social organization.[32] As Ibn Khaldūn explained, in the early days of Islam, 'asabīyya was combined with religion to create a new form of civilization; similarly, Islamic movements may emerge in the current context of globalization to become a more worldwide project. With support from local or religious forms of group solidarity — sources of identity — they try to generate a sense of cohesion among segments of the population that have been alienated by globalization (economically, socially, or both). Building on local or religious groups, they try to play a civilizing or development role for all communities.

In relation to the appearance of identitary projects today, whether they are the product of Islamic fundamentalism, territorial communities, or local nationalism, there is a final analogy linked to the idea of 'asabīyya as a mechanism of redistribution. I have noted that 'asabīyya, by defining the social connections within the community, also determines the position and role of its members and the forms of social and economic interaction allowed within the group, setting up an entire order of reproduction and redistribution. It defines who is inside, who is outside, and how those who are inside plan to interact as elements of the group. In Ibn Khaldūn's view, this reflects clientelist relations based on the principles of reciprocity and redistribution, which form one of the characteristics of Polanyi's premodern economies — in other words, economies in which the markets have not yet become a connective force. This particular dimension of 'asabīyya is not only in conflict with global market principles but also promotes its own forms of exclusion or creates new ones — forms of exclusion that are not introduced only by globalized or self-regulated markets. The traditional, religious, or local forms of organization or socialization on which these projects are based also contain redistribution mechanisms, which depend on race, nationality, religion, or sex. Thus, the search for autonomous generalized markets may produce alternative forms of interaction and social redistribution, but it may also create or re-establish other models of exclusion. Globalization encourages a certain degree of homogenization in modes of consumption and socio-economic exchange. Under traditional or local forms of social organization, however, consumption models are attached to local values and customs and are based on respect for certain set social norms and, as a consequence, involve mechanisms of both exclusion and social control.

Conclusion

The current globalization process has been seen as a supplementary step in Polanyi's "great transformation." At the cultural level, the expansion of markets and consumer society creates tensions in that those communities and regions that reject these forms of exchange demand more autonomy with regard to this process. These conflicts and tensions may be considered reactions against the domination inflicted by markets through the social, cultural, and religious systems; in Polanyi's view, these reactions led to the emergence of socialism, nationalism, and Nazism in the early twentieth century. Such conflicts may also be extended into the reactions and tensions that arise within local communities as civilization expands, as Ibn Khaldūn so rightly observed.

In his introduction to history, Ibn Khaldūn tried to explain the tensions between local groups and broader societies that appear cyclically throughout history, in parallel with the expansion of civilization. His "ideal types" and categories are relevant to the current situation for different reasons: first, they are part of the contemporary imaginary, because of the relationship between Ibn Khaldūn's ideas and the development of the social sciences in Europe. Those who use contemporary sociological theories to understand globalization and autonomy regard these phenomena, in effect, through the prism of his work. Second, this imaginary also belongs to a common intellectual tradition stretching from Aristotle to contemporary alter-globalists, via South Mediterranean religious systems, that regards markets and monetary exchanges with suspicion. Third, parallels can be established between the social rupture that Ibn Khaldūn tried to explain and the changes that contemporary globalization induces. Finally, markets and consumption play similar roles in both cases, by transforming the equilibrium and the social forms of redistribution.

Discourses confronting globalizing trends denounced the pervasive impact that the expansion of markets and consumption society are having on local values and religious or cultural systems. These indictments are analogous to the "corrupting" character the Tunisian scholar saw in the increase of the pursuit of luxury goods that was brought about by the expansion of civilization.

We have seen how Ibn Khaldūn's concept of 'asabīyya is a multivalent category applicable to various forms and stages of social organization. I argue that it may apply to sources of "natural cohesion" and social mobilization in reactions within local and religious groups to globalization in the Mediterranean region. 'Asabīyya may apply in this context to the existence or re-emergence of communal and tribal ties, or to other kinds of loyalties and partisan adherences, including religious forms of identity and religious movements. While existing forms of social cohesion are undermined (the welfare state, communal groups, family networks) and civilization expands towards bigger social and economic entities (regional entities like the EU, transnational corporations, international organizations), certain social groups or communities claim higher levels of collective autonomy and return to local, religious, or traditional forms of social cohesion to create their own forms of development and social organization. In this way, current local and religious movements against globalization could be seen as reactions or competing forces that, like in Ibn Khaldūn's vision, appeared in moments of social distortion. Those movements appeal to different forms of cohesion, 'asabīyya, based on local identities, religion, or culture, to call for mobilization against centres of power and defend their collective autonomy.

However, we also saw how 'asabīyya entails a particular mechanism of redistribution that determines the "victims and beneficiaries" of a given social system. As a result, new forms of 'asabīyya may appear among those groups who benefit less from the new rules introduced by globalization, or they may also be a way of mobilization among those social groups whose former privileges are threatened by the appearance of new forms of distribution and social intercourse. Although it suggests a positive, binding component, it also can be used socially in pursuit of negative, reactionary, or exclusionist mechanisms.

In the same way that tribal or Bedouin communities resisted or co-existed in the margin of the dynasty in Ibn Khaldūn's vision of history, in the current context, 'asabīyya may take a reactionary form as resistance identities, following Castells' terminology. As the new 'asabīyya taking over after the decline of the dynasty, it may also take an expansive form as new project identities, which attempt to build a new social order. There are some moves among Islamist groups in the different countries of the Mediterranean region, which have turned to participate in the democratic game and adapted to offer more global projects. These moves seem to reflect a transition from resistance identities to project identities, from the 'asabīyya of the local defensive group to the 'asabīyya of the active expansive community. The final outcome, however, is uncertain. Those reactions and moves may create a sub-society or sub-economy; they may create alternative forms of social organization challenging the model of globalization; or they may be, simply, desperate reactions to the transformation of society, similar to the ones Polanyi observed in the second quarter of the twentieth century.

chapter 4

Transmission of Texts and Globalization of Knowledge: Inter-religious Dialogue in Castile in the Fifteenth Century

Sonia Fellous

AT FIRST GLANCE, a chapter on fifteenth-century translations into a Romance language seemed to me to be off topic in a work on autonomy and globalization. But I became convinced that the political project that led to the creation of these works has its place in the context of analysis of the globalization of knowledge in Mediterranean cultures. My focus is the relationship between knowledge and power — more specifically, knowledge as a factor in national unification serving political power. The humanist-type venture that I discuss here, the only one of its kind in any region or period, took place in the Iberian Peninsula, the last European region in which three monotheistic religions still cohabited — each designated as a *naçion* (nation) in the *Biblia de Alba,* the manuscript that marks the starting point of my analysis.

In the fifteenth century, some intellectuals thought that peaceful co-existence based on mutual understanding could be re-established between Castilian Jews and Christians. They sought to create a common cultural terrain based on the great religious, literary, philosophical, and artistic works of the three monotheistic "nations." Their fertile soil was a common language (vernacular), Castilian, that conveyed, through syncretism, the pluricultural knowledge of a composite nation organized around a centralized power identified with its language. Thus, in the early fifteenth century, the tradition of translation of great works into vernacular language was revived — a tradition that had begun with Alphonse the Wise (1252-84), who saw such translations as a means of imposing the hegemony of Castile on the other Christian kingdoms of the peninsula. For intellectuals and political leaders of the thirteenth and fifteenth centuries, translation had a role to play in the formulation of a universal language that would bring peoples together. This theme was a major one of the Renaissance but also pointed to a process that would resurface centuries later with the attempt to establish Esperanto and then the gradual and more or less successful imposition of English as the majority language of exchange, although it is not yet universal.

In this ideological current, the Grand Master of the Order of Calatrava,[1] one of the three great military and religious orders of the Christian kingdoms, commissioned translation of the Old Testament into Castilian.[2] The text was to be accompanied by commentaries by "modern" rabbis and to be richly illuminated, so that the manuscript would become the great work of its times. The central idea of this project, which was visionary, if not revolutionary (although the term is anachronistic), was that in addition to the transposition from Hebrew — and sometimes Latin — to the vernacular, the translation of the twenty-four books of the Hebrew Bible and its commentaries would reconcile, as much as possible, Jewish and Christian views! The stated goal was to unite or synthesize the two dogmas and form the basis for a centralized "national" culture based in the Castilian kingdom, into which minority cultures would be integrated to form a nation unified by language, territory, and faith. And this is no doubt why the architect of the project, Rabbi Moses Arragel de Guadalajara, who had accepted the commission after much equivocation, decided to record in a prologue all of the steps in the creation of the work, in which he also evokes Islam, at a time when the Christians were preparing to leave to conquer Grenada.

The *Biblia de Alba* comprises the history and the result of this one and only attempt at religious syncretism through universalization of knowledge about the Bible.[3] The twenty-five-page (in folio) prologue reports all of the exchanges — by letter and in person — among the people involved in the commissioning and production of the work; it also contains a sort of methodological discourse concerning translation choices — grammatical and semantic, philosophical and religious.

Moses Arragel de Guadalajara (ca. 1385 — before 21 September 1456) was a man of the Renaissance, and his knowledge extended to many areas of scholarship, both sacred and profane; in the domain of the sacred, aside from translation of the Bible, he was responsible for illuminating the text, gathering a corpus of commentaries from "modern" rabbis, translating them, and adding to them those of the Fathers of the Church, whose language, Castilian or Latin, we do not know. He was, according to the patron, one of the great scholars of his time, an experienced translator, and a renowned exegete: "We are pleased to have among us a wise man very knowledgeable in the Law of the Jews" (muy sabio en la ley de los judios).

The Grand Master of the Order of Calatrava asked Arragel to produce this work with his cousins, Don Vasco de Guzman, the archdeacon of Toledo, and Brother Arias de Ençinas, superior of the Franciscan Convent of Toledo, who was in direct contact with Arragel to develop their collaboration. The illuminations are unique. The 324 gold- and purple-highlighted miniatures that illustrate the text are related to no known model and do not seem to have led to copies. Some bear the mark of a remarkably singular religious syncretism (Fellous 2001, 231-43). They accompany an extremely dense rabbinical commentary followed, when applicable, by Christian commentaries, most of them concise. As a whole, the *Biblia de Alba* forms a true treatise on comparative doctrine, the only one that has survived from its time.

This manuscript was to be the work of its times. Arragel, an accredited master craftsman, aware of the ideological and political stakes that such an undertaking involved, supplied in his prologue a unique testimonial on the state of relations between Jews, the political powers (represented by Don Luys de Guzman, the Grand Master of Calatrava, and Juan II, king of Castile [1406-54]), and the religious powers. These came in the person of the two eminent supervisors of the work, the great religious and intellectual forces represented by the Dominican Don Vasco de Guzman and the Franciscans Arias de Ençinas and Johan de Zamora, of the university in Salamanca.[4]

During this period, a great number of converted Jews could be found within the church, some of them at the highest level. Pablo de Santa Maria[5] (or Paul de Burgos, ca. 1350-1435, formerly Salomon ha-Levi) and Jerónimo de Santa Fe, the champion of the Christians during the Disputation of Tortosa (Pacios Lopez 1957) (Joshua ha-Lorki before his conversion), stood out for their religious fervour. They maintained that the practice of Judaism was in itself the source of the Jews' error. Salomon ha-Levi knew the Talmud, as well as classical and scholarly philosophy; he belonged to the intellectual elite. As Pablo, he embraced his new religion with a conviction that took him to the episcopate. Pope Benedict XIII made him bishop of Burgos, where he had been the rabbi.

Don Luys de Guzman certainly knew the opinions of Bishop Paul of Burgos, who reproached Christian commentators — Nicolas de Lyre in particular — for having been influenced by Rashi and neglecting other scholars, including Maimonides, Nahmanides, and Abraham Ibn Ezra (all of whom are cited in Arragel's commentaries). When work on the Bible began, in 1422, Paul of Burgos was still alive, at seventy-one years of age; he may have influenced Don Luys de Guzman in his choice to accompany the biblical text with commentaries by modern rabbis. Like Paul of Burgos, numerous converts, many of whom championed Christianity in conflicts with the Jews, understood Hebrew and had access to rabbinical texts. But it was, nevertheless, a rabbi who was commissioned to produce this translation by a senior Christian dignitary, the third most important man in Castile after King Juan II and his minister Alvaro de Luna (Baer 1998, 529-31, 533, 549; Rucquoi 1993, 221, 223-24, 243, 245, 273, 274). This project, emanating from the highest level of the state, may have symbolized the continued hope of some Jews and Christians for a national reconciliation. Seventy years before the final expulsion of Jews, however, controversy was brewing between Jews and new Christians, since members of each group had to justify their choice. Indeed, the reasons for conversion were diverse: for some, it was a case of saving their lives and families; for others, who did not find themselves at the centre of the riots, there were socio-economic reasons; for a smaller group, it was a philosophical choice. The memory of their Jewish origin did not disappear, though, because Christian society proved incapable of absorbing so many converts all at once. This situation was behind one of the most serious confrontations in Spain's history.

After the deadly persecutions in 1391 and the Disputation of Tortosa in 1412-13, and their ravaging consequences for Jewish communities, most of what remained of the Jewish population and its intellectuals resettled in Castile, mainly on the land of the Order of Calatrava. The majority moved from cities to small towns where they could live more freely; this decision was probably the case for Moses Arragel, who settled in Maqueda.

Because the church had not yet approved an official Latin version of the Bible, the *Hebraica Veritas* remained the essential reference, which explains the repeated recourse to Jewish translators. That a Christian would commission a Jew to translate the biblical text into vernacular language was still conceivable in the fifteenth century, and the discovery of other translations of the great works of Judaism confirms this conclusion.

Jewish, or new Christian, translators continued to be the natural choice for all translations of Hebrew and Arabic texts. Multilingualism was common among Jews of the diaspora.

According to the prologue, Moses Arragel was himself known to Christians, who treated him with respect, even with some deference, for his mastery of Castilian and his knowledge of rabbinical exegesis. Don Luys de Guzman and Brother Arias de Ençinas, knowing and valuing his scholarship, even gave him the title of rabbi, a term up to then reserved by Christians for Maimonides and Nahmanides.[6]

In the early fifteenth century, the commissions for these major translations were always issued by the government or people close to it. The goal was to impose Castile's hegemony; its cultured language was to act as a catalyst for the centralization of forces of a divided kingdom ravaged by dynastic wars. After the aborted attempt by Alphonse the Wise in the thirteenth century, the process was re-established under the reign of Juan II.

The prologue written by Arragel gives information that allows us to better assess the stakes of this collaboration between Jews and Christians, and it shows that expulsion was not yet in the air. It remains the last testimony to an attempt at communication between cultivated Jews and Christians during one of the rare periods of calm, from 1422 to 1433, in a tempestuous fifteenth century.

The Prologue of the *Biblia de Alba*

The prologue is full of information. It shows that the commission was originally part of a large political and humanist plan that was intended to unite Jews and Christians around an agreed-upon reading of the Bible. But whereas the commission seemed to emanate from a single person, the completed work was apparently destined for a broader public. In fact, Arragel addresses not only Christians but also Jews, converts, and even Moors, in the introduction to his work, in his commentaries, and in the iconography based on rabbinical sources that only scholars of Judaism would recognize.

The visionary idea of this translation — and it was Arragel's initiative alone — was to present Jewish and Christian biblical commentaries that were not opposed at the level of dogma as a source of a common cultural heritage; thus, he is said to have deliberately omitted their provenance when he cited them. Because they were presented as "universal" commentaries acceptable to Jews and Christians, it was not important to specify the source — or, to put it another way, it was important to not specify it.

Nevertheless, this Bible, which was intended to be conciliatory, if not ecumenical, was seen as Christian by inquisitors and researchers up to the twentieth century. Nonetheless, it was revealed to be a profoundly Jewish work to those who knew Hebrew and the rabbinical texts. Was this ecumenism deliberate? Had the manuscript been coded, or was the degree of cultural interpenetration in these scholarly circles greater than has been thought?

Arragel's text is articulated around four major, intrinsically linked themes: the political context from which the commission was issued; the content of the text, criticism of which could have had disastrous consequences both for the author and for the community for which he was the spokesperson; the terms of his collaboration with the Christian supervisors; and the review of the work by the religious authorities (Fellous 2001, 71-102).

The inclusion of copies of all of the letters exchanged among the main figures involved in the commission gives the prologue the sense of a dialogue. The author thus prepares the reader for the arrangement of the commentaries on the biblical text in the lively and flexible form of a debate. Some passages form a historical testimonial of considerable value: the author forcefully relates the entire process of creation of the work; he lists the titles and the nature of all of those involved; and he outlines the social and political context (the virtues of the Order of Calatrava; his arguments with nobles, whose domestic wars were dividing and ruining the kingdom; the economic and social problems that these struggles were provoking; and the situation of the Jews).[7] He speaks of comparative doctrine and not of polemic, because "this is not the place for that." The prologue also contains a dictionary of scholarly terms, neologisms, and words lending themselves to debate or equivocation, which is an important philological contribution. He explains that he chose not to translate Latinisms that had come into common usage and defined the Hebraisms that he did not want to translate (Fellous 2001, 93-99). It seems that from the start the "modern" language of the *Biblia de Alba* was marked by the specific characteristics of this multicultural, polyglot nation, whose language was coloured by Latin, Hebrew, and Arabic.

Sonia Fellous

Figure 4.1　Ceremony of presentation of the manuscript to the Grand Master of the Order of Calatrava, fol. 25v, fig. 1.

Finally, the prologue also contains a commemorative historical icon-ography that shows all of the people involved in commissioning the manuscript. The images clearly illustrate the role of each player: Moses Arragel, being instructed by the Dominicans and the Franciscans (fol. IV), then taking his registers from Brother Arias (fol. IIr). The miniature portraying Moses Arragel kneeling before Juan II of Castile (fol. IIr) indicates that the commission for this Bible was part of a vast political strategy that went beyond the academic project. This hypothesis seems to be confirmed by the sumptuous double-page miniature portraying the ceremony of handing the manuscript to the Great Master of Calatrava, which closes the prologue and confers an official status on the enterprise (fol. 25v) (see Figure 4.1).[8]

The *Biblia de Alba* and Contemporary Translations

The early decades of the fifteenth century, in particular the years during the reign of Juan II, were marked by the return to a policy of translation into Castilian in order to establish the language as the hegemonic lan-guage of the kingdom. The desire to integrate into "national" culture the great texts of Judaism seems to have fallen within the same ideo-logical current, whether such integration was at the instigation of the new Christians who had joined the clergy, in order to have these texts' richness and true value recognized, or of those (perhaps the same ones) who wished to lead still-hesitant Jews to a gentle apostasy.

Did all of these translations emanate from a single circle of scholars and a single intellectual process that was midway between humanism and a political rationale? It seems to me that identification of the type of writing could constitute a reliable guideline for recognition of texts translated by one circle of scholars. Indeed, the writing in the *Biblia de Alba,* although it is in Latin characters, bears the mark of Jewish scribes accustomed to writing in Hebrew characters.

Paleographic Study

Handwriting is an object of study in itself. It makes it possible to identify texts, place them in a hierarchy, localize them, and date them. The iden-tification of a writer's hand sometimes contributes to knowledge about a text and its distribution, and it often adds aspects of the copyist's biog-raphy that had not been known previously (for example, a scribe trained in Sephardic — Iberian Peninsula — writing in Italy in a technique used in his country of origin).

Until 1992, the *Biblia de Alba* was considered a Christian Bible executed by a workshop of Toledo scribes and painters. But paleographic study has enabled us to determine that it was copied entirely by scribes accustomed to writing in Hebrew. There is thus room to speculate about the true makers of this work, and certain clues have revealed that Jews not only copied the text but also executed some of the illuminations and participated in planning the iconographic program.

The Hispanic-type writing in the *Biblia de Alba* is, in the term used by Angel Canellas, a textual bastard that involves the repeated use of certain cursive strokes.[9] In Latin manuscripts, a line of writing required two rule lines, and the lower rule served as the vector for the letters. Here, the letters are hanging from the upper rule line throughout the text: the prologue, the Bible, the commentaries, and the rubricated and gold-tooled legends. It is the only manuscript in Latin characters yet found, to my knowledge, that is written in this way. This writing technique, applied by Eastern scribes of Hebrew characters (in Hebrew manuscripts both from Qumran and from Egypt and Yemen) was also used by scribes in the Iberian Peninsula. These scribes, perpetuating this Asian tradition, also used the upper ruling line exclusively as the vector for the writing of their letters.

No "professional" Latin copyists were involved with Arragel's manuscript, and the calligraphy is by the hand of an indigenous "professional" of Hebraic writing. The copying, which took at least eight years — from 1422 to 1430 for the text of the Bible and the commentaries — is stunningly homogeneous from beginning to end of the manuscript. Folios 60r and 100r give good examples of this technique, applied to both the biblical text and the glosses and legends (see Figures 4.2 and 4.3). The legends that accompany the images are inscribed with rubricated ink for the scene of Moses before God's Angel in the Burning Bush, and in golden ink for the scene portraying the sacrifice of the two goats, linked to the Yom Kippur liturgy. The writing is suspended above the upper rule line — gone over in ink — in all cases. The second gold-leaf legend mentions the name of God in the Hebrew transliterated form, *Adonay*.

This technique was applied to all Hebrew manuscripts produced on the Iberian Peninsula and subsisted in Hebrew manuscripts written in the peninsula's Christian kingdoms until the end of the fifteenth century (see Figure 4.4). Other Hebrew manuscripts testify to this tradition,

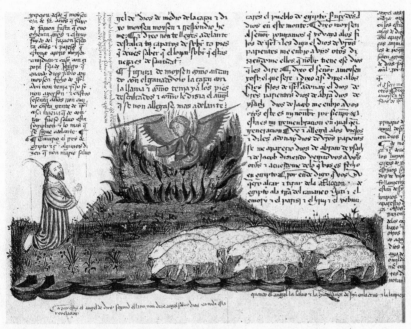

Figure 4.2 *Biblia de Alba,* fol. 60r, Exodus, Moses at the Burning Bush.

Figure 4.3 *Biblia de Alba,* fol. 100r, Leviticus, Sacrifice of the two goats.

Figure 4.4 Navarro, Tudela, circa 1300: Bible inscribed in square characters, the writing — the initial word as well as the rest of the text — suspended above the upper rule line, which is drawn in ink. Bible, Paris, BnF, Hebrew 20, fol. 129r.

which was exported by scribes in the peninsula during their exile and perpetuated up to the time that the printing press was invented.

I tried to find other texts written in Castilian in this specific technique, a textual hybrid, both sacred and profane, that seems to classify these texts — sacred because Hebrew in origin, and profane because conveyed in vernacular language. My research criteria were based on themes of works, names of scribes and translators, and type of writing. The great texts of Judaism that were translated during the same era, and that I have found to date, in addition to the *Biblia de Alba,* are a manuscript of *The Guide for the Perplexed,* translated into Castilian by Pedro de Toledo, a Jewish convert; four inventoried fifteenth-century copies of a manuscript titled *Proverbios Morales* by Shem Tov Ibn Carrion, written directly in Castilian in the fourteenth century; and an anonymous translation of *Sefer ha-Kuzari* by Judah ha-Levi.[10]

Paleographic examination, analysis of the texts, and the similarities in the writing and translation techniques in these manuscripts allow us to envisage the existence of a group of Jewish scribes — or converts (Rodríguez Díaz 1998) — specializing in the translation of Jewish works for Christians, converts, and Jews who liked works in vernacular language (Reinhardt and Santiago-Otero 1986, 21-25, 28-34). These scribes wrote in Castilian in a technique proper to Hebrew, because they were trained by masters who wrote and produced works in Hebrew. One might have thought that the demand for such works would fall off after the exodus of Jews following the riots of 1391 and the waves of conversions that followed the Disputation of Tortosa in 1413 (Fellous 2001, 36-51). But the demand continued to emanate from high society — aristocrats close to the government and literate people with a passion for translations of the great classical and literary works, among them Jewish works. Indeed, literary activity grew when Juan II (1406-53) ascended to the throne of Castile. This fact is related by the Spanish historian Fernando del Pulgar,[11] a Jewish convert, in his book *De los Claros Varones de España* (Castro 1984, 193-96, 517-18, 543-44, our translation), in which he explains, "It pleased the king [Juan II] to hear, read, and understand the explanations and secrets of the Sacred Writings"; the tastes of this "literary" king no doubt had an influence on the society of his times.[12]

Finally, three of these works — the fourth one having an anonymous author — have several points in common: they were intended for the highest level of the kingdom (King Pedro the Cruel, the Grand Master of the Order of Calatrava, and the son of the Grand Master of the Order of Santiago), and they were produced by people reputed to be great scholars and the best translators of their times. Furthermore, they were adaptations of Jewish texts: a Hebrew Bible; two philosophical works, *The Guide for the Perplexed* by Maimonides and the *Book of the Kuzari* by Judah ha-Levi; and a prophecy-inspired liturgical and literary work for Alphonse XI and then Pedro the Cruel *(Proverbios Morales)*. All four featured Hebraisms, transliterations from Hebrew, and a syntax similar to that of Hebrew. They were copied or translated by Jews and one *converso* (Pedro de Toledo) in a "hybrid textual" writing technique.

Production of Art

The Hebrew language and rabbinical tradition also made their mark in the production of art in the Iberian Peninsula. In the *Biblia de Alba,* the illustrations are quite representative of the ambient cultural interpenetration. The full-page painting of the giving of the Torah at Mount Sinai

Figure 4.5 *Biblia de Alba,* Giving of the Torah at Mount Sinai (fol. 72v, Exodus 34, 29).

contains the complete text of the Ten Commandments in large-module Hebrew letters (fol. 72v, Exodus 34, 29, fig. 13), which was an innovation (see Figure 4.5). In fact, in both Latin and Hebrew manuscripts, the text was rarely written in Latin or Hebrew; when it was, it was always abridged (the first one or two words in each commandment); moreover, no portrayals in this or previous periods illustrated the Tablets of the

Law in such monumental size. Moses is portrayed in compliance with rabbinical tradition: standing on Mount Sinai, barefoot because walking on hallowed ground, an aura of rays around his head (Ex. 34, 29). As Arragel's translation, which uses the rabbinical interpretation, emphasizes, "En desçendiendo del monte Moysen, non sabia que rresplandeçia asy como rayos rretrogados como a manera de cuernos el cuero de su cara en fabalando con el" (As he was descending from the Mount, Moses did not know that he was resplendent as if rays encircled his head like horns around his face, because he had spoken with Him). Moses holds the Tablets of the Law, monumental in size and rectangular in shape; they are disproportionate to all other elements of the illumination. The text of the Ten Commandments is written clearly in two columns of five lines each (Metzger 1975, 136). The image strictly respects Jewish interpretation and tradition, although Arragel refers indirectly in the text to Jerome's translation: "in the manner of horns," *horn* being his translation for the Hebrew *keren*, "ray," which explains the Christian imagery of Moses wearing horns. The word *keren* may in fact have two meanings. Rashi's interpretation tended towards the meaning of ray of light and was to influence Jewish iconography of Moses, whereas that of Jerome inspired the portrayal of Moses with horns in Christian art.

The iconography of the *Biblia de Alba* is exceptional for both Christian and Jewish manuscripts. Overall, however, it seems to draw on Jewish tradition, because of the number of edifying rabbinical sources that underlie the image. I therefore looked for works, both Jewish and Christian, that could have served as a model or that follow the same iconographic pattern. Although most of the illustrations in the *Biblia de Alba* have neither model nor copy, part of the pattern, that of the Exodus in particular, led me towards Jewish works, the Sarajevo Haggadah (early fourteenth century) in particular. And, for Christian works, I was drawn towards the bas-reliefs in the Toledo cathedral (late fourteenth century). Because numerous scenes illustrate the books of Exodus, we can presume that they were not all created ad hoc. I compared them with those in Haggadoth; they were used mainly for illustration of the ten plagues of Egypt, the complete treatment of which in the *Biblia de Alba* would inevitably be compared with that in the Sarajevo Haggadah.[13] The rood screen in the Toledo cathedral has fifty-six bas-reliefs dating from the late fourteenth century (Schonfield 1992, 94-96). It is unique in Christian art and bears a certain resemblance to the iconographic program of the *Biblia de Alba,* at least for the Exodus. I examined these bas-reliefs, and it seems that their treatment is similar to that in the Sarajevo Haggadah, and that they include almost no sacred images. The miniatures are so similar to these ritual books and bas-reliefs, in Angela Franco's view, that one might posit that they constitute an almost exact thematic biblical repetition — with the exception of the legend of the deaths of Cain, Seth, and Adam, and with differences regarding the extent of the cycles. For instance, the presentation of the ten plagues of Egypt in seven bas-reliefs is exceptional in the Christian context, although it is common in Haggadoth. The profusion of scenes from Genesis and Exodus in the Toledo cathedral, as well as in the *Biblia de Alba,* may come from the same iconographic current. The Exodus scenes situated in the north part of the rood screen are distributed as follows:

- Seven are devoted to the plagues (36-41 and 45); the second and fifth plagues receive treatment similar to that in the Sarajevo Haggadah and the *Biblia de Alba,* while the tenth is similar to the *Biblia de Alba* but different from the scene in the Haggadah.
- Two scenes devoted to the institution of Passover (42-43) are similar to those in the two other works.
- Two are devoted to the crossing of the Red Sea (45-46) and three to the Wandering in the Desert (47-49), also present in the other works.
- One bas-relief is devoted to the golden calf and its making in the flames, as in the *Biblia de Alba,* while this scene is absent from the Sarajevo Haggadah (by ideological choice?).
- Four scenes are devoted to the Alliance in the Sinai Covenant (50, 53, 51, 52) and two to the New Covenant (55-56).

Jews played a prominent role in the book world (Fellous 2001, 55-66, and, in particular, 58-59, on "the artisans of the book in Castile" [our translation]). It seems quite possible that illustrations of certain themes of the Old Testament, commonly portrayed in deluxe manuscripts designed for Jews (whether they were in Hebrew or vernacular), were taken up by Christian artists when these themes also held an important place in the Christian religious context. However, the existing models, both Jewish and Christian, do not encompass the many variants that appear in the *Biblia de Alba.* According to Brother Arias, Moses Arragel must have used as a model "the illuminated bible from the treasury of the Major Church of Toledo."[14] If the miniatures come from this manuscript, which has not been confirmed to date, it may also have served as a model for the reliefs on the cathedral's rood screen. The miniatures might have been inspired by Jewish sources or models, probably Haggadoth, inasmuch as in Spain these were the only Hebrew manuscripts that were abundantly illuminated. One might also posit, however, that they came from a Jewish production in Castilian that has not been identified as such, or that has not survived. In any case, Arias did not know that the miniatures were influenced by rabbinical sources.

According to the terms of the patron, the Grand Master of the Order of Calatrava, the manuscript was to become "the work of its times." As the illumination of the *Biblia de Alba* had to be sumptuous, a studio of artists capable of producing it would inevitably have to be recruited. Two other possibilities may be envisaged: either the images were created ad hoc, or it was a copy of a model in Hebrew or in vernacular language. Indeed, certain images in the Castilian manuscripts contain clues that support this latter hypothesis. For example, two scenes — one of Jonas sitting under an ivy bower or a vine, and the other of the king of Nineveh throwing his crown to the ground and tearing out his hair — are illustrated in a manner similar to those in the *Biblia de Alba* in a fifteenth-century Castilian manuscript of the *Siete Partidas* that belonged to Alphonse X. A comparison of the images in these two manuscripts seems to indicate that the illustration of this theme conforms with a local tradition underlain by rabbinical sources.[15]

All of these elements make the *Biblia de Alba* a unique work in terms of its text, its images, and the exceptional collaboration that led to its execution. However, the project behind the work does not seem, as has been thought up to now, to have been an isolated initiative.

- The fact that there were other translations shows that there was a political aim at the highest level of power. The project was a humanist one in many ways, visionary and hopeful, unexpected in the Iberian Peninsula in this period of constant crises. The work tended to integrate the great works of Judaism with a national culture still in formation. This Bible was to become the common ground for the Jewish and Christian cultures, already largely interpenetrating each other, in a peninsula where the coexistence of three monotheisms was the oldest and last in the Western world.
- These translations and transmissions of texts prove that there still existed, in the fifteenth century, an active group of Hebraizing Jewish translators, scribes, and illuminators who were sufficiently

well known that they were commissioned to produce major works. Thus, it appears that Jewish scholarship was not in decline in Spain until the Expulsion. Great works appeared until the late fifteenth century, such as Joseph Albo's *Sefer ha-Iqqarim,* which was written after the Disputation of Tortosa. In addition, splendid illuminated Hebrew manuscripts continued to be produced until the eve of the Expulsion, such as the Bible of Kennicott, copied at La Coruña, in Estremadura, in 1475,[16] and the magnificent Bible illuminated in Portugal in 1496, the ornamentation of which was not finished before the Expulsion. Its patron immigrated to Italy, where it was completed.[17] Christians continued to seek out Jewish scholars for translations of sacred and profane texts. They were masters of Romance languages, Arabic, and Hebrew, and some also knew Latin. Arragel's intention to make his work a reference text for the Castilian language is confirmed by the presence of the glossary and the constant concern in the glosses with defining ambiguous terms. In this work, he developed the original idea that disputes arose when particular meanings were inferred from general terms, and he tried to formulate a common language with which to resume the religious dialogue that had suddenly been interrupted in the fourteenth and early fifteenth centuries after the Disputation of Tortosa. Thus, he was addressing a theme typical of the Renaissance.

The copying of texts in Hebrew and vernacular language establishes that production of Jewish works did not stop in the peninsula with the Jews' departure but persisted with the *conversos,* who continued to work in the cultural sector.

The bas-reliefs in the rood screen of the Toledo cathedral chancel show that the Jewish literary sources underlying the iconography, even the iconographic program, were not necessarily known to the artists who used them. Indeed, it is entirely possible that borrowings were made without taking account of, or knowing, the origin of the work, as long as the images were intelligible to those who were viewing them.

Conclusion

These cross-currents provide ample evidence of the deep cultural synthesis that took place in Spain among three religions and the existence of a common cultural heritage, a heritage that took time to erase from the collective memory, at least consciously, and that endured in Sephardic Jewish memories. Today, in a period of globalization propitious to cultural opening, Spain is trying to rehabilitate and restore this lost heritage.

As for the Sephardic Jews, they settled throughout the Mediterranean Basin and Europe. They took with them a culture that they preserved and a language that they kept alive during their exile and transmitted from generation to generation. Turkey, Morocco, Tunisia, Greece, the Balkan countries, the Netherlands, South America, and Israel are some of the places where Spanish and Portuguese entered the local language (Gutwirth 2003; Hagège 2003, 132), and where fifteenth-century Castilian (better known as Ladino) is still spoken by the last descendants of the exiles of the fifteenth and sixteenth centuries.

The Jews of Spain and Portugal kept their Iberian roots alive beyond the peninsula. They seeded the Sephardic culture in a world where Spanish did not exist, and where they became a vector of Latin-ness. They exported, with themselves and their books, a culture that made its mark on the societies that received them, and they were early players in a phenomenon that was to accelerate with modernity and the opening of borders.

PART 3

Religions and Globalization

The principal monotheistic religions — in particular, Islam and Christianity — have stated universal values, and they consider it an integral part of their mission to promote and circulate these values and find ways of putting them into practice on a global scale. Over the last two millennia, this mission has resulted in a range of transplanetary links that were the product of proselytizing activities and conquests of distant lands by various groups in the name of their respective faiths. With contemporary globalization, religious practices and beliefs have taken more fundamentalist forms in the Christian, Jewish, Muslim, and Hindu religions, among others. Fundamentalism tends to rely heavily on the principal religious texts, especially when it comes to structuring daily life and religious practice. Manuel Castells (1999) suggests that fundamentalists participate in the formation of resistance identities: self-identification systems based on resistance and survival, following principles that diverge from and, in some cases, oppose dominant global modern values.

These forms of resistance are visible, but in different ways, on the north and south shores of the Mediterranean. In Chapter 5, Mohamed Yassine Essid examines how a distinct form of Islam, which he calls global Islam, has reached out to more and more members of the Muslim diaspora living in western Europe, as well as the populations of the Muslim Maghreb states and Egypt. Global Islam, especially its aspects critical of modernity, has spread to and taken root in both Muslim and non-Muslim societies.

One common issue in the confrontation between Islam and modernity has been control of women's bodies and the degree of individual autonomy among women in relation to men, for which women have constantly struggled. In Chapter 6, Latifa Lakhdhar discusses this issue through the prism of patriarchal systems that preceded the era of national independence and globalization.

chapter 5   ## Islam: Globalization, Autonomy, and Internationality

Mohamed Yassine Essid

LET US FIRST AGREE to define globalization as the conjuncture of a group of factors — such as liberalization, market deregulation, and new communications technologies — that lead to densification of trade in goods, services, capital, persons, and ideas and promote the formation of a global economic and cultural field. Increasingly, rapid integration into a vast market is accomplished at the cost, it is said, of a decline in a nation-state's political, social, and cultural sovereignty. Nor is integration without consequences for governments in both underdeveloped countries and Western democracies, which are often accused of playing a passive role in the process of (mostly trade) liberalization that generates economic crises and social inequality. And yet, when one looks more closely, one sees that the effects of globalization (Sachwald 2003) are always filtered through institutions, economic reforms, or outright protection measures that violate or, at least, contradict the commitments made within international regulatory bodies.[1] This observation proves that national policies always play a role in the influence, positive or negative, that globalization may exert on a country.

Why this preamble on the economic aspect? Most works on globalization deal mainly with the economic dimension, despite the fact that present-day globalizing processes have created an unprecedented historical situation that also involves the cultural, social, symbolic, and political spheres. In this complex picture, culture (which includes knowledge, beliefs, the arts, laws, morals, customs, food and culinary traditions, and all other capacities and customs acquired by human beings as members of a society) has a relationship with globalization similar to that of economics. Thus, no one field of human activity is subordinated to another. Rather, each field is distinct and relatively autonomous from the other (Appadurai 1996, chap. 2). In other words, what happens in the political, linguistic, or religious fields is not necessarily controlled by what occurs in the economic field. Integration with globalization may, therefore, in some (Northern) countries, be strong in the economic field but weak, or even absent, in the cultural field. In other countries, such as those south of the Mediterranean Sea, for example, globalization may be weak in the economic field but strong in the cultural field. There are various reasons for this situation, some of which are discussed in this book:

- Globalization means, above all, freeing the economic system from all regulation and allowing it almost complete autonomy (free circulation of currencies and capital, autonomy of central banks, and so on). This situation does not yet obtain in countries south of the Mediterranean Sea, where national institutions have been slow to liberalize the economy.
- There is little vitality in foreign direct investment in southern Mediterranean countries (compared, for example, to foreign direct investment in China).
- Although they have increased their participation in multilateral trade liberalization, Southern countries have economies that are still largely protected and regulated.
- There is evidence that the informal sector is surviving in Southern countries.
- Finally, there is an absence of good governance, indicated by the persistence of corruption and a lack of transparency on the part of political elites (see Chapter 1, this volume).

Rather than looking primarily at globalization-related economic changes in Southern countries (see Chapters 15-20), I shall demonstrate that what is happening in the economic field is isomorphic to what is occurring in the cultural field.

One of the effects of globalized trade is the extraordinary circulation of cultural products worldwide, including dissemination via new communications technologies. Some interpret this circulation as bearing the promise of an emerging universal culture; others see it as leading to a loss of identity because many non-Western cultures have neither the ambition nor the means to disseminate their culture to the world. For the latter group, such a situation raises the question of their capacity to produce, keep dynamic, and perpetuate their own cultures in the face of the cultural hegemony of the West and the selective yet increasing invasion of Western cultural goods.[2]

The new technologies also pose the question of a culture's orientation. Before the 1980s, institutions such as the family, the school, places of worship, and different "civil" or "state" social agencies (in Southern countries) functioned to sort, prioritize, evaluate, transmit, and control information and cultural content disseminated by the media. With the explosion of new mass communications technologies, these authorities and institutions are gradually losing control and being discredited. In the process, individuals and groups gain a greater capacity to sort, prioritize, and order cultural content for their own purposes — whether ideologically, commercially, or artistically. No cultural field, including that of symbolism, is insulated from this new reality. It goes without saying that discussion of the religious sphere in the Mediterranean region today focuses primarily, though not exclusively, on Islam.

In this chapter I will pay less attention to the other Bible-based religions, even though they, too, are imbued with the universalism of a foundational message. For instance, followers of Judaism form a separate, autonomous community that has a different set of beliefs in what they understand to be a universal project. Similarly, missionaries and migratory flows since the sixteenth century have made Christianity the predominant religion in the Americas, the Philippines, Australia and New Zealand, central and southern Africa, and other world regions.[3] However, although the Roman Catholic pope still proselytizes to bring the faithful together across denominational lines, many Christian denominations have renounced such activities, which are widely criticized for their attitudes of cultural superiority and Eurocentrism and seen as anachronistic. Furthermore, laïcité in France and secularism in other countries of the Christian West have challenged proselytizing practices, often successfully. Nonetheless, orthodox revivalist, activist evangelism has prospered for two decades in Europe and North America against "what is perceived as a dissolution of the Christian identity and the church in the 'world' and refocused the church on its message and its faithful, those who truly have experience of the faith" (Willaime 2001, 171-72, our translation). Another manifestation of rupture with established religions is also underway in Latin America and the Caribbean. Pentecostalism is surging among formerly rural populations congregating on the fringes of large cities, in which individuals are constantly "immersed in a general movement toward deregulation of the economy, political life, and symbolic systems" (Hurbon 2001, 130, our translation).

In the Mediterranean region, in contrast, only Islam, with the growth of fundamentalism, has taken up the idea, differently expressed in the foundational texts, of Islamizing the world. The globalization that accompanied the wave of re-Islamization of Muslim societies, notably in the Mediterranean, has boosted the internationalization of Islam, which has evolved in three stages: local Islam, then political Islam, and finally the deregulation and internationalization of Islam.[4]

Local Islam

The daily experience of Islam in the Mediterranean region before the wave of re-Islamization varied widely from one society to another. When it came to worship, there was a popular Islam that completely bypassed Muslim penal law (which has been resuscitated today by Islamists). It did not involve stoning, honour killing, flogging, execution for blasphemy, amputation of the hand to punish theft, slavery, segregation, censorship of lifestyles,[5] or combat on the road of God — jihad. Laïcité is defined, among other things, as the commitment to guarantee to all individuals the possibility of freeing themselves from their religious affiliations and origins. Although this situation did not obtain in the Islamic world,[6] the vast majority of Muslims in the Mediterranean region were free of the obligations arising from social pressures associated with open and public demonstrations of religious faith.

One feature of popular Islam was maraboutism,[7] or saint worship, a Maghreb variant of Asian Sufism.[8] Local foci of intense religiosity, planting their standards in Maghreb soil, the marabouts, or wouli, were beatified by the vox populi alone. They established themselves among the rural masses and the urban underclasses, to whom the Islam of the ulama was not accessible.[9] The wouli fashioned themselves as intercessors with Allah, sometimes benefactors, but always steadfast protectors of those who invoked and honoured them. They were condemned in the past[10] by orthodox believers and are condemned today by Islamists — considered by the former to be a factor in the fragmentation of Islam and by the latter a reprehensible *bid'a*[11] innovation. Nevertheless, the occupants of humble *zawiyahs* (niches or cupolas), scattered throughout the most remote countryside, were among the most active expressions of Maghreb and African Islam and the earliest manifestation of Islamic deterritorialization and networking.[12] Some holy men had a universal reputation, whereas others, with popular or local origins, enjoyed some prestige among the public for their knowledge or for the numerous miracles that they had performed. Many holy men were more important to the faithful, in all respects, than were Allah and Muhammad. This passion was surprising, given that "the Muslim theologians had made sure to prevent the intrusion of anything that might resemble, in any way, an alteration of the monotheist principle in either general doctrine or the smallest details of worship" (Goldzihedr 2003, 145, our translation). Concerned with modernization and economic development, the newly independent Muslim states dismantled the old forms of solidarity and accelerated the abolition of corporations and fraternal societies and the breakup of village communities, whose members were now propelled into what was, in essence, an obligatory exodus from rural areas.

In almost every Mediterranean Arab country, from Morocco to Syria, there were also large foreign communities that transformed certain cities into truly cosmopolitan urban centres. The variety of neighbourhoods and places of worship made coexistence with people of different religious persuasions a familiar concept. Nuns in wimples, who administered schools, infirmaries, and nursery schools, were part of this world, and their extreme devotion was never seen as proselytizing or as the expression of their monastic vows, and it was not equated with the presence of churches; thus, the nuns did not pose a threat in the eyes of popular Islam. More surprising, perhaps, is that family life in the Muslim community involved no institutional discrimination against women — mothers, sisters, or daughters. They gradually made a space for themselves in the city just as men did, sometimes surpassing them in academic and professional achievement. Both Tunisia and Turkey were exceptional in this regard.

The Qur'anic injunction to wives, girls, and women to "cast their outer garments over their person" (Qur'an 33:59; see Yusuf Ali 2004, 278) cannot be understood literally outside of its historical and geographic context in the ancient Near East, where most women were veiled when they were outside of the gynaecea (El-Cheikh 1997). The veil is called *burqa*[13] in Afghanistan, *hijab*[14] in Saudi Arabia, *chador*[15] in Iran, and *niqab*[16] in the Persian Gulf region, as well as *khimar,*[17] *'abaya,*[18] or *sefsari,*[19] and these different terms evoke traditional ways of dressing rather than religious affiliation. They are the female equivalent of men's garb — the customary clothing. They were, and are, part of the tradition of not mixing the sexes according to ancient morals — not a religious code — that stipulated that women and men should not encounter each other in public spaces. For instance, the struggle of Tunisian women against wearing the sefsari immediately following independence was an attempt both to free themselves from the patriarchal straitjacket and monitored liberty that they lived under until they married and to obtain financial autonomy. It was not religious in nature. In the countryside, peasant customs did not include the severity of *sharia*. Bedouin women were not forced to wear the veil or live as recluses. One characteristic of Muslim jurisprudence, in fact, was that it applied only to urban dwellers; in entire regions, such as Kabylie, Bedouin women had never known anything but customary law, *'urf,* and worked alongside men in the fields. 'Urf, or established tradition, was what defined each person's sense of belonging and release from the burden of dogma. Muslim law recognized customary law: each social grouping could preserve its own rules. The law took into consideration local customs and, through them, the specificities of each group. In the cities, the law was stricter but not excessive, and the wearing of the traditional (not Islamic) veil did not impede women's emancipation.

Until just after independence, this was the experience of religion for most populations. The state remained faithful to Islam, and the population remained attached to its religion — except that popular Islam was very different from what was taught in the books. It is true that the idea that some people, activities, or aspects of human existence might escape the grasp of the Muslim religion and divine law was foreign to Muslim thought. There was only one Law, and that Law governed diverse legal issues. But, slowly and surely, its severity was attenuated; there were neither inflamed fatwas nor excessively strict forms of legal punishment, *hadd*. Muslims did not always conduct themselves according to the prescriptions of the sages and theologians, or even according to the prescriptions of Islam. However, customs, traditions, and the social environment exerted their own pressure.

Finally, modern lifestyles played an important role in determining individuals' viewpoints and behaviours. In the Book, the source of all interpretations, there are three clearly defined statuses of Islam: a conservative Islam, perceived negatively, followed strictly by the faithful; a social and political Islam, drawn chronologically from the foundational texts (all of the verses addressed to believers, *mu'minun*); and a legitimately universalizable Islam — the text calls people to an Islam to which all beings of the earth and heavens are subjected.[20]

It is important to note that during the struggle against British colonialism, in which Islamists did not take part, there was no reference to Islam or jihad, only a movement of national resistance against the occupier, launched for the country's freedom and independence. In making wide use of the term *jihad,* the Islamists are now asserting that they are engaged in a struggle for a civilization, or even a religious war.

Thus, Mediterranean Islam was appreciated for its egalitarianism, tolerance, and simplicity. It was satisfying because it respected the individual. It was, as Fathi Triki (1998, 90, our translation), observes, "a customary Islam, rooted in the folds of Tunisian society — essentially a social ethic characterized by mutual assistance, hospitality, tolerance, generosity, moderation, and piety." Today, the globalization of Islamic discourse tends to generate a single Islamic model that holds local specificities in contempt. The mobilization of fundamentalists to promote the veil, for example, enables them to occupy the entire space of the individual in order to impose it on the community.

Regulation of the religious sphere was mostly the province of the *ulama* (plural of *alim*), the literate or wise men, who possessed *'ilm* (literally, knowledge of divine law, sharia); were versed in questions of jurisprudence, *fiqh;* and used great creativity, *ijtihad,* to understand and interpret the law in the changing contexts in which Muslims lived. Not everyone could claim this status and elevate him- or herself to authority in this area; an apprenticeship in a prestigious university, such as Al-Azhar[21] in Cairo or Al-Zaytuna[22] in Tunis, was necessary before ulama could assume the right to lead religious services, teach and train future postulants to the title of sheikh, issue fatwas that were likely to affect the lives of believers, and dispense justice in all matters regarding the personal status of Muslims. For centuries, such power raised them to a privileged caste as uncontested guardians of the text[23] acting in the name of God,[24] whose dominant intellectual posture remained, despite the changes that the world underwent, emulation more than innovation.[25] They also owed their status as an instrument of regulation of dogma and their credibility among their flocks to their independence from political authorities, their financial autonomy, and their exclusive control over the project of training aspirants to the status of ilam.

With the emergence of the national state, the status of these guardians of the faith was seriously shaken by social transformations in the sphere of the family and by reforms of the education and training system to create modern lay schools and colleges. Not only did the ulama see their monopoly eroded and their financial means reduced, but their authority was also diminished as the national state encroached heavily on their reserved domains. They were forced to accommodate and justify the state's political and social choices, even though these no longer corresponded to their sometimes reactionary social vision. The abolition of sharia courts in Egypt in 1955 eliminated a traditional outlet for graduates of Al-Azhar; furthermore, they did not have access to state universities. The 1961 statute reforming Al-Azhar ended the institution's age-old hegemony, subjected it to state control,[26] broke its monopoly on education, and downgraded the ulama to the status of civil servants. In Tunisia, Al-Zaytuna University was actually shut down, all types of teaching considered obsolete were eliminated,[27] and the Personal Status Code reform, a true social revolution for a Muslim country, was instituted. This step created friction between the controlled ulama and the intellectuals who spoke in Western terms of modernism, socialism, and economic development.

Political Islam

The 1979 Iranian Revolution revived the Islamic principle of combining politics and religion. It was, in effect, the first political revolution that demanded religious allegiance, at a time when third world countries were beginning to despair of a socialist or liberal revolution. It was also the first sign of a conflict of civilizations, giving rise to religious militancy and invocations of jihad. Once the first shock had passed, Iran, now an Islamic republic, quickly established its legal status internationally, and the world accommodated its existence. Although its Constitution was ruled by scrupulous respect for Shiite Islam, this nevertheless gave hope to millions of Sunni Muslims in the Arab and Islamic world. An Islamic state, ruled by the Law of God, could now be envisaged, and even viable.

The massive urbanization of cities south of the Mediterranean Sea, their disintegration under the combined pressures of demographic growth and the rural exodus, the dismantlement of traditional solidarity systems, and the domination of national governments "more concerned with monopolizing legal violence than constructing modern legitimacy" (Arkoun 1998, 52, our translation) profoundly changed the relationships that individuals had with their belief system. Development policies implemented successively over three decades led to major economic, social, and cultural upheaval: aggravated unemployment, lower standards of living, and degradation of educational and health services.

Geopolitically, the model of a unified Arab nation gave way to the fantasy of Islamic unity, the advent of which had previously been impeded, it was argued, by Western imperialist manoeuvres. The West had gained a foothold because of the weakening of the Ottoman Empire, which in turn weakened all Muslims by causing the Islamic world to be splintered into nations. Culturally, the withdrawal of modernist Arab nationalist movements from all Muslim states created a space for opposition to Arab nationalism. Rather than encouraging peoples to reconcile with their former identity, radical Muslims everywhere conducted a battle against pre-Islamic culture, which was erroneously associated with Western culture. Interventionist governments threw up obstacles to democracy, and all contestation of the political regime and its social values had to be expressed outside of political institutions.

On the level of individual identities, this period was one of tensions between an aspiration to universality and a fruitless quest for unobtainable authenticity. Neither liberalism nor third-worldism could provide Arabs or Muslims with a specific cultural identity. The claim to an Islamic identity was evidence that this genealogy was both uncertain and inaccurate, and for these very reasons the demands that it expressed were often irreconcilable (Arkoun 1998, 29-62).

The disenchantment with liberalism and the third-world concept was all the greater because it was accompanied by the perception that a single model of civilization was expanding and being forced *culturally* on everyone but remained *materially* less and less accessible to a large part of humanity. Islamists advocated the reversal of cultural identity, and they used the famous "return to the source" slogans of *hawiyya* (identity) and *'asala* (authenticity) to attract the adherence of acculturated masses seeking a religious alternative (Islam) to nationalist or nationalist-socialist (Arab) ideologies. Given all of these factors, the social, political, and cultural spheres were gradually Islamized: mosques were built thanks to private contributions and prayer rooms were provided in public facilities and even within university buildings. Official discourses were punctuated with Qur'anic verses and opened with the inevitable *basmallah,* and even the spoken language was replete with references to the Qur'an and to *ahadith.* Threadbare traditions, old beliefs, archaisms, and even charlatanism were revived, becoming a source of inspiration for new artistic productions.[28] In Islamic social sciences, especially history, any reference to a pre-Islamic past — whether Babylonian, Chaldean, Greek, or Roman — from which, for better or worse, Islamic civilization had sprung was banished. This history, linked by theorists to the age of ignorance and barbarism, was of no interest. Islamists, in what Youssef Seddik (1994, 9, our translation) calls "the crushing, flattening strategy of orthodoxy," rejected any history but that of an expurgated orthodox Islam. In their view, an open Islam, confident in itself and in its past, would be likely to lead to Mediterranean peoples' rediscovery of their pre-Islamic identity — an unacceptable outcome.

The Islamic economic system, as conceived by its proponents, was to ensure economic and social justice by applying the precepts of Islam in the economic domain and make certain that social relations conformed to divine injunctions. The call was issued to adopt "economic" behavioural norms inspired by Islam and enact what had previously been completely theoretical political, administrative, and legal institutions such as morals police, the *beyt mal al-muslimin* (public treasury), and so on. In the 1980s, such theories began to be embodied in the creation of "Islamic" banks that were to apply Islamic financial theories by banning interest on loan. As a corollary, institutions such as the Islamic Development Bank promoted the dissemination of these theories to Muslim countries through colloquia and seminars.

Similar to the goal of gestural and religious emulation of the Prophet and the caliphs known as clairvoyant *rashidun,* which was sometimes taken to the point of obsession, the primary goal of Islamic economic institutions was to define their distinctiveness — even if, objectively, other systems proved to be more rational and efficient. For theoreticians of economic Islamism, there was no need to justify this social system, modelled on a religious literature written entirely in the Middle Ages, or to prove its effectiveness or its superiority over current systems. Similarly, there was no need to prove its coherence or scientific accuracy. People were expected to subscribe to it as to an act of faith, although recourse to forms of coercion was not excluded, if necessary.

The wearing of the veil "arises from a domain of invented tradition that has not spared certain pillars of Islam" (Seddik 2007, 24-25, our translation). There is no explicit and constraining prescription in the Qur'an forcing women to wear it. Nevertheless, the veil has gained more and more proponents throughout the Muslim world and in the Muslim diaspora in the West.

In the area of literature and in the name of a return to origins, books highlighting the Islamic heritage proliferated, as did books on mysticism, eschatology, the irrational, and the Islamic viewpoint on questions of the day such as women, economics, and biology. Some Qur'anic verses were sublimated into scientific truths. All such books, containing naive and indulgent content, were sold at very low prices to credulous unilingual readers with little education but eager for knowledge about Islam. During this time, other works, such as those by Taha Hussein,[29] Khalid Muhammad Khalid,[30] Ali 'Abd al-Raziq[31] and Kacem Amine,[32] disappeared from bookstore shelves or simply did not find republishers.

Intellectuals with a classical education, who graduated from the same establishments as the institutional scholars and were as well versed in the science of the fiqh as the ulama of Al-Azhar (considered throughout the Muslim world as the reference with regard to Sunni orthodoxy), challenged the ulama, who were largely discredited for their support of existing regimes' policies for managing the symbolic sphere. These intellectuals were critical both of the authoritarianism of national states and of the large Islamic institutions controlled by these states. Using ever-expanding media coverage, they gained new followers and drew the attention of the Arab public through their Friday sermons, their *tafsir* exegeses of the Qur'an, and their analyses of questions linked to Muslim law and religious beliefs. Charismatic sheikh preachers such as al-Sha'rawi,[33] Ghazali,[34] Kishk,[35] and Al-Qaradawi[36] reigned triumphant throughout the Arab world. Both the Egyptian state and official Islam, whose institutions had remained impervious to worldly developments, saw Islamists contesting their monopoly of access to the transcendental order and formed a common front to oppose the sheiks' fundamentalism.

During this period, society began to draw its guidelines and new references from religion. Illusions about the project of Arab unity were extinguished, replaced by the fantasy that the Caliphate would restore daily living to how it had been at the beginning of Islam. In the area of thought in general, Islamist ideology took over from modernist, liberal, and third-worldist theories, while sometimes preserving the discursive forms of third-worldist ideology. The identity that Islamists claimed was no longer Arab nationalism but Islamic supranationalism, and they brandished an alternative plan drawn from the religious heritage. Thus, Arab nationalism, often secular, was challenged by the unifying and pan-Islamic interest of a vaster community — that of believers who sought to bring justice and harmonious relations not only to the Islamic world but also to humanity as a whole. In mobilizing for this agenda, and in the context of pre-established ideological imperatives, they used the greatest number possible of audio-visual means, centres, and institutes, through which Islamic specialists and experts of all sorts were called upon to define what was now called *Islamic society*.

For instance, Islamism expressed an extravagant claim to spiritual authenticity, and even superiority, that took priority over the search for conformity with any particular orthodoxy. There was therefore an "institutional demonopolization of the universal" (Hervieu-Léger 2001, 92, our translation), in which the system of truth was no longer the exclusive preserve of the great institutions of belief, such as Al-Azhar. Instead, it was personally appropriated, especially because the number of those promoting themselves as a source of truth became extremely numerous, and they spread their message effectively thanks to new technologies. This new status of truth was at the core of the institutional deregulation of belief. It strengthened the autonomy of the believing individual and contested the old mechanisms of authority, such as the family, for control of the symbolic sphere. "The reality of religions," observes François Thual (2003, 192, our translation), "led, moreover, to a rise in deregulation: not a revival of non-belief or atheism, but the establishment of a practice that, while continuing to be based on adherence to religious truths, was conveyed by a loss of control by religious apparatuses over individuals and groups."

Faced with the deregulation of Islam, the state had responded by strengthening official Islam. Among the authority mechanisms implemented to supervise religious affairs were ad hoc government ministries, as in Tunisia and Jordan, and official bodies for training and appointing imams, as in Algeria, Egypt, Morocco, Syria, Tunisia, and Turkey. In Egypt, for example, there were eighty thousand places of worship, but there were only forty thousand state-appointed preachers. Under such circumstances, when an urgent societal question, such as population control, arose, government plans were constantly countered by independent preachers, who asked their flocks to reject the policy — in this case, by declaring it contrary to Islam and invoking the verse that says, "And there is no creature on earth but that upon Allah is its provision, and He knows its place of dwelling and place of storage."[37]

In this phase, institutional Islam was in fear of being overwhelmed by the clearly more effective rhetoric of political Islam, especially because the Islamists no longer recognized the authority of this guardian of the dogma. In order to preserve its power and authority, Al-Azhar University (Orelli 2002) tried to safeguard its institutional autonomy and preserve its respectable status in Egyptian society by maintaining its primary role of eminent authorized interpreter of Islamic text and traditions. It could be said that the rise of Islamism restored the image of Al-Azhar as a centre of religious expertise and interpretation and as an interlocutor with power. It thus strengthened its once-waning autonomy (Kepel 1985). It even began to manipulate the government into advancing the Islamization of Egyptian society. For instance, it opposed government policies in 1992-96 that suppressed female circumcision and birth control, and it censored films, such as Youssef Chahine's *L'émigrant,* and banned the novel by Nobel Prize winner Naguib Mahfouz *Awlâd hârat-inâ* (Children of the alley, published originally in 1959) as part of its new mission, granted in 1994 by the Egyptian government, of controlling cultural products. Al-Azhar's desire to preserve, at any cost, its monopoly on regulation of religious order pushed it to escalation. A good example is the case of Faraj Foda, lay intellectual and essayist, who was assassinated soon after he was declared an apostate by the rector of the university, and the less dramatic, but still disturbing, case of Nasr Hamed Abu Zayd,[38] in which Al-Azhar showed itself to be much more virulent than the Muslim Brotherhood.

The creation in France of the French Council of the Muslim Faith arose from the same logic. Aside from thrusts towards fundamentalism, the practice of Muslims living in France and in other European countries followed a path to deregulation that was similar and parallel to those in Muslim countries. The French interior minister, who was also responsible for religious affairs, actually went to Cairo to obtain the approval of the rector of Al-Azhar University, Mohamed Sayyid Tantawi, for France's new law regarding wearing the scarf in schools and public establishments — which he did indeed obtain. Despite its attacks on the credibility of institutional Islam, France felt that it was a good idea to seek the backing of Al-Azhar — forgetting, incidentally, that it was addressing an institutional actor that was now barely heeded in its own country and even less by the Muslim diaspora in France.

There is social legitimacy in the wearing of the veil in Southern countries. Women who work in factories are poor, and the veil is an inexpensive way of covering themselves. They escape discrimination because the veil conceals them from both the contemptuous gaze of wealthy women and the provocative gaze of men, and it thus becomes a symbol of pride that shelters them from the judgment of others. But what about Muslim women in the diasporas, women who live in modern secular European countries, where women are theoretically emancipated and autonomous? Thanks to mass communications, these women are as exposed as are their sisters in religion in the South to Islamists' arguments — in other words, to the effects of globalization, considered here to be the perfect expression of the new relationship between local and global realities. The migratory context, politically different from Southern political regimes, illustrates best the difference between Western democracies and the southern Mediterranean countries. In the former, the technological reality of communications allows free, autonomous individuals to organize information spaces, express themselves freely without government control, and avail themselves of religious knowledge circulating on uncensored channels. In contrast, the reality of Southern countries includes authoritarian regimes, in which only an autonomous civil society, where it exists, may oppose the omnipotent state. In an environment that is objectively favourable to at least the claim, if not the assertion, of individual autonomy, Muslim women who have adopted the hijab hold it up not only as an affirmation of the modernity of Islam but also on behalf of a principle of autonomy.[39] However, this principle does not articulate a desire for freedom, for assuming life choices, for equality between men and women, for the search for truth, for personal reflection, or for formulation of and respect for the laws that one has created, as is the case in the West. Rather, it is related to becoming aware of the dominant socio-cultural influence, from which there is the intent to disengage by claiming an identity through scriptural religiosity. The veil then becomes the symbol for a demand for individual autonomy in reaction against a society that is not receptive to cultural diversity.[40]

The Internationality of Islam

Up to the 1990s, the practice of Islam continued to be characterized, notwithstanding confrontations and violence, by bipolarity between a pro-state Islam and a political Islam. The birth of Islamism gave free rein to multiple Islams, each claiming to be the true Islam, dissociated from societies and governments and not obedient to any authority. However, it was agreed that the practice of Islam followed a single model, with consensus on how it should be practised and, what is more, that it should be limited to within the borders of a territory and a nation.

At the end of the 1990s, economics and culture became planetary, organized through networks and no longer by territory — the principle upon which the nation-state had been founded. In this context, globalized Islam found a raison d'être and a path to emergence. It was no longer confined within borders, or censored by states, or challenged by national culture, and it took full advantage of this situation by using all of the springboards offered by globalization, including satellite television, websites, cellular telephones, and the English language. Ideologically, the movement, more virtual than real, called for a return to the religious, political, and sociological purity of original Islam. Unlike the ideology of Jamaat-e-Islami, founded by al-Maududi,[41] or that of the Muslim Brotherhood, which has always been concerned mainly with political power, transnational Islam ignores national societies and cultures, rejects all local specificities, and has only an instrumental relationship with science. None of these dimensions impedes the adherence of the masses to its religious truths.

The prescriptions of these thousand and one Islams — whether related to the hijab (Tersigni 2005), the unearthing of numerous observances that had more or less fallen into obsolescence, or *mu'amalat* social interactions — are gaining increasing numbers of Muslim followers. As the old religious frameworks of the Islamic world have lost their social, moral, and pedagogical authority, they have given way to new media figures of religious prescription: intellectualized ones such as Tariq Ramadan[42] in Europe and popular and "new look" Amru Khalid[43] in Egypt, as well as more and more cyber-preachers and new sharia interpreters. Well versed in classic texts on Muslim theology but educated beyond the curriculum of the ulama, they have built effective religious-cultural enterprises throughout the Arab Muslim world. In contrast to the superstitious and superficial nature of their parents' religious knowledge, they have built a pseudo-scholarly religiosity for a clientele formed of young Muslims. The traditional religious institutions and the state have lost the fight for control of the symbolic sphere, which they had previously been able to manipulate to their advantage.

Autonomy by Fatwa?

Of all the Islamic institutions that are promoted through broad dissemination and that draw on globalizing processes, the fatwa, or legal opinion, has certainly become the most ubiquitous. Traditionally, interpretations of the Qur'an and the sunna about what was licit and what was illicit were made exclusively by a man of law, called a *mufti*. He would issue a legal statement called a fatwa, in which he expressed his view on the case proffered.[44] In institutional Islam, because issuing legal opinions was so difficult, the ulama were, theoretically, the only ones authorized to do so; the person consulted had to have discernment and wisdom, because he provided the synthesis between the ideal of the law and the necessity of the moment. The usual procedure in official bodies for interpretation of the law began with a question submitted by an individual or organization that, in turn, set in motion a complex process. The opinion issued was the result of the intellectual effort of a single person or a group synthesis. Scholars, meeting within commissions, academies,[45] or assemblies,[46] took into consideration not only the letter of the law but also the interests and dynamics of different groups, as well as factors such as economic development, political pressures emanating from both governments and society, and the common aspirations of Muslims. The procedure might even require recourse to Ahl al-Dhikr experts, those who had specific competencies in a given matter but were not ulama.[47] More recently, however, the fatwa has become detached from its local and institutional context and can claim a worldwide jurisdiction. Initiated by Khomeini as a death sentence against the Indian-British novelist Salman Rushdie, who was accused of apostasy following the publication of his book *The Satanic Verses* in 1989, the term has now come to mean, in Western minds, a contract on the life of anyone who does not submit to a Mafia-type diktat.[48] There was also the emergence of counter-fatwas to thwart and contest the monopoly on fatwas held by Islamist groups.[49]

The current highly lucrative proliferation[50] of fatwas, some of which are justly called "commercial" or "industrial,"[51] and the promptness with which they are issued offers the best illustration of the deregulation of

Islam. A space has been created for communication and expression without any borders or political control; within that space, the religion is constantly debated and redefined. This space represents an increase in autonomy for Muslim individuals in comparison to their position under traditional bodies for managing the faith. In contrast, it is narrowing their vision of the world, reducing it to what is licit or illicit and to pointless questions that bear no relation to reality. The rash of consultations on questions from the simplest to the most unusual denotes individuals' incapacity to take charge of their lives and make free, well-informed choices. Worse, it emphasizes their withdrawal to a mythical past and their loss of confidence in the future, inaugurating what one author has called "the step of post-underdevelopment" in the Arab world.[52] One eloquent example is the fatwa issued by Sheik Izzat Attiyah, eminent dignitary of Al-Azhar University, over a question that has always haunted the ulama: segregation of the sexes. In the work world, Muslim women are advised to choose "female" professions and to concentrate on a clientele of their own sex, limiting as much as possible the opportunities for contact with men. The ulama cite a *hadith* that has become proverbial, according to which a man and a woman may not be alone together without being joined by the devil (maj tama'a alrajul wa 'imra'a illa wa kana thalithuhuma al-shaytan). What can be done, then, if in the workplace it is inevitable that colleagues of opposite sexes find themselves alone together and thus are, by definition, promiscuous? In this case, answers Izzat Attiyah, basing himself on a hadith whose authenticity is doubtful at best, a woman is allowed to breastfeed her colleague five times in order to seal with him a fraternization by breastfeeding. This solution would ultimately solve the problem of mixed sexes in the workplace.

Conclusion

Islam in daily life was once contextualized by authority mechanisms — family, social traditions, and local customs — and the great religious institutions provided concrete expertise with regard to truth. Each family, village, city, and country had its own Islam. At a certain point, for reasons discussed above, local connections and official operators were discredited by political Islams, which were in turn overtaken by globalization. Religious, media-related, transnational entrepreneurship competed with traditional religious authority and quickly adapted to the strategies of the market for symbolic goods, satisfying demand for individual autonomy. It is the revenge of the local over the national and institutional. This market-based Islam, as it has been called (Haenni 2005), has induced a trend towards multiplication of limited belief systems that are merging into a planetary-scale religious network in a context of general cultural globalization.

chapter 6   Muslim Women in the
                Mediterranean Region:
                Discriminatory Autonomy

Latifa Lakhdhar

WHEN ONE LOOKS AT the question of globalization and autonomy in
relation to the condition of Muslim women in the Mediterranean region,
including those who live in Europe, one is confronted with an unusual
situation, engendered by an unprecedented socio-economic and cultural
order. This order is seen as the most advanced, if not the final, stage of
liberal market capitalism.

Although it is hegemonic, globalization is distinct from imperialism
and colonialism in that it is based on a completely deterritorialized power
apparatus. In the religious domain of Islam, deterritorialization throughout the Mediterranean region, from Morocco to Albania, has encouraged
the re-Islamization of societies and exacerbated the rise of a religiosity
that follows, more and more faithfully, the strictest norms of Muslim
orthodoxy.

It is important to underline that this reassertion of a well-established
historical (Arab) and religious (Islamic) identity and character goes hand
in hand with a power relation of domination over women in this part of
the world. Incapable of evolving towards an egalitarian ideology or a
more secularized vision of social relations, globalized Islam has revived all
of the archaic norms governing relations between the sexes — relations
thought to have been left in the past. The "Islamic veil" is its most obvious expression. According to certain estimates, the overwhelming
majority (more than 80 percent) of women in Cairo today are veiled
(Al-qâhira wal hijâb 2006). This is neither an isolated phenomenon nor a

passing trend in Egypt but arises from a reality that is more broadly Arab and Muslim. More and more women wear the *hijab* and do so more and more conspicuously. Islam is also ostentatiously displayed in visits by huge crowds to prayer sites and in the infatuation of younger and younger followers with accomplishing the minor Umrah pilgrimage,[1] as well as the great pilgrimage, the Hajj. Receptions are organized for these pilgrims when they return home. Increasing numbers of middle-class homes are hosting *halakat,* or religious-instruction sessions run by professionals. To these activities are added dozens of Islamic satellite television stations that owe their prosperity to the thousands of viewers who pay a fee to solicit the opinion of cyber-*ulama* on various subjects of private life. In some cases, such endeavours lead to an extraordinary display of intellectual and social poverty that bears no resemblance to *taqwa,* the spiritual discretion and humility advocated constantly in the Qur'anic revelations.

It must be recognized that this return of the holy is not simply a reaction to the crisis in modernity, social inequalities, or the armed conflicts in which certain Arab peoples in the Middle East are currently involved. It is an effect of the triumph of globalization, which is making it possible to fashion a free-market Islam throughout the Arab and Islamic Mediterranean region. How women in this region have fared under this most dogmatic expression of Islam can be seen through an analysis of the evolution of gender relations during three historical periods: the colonial period, the period of national construction, and the period of globalization. It appears that, beyond discontinuities and constancies, a religiously inspired guardianship over women endures, justified today by the struggle against Western and globalist laws.

The Colonial and Postcolonial Contexts and Their Impact on Women

Integration of the countries of the southern Mediterranean into the world market during the colonial period had an effect, though indirect, on the fate of Muslim women in the region. It should be noted, first of all, that the issue of women did not figure in the stakes of the colonial process. Gender relations continued to follow ancestral religious norms characterized by the undervaluing of women. Girls were not admitted to schools until 1839 — when the Tanzimat reforms, influenced by liberal European thought, were instituted — a symbol of the permanent inferior position of women. Moreover, girls' education was limited to Turkey, since the Arab provinces of the Ottoman Empire were not affected by the reform. The girls' school started by American missionaries in Beirut in 1835 long remained an isolated institution.

The colonial powers in these provinces showed little concern for this situation. In the parent countries, socio-economic conditions had led to a certain degree of female autonomy. Paid work for women and education for girls began in the second half of the nineteenth century with the appearance of state education in England and universal, obligatory lay schooling in France. These opportunities for women and girls existed only in a limited and restricted form in the colonies.

Women were also marginalized through a policy of religious education instituted by the colonial power. In this sense, French colonialism, faithful to its anti-clerical ideology, evinced in the Maghreb countries a strategy of systematic control that included a thorough knowledge of Islam, mobilizing for this purpose both scholarship and practical policy. For the colonial power, Islam was a source of suspicion, or even fear. Travellers, administrators, academics, and scholars were all engaged in learning more about the local religion, and studies, censuses, and reform projects were undertaken with a view to establishing a practical Islamic policy that would correspond to the interests of colonization. This approach led the occupier to undertake the reform of religious institutions and the dismantling of statutes governing land ownership in order to facilitate expropriation of land.

The Islamic conception of social relations posed a challenge to Western humanism. However, the modernist vision did not go so far as to question the status of Muslim women, which remained unchanged and the sole prerogative of religious leaders. Thus, under colonial rule, Islam was subjected to all sorts of reforms, except those involving the status of women. In colonial Tunisia, for example, this omission could be seen in the reform of the justice system and the courts: all affairs regarding personal status and inheritances continued to be under the jurisdiction of religious *sharia* courts, but they were relieved of the rest of their prerogatives. Although the reforms created momentum towards modernity in various spheres, they fixed the nature of gender relations by keeping women in the straitjacket of their traditional status.

The greatest impact that the triumphant West had on gender relations in the nineteenth century was the birth of the Al-Islah reformist movement, indirectly provoked by the "shock of modernity." During the pre-colonial period, this movement spread to all countries on the

Mediterranean south shore, although it was not expressed in the same way from one country to another. Following the campaign in Egypt, Napoleon Bonaparte had been the first to understand the culture of awareness of the advances in the West. The relative growth of Muslim bourgeoisies following the liberal reforms undertaken in Turkey starting in 1839, in Egypt under the rule of Mohamed Ali Pasha from 1801 to 1849, and in Tunisia from 1837 to 1877 reinforced this new awareness — and the desire to accede to modernity.

One reformist current of thought was concerned with the imbalance between the two sexes. The reformist elite was attentive to women's access to education and public spaces and their contribution to the progress of civil life, and it suggested that Western models be emulated. During the colonial period, polygamy and women's right to education were subjects of debate alongside the question of national liberation.

The changes became more significant after countries gained independence. From Morocco to Syria, the more or less enlightened leadership elites emerging from national liberation movements were able to increase the state's control over society and the religious experience by encompassing them within state projects for the construction of a modern nation. Traditional structures, both political and economic, were affected by these changes.

By associating women with the process of national construction, these states introduced some modifications to their legislation in order to reduce the importance of religious factors impeding women's participation. In the first months of independence in 1956, Tunisia promulgated a relatively modern personal status code, modelled on that of Kemal's Turkey. However, the limits to development policies were quickly reached. Construction of the state, the means of development at the beginning, became an end in itself.

The Repercussions of Socio-economic Policies Linked to Globalization

The socio-economic conditions inherent to recent development policies presage even more difficulties for Arab women in the Mediterranean region. According to the United Nations Development Programme (UNDP) report on human development in the Arab world, the region is in a state of regression when it comes to women's status (UNDP 2003). It has the highest proportion of women not on the job market; out of a total of fifty million women of working age — one quarter of the total population on the job market — barely 25 percent are employed.[2] Thus, a crushing majority of women in these countries are excluded from the job market and stripped of one of the major gains of modernity: access to the public space and to the financial independence that allows for separation between paid work and home life. The illiteracy rate among women is highly indicative of segregation: in the late 1990s, this rate was 58 percent for women, compared to 35 percent for men, in Egypt; 66 percent, compared to 40 percent, in Morocco; and 42 percent, compared to 21 percent, in Tunisia.

This socio-economic reality underlines the dangers of neoliberal ideology when it recommends disengagement by the state. There is no need to recall that the history of gender relations shows that a policy of social injustice always leads to greater injustice for women (CAWTAR 2001). From a sociological perspective, these difficulties, added to the crisis in the nation-state, create a transfer of power towards old forms of mechanical solidarity, such as tribalism and regionalism, that accentuate the gaps between the sexes.

Meanwhile, the pauperization of rural zones has led to increased rural migration to cities. In urban environments, reference points are lost, spaces are more restricted, and women are more confined than had been the case in the countryside. These transplanted rural people attempt to construct a new type of cohesion by the formation of groups of cousins and brothers, the wearing of the protective veil by women, and recourse to the integrative force of religion. The wearing of the veil by women in working-class neighbourhoods has become generalized.

The situation of women in the colonial, postcolonial, and globalized contexts in the Mediterranean region is characterized by contradictory elements — limited emancipation on the one hand and fragility on the other. Yet, far from guaranteeing them immunity from regression, this fragility could, paradoxically, encourage it. The paradox is even more manifest in countries in the Mediterranean region because globalization involves a public struggle between one Islam, inscribed in each country's tradition, and another, global Islam, with no local values at all.

Women have always been the traditional instruments of Muslim identity distinction; they also give visibility to this distinction through the wearing of the veil. This situation of historical continuity, marked by their subjection to a status tinged by religious sexism, does not facilitate the task of current Islamist discourse, which demands the restoration, pure and simple, of their former status. On the other hand, the emerging difficulties that autonomous feminist associations are encountering, as well as modern expressions of civil society (for reasons that involve the democratic failure characteristic of these countries), are creating a void favourable to the propagation of Islamist discourse.

Globalization and the Effects of the New Islamic Order on Women

This situation of fragility is integrated into a new and broader Islamic order. One characteristic of this order is the reappearance, in response to the deterritorialized power of globalization, of a foundational theological notion of the religious and geopolitical space of the former Dar al-Islam (Abode of Islam), *ummah*. In the Muslim belief system, the notion of ummah, which today includes the idea of a virtually transnational Islamic state, has been and remains important in the Islamic conscience.

The breakdown of national experiments seems to weigh in favour of the return of the supranational pan-Islamist reference of ummah. As their modernist projects failed to live up to the universalist referent of democracy as a source of political legitimacy, the Arab states in the Mediterranean region condemned modern notions of homeland and nation that would incorporate a moderate Islam within the national idea. In doing so, they left room for the return of old representations and for a claim to belong to the pan-Islamist movement.

Propelled by mass communication techniques allowing for real-time accessibility to information and the circulation of ideas, globalization provides an appropriate framework for the return of Islamic supranationalism. It becomes part of a theological and political space that transcends the borders of profane history and places the community in a spiritual space in which believers feel closer to God. In this transnational space, the precepts of Islam are no longer transmitted via the paths created for this purpose by the national state: departments of religious affairs, religious educational institutions such as Al-Azhar University in Egypt and Al-Zaytuna in Tunisia, and imams in the neighbourhood mosques. Instead, mediation between religion and society is increasingly the province of bodies that seem to transcend these institutions, such as satellite television channels, Islamic websites, and electronic distribution media. These technological developments have opened up a virtual society maintained by religious hosts, who, from Amman to Sydney, are rushing to revive the sense of belonging to a common space — a feeling well rooted in Islamic conscience and sustained today by a religious discourse freed from all national culture (Kepel 2000).

This new order has had a major impact on the situation of women. The return of ummah, expressed as a desire for autonomy and for aggressive demarcation in relation to globalization, goes hand in hand with a strong resurgence of a second form of Islamic integration: the family and, more specifically, women. The veil has become an issue and an emblem, as evidenced by the passionate debate that surrounds women's wearing it conspicuously. Tele-preachers evoke the idea that any woman leaving a single hair on her head visible to a stranger is exposed to hell and damnation. This discourse, which is reproduced in daily life, seeks to make the wearing of the veil a sixth pillar of the Muslim religion, at the same level as prayer or profession of faith, and accuses any woman who does not wear it of being a non-believer.

The Veil, or Alienating Visibility

Sociological studies in the Mediterranean Arab world, when they are available, suffer from a lack of transparency. The exact proportion of veiled women is available only for Egypt. There are other clues to the scope of the phenomenon, such as observation of what is actually worn on the street, sexist tele-preaching and its growing female audience (for instance, Amr Khaled, one of the most famous Egyptian tele-preachers), the disproportionate mediatization surrounding the Islamic veil, and measures to ban wearing the veil in public spaces adopted in several countries.

The veil, thus raised to an emblem of autonomy and Islamic authenticity in the face of the diluting effects of globalization, requires close study. Such study is even more important because Islamist discourse focuses on this phenomenon based on two sorts of dissimulation. One concerns the history of the veil, which stretches back several thousand years, to well before the advent of Islam; the other involves the misogynous theological structure that has surrounded the veil, the importance of which has been amplified even though the veil is discussed only briefly in Qur'anic discourse.

The endowing of a way of dressing with spiritual, and political, meaning is justified at a broader level by the strong resistance to distinctive ways of dressing throughout the history of the Muslim world. The great theological debate surrounding the Transvaal fatwa of 1903, in which Mohamed Abduh, a great Egyptian mufti of the time, declared that it was legal for Muslims in that part of the world to wear European-style hats, gives a sense of the religious significance that Muslims attach to clothing as a distinguishing feature of their identity.

Orthodox Islam has always made rules about licit and illicit clothing and insisted on the maintenance of an Islamic clothing identity; men long resisted giving up the fez and the *chechia* for the European suit (jacket and pants). Muslim orthodoxy raised the religious identity connotation of clothing to a dogma because, according to the *hadith,* "that which is identified with a people is part of it"; moreover, imitation by infidels was considered apostasy.

For women, the issue is more serious because they must veil themselves to distinguish themselves from non-Muslims, to mark the passage from childhood to puberty and from being single to a spouse, and to manifest restraint and moderation as a sign of submission to God. Ironically, the most widely broadcast preachers on Islamic satellite television channels — who appear dressed Western-style, as do Islamists in the Parisian suburbs, and who are so supercilious when it comes to forcing the veil on women — are often the most faithful followers of the big European fashion labels.

It is important to point out, however, that, historically, the wearing of the veil was challenged at a time when Muslim elites, both male and female, were becoming aware of modernity. At the turn of the twentieth century, Kacem Amine in Egypt, Tahar Haddad in Tunisia, Hoda Chaaraoui (founder of the Egyptian feminist movement, who removed her veil in public during a meeting in Cairo), and Manoubia Wartani, a Tunisian feminist, all wanted to prove through their enlightened nationalism their break with social conceptions from the dark ages of Islam and their desire to make the transition into modernity. Through their struggles, they sought emancipation and the end of supervision, including the supervision imposed on women through the prescription of the veil. In a strange twist of history, the granddaughters and great-granddaughters of the generation of women of the 1920s and 1930s who had taken off the veil and fought for a modern status for women are fighting today to wear the veil. This regression is explained no doubt by Arab societies' new historical conditions and relations with the world.

Genealogy of the Veil

To find the underlying meaning of the wearing of the veil, it is not enough to discuss its clothing- and identity-related dimensions. Germaine Tillion (1966, 199), in her book *Le harem et les cousins,* metaphorically analyzed the issue of the veil in a chapter called "La dernière colonie" (The last colony). Looking back at the historical origins of the veil, one can easily grasp the meaning of this metaphor: subordination, control, and oppression were once major factors in the meaning of the veil.

Cultural theorists posit that the phenomenon of the "Islamic" veil is perfectly integrated with the Muslim community's demands for cultural rights in the West. In their view, it represents, for women in Islamic countries, a female claim to respectability and a means of access to the public space and mixing of the sexes (Lutrand 2003). Looked at as a sociological phenomenon, setting aside its historical origins and theological foundations, the veil is presented in a positive light, conveying harmony and a form of adaptation to the requirements of modernity. Tillion (1966, 201, our translation) observes that, historically, "Any foray into the past shows that the harem and the veil are infinitely older than the revelation of the Qur'an."

The veil is a phenomenon that precedes by far Mohammad's revelation. It dates back to Mesopotamian civilization; tablets of Assyrian law attest that it was obligatory for married women, whereas prostitutes who dared to wear it were punished with fifty strokes of the stick (Vallet 2003, 44). Evidence of its existence in the Semitic Middle East is also found in one of the oldest texts in the Old Testament, the Canticle of Canticles. In that ancient Middle Eastern civilization, the main rite of divorce consisted of either removing the wife's veil or symbolically cutting off a piece, since the deep meaning of the wearing of the veil was alliance through marriage.

This same meaning was even more explicit among the Greeks and Romans, who perpetuated the tradition. For the Romans, wearing the veil and being married were synonymous, and they were designated by the same term, *nubere.* The veil, *nubes,* was made to protect nubile women against the desire of men, and it was also the sign of a woman who was married and therefore honourable. Moreover, women who dared to go in public without a veil were no longer protected by Roman law against possible assaulters, who would benefit from extenuating circumstances.

Men had the right to divorce if their wives appeared in public bare-headed (Tillion 1966, 202).

In these ancient civilizations, in addition to being a symbol of inviolable ownership, the veil had a more religious meaning of fidelity to a mystical alliance. The Vestal Virgins, who were Roman priestesses, covered their heads as a sign of their mystical marriage with the goddess Vesta; later, Catholic nuns, taking inspiration from the Vestal Virgins, covered their heads as a sign of their betrothal to Jesus Christ. This inspiration leads to the supposition that St. Paul, the first Christian theologian, was inspired, in his known injunctions to wear the veil,[3] by the Greco-Roman culture from which he came and that he knew so well. The veil was the rule for married women throughout the Mediterranean region in ancient times, and the practice survived on the north shore until modern times. It is mentioned, for example, in an eighteenth-century Corsican code (Tillion 1966, 202).

The Qur'an therefore did nothing new in invoking the veil. The word *hijab* is used in the Qur'an but not emphatically, as it is mentioned a scant seven times, and only three of those in relation to women.[4] A reading of the Qur'an shows that the custom of wearing the veil did not exist in Medina. Further, evidence that Islam revived this ancient tradition can be found in the similarities between what the Qur'an says and what was customary in the civilizations discussed above. Pliny the Younger (61-114), a jealous man, rejoiced that his wife had come to listen to him giving a reading of his works, "lending an eager ear behind a curtain" (Duby and Perrot 1991, 339, our translation). This description seems to be echoed in verse 53 of sura 33, "The Coalition": "And when ye ask [his ladies] for anything ye want, ask them from before a screen" (Berque 1957, 5, our translation). The fact that the Caliph Omar, known for his strictness, walked the streets of Medina to banish all veiled slaves (Al-Qurtubî 1978, 183) can be seen only as a straightforward adoption by Muslim men of a Middle Eastern tradition that pre-existed the Qur'anic revelation. All indications are that the veil was related less to standards of spirituality and faith than to controlling women in order to defend the patrilineal family.

During the Abbasid era (eighth to tenth century), Islamic jurisprudence began to surround the wearing of the veil with a misogynous ideology and went so far as to make sexual pleasure an act of faith. Female pleasure became a thing of fantasy, sexual obsession,[5] pathological jealousy, suspicion, and accusation.[6] Marriage was defined by the early scholars of Islam to cohere with this conception.

Social Intermediaries for a Discourse of Segregation

Propagated on a global scale, this discourse, which defends the autonomy of the Islamic ummah by imposing an "Islamic" status on women, is now borne by new, more influential, and much more powerful social intermediaries. In the 1980s, Islamism was simply an expression of rural and working classes frustrated in their social aspirations by the failure of the welfare state. In essence, it was an avenue for expressing social discontent without real economic force, whereas today Islamism seems to be rallying to its cause not only the working classes but also the middle class and entrepreneurs. Things have changed a great deal since the 1970s and 1980s with regard to the economic profiles of the promoters of combative and media-based Islamism. Saudi Arabia and other oil-rich countries, although integrated into globalization, are demanding religious autonomy.

It should be noted that women themselves are increasingly becoming social intermediaries for traditionalist discourse. In 1999, Al-Azhar University opened a section for women preachers, some of whom are currently preaching in Cairo mosques. In April 2005, Egypt's minister of religious affairs announced that he would select, from among eight hundred candidates, fifty-two women to be trained to perform "the function of imam in the prayers reserved for women" (Kristianasen 2005, 6-7, our translation). Al-Azhar University dispenses diplomas to female legal advisers, or *muftiyyat* (Kristianasen 2005). But, in the absence of an egalitarian theology, this feminization of religious personnel, which seems to recognize the right of women to exercise religious power, appears to be a means of instrumentalizing women in the battle that Islamism is waging against the all-embracing meaning of globalization. These women can organize only on the basis of upgrading their "Islamic" status in lockstep with the imposition of the veil, polygamy, repudiation, being subjected to guardianship, and inequality of succession. Thus, the autonomy claimed by globalized Islam underlies serious discrimination against women by presenting it as a discourse of resistance to cultural homogenization in a time of globalization.

States carry out the same strategy of sexual segregation by other means, such as expressing reservations about international legal models governing relations between the sexes. These states evidence their desire for autonomy from globalized law, in the name of their cultural, social and, especially, religious values, when it comes to the right of women to be in charge of their own bodies and reproduction. Further, they balk at fully adhering to conventions that condemn discrimination against women with regard to succession, marriage to non-Muslims, equality with regard to child care, and other matters. International conventions on women's rights are said by these countries to be incompatible with "Islamic sharia" and to be applicable only within the limits prescribed by religious law (Chkir 2000).

Conclusion

The Muslim Mediterranean region offers the world empire an opposing religious model of resistance and autonomy. This model obviously poses the question of the reasons for so religious and backward-looking a reaction, more appropriate to conflictual behaviours in the Middle Ages, given that the values of modernity supposedly took over the world since decolonization movements swept around the globe.

The resurgence of religion is fed by disenchantment and skepticism resulting from the modernist and democratic deficit in countries on the Mediterranean south shore. Women are the obvious victims of these contradictions. The autonomy claimed on the basis of the socialization of women by a dogmatic and backward-looking Islam contradicts every understanding of internationally recognized human rights. As a consequence, women are barred from any possibility of being autonomous subjects.

PART 4

Cultural Autonomy: Music and Food

The accelerated growth of transplanetary connections and social relations characteristic of contemporary globalization has had profound effects on how individuals, communities, and institutions create meanings and on how these meanings, in turn, change individuals, communities, and institutions. Whereas meaning-creation activities — what are generally called culture — were once shaped powerfully by the senses of belonging, identity, and territory associated with nations, many of the new connections and relations transcend the territorial limits delineated and controlled by nation-states. Networked capitalism is characterized by the central role of information and communications technologies, the dominance of financial capital, and the power of transnational firms — forces that have led to the commercialization of ever more facets of daily life, including cultural practices. The authors in this part of the book study the relationships between old and new forms of power and their impact on cultural autonomy — the capacity of individuals, communities, social movements, and other forms of organized collectives (including states) to create meaning and respond to the crystallization of signification that may model who they are and how they live.

In a context of cultural hegemony, one expression of autonomy is a country's capacity to support its own musical culture and have it endure in the face of the selective invasion of mass-produced music. What aspects of globalization are likely to have an impact on the music world? How does the Arabic music sector reorganize in a context of globalization? How does it react to the new world order? Can local forms of music in small countries south of the Mediterranean Sea preserve a form of autonomy in the cacophony of globalization? Answering these questions is Myriem Lakhoua's objective in Chapter 7.

Although the paths to change are different, the consequences for cultural autonomy in the domain of food are similar to those for music: a loss of collective cultural autonomy but, in various ways, possible gains in individual autonomy. In the Mediterranean region, and given the industrialization and globalization of markets, the Southern countries — which import more and more basic foods — are less and less able to preserve genetic diversity or, just as important, diversity of food production and consumption. The question is therefore whether the trend towards standardization is compatible with the persistence of cultural differentiation. In other words, can globalization co-exist with collective autonomy when it comes to food culture? If not, how can the cultural identity of peoples be secured in the long term? How can peasant agriculture, for example, be preserved as an autonomous space in material culture? The authors of Chapters 8, 9, 10, and 11, each in her or his own area, have pursued two objectives involving the populations of five Mediterranean countries: first, they analyze the effects of globalization on food practices and representations among communities and individuals and their consequences for autonomy; second, they describe the main factors affecting the maintenance or modification of these practices.

chapter 7

Local Tunisian Music and Globalization: Between Musical Autonomy and Commercial Autonomy

Myriem Lakhoua

IN THIS CHAPTER, I define how the new environment of globalization has affected the music field. My study deals with music production in the Arab world — more particularly, in Tunisia. I maintain that analyzing how music is created — the nature and mode of production, distribution, and perception — is the best way to measure the impact of globalization on a given musical sphere and, simultaneously, its degree of autonomy from globalization.

Such a project naturally raises the following questions:

- What aspects of globalization are likely to have an effect on the music world?
- How does the music world organize in a context of globalization?
- What is the specificity of Arabic music in a globalized world?
- How does Arabic music react to the new facts of globalization?
- How can we define the notion of autonomy in the context of music?
- How can local forms of music in small Southern countries such as Tunisia preserve a form of autonomy?

About Globalization

A look at the literature on globalization yields the following observations. Change based on technological innovations has swept us into the modern globalized world, which is accessible to everyone in real time.

The extraordinary advances in communications technologies (transmission of information by audio and video signals) and transmission through multiple forms of new electronic supports (television, movies, computers, telephones, MP3 players, and so on) have given populations all over the world an opportunity to transcend physical borders and create "hybrid" cultures. New cultural alliances, born of the aesthetic encounter of the modern and traditional worlds, represent the ideal of the new globalist and cosmopolitan view.

Concretely, globalization offers industrial and commercial structures tools with which to control and manipulate cultural capital in order to transform it into economic and trade capital. These structures encourage the creation of hybrid cultures and build international systems for the circulation of goods. Thus, the new world culture is based on new production techniques and largely supported by modern means of electronic distribution.

About Music

The introduction of new technologies for music production and distribution is stimulating increased hybridity, which is reinforced by the mass migrations of people facilitated by improved means of transportation. So many multilateral connections have been established that musical styles and genres have become less and less distinct, resulting in a syncretism of genres and styles from various repertoires (urban, rural, Bedouin, traditional, pop, modern, and so on) and musical cultures (Arabic, Western, South American, and so on). At the same time, increasingly aggressive commercialization takes advantage of every possible marketing springboard to transform music into a consumer product.

This context has given rise to a new musical genre bearing the label "world music," which enables the Western music industry to sell different types of musical products, ranging from heterogeneous contemporary pop music to "exotic" third world sounds. Although initially addressed to a Western and diaspora audience, this music has managed, as if by boomerang effect, to reach audiences in southern Mediterranean countries as well as to invade the world's audio space. How has the highly publicized distribution of world music affected the system of perception of traditional and local musical cultures? Does it threaten traditional modes of musical creation? I address these questions using the example of Arabic music.

About Arabic Music

A phenomenon comparable to world music already exists in the Arab world. A new musical genre, which I call commercial Arabic music, was born in the context of globalization, and it has come to represent all so-called modern Arabic music. Its industrial and commercial bases are Egypt, Lebanon, and the Gulf countries, which are its financial backers. These countries have appropriated the tools of globalization, such as new means of distribution and new technologies for music production (computer-assisted composition), to exploit the resources of different Arabic musical cultures and meld them into a single, marketable Arabic musical culture.

Upon closer examination, it is obvious that the marketing strategy for this type of music induces a certain degree of standardization of taste (perception) and modes of production in order to reach the largest number of listeners. New forms of Arabic music have been created, leading to changes to, or even the disappearance of, traditional styles and modes of musical production and perception specific to different local and traditional Arabic cultures. Promoted through aggressive commercial techniques, this new musical product, considered an evolution in classical Arabic music, is coming to resemble ever more closely the American pop music that dominates the Western and international scene and is now invading the Arab market.

How does commercial Arabic music influence local and traditional musical forms in different Arab countries? Does it threaten their autonomy, or even their very existence?

About Autonomy

For the purpose of this study, I have distinguished two types of autonomy:

1 *Musical autonomy:* the capacity of a form of music to preserve its local, traditional creative mode, production, and reception. A repertoire of traditional and popular music and the mastery of ancestral lore linked to this form of music are essential creative sources. Thus, in the case of traditional Arabic music, the mode of creation is related closely to the preservation of *simmi'* (superlative of one "with a musical ear"), who are expert listeners, connoisseurs of the rules of the musical art, and capable of feeling its profound meaning.

2 *Commercial autonomy:* the capacity of a musical form to adapt to (in order to create) a new, globalized environment by using that environment's technological, technical, and commercial resources. These resources are needed to create loyalty among consumers who are constantly following the latest trends and whose taste is constantly changing. The adoption of new tools offered by globalization, as well as the constant rejuvenation of audiences, will in turn exert an influence on the musical product, spurring further transformations to enable it to adhere to new forms.

The challenge to composers and musicians is to develop a creative mode that reconciles these two types of autonomy in a way that preserves authenticity (musical autonomy) without depriving them of modern means of distribution and production (commercial autonomy).

About the Audience

With the globalization of culture, a local musical form (which we could call traditional or "authentic") may be played for a heterogeneous audience that is foreign to the particular musical culture (we might call this audience "multicultural" or "international"). Through globalization, this music will therefore have a certain *commercial* autonomy. However, by losing its original homogeneous listeners, who know the rules of the music and how to interact with and appreciate it, it is deprived of all of its intrinsic meaning — its *musical* autonomy. We therefore move from a coherent and stable musical system to a hybrid musical culture without defined rules.

In Arabic — and more specifically, Tunisian — music, the presence of simmi', who are supposed to ensure the quality of the musician's execution and interpretation, is a good illustration of musical autonomy. In an interview with the musician Tahar Gharsa, who was a master of Tunisian *malouf,*[1] I asked about the musical techniques that he used in his improvisations. He spoke about the type of audience present, which had to be composed of knowledgeable listeners — simmi'. His response took me aback. Had he misunderstood? I had asked him about his technique, and he told me about his audience! I later realized the significance of his reply: he could hope to provide a good musical performance only in the presence of an audience capable of hearing and understanding the full meaning of the music that he was playing. It was the effect produced by his music and the emotion that it aroused that encouraged him to give the best of himself. The authenticity of the performance was the fruit of this subtle exchange, which made each presentation unique. An international audience (euphemistically called "multicultural"), although ignorant of local and traditional musical styles (labelled "world music"), is perfectly capable of appreciating the "exotic" sounds of these musical styles that are foreign to their own culture. However, they remain completely deaf to the deeper meaning of the music.

The issues of how the music is heard and the interaction between musician and audience do not figure directly among the themes linked to globalization and autonomy. They remain, however, at the centre of the process of change wrought by globalization on local musical forms.

About the Method

The innate characteristics of a musical form are remarkably different from one Arab country to another, and even more from Northern to Southern countries. They include the following:

- the status of the musician
- the organization of music production and distribution
- respect for intellectual property rights and the legislation that protects them
- the specific provisions taken to protect local production
- the economic and social context within which a piece of music sees the light of day.

Music production, particularly in a globalized context, cannot be defined solely through purely musical characteristics. Other factors, such as the environment within which the music is created, the means used to produce and distribute it, and how it is perceived by different audiences must also be taken into account, as they interact to distinguish any production.

To address all of these ideas, I built a corpus that includes the following:

- *data related to the musical environment* on the basis of observing the existing musical environment and commercial systems through recordings of local Tunisian music, classical Arabic music, and commercial Arabic music in the variety and world music styles

- *data related to musicians* on the basis of interviews conducted with renowned musicians in different spheres: Tunisians producing local music in Tunisia; Tunisians producing world music in France; Tunisians producing Arabic variety music in the Arab world; and French people producing world music with Tunisians in France
- *data related to listeners:* simmi', knowledgeable public, experts in the musical genre offered; "general public" listeners in Arab countries, with no particular qualifications in the field; "nostalgic" listeners, members of the Southern diaspora living in the North; Western intellectuals seeking a musical journey, new age musicians looking for new experiences; purists seeking "authentic" or "exotic" music that is not contaminated by modernization or globalization.

First, I address the question of music production through the use of certain analytic tools and methods. I gathered musical samples and organized them for analysis. (Many of these samples can be found on the Internet by conducting a web search. Some general URLs are given below.) On the basis of recorded data, I conducted diachronic and synchronic analyses.

Through diachronic analysis, I explored the evolution of Arabic music from the beginning of the twentieth century to the present. For this analysis, I established certain chronological criteria so that I could better grasp how globalization has affected the world of Arabic music. The study of diachronic change between the colonial era and the globalization era reveals both the transformations that Arabic music underwent on the path to modernity and the musical elements that were not affected by modernization.

The synchronic analysis revealed the strategies employed by musical creators from different environments to adapt to the new order of globalization. My analysis distinguishes among three musical genres arising from three distinct environments: world music (Western); commercial Arabic music (Egypt and Lebanon); and local Tunisian music. This approach allowed me to describe the modern norms for contemporary musical creations in these three categories. The comparison and cross-referencing of different data — musical (from the composer), commercial (from the producer), and receptive (from the listener) — reveals the strategies used by players in the different musical categories to ensure their autonomy.

About the Evolution of Arabic Music

Diachronic Study: Specificity and Evolution of Arabic Music from Colonization to Globalization

To illustrate the evolution of Arabic music from the colonial period to the present, I compared samples of musical creations from the 1930s and the 1950s and their reprising by contemporary musicians. For instance, I compared two versions of a composition by Mohamed Abdel Wahab[2] performed in two different periods: one in 1930, in the traditional music genre, and one in 1960, in the classical Arabic music genre. These two versions involved a modernization of both the creative and interpretation modes.

Examples 1 and 2: Mawwal (individual vocal improvisation), "illi rah rah ya albi," 1930 and 1960

[http://www.tulumba.com/]

A comparison of Mohamed Abdel Wahab's performance dating from 1930 to one dating from 1960 provides a good illustration of the changes that occurred in the modes of production, execution, and performance of Arabic songs in terms of the composition of the band, the types of instruments used, and the type of interaction with the audience, inasmuch as the live recording allows us to discern these aspects. For instance:

- The number of instruments has grown considerably, and the *takht,* the traditional ensemble composed of a violin, *'oud* lute, *riqq* percussion instrument,[3] and *nay* flute,[4] has been replaced by a large orchestra in which Western instruments, such as the flute, are introduced, while basic Eastern instruments, such as the *qanun* zither, the 'oud lute, and the violin, are retained.
- New functions appear for the instruments; the qanun zither, a *mousahib* accompaniment to the song, becomes a solo instrument (an instrumental section is reserved for it).
- The composer uses new rhythms, such as the samba and the rumba, in fashion in the West at the time.
- The instrumental performance is no longer heterophonic, and there is an attempt at orchestration. Each instrument is played according to

157

a written part, and improvisation is distributed among the solo instruments.

- The quarter-tone *maqam*[5] modes, such as *rast* and *bayâtî,* are still used.
- Abdel Wahab's maqamic performance mode remains identical, as does the language used.
- Improvisation, the proof of the singer's expertise in the art of Arabic music, occupies an important part of the song.
- The instrumentalists and the singer belong to the same Arabic musical culture.

Now, I compare two performances of a composition by Abdel Wahab in two different eras: colonization and globalization. This clip is a reprise of a song dating from the 1950s and its adaptation to the world music style.

Example 3: "'Ala bali ya nasini," song by Abdel Wahab dating from the 1960s, performed in 2001 by the Lebanese singer Hanine, accompanied by a Cuban orchestra.[6]

[http://www.arabooks.ch/]
[http://www.lepost.fr/]

In the colonial era, Tunisia's opening to the world was conveyed music-ally by borrowings from Western musical culture and, in extreme cases, by the adoption of a new music system. In world music, a pure product of globalization, borrowings no longer occurred. Songs were the prod-uct of shared experiences among musicians with neither the same home-land nor the same musical culture. Concerts brought together musicians of different nationalities, each expressing her or his own musical culture, for an audience that was also culturally heterogeneous. The goal was to find a point of accord and a common musical language with which to interact before a single, large audience. What was important was the search for expression and emotion to communicate to the audience, in a way that reached beyond musical and listening specificities. The per-formance was not the result of unique and localized musical cultures, or mixed and combined musical cultures giving rise to a new musical genre or style, but culturally differentiated musicians producing a common musical experience. The formula "inspired by music x," valid for the colonial period, gave way to the formula "having an experience with musician x" in the globalized music world.

The public reacted to the 2001 version of Abdel Wahab's song in different ways, depending on the respective underlying musical culture. For a simmi' audience, this experience, though unusual and original, considerably impoverished the musical language of the first version for the following reasons:

- The passages improvised by the singer, proof of his mastery of this musical culture, are eliminated.
- Abdel Wahab's performance, based on a maqamic modal interpretation and on rich and nuanced variations, is replaced by a simpler but more rhythmic melodic interpretation.
- Passages using quarter-tones are almost eliminated.
- The South American rhythm, used by Abdel Wahab as a borrowing from South American music in the first version, is accentuated in the second version, which is performed by a Cuban musician.

For an audience other than simmi' listeners, this version of Abdel Wahab's song had the merit of bringing the music of a singer up to then unknown to younger generations to a large audience. It also integrated Tunisian music into the world repertoire by facilitating listening for a Western audience that did not know Arabic musical culture. Whereas an audience of simmi' would be moved to *tarab*[7] by the singer's modulations, the finesse of his performance, his excellent control of the maqam, and his perfect diction, and would express this appreciation at the least by a respectful tribute and at the most with emphasis, the audience for the 2001 version reacted to the music mainly by dancing to its Cuban rhythms. This version, recorded digitally, bore the label "world music" in the West. The singer Hanine, accompanied by her Cuban orchestra, performed at music festivals throughout the world, including France and Beirut, where her concerts were sold out.

Examples 4 and 5: Comparison of two performances of a song by Farid al-Atrash,[8] "'Ya salam 'ala hobbi ou hobbak," dating from the 1950s and reprised in 2006 as Arabic commercial music, performed by Hichem Abbès (Egypt) and Hayfa Wahbi (Lebanon).

[http://www.wat.tv]
[http://www.youtube.com]

In this arrangement of the song, one electric organ replaces almost all of the traditional instruments once used in the Arabic takht. The *darbouka*[9] is still used, but it is accompanied by castanets. The tempo of the song is slightly accelerated. The mode of performance is no longer based on the maqam but has become melodic, and the singer no longer respects the quarter-tone rast mode in which the song was composed. Again, a simmi' audience would have a hard time recognizing the original melody. To ensure maximum coverage of the song on satellite stations, the new version is enhanced by a music video, the modern version of the old Scopitone films in which the song performed by Farid al-Atrash was disseminated in the 1960s.

The Globalization Effect

These diachronic examples show that Arabic music underwent significant changes from its traditional local form. The first change took place through colonial influence and produced the Arabic music or classical Arabic music category. The second change was brought on by globalization and produced the Arab variety music or commercial Arabic music category. Comparing the characteristics of musical productions in the three periods — colonial, postcolonial, and today — it is obvious that Arabic music has evolved into profoundly different registers.

In 1932, King Farouk I of Egypt commissioned Baron d'Erlanger[10] to organize the first Congress of Arabic Music, which was held in Cairo from 28 March to 3 April 1932. The general goal of this gathering was to preserve and modernize Arabic music. More specifically, the idea was to organize a congress in which Western researchers would participate in order to discuss all aspects of *rouki* progress and the transmission of Arabic music, and to provide it with fixed *thabita* scientific bases through a language that everyone understands. In fact, "modernizing Arabic music" meant, in essence, following the model of Western music, Westernizing Arabic music, or replacing the system of oral transmission of music with written transmission. "Language that everyone understands" meant the recordable language of *Western classical* music.

A first series of concrete changes were adopted:

• Arabic music theory was simplified and normalized using the Western music-notation system.

- Music institutes and conservatories replaced the traditional oral mode of transmission with written methods. According to the creators of the reform plan, this notation system would ensure the sustainability and preservation of Arabic music.
- Institutions for the preservation and revival of the *'ihya' al tourath* heritage were created in different Arab countries; for example, the Rachidia Institute was founded in Tunis in 1934. This organization took charge of reviving the repertoire of malouf, which it chose to represent Tunisian national music, and "modernizing" it — that is, having the music performed with large orchestras and transcribed into a single version to elevate it to the rank of "classical Tunisian" or "classical Andalusian-origin" music.
- The takht, a band formed of three or four instruments and a *mutrib* singer — once the composition of all Arab traditional bands — gave way to a large orchestra formed of a mixture of Western and Eastern instruments and led by a conductor.

Accordingly, profound changes took place in the very nature of the music and how it was produced and heard. Producers of Arabic music now began to adopt Western composition tools, such as orchestration and harmonization. Arab composers' openness to Western musical culture was manifested, during and after independence, by borrowings from all types of Western music and by changes in band formations, musical form and genre, performance, teaching methods, methods of analysis, and working methods. These Western influences have extended down to the present day.

The modernization of Arabic music led to an increasing convergence with the aesthetic and musical techniques of Western music. A new musical categorization was created. "Classical Arabic music" and "classical music of Andalusian origin" were labels applied to malouf; to modernized music, *mutatawwira;* and to outright modern music, *haditha.* Musical forms or genres considered "too popular," or even "vulgar," were pushed to the background and judged by Tunisian or Arab elites to be "non-music," music that could not be elevated to the rank of "classical music." Such judgments did not, however, keep new composers from being inspired by it. For example, *mezoued,* a type of popular Tunisian music (named after a traditional Tunisian musical instrument), was long scorned by Tunisian urban dwellers because it was associated with the fringe elements of the city — so much so that for a time it was banned from broadcast by Tunisian official agencies.[11] Since the 1980s, with the progressive ruralization of Tunisian urban society, mezoued has finally invaded the city, and it was rehabilitated in the early 1990s thanks to the show *Nouba,* which brought it into the era of globalization.

Postcolonization, Arabic music underwent a first profound change involving the composition of the band (number of players and instruments used), teaching method, and context for production and reception. Nevertheless, under the nationalization movement, certain aspects were preserved: language, dialect, instruments used, composition method, mode of vocal and instrumental performance, and mode of reception. Tarab and chosen lyrics remained absolute criteria for Arab listeners. With globalization and the emergence of new technologies, change came to the mode of creation (computer-assisted composition), distribution method (by satellite), and thus the reception and audience ("watching" music on videos). It was no longer music that was "too popular" or "vulgar" that was banned; rather, paradoxically, music that was not "popular" enough in the commercial sense of the term was set aside.

About "Glocal" Music

Most of the new trends in music production are the result of a globalized environment that, through innumerable technological innovations, has given rise to new ideas and new ways of producing, distributing, and listening to music. Each country responds to this environment differently depending on its degree of integration with it. This difference is conveyed through musical creations.

Here, I give a synchronic reading of new Arabic music productions in different contexts: first, the world music environment; second, the environment of Arab commercial or variety music; and finally, the environment of local Tunisian music. For each case, I present and comment on the environment of the sample chosen (legislation, market organization, distribution system, technology, and so on) and offer some further thoughts (strategy, specificity, categorization, autonomy, and so on).

World Music

"World music" is a new label that appeared with globalization. Although invented by musicologists to designate all music that is not Western, the term has been adopted and used broadly in the music industry. A number of new productions inspired by Arabic music are called world music today.

The music environment is presented in the West as follows:

- sophisticated technology
- respect for intellectual property law
- a new mass migration culture
- an aesthetic encounter between third world and first world technologies
- a context that is more and more urbanized and cosmopolitan, with heterogeneous listeners sharing the same geographic space
- a constant search for new niches to penetrate new markets and gain a larger audience
- the existence of international music industries: the pop music industry, the world music industry, and so on
- the existence of a structured market for music commercialization
- the proliferation of festivals of world music, traditional music, sacred music, and other musical styles.

Here is a sampling of songs catalogued as world music, marketed in the West, and presented at festivals as such.

Example 6: "Così celeste," duet by Zucchero (Italy) and Cheb Mami (Algeria), new production 2004 (Universal Music Italia).

[http://www.starzik.com]

The internationally renowned Italian singer Zucchero released an album of eighteen duets with singers of different nationalities: French, English, American, Algerian, and so on. The singers had careers in different musical categories, including jazz, soul, opera, and pop. The Franco-Algerian singer Cheb Mami performed in the above example with a vocal interpretation typical of Algerian *rai,* using the melody sung in Italian by Zucchero and Algerian lyrics. Although all of the musical elements belong to pop music, the perceived mode in the part performed by Cheb Mami is that of rai.

Example 7: Arrangement of the famous "'Andak bahria" by Wadii Essafi (Lebanon) in a duet with José Garcia (Spain), produced in 2001 during a private concert.

This example is a good illustration of the kind of musical experiments and cultural exchanges that proliferated with world music. Wadii Essafi, a star of classical Arabic music, sings, in a duet with a young Spanish performer, a well-known song that he previously performed in the 1960s. The exchange begins with vocal improvisations performed first by Essafi, in classical Arabic style, and then by Garcia, in Spanish flamenco style. Then, a piece of Arabic music is performed in Arabic and Spanish with Arabic and Spanish vocal interpretations, which, despite their differences, are curiously similar.

Example 8: New version of a song by Oum Kalthoum,[12] "'Alf leila wa leila," produced in 2000.

[http://www.youtube.com]

The song by Oum Kalthoum, the great figure of classical Arabic song, is reduced to a mix. The music from the original recording is mixed with techno rhythms, ensuring the piece a legitimate reception in all discotheques the world over. This example shows the potential of new recording technologies to manipulate, reinterpret, and reuse original versions in different ways. A song appreciated in the 1960s by an educated Arab audience becomes a techno beat that can be appreciated by an international heterogeneous audience.

Example 9: Nusrat Fateh Ali Khan (Pakistani Sufi musician), concert at the Centre des cultures du monde theatre in Paris.

[http://www.deezer.com]

The sacred Pakistani music performed by Nusrat Fateh Ali Khan in front of a heterogeneous audience in Paris is considered, in this production context, to be world music. This genre owes its visibility and increasing popularity in the West to globalization alone, and it is now classified among the "local" music styles of the world.

The expression "world music" is quite vague, since it seems to cover everything that does not fall into a traditional category. It encompasses a variety of experiences, strategies, and musical genres in a single marketing policy. A description of a series of musical creations in terms of musical components, means of distribution, and modes of reception provides a preliminary categorization.

"Authentic" or "exotic" local music: music produced in a context of production and perception that is not its own. An example is Nusrat Ali Khan's music performed in a theatre in Paris.

New version: a new arrangement with the mixing of musical elements from two different cultures. The new version is a reinterpretation of a traditional musical genre in a contemporary musical genre (disco), produced using new tools (electronic instruments, computer enhancement, and so on).

Reprise: a reinterpretation of a known song by players from different musical cultures using the latest technical means, in the context of a cultural exchange or a commercial production.

New production: a musical hybrid or mix, a musical style melding two different musical cultures, generally one from the North and one from the South.

Musical exchange: a musical experiment improvised at a world music festival by players from different musical cultures assisted by modern technological means.

International pop music: local music that has international popularity (access to the general public) because of specific mediation provided by the music industry: rai, jazz, pop, rap.

Commercial Arabic Music (Lebanon, Egypt)

Commercial or variety Arabic music has expanded exponentially in recent years. Countries such as Egypt and Lebanon, which have always been major centres of production of commercial Arabic music, rapidly adjusted to the new situation by doing the following:

- adopting a sophisticated production and distribution technology: the making of music in the studio and with recording methods allowing for all sorts of adaptations
- using an effective promotional strategy
- adding numerous satellite music stations financed by Arab capital, ensuring the widest possible distribution of this new musical genre
- creating a promotional structure for the making of "Arab stars," young women or men who meet all of the international norms of beauty and behaviour
- gaining access to an audience composed of listeners and viewers of all Arab nationalities

- gaining access to modern performance venues: festivals and concerts organized by Arab countries and broadcast by specialized satellite channels[13]
- finally, organizing a market to promote and commercialize music.

I have chosen a representative sample of commercial Arabic variety songs.

**Example 10: A song by Elissa (Lebanon), "Bastannak'":
new production (2006), Rotana production, Lebanon.**

This is a good example of the specific features of current commercial songs. On the visual level, a young, beautiful singer, star of videos broadcast on playlists of satellite music channels, addresses an Arab audience, all nationalities combined. She sings and dances to a rhythmic sentimental air, in Egyptian or Lebanese dialect. Specifically Arabic rhythmic or melodic musical elements, such as the *daff*,[14] sometimes double the tune, composed essentially of synthetic sounds and mixing effects.

Example 11: "'Allah 'allah ya baba," a song from the Tunisian popular repertoire, reprised in 2001 by Saber Errebai (Lebanon).

[http://www.bomb-mp3.com]
[http://www.maghrebspace.net]

This song was the first pan-Arab commercial success by the Tunisian singer Saber Errebai. A video was produced to promote the song. It is interesting to note, on the musical front, that the most noticeable alterations are produced in the orchestration by use of the organ, the zither, and the Turkish *bouzouki*[15] instead of the *gombri*,[16] as well as rhythm instruments that are totally foreign to the original version but nevertheless familiar to an Arab ear. The musician's vocal performance remains faithful to the Tunisian *tba'* (vocal performance style). The lyrics are in rural dialect, today well rooted in the linguistic usages of the Tunisian population and more accessible to the Arab population in general.

Example 12: "Barcha barcha," by Saber Errebai, new production (Lebanon 2001).

[http://www.dailymotion.com]

Saber Errebai had a second success with a new song titled "Barcha barcha," a typically Tunisian expression. The expression gave the music video originality, even as the song met the standards for Arabic commercial music.

Example 13: "Ajmal Nissa'el Dounia," by Saber Errebai, new production, Rotana (Lebanon 2006).

[http://www.itunes.apple.com]

This song by Saber Errebai perfectly fits the standards for Arabic commercial music, and his style owes nothing to his Tunisian origins. He continues to have commercial success thanks to Rotana, a production and distribution company that dominates the Arab market.

The samples chosen from among a number of pieces of variety music have a certain number of shared traits. Songs are accompanied by music videos, a marketing technique that shows that commercial music is now watched as much as it is listened to. It is essentially music with a beat. The lyrics are in Egyptian or Lebanese, which have become the preferred languages for commercial Arabic songs. The tune is based on a melodic interpretation of popular lyrics and litanies and not on maqamic interpretation, which has earned it the additional label "light music." Interpretation based on emotion is gradually replacing the traditional modulations and variations of the maqam:[17] the singer simply performs a melody and therefore no longer needs to understand Arabic musical culture. Production is characterized by the simultaneous use of synthetic, electronic, and traditional instruments. Fabrication in the studio allows for all sorts of artificial adaptation: vocal arrangements, multiplication of instruments, mixing, and a disco beat overdubbed on a darbouka rhythm. There is therefore no need for a large Arab orchestra. The instruments are becoming predominant in the song, to the detriment of the singer's voice, which has become ancillary. The darbouka, offering a rhythm specific to Arab culture, is often used in new productions, but its function is sometimes limited to providing a reference to the Arabic origin of the music and a beat to which all Arab listeners can dance. Acoustic instruments used in Western pop music, such as guitar, piano, and drum set, are very much in evidence, as are certain electric and synthetic instruments, such as beat box and organ. Certain foreign traditional instruments, such as the Turkish bouzouki, are appropriated. Computer-assisted composition incorporates synthetic samples from sound banks and increasingly uses sound effects from American pop music.

There are two poles of production of Arabic commercial songs, Egyptian and Lebanese, depending on the language of the lyrics. We can distinguish the following:

- songs sung in Egyptian dialect
- songs sung in Lebanese dialect by Arab singers of all nationalities combined
- songs sung in one or the other of these two dialects with the introduction of one or more musical features of another Arabic musical culture (generally the singer's Arab country of origin)
- reprises of songs in the "classical Arabic music" genre
- reprises of tourath songs from an Arab country, dressed in new commercial clothes.

A third, less-well-known pole should be added to this list, *khaliji* music (Gulf Arab countries), which largely retains its Bedouin/Arab desert musical specificities (musical autonomy) while using the new means of distribution offered by globalization.

Another way of categorizing musical creations is according to the interpretation:

- Melodic mode of interpretation, a complete break with tradition
- Maqamic mode of interpretation, in continuity with tradition but produced with new means of recording and distribution.

This broad sampling of different categories and modes of interpretation seems to show that in the globalized economic and social environment, Arabic commercial music is attaining commercial autonomy at the expense of musical autonomy. Like international music styles that benefit from wide distribution, Arabic commercial music no longer obeys strict musical rules, as does traditional music. Rather, it incorporates all forms of musical borrowings, as long as they provide a vehicle for reaching the largest Arab audience possible, and perhaps for expanding beyond its traditional area of influence.

Tunisian Local Music

The Tunisian environment is characterized by the following:

- use of unsophisticated technology
- commercialization that does not respect intellectual property law
- proliferation of the trade in pirated musical products
- the absence of a state policy for encouraging musical creation
- the absence of music distribution companies
- the absence of a marketing or media strategy for Tunisian music
- a multiplication of world music festivals (jazz at the Tabarka festival, world music at Hammamet, classical music at El-Djem, and so on)
- stars of Arabic music gaining in popularity at the expense of Tunisian singers
- local radio and television stations broadcasting Arabic commercial music to meet the expectations of a public greatly influenced by "Arabic" products.

To analyze the major trends in local Tunisian musical production, I selected albums produced in 2006 by the Tunisian singers Mohamed Jebali, Samir Loussif, Zied Gharsa, and Hédi Donia, who perform urban, popular, and rural songs.

Example 14: "Hathaka kâtibtib liyya" by Samir Loussif, Tunisian pop song produced in 2006.

[http://www.ilike.com]

In this song, the only elements foreign to Tunisian popular music are the timid use of an instrument from Arabic classical music, the *nay,* synthetic sounds (organ, beat box), and a melody in *charki (nahawand)* mode.

Perusal of six songs from Samir Loussif's album reveals some borrowings of popular music from other cultures: Asian for melodic modes, Tunisian urban for use of the nay, and Western for use of the piano, the organ, and the beat box. However, these borrowings have no impact on the general reception, because the elements specific to popular music are still present. Moreover:

- All of the songs are sung in Tunisian dialect.

169

- The rhythmic interpretation is authentic, and in all songs the acoustic sounds of the darbouka and the daff are used in a Tunisian *fazzani, bou nawwara,* or other pop beat.
- The songs deal with human subjects, such as misery, love, betrayal, and the difficulty of social relations, in a metaphoric style proper to Tunisian culture.
- There is systematic use of the instrument that gave its name to this popular music, the *mezoued,* here played as a solo instrument, with passages of improvisation, or in a *lezma* interlude to the vocal parts to allow the audience to interact by dancing.
- The melodic modes, although borrowed from the Asian *nahawand, jaharkah, rast,* or *kordi* modes, have their equivalent in the Tunisian *mhayyir sikah, mazmoum,* and *rast al-dhil* modes. The vocal perform-ance, in Tunisian dialect, is perceived as Tunisian.

In regard to musical autonomy, there are timid attempts at borrow-ings from Western acoustic (piano and accordion) or synthetic (organ, electric bass) instruments and references to classical Tunisian urban music by recourse to the nay or the daff. However, the sounds remain Tunisian, dominated essentially by the mezoued, the darbouka, and the human voice. In regard to commercial autonomy, the songs on this album, produced by a local Tunisian company (Phonie) and distributed through local channels, had a popular success that translated into record attendance at Lussif's concerts and his appearances at national (Carthage) and regional festivals.

Example 15: song titled "Na'atîk jwab," by the singer Hédi Donia, reprise of popular rural patrimony.

Example 16: "Sidi dlali," Hédi Donia, new production in religious style.

Example 17: "'Îcha," Hédi Donia, new production in traditional and popular style.

[http://www.mp3tunisie.com]

The album by Hédi Donia, who is considered an excellent performer of both profane and sacred popular music, is a mixture of new music and reprises of Tunisian popular songs. Three of the six cuts on the album are reprises of popular songs, and the other three are new productions in the same genre. The sounds used are those of popular Tunisian music, composed of acoustic instruments of the mezoued and darbouka types. The modes used are mazmoum and rast al-dhil, and the rhythms, such as fazzani and bou nawwara, belong to Tunisian musical culture. Improvised variations are reserved for the mezoued. Thus, this music is devoted essentially to trance building.

Comparing some aspects of Loussif's and Donia's albums, we find that Donia is popular for her interpretation of popular and sacred tourath songs, respecting the original musical specificities of popular music (rhythm mode, instruments, dialect, lyrics) that resemble ancestral sounds likely to transport listeners to a state of collective trance. Loussif, in contrast, addresses societal and human relations issues (immigration, male-female relations, attachment to mother) with which the same listeners can identify. Although he has sometimes used Asian modes, his music retains the Tunisian popular style through the specifically Tunisian rhythms that he uses, the rural Tunisian words in his vocal interpretation, the presence in all of his songs of basic instruments in popular music, such as the mezoued and darbouka, and the *tat'im*, borrowings of instruments of foreign origin, such as the organ, the piano, and the accordion. In both albums, there is a similar purity in the use of elements specific to Tunisian popular music.

Example 18: "Trahwija," song from Zied Gharsa's album, new production in the traditional *watariyya* style.

[http://www.fann-cha3bi.com]

It should be noted here that the mezoued is not generally used in the traditional music called *watariyya* (literally, stringed). It is introduced by the musician, who is also the composer, as a strategy for success with a Tunisian public.

Example 19: "A'lâch tjâfînî," Zied Gharsa, new production in traditional watariyya style.

[http://www.zikamp3.com]

The use of the harmonium is a characteristic of early twentieth-century urban Tunisian songs.

In regard to musical autonomy, the sounds on the album are related to traditional Tunisian urban and popular or sacred music. By integrating the mezoued, the composer breaks a taboo on never using this instrument in traditional urban music, creating a mixing of genres. In regard to commercial autonomy, the musician achieves this goal by composing two songs with a popular sound (mezoued and rhythmic) while reprising songs that are common at Tunisian celebrations (weddings, circumcisions, graduations, and other occasions), which constitute the main source of employment for musicians.

Example 20: Song titled "Habîb 'ouyouni" from the album by Mohamed Jebali, new production in Arabic commercial music style.

[http://www.tunisia-today.com]

The music is composed, arranged, and performed by Egyptian musicians. The sound of the song is not specific to Tunisian music but meets the norms of Arabic commercial music (Egyptian dialect) and is sold through Tunisian distribution circuits.

Example 21: "'Ijbik ma 'ijbikchi," Mohamed Jebali, new production in disco style.

[http://www.dyalbasah.com]

The only form of musical autonomy resides in the dialect used; all the rest is borrowed from Western disco music.

Example 22: "Kmar," Mohamed Jebali, new creation.

[http://www.beemp3.com]

Here, the performer tries to ride the wave of modern commercial Arabic music, which weakens his musical autonomy. Out of the nine songs on the album, only three are sung in Tunisian, and "Kmar" is the only one composed in a Tunisian musical language. Commercially, this album did not benefit from a modern distribution system and received only limited play on Tunisian radio stations. This situation caused it to be a commercial failure, which led to an absence of commercial autonomy. This is a good illustration of the influence of Arab commercial music on the behaviour and musical choices of certain Tunisian musicians; thus, success requires a double strategy, both musical autonomy and commercial autonomy.

Conclusion

How does local Tunisian music fit into the debate over globalization and autonomy? I methodically analyzed different productions by known singers of contemporary Tunisian songs — classical with stringed instruments, popular using the mezoued, rural, and traditional — in order to define the degree of musical or commercial autonomy of the Tunisian musical environment under the influence of globalization. My diachronic analysis of the evolution of Arabic music from the early twentieth century to the present revealed elements that have transformed how Arabic music, including Tunisian music, is created and the musical elements most affected by the transformation.

The musical autonomy of Tunisian music may be measured through five independent criteria, listed in order of importance:

1 The vocal interpretation: lyrics, language, or local dialect. This is the best-preserved aspect of Arabic music. Even though the musical language sometimes changes completely, the use of a specific dialect, and thus the mode of vocal interpretation, signifies a minimum of musical autonomy. For Arab listeners, expert or not, this is the element that is the most important to preserve and the most difficult to standardize. Although there is a gap between commercial Arabic music and classical Arabic musical language (mode of traditional creation), that the music is performed in Arabic or one of its dialects makes it completely authentic to the ears (and eyes) of (non-expert) Arab audiences.

2 The rhythmic element: the use of rhythm and percussion instruments specific to a given culture. This element is very important to listeners, because it allows them to react according to their respective cultures. In Tunisian music, popular dance rhythms are used in new productions and may determine their success. In commercial Arabic music, the wahda rhythm, interpreted by the darbouka, dubbed over the regular rhythm provided by the beat box, is used almost systematically to mark the Asian touch. Unfortunately, among the dozens of rhythms in Arabic music, only this one is used. In khaliji music, traditional rhythmic elements and vocal interpretations have been retained, preserving musical autonomy, even though the type of orchestration, the mode of composition, and the interpretation have changed considerably. This finding shows that adoption of new

creative technologies (creative assistance software) does not force abandonment of the traditional elements of Arabic music.

3 The melodic element: the use of a melody specific to Arabic musical culture, known quarter-tone modes, specific ornamentation, maqamic interpretation, and so on. For an expert listener, this element is essential. The musical language, the variation in modes, and their richness are used to evaluate a musical composition — except that commercial music is not evaluated by expert listeners. Modal variations are no longer necessary for the music to be appreciated. The songs are often limited to a repetitive melodic phrase and depend on visual effects in music videos to fill the gaps. Quarter-tone modes are almost never used; most compositions are in nahawand, ajam, or kord mode, very similar to the minor and major modes in Western music. In addition, these modes allow for Western-style harmonization created with composition-assistance software. In Tunisian music, however, specifically Tunisian and Arabic modes are retained.

4 The instruments: the use of instruments not specific to the musical culture such as electronic instruments. Today, no festive gathering takes place without an organ and an amplifier!

5 The traditional mode of composition and performance: this element includes the composition of the band (the takht), the place made for improvisation, heterophonic play, the type of accompaniment and arrangement, and the musical language.

Despite attempts to emulate the world music commercial model, Tunisian music has managed to preserve its characteristic musical elements: dialect, rhythm, and instruments. Its degree of musical autonomy is thus relatively intact.

Globalization is characterized, in my view, by the technologies that have induced new modes of production and commercialization of musical products. Based on the degree of adoption of new distribution supports, we can observe whether a local musical style, such as Tunisian music, has entered the logic of globalization. By measuring how much it resists the new environment by not taking advantage of the opportunities offered by globalization, we can determine its capacity to preserve its autonomy faced with the invasion of world music.

Unlike some Arab countries (Lebanon, Egypt), which have built a production and commercialization system that has reached the entire

Arab world, Tunisia lacks specialized satellite TV stations, organized production circuits, and a workforce in the trades related to musical production. The lack of these aspects has prevented Tunisian music from spreading throughout the Arab world. In contrast, the Tunisian public has had access to world music. Tunisian music, like other Arabic musical styles, has had trouble achieving commercial autonomy, even on the national scale. Commercial autonomy does not go beyond the local level and therefore is outside of the globalization process.

Computer-assisted composition gives composers the means to use sounds from all over the world, as well as new synthetic sounds, at a low cost. Because this technique is designed for Western musical language, Arab composers are forced to give up certain specific musical characteristics: quarter-tones, variable notes, maqam, heterophony, improvisation, and so on. The disappearance of these elements changes composition standards and processes, giving rise to the easily memorized melodies that dominate the Arab, and global, musical space today. This technique is rarely used by composers in Tunisia.

The reception of music in the Tunisian musical environment has changed profoundly. Private Tunisian radio networks (also broadcasting on the Internet) and specialized satellite networks, which have become popular, reserve more than 90 percent of their air time for Arabic and international commercial music. Tunisian listeners and viewers are subjected to permanent audiovisual overkill. Tunisian musicians, meanwhile, have access only to national networks that lack an effective marketing policy. Furthermore, the organization of world music festivals, more and more frequent with globalization, is leading to the formation of Tunisian groups that perform international musical genres such as rock, rap, or "Tunisian" jazz.

Popular music, dominated by mezoued, is the most commercially successful genre in Tunisia. This music has not, however, incorporated the new technological means of recording and distribution made available by globalization. It has kept the basic elements specific to the national music: popular dialect, rhythms, and instruments and themes close to the reality of Tunisian social and cultural life. Other Tunisian musical genres, both traditional and modern, borrow elements of the Tunisian popular genre in an attempt to achieve commercial success.

Given all of the elements imposed by globalization, composers of Tunisian songs try desperately to preserve some musical autonomy, which is threatened by an absence of commercial autonomy. The choice today is between reasoning in terms of globalized Arabic music, and therefore following the model of commercial Arabic music, and reducing all genres to the single mezoued genre that is a commercial success, but only at the local level.

chapter 8   **Globalization and Food Autonomy in the Mediterranean Region**

Amado A. Millán Fuertes

IN THE MEDITERRANEAN COUNTRIES, food is a culturally significant field for investigating the relationship between globalization and autonomy. The Mediterranean region is a site not only of exchanges and encounters but also of conflicts. Cultural diversity is limited by common geographic conditions; climate and landscape provide the framework for a shared history. Food in the Mediterranean is not unchanging, but it is identifiable — differentiated and acknowledged within the globalization of nutrition. First, there are predilections for certain foods: wheat, olive oil, vegetables,¹ fruits, mutton and lamb, fish, spices, herbs, and condiments. Plant foods and frying predominate in all culinary preparations, and salt and oil are used for preserves. Finally, common ingredients and preparation methods are used in sweet dishes and pastries. On the economic side, there is a parsimonious approach to food consumption: fasting for Ramadan and Lent, husbandry of small herds, agrarian systems adapted to limited water resources, and fishing with tunny nets. These are the dominant alimentary characteristics of the peoples around the Mediterranean Sea.

Wine growing, first practised in Asia, was spread by Romanization and then by the extension of the liturgical practices of a conquering Christianity. It is now globalized. Wine is a product typical of the shoreline countries in the Mediterranean region, in which it is either a sacred or a forbidden product, depending on the national religion. It is now consumed all over the world; in some regions, it is seen as health enhancing. Conviviality rules wine consumption in the Mediterranean region; it accompanies not only meals but also various rituals and major occasions. This status is far from its reductive function of intoxication in northern European countries — a function that justifies its repression and contributes to the global domination of a local morality, poorly concealed behind prescriptions of prevention that are foreign to daily life in the Mediterranean region.

Evidence of trade in general, and of foodstuffs in particular, can be dated back to when the human species began to spread. Local cuisines, in continual evolution, were typified by sustained but dynamic food models. The Mediterranean socio-alimentary zone was configured by successive historical contributions. Some elements came from the East (Phoenician, Hebraic, Greek, Arab, Ottoman, Berber), others from the North (Iberian, Celtic, Roman, Germanic, Andalusian), and still others from the West, with an American component. These contributions formed a regional food syncretism built on ecological foundations and cultural requirements. Nevertheless, the Mediterranean food space remained unique.

This system of cross-influences was acted upon by modernization through the industrialization of food production, processing, and distribution, resulting in mass production, on the one hand, and planetary dissemination, on the other. This change in how an essential need was fulfilled could not help but have a profound impact on the autonomy of subsistence farming, provoking an increase in dependency and a reduction in local differences. Although the diversity of comestible species was dropping, the variety of products consumed was growing constantly. Both north and south of the Mediterranean Sea, modernization, conceived today as globalization, has affected local food. Under the aegis of globalization, large transnational firms determine individuals' food preferences, choices, practices, tastes, and representations, thus reducing those individuals to the single function of consumer.

Food and Anthropology: Advantages for Research

Food is interesting as an object of study because it is a transversal phenomenon — not only socio-cultural but also biological and ecological. Food involves a multiplicity of cultural variables, and it allows for direct observation of fragmentary aspects of social life that are difficult to pin down. For instance, culture as abstraction is materialized in the food served on a plate, which can be seen as the final link in a long alimentary chain that extends from the International Monetary Fund (IMF) to the guest at the table. With its transversal and differential nature, food is a perfect fit for the global and comparative anthropological approach.

Food

As a transversal fact, human food is at the intersection of the biological, environmental, technological, societal, cultural, and individual fields. It thus provides an entry point to socio-cultural research on globalization and autonomy. A dependent variable because of its transversality, food opens a path to the comprehension of general socio-cultural facts and not solely food-related ones. It is the result of a complex ensemble of elements, including the following:

- the environment and social relations of the milieu, configured by both local food-production techniques and the tools or manual techniques associated with them
- the social structure and, thus, the access to food resources, the conditions for economic exchanges, and even the distribution of these resources within the group of guests
- the selection by class of a hierarchical range of foods and the rejection of products that are biologically or economically more accessible or abundant
- the norms that rule the food system and the values attributed to foods and to their culinary preparation
- nutritional or religious beliefs
- cultural and food-specific traditions.

Food is both material and symbolic, both individual and collective (Fischler 1995, 12-13). It is also reiterative, ephemeral, and emotional. Neither hunger nor satiety can be transferred (Simmel 1986) or sublimated (Kardiner and Linton 1939). Food is functional and convivial, statutory, ostentatious, ritualized, sacred, and associated with festive seasons. It has immediate or deferred effects on the health of the body or soul, and food behaviour is subjected to norms that are both ethical and aesthetic, under informal social control. It represents a unique link between outside and inside (Farb, Armelagos, and Desmond 1985).

Thus, food distinguishes and identifies as much the human species as a whole as the members of a given culture or social category (Geertz 1987; Léroi-Gourhan 1973, 171). Although the need for food is common to all living beings, humans have differentiated socio-cultural responses to it. It establishes and actualizes the foundation of society, foments trade,[2] and generates cohesion or conflict.[3]

Globalization

Globalization may be thought of as a process of socio-cultural change that operates throughout the world in unequal ways. It is not a matter only of capital or goods circulating through and occupying the planet but also of ways of doing, perceiving, feeling, desiring, thinking, and organizing structured according to an expanding cultural model with a local origin (probably neo-imperialism) and not a synthesis of cultures. Under globalization, the world is conceived as an enterprise, and unlimited acquisition of economic benefits is substituted for the attribution of divine grace. Consumption thus becomes the criterion for creating a social hierarchy.

The local and the global coexist. The merger of the two produces a third attribute: the glocal (Robertson 1997). As globalization advances, certain local differences are selected and certified so that they may continue to subsist. Global homogenization adopts different strategies to occupy the local.

Despite advances in technology and transportation, certain conditions for the localization of food cannot be ignored.[4] Unlike financial capital, images, and information, foods have a materiality — the production environment that they require and their perishable nature — that affects their degree of globalization. Culinary traditions and reiterative food practices shape tastes and raise barriers to rapid change, but these act on the periphery of the system. Traditional holiday foods may change depending on whether the holidays are in Tunisia or Jordan, for example; here and there, globalized dishes appear at celebrations because of the attractiveness of imported customs. For instance, under the influence of Western dietetics related to the globalization of health concepts such as the demonization of cholesterol, the traditional sacrifice of a sheep is sometimes replaced by that of a cow at the great festival of Eid al-Adha (Tunisia).[5] This trend is still limited to upper social classes in certain modern social circles, but in the daily diet, autonomous foods are being replaced by global preparations.

For a global innovation to be adopted, however, it must respect certain rules by which the food system is structured. A meal must meet precise standards: composition, sequence, simultaneity, combination, and possibilities for substitution. There are culturally appropriate times and places to drink and eat despite the food-related restructuring wrought by globalization. For instance, foods have an appearance, shape, texture, colour, temperature, flavour, aroma, type of preparation, quantity, and quality (difficult to define) that may or may not comply with habitual food practices (Millán 2000b).

The pace of life has changed because of industrial development and urban concentration. A context favourable to food globalization is formed by women working outside the home (along with little participation by men in domestic tasks), changes in family structure, the individualization of meals, the devaluation of primary activities and a reduction in the time devoted to them, the simplification of nutrition, the automation of household tasks, and the consumption of prepared products.

Local/Global

Opposing the process of globalization is that of localization: in the face of dependency is autonomy. Although the local is determined by the global, the reverse is also true.

Perishable materiality is one obstacle to food globalization; the symbolic dimension of food is also an important barrier. Globalized foods are sold under and recognized by commercial brands that belong to private economic organizations, while institutionally branded products are the result of joint private-public councils. Adopting fast food — eating a hamburger or drinking certain carbonated beverages — means choosing an ideological option associated with an Anglo-American lifestyle. Such products become *edible icons*. Thus, the play of transfers made between food and guest serves as their mutual identification ("Tell me what you eat, and I will tell you who you are"). Consumption of local products also means taking a position, expressing a preference opposed to a previous choice. It must be remembered, however, that we are plural guests and that, by desire or by necessity, our food styles are changing. Similarly, globalized foods are consumed in a local context awash in signifiers.

Local foods acquire their prestige from their place of origin, and commercial brands become secondary in relation to guaranteed provenances. In central and northern Europe, quality is reduced to health safety criteria, and the reference is the brand; on both shores of the Mediter-ranean Sea, by contrast, quality is associated with place of origin (Lorente 2001, 40) — that is, with institutionalized local products, many of which are part of the cultural heritage (Espeitx Bernat 1999).

The local-global duality involves polarities and interactions. For in-stance, to counter fast food, Slow Food, a movement to preserve food diversity, has appeared. Faced with modernity, culinary tradition is strengthened: opposing industrial "machine-made food" are artisanal foods, which are represented as "natural." Finally, alongside Anglo-American fast food, other products from less dominant countries are now emerging, such as Gyros, hummus, and so on.

Strategies and Forms of Interaction between the Global and the Local

On the one hand, globalization progresses in a decentralized, diffuse man-ner: it subtly infiltrates cultural spheres and modes of consumption. On the other hand, globalization is negotiated and planned, and it concerns economics and governance (see Chapter 15, this volume). It is insinuated into the local level in association with industrialization — modernization of production and distribution — through borders that are opening to capital, goods, and services and thanks to the adoption of favourable political measures. Its implementation is facilitated by expanded travel and tourism, as well as by strategies ranging from enticement to imita-tion. It may be imposed through political and economic pressure or by means of technical standardization measures, which are, in fact, only hom-ogenization of the local within the parameters of the global.

Food globalization may sweep up emblematic local products and de-territorialize them. Examples include couscous that bears the Knorr or Maggi brand, pizza from Pizza Hut, Old Paso chili con carne, and El Paellador paella and tabouli — dishes with a local identity removed from their original context. But whereas the product may be globalized, its context remains local. Tapas may be consumed from Tokyo to Cape Town, from New York to Paris, but the sociability that accompanies the action of "going to eat tapas" cannot be globalized. It is a local food culture. At the same time, and in relation to this expression of local food culture, the modality of franchising is adopted as a global implementa-tion strategy (for instance, the Lizarran and Sagardi tapas bar chains). Not only are local products from peripheral cultures globalized, but consumption techniques are also standardized (for example, eating with the fingers or with cutlery). In contrast, coffee, a globalized product, is consumed locally with different preparation methods (United States, Italy, Germany, Turkey, Jordan). Similarly, the hamburger, a product emblematic of globalization, may be transformed in a preparation that is made as local as possible and called "homemade."

Traditional products, in the grasp of global trends, may become "neo-traditional"; on the other hand, globalized products may be territorialized. McDonalds, for instance, serves beer in France and Spain but not in the United States. In Muslim countries where it has outlets (for example, Jordan), it serves a special breakfast for the month of Ramadan. The local Coca-Cola company markets three-litre bottles for large Brazilian families, and Nestlé diversifies its coffee to match the specificities of the countries in which it is sold. Some globalized products are replaced by others with similar characteristics but manufactured regionally (Méca-Cola). Sometimes, traditional dishes are made with globalized ingredients, such as Maggi concentrated soup cubes in sub-Saharan African dishes.

Thus, under the effects of globalization, tradition is merged with innovation. A *tajine,* or terracotta pot, is used to cook on a gas stove; DIN A4 eggs[6] are fried in high-end olive oil; people drink *calimocho,* a combination of local red wine and Coca-Cola; a Spanish omelette is seasoned with ketchup, and so on. Globalization may also bypass local food culture. Auchan, a French supermarket chain called Alcampo (translated literally as "in the country") in Spain, sells ingredients for pot-au-feu but not those for *cocido* (a literal, but not culinary, translation). Similarly, the cultural translation is lacking in an ad on the label of a product that combines Marseille soap and talc; this makes no sense in Spain, where the brand imitating homemade soap is Lagarto (literally, "lizard").

The local character of some food products persists thanks to ecological particularities, growing difficulties, or seasonality. An example is gurumelo wild mushrooms, cultivated in the Sierra de Huelva in Andalusia and harvested in March and April.

The economic need to grow local crops despite the advance of globalized products, on the one hand, and the need to exist on the symbolic, identitary level, on the other hand, causes local resistance to emerge. Revitalizing, recycling, protecting, institutionalizing, and preserving the patrimony are strategies used on the local level with the simple goal of self-preservation; expansion is the guarantee of this survival. Thus, local products, such as the Fuentes de Ebro sweet onion, stand out from delocalized brands. The identification of certain products and dishes with regions and communities is presented as an adaptation by the market to local and denominational requirements.

Effects

The local level is conceived as an identitary value, while the global level is perceived as dissolving cultural distinctions. Local products are differentiated, autonomous; globalized products are mass-produced and subjected to economic and industrial imperatives. Thus, variations in uniformity are required by the reductive technology of the diversity of tastes. Authenticity, difficult to establish and sometimes ambiguous, is considered a local attribute, even if it is the result of ancient ingredients or preparation modes. Identity and autonomy are perceived as being in danger of extinction, and so traditions are revived as dependencies increase. Food nostalgia is emotional and does not take account of social changes, tastes, socio-cultural values, or differences between yesterday's and today's consumers.

The process of globalization involves the abolition of time and space: foods are produced and consumed out of season, and it is possible to have access to a single product throughout the world. Food localities and borders are more and more diffuse. Foods and dishes become ambiguous and are freed of their symbolic weight to become pure consumer products. Furthermore, health risks increase because of the global circulation of foods.

With the disappearance of subsistence farming (Dupin et al. 1997), food provisions are now gathered mainly through purchases at different retail sites. These stores concretely display the contrast in levels of globalization in the food retail sector — for example, markets and supermarkets in east and west Amman (see Chapter 10). Under the grasp of globalization, consumption of meat, for example, is democratized, but this is at the expense of the animals' health, degradation of the environment, loss of biodiversity and of the sensory qualities of the food, and the disappearance of seasonal cycles and rituals.

Conclusion

Globalization is not a synthesis of cultures. Food globalization certifies and homogenizes differentiated local products to fit conditions required by industrial technology and the marketing strategies of large transnational retail chains. The symbolic aspects of food thus become secondary. Transnational firms, which have a complete marketing apparatus at their disposal, show an incapacity to understand local, regional, and cultural food differences, causing them huge economic losses. One example is Nestlé's fruitless attempt to introduce Nestea into Great Britain.

When products are deterritorialized, their context is abolished and becomes a non-place; they are adapted to the globalized non-context. The localized space is a constriction that tends to dissolve as globalization expands. The industrial agrofood system increases both dependencies and the distance between sites of production and consumption. It limits consumer choice to what is available in the large retail chains, homogenizes tastes, and reduces biodiversity, even though the variety of processed products on the table is increasing continually. Strategies for the implementation of globalized foods, processed or not, focus on the attraction exerted by global reference models in challenging the position of locally defined and prepared foods. These strategies are thus based on the appropriation of local products, as well as on ethnocentric and maladapted imposition caused by the inequality between local and global power. The actions of media and advertising mechanisms influence local food consumers, most of whom belong to the rising middle classes. As a consequence of middle-class influence, the products sold in large, multinational shopping malls become valued over more traditional local foods.

chapter 9

The Fuentes de Ebro Sweet Onion: Autonomy through Globalization

Rulof Kerkhoff

THE VILLAGE OF FUENTES de Ebro[1] is situated on the shores of the Ebro River some thirty kilometres from Saragossa, the capital of the department and of the Autonomous Community of Aragon, in northeast Spain. Like the majority of Spanish villages, it was a mainly agricultural locale until the 1960s, when a wave of generalized modernization rolled through the country. At the time, Fuentes combined small local industry with mechanized farming for the local market, the main products from which were wheat and olives on non-irrigated land, and corn and alfalfa on irrigated land. Fuentes also has a rich zone devoted to market production, irrigated by a tributary of the Ebro and by the Ginel, a stream that, according to the local people, has special properties that enhance the quality of vegetables, especially the famous Fuentes de Ebro onion *(Allium cepa)*.

The Fuentes white onion, also called the sweet large onion, has a reputation both in its zone of production and on the national level. I was told that this variety of onion has been cultivated in Fuentes and its environs since the dawn of time — "since the world was the world," as it is said — although Pascual Madoz, in his *Diccionario geografico, estadistico y historico* (1845-50), does not mention the onion when he refers to the population of this region. The Fuentes onion is formed of a rounded bulb and a wide stem. The outer layer is white, and the flesh is tender and crunchy. Eaten raw, the onion is sweet, with a slight underlying piquant flavour. Although many local informers insist that the conditions in the area (soil, water) are essential to obtaining these qualities, scientists suggest that it is the genetic variety that distinguishes the onions. Its uniqueness is probably due to a combination of genetic factors and the growing environment.

The cultivation cycle for the Fuentes onion is annual for bulbing and biannual for obtaining seeds. Traditionally, seeds in the nursery were irrigated with water from the Ginel before a subculture was prepared. Today, the onions are sown on land irrigated by the Ebro, and some sixty producers cultivate the sweet onion on a total of 600 hectares. In 1999, Fuentes onion cultivation took up 250 hectares out of the 1,300 hectares devoted to onions in the Aragon region, which is ranked fifth in Spain, with 4.5 percent of the national total, or 43,000 tonnes. Thus, cultivation is expanding; 1,500 tonnes of Fuentes onions were sold in 2004. Cultivation of another variety of onion (Valencia) has also increased over the last twenty-five years. Production is only partially mechanized. Fuentes onions are harvested and packed by hand since they must be handled carefully. I observed that much of the labour is supplied by elderly people who are related to the owners of the operations. With their long agricultural experience, they know how to handle this fragile product. They also provide the cheap labour that enables this crop to be profitable. The onions are harvested from late June to mid-September. Current conservation conditions allow them to be marketed from July to December, making them a seasonal product.

During the summer, producers sell directly to consumers, but most of the crops are processed through five local enterprises: Jumosol Fruits, Cooperativa San Miguel, Hortal Ebro, Fuencampo, and the SAT Couronne des Fuentes de Ebro. Most of the onions are consumed in Saragossa and its environs and in Huesca province and sold through supermarket chains and Mercazaragoza. In recent years, the onions have invaded the large Catalonia market (Mercabarna), and they are occasionally sold in other parts of Spain, such as Madrid and the Basque Country.[2]

Surprisingly sweet when eaten raw, savoury when cooked, and easy to conserve, this traditional product has gradually gained a toehold in the market and, over long years of production, has ended up earning a well-deserved reputation among consumers in the immediate vicinity. Alongside other varieties that are available year round, consumers appreciate its culinary qualities in salads, soups, and stews and with roasts.

To understand the changes that cultivation of the Fuentes onion has undergone over the last twenty years, we must recall the transformation of Spanish society and the changes that have taken place in the distribution and the seasonal availability of foods. The globalization of markets and the delocalization of some production have caused consumption models to change.

The quantity of sweet onions cultivated in this geographic area has increased in recent decades. This increase is attributable, among other things, to the drop in profitability of the dominant crops, alfalfa and grains. However, fluctuations in the price of sweet onions have led to considerable variations in quantity produced from year to year. In the 1990s, producers and firms that marketed the Fuentes onion became aware of the need to differentiate their product on an increasingly competitive market, in which it was difficult to make a seasonal product with higher production costs profitable while making price the main sales pitch.

In collaboration with the technical department of the Aragon General Caucus, research was conducted to quantify the Fuentes onion's degree of piquancy, the characteristic that distinguishes this product from other varieties. The results established a maximum level of 3.5 moles/litre of pyruvic acid. In 1997, under the technical regulations, the Fuentes onion obtained the Aragonese quality label "C" *(calidad)*, based on its flavour and the care given to its cultivation, the limited use of chemical products, and a minimal level of piquancy, which guaranteed consumers the famous sweet taste. Furthermore, the protection of this variety meant that its cultivation continued to involve non-standardized traditional cultural practices in which each farmer worked with his own seeds, thus offering considerable diversity in size, bulb shape, piquancy, and aptitude for conservation.

Because of the seasonal nature of the Fuentes onion, producers in the region began to cultivate other varieties that could be conserved for longer. This change caused confusion among consumers, because the product became an onion that was grown in Fuentes but did not have the characteristics expected of a Fuentes onion, raising the possibility of hybridization and the danger of losing the native variety. (One expert told me that farmers in the region had begun to recover seeds of the original variety, but it already no longer existed.) In addition, some have observed that producers in the zone had been very generous with their seeds in the past, which explains the presence of the Fuentes variety in other regions, such as Valencia, Catalonia, and even Chile — in spite of the belief that ambient conditions would cause the rapid "degeneration" of the onions when they were cultivated in locations other than their native soil.

Circumstances led farmers, processors, and commercial companies, among others, to organize the Association for the Promotion of the Fuentes Onion of Ebro (Acefuentes), in February 2005. The association's objective was to obtain the designation of origin label,[3] the highest level of protection of food products allocated by the European Union. The main promoter of this operation was the Fuentes town council, with the support of the regional government. The designation of origin is essentially a legal tool designed to protect agrofood products that, because of their particular quality, attributed to the influence of the local production environment, have achieved a certain prestige. In addition, it was consumers who named the onion Fuentes, thus emphasizing the locality as a particular growing environment (Lorente 2001, 54). It is thus necessary that all production and processing be done within the determined geographic zone.

The designation of origin may be seen as an instrument for development of a territory and as a valuable tool for protection from the forces of globalization. The objective is to protect not so much the products but the local territory, which is understood as a homogeneous geographic space because of its resources and agricultural specialization and its interaction with natural and human factors in the production standards that ensure the characteristics of the product. It is precisely this environmental aspect that distinguishes the designation of origin from a commercial brand. The latter is based on a commercial philosophy, arises from private ownership, and is situated opposite the concept of patrimony. Brands in general do not maintain links with a particular territory or offer a guarantee with regard to production methods or quality beyond what is stipulated in terms of food safety, the standards for which might vary by country, region, or territory. Designations of origin operate through an agreement between producers and the government. In the case of the European Union, Brussels grants the certification through a regulatory council whose functions, in addition to certification, are to guide, monitor, and control production, development, and quality. Inspectors authorized by the corresponding administration perform impartial monitoring of the product's producers and processors.

In the case under discussion here, the designation of origin concerns the geographic zone of production of the onion, the seeds, seed size, the harvest, and the growing methods. It also guarantees phytosanitary processing that respects the environment and the sales period, minimizes the difficulties with conservation, and guarantees the maximum sensory qualities. The designation of origin plays a decisive role in the struggle against fraud, both external and internal; it is meant to be a sort of shield against imitations, substitutes, and falsifications. Moreover, it makes the product, its producers, and the territory where it is cultivated more important. Although the sweet onion is a significant element of identification for inhabitants of the Fuentes region, it is hoped that the designation of origin will make this identification even clearer. In this context, it is interesting to note the result of a survey conducted in 1999 among Aragonese consumers (Llamazares and Martínez 2000), who appreciated the Fuentes onion most, after its lack of piquancy, for its origin or provenance (37 percent).

The increased protection for the Fuentes onion (and other indigenous varieties) is amply justified given the threats to which it is exposed, as the following example illustrates. In recent years, the American company Keystone Fruit Marketing Inc. began to market in Spain and other parts of Europe onions with characteristics identical to those of the Fuentes onion, including the sweetness. These onions were produced in Peru under the name Mayan Sweets from seeds originating in the Vidalia district of the US state of Georgia.

Certain aspects must be addressed in the process of obtaining the designation of origin label:

1 Technical and legal conditions involve the obligation to define the characteristics of an indigenous product and the cultivation practices associated with it, in order to guarantee its survival.
2 These conditions require approval of the product by reducing the number of existing varieties and subjecting production to standardized criteria throughout the European Union.
3 The production area of the designation of origin is expanded to six thousand hectares, which involves new markets, extending beyond the product's traditional zone of consumption. A limited attempt will be made to globalize the Fuentes onion, a local product.

Beyond the technical and legal steps, efforts are being made to promote the product. A communications company (Adico) has been hired, and the Fuentes onion is constantly in the Aragonese media. The Fuentes onion was also used as a pretext for agrofood festivals. Gastronomic days were organized with the collaboration of twenty-one restaurants throughout the region and, most important, participation by the public. Finally, courses were organized for inhabitants of Fuentes and the environs to improve their knowledge of the indigenous onion's designation of origin and culinary applications.

One problem that must not be underestimated is the cost of maintaining the administrative mechanism for quality control, certification, and the fight against fraud. The territory is small, the onion is a relatively cheap product, and producers are expected to take on a variety of important responsibilities without being assured of realizing substantial profits. Thus, better organization and greater cooperation are necessary between the members of Acefuentes, the town's bureaucrats, Adico, and the inhabitants in general to strengthen the region's identity and social cohesion.

chapter 10   **Globalization of Food Practices in Amman**

Almudena Hasan Bosque

GLOBALIZATION (SEE BECK 2002, 31) has an impact on all aspects of life today. Socio-cultural practices and representations associated with food are changing on both the local and global levels,[1] and norms and values are in a state of constant transformation. Jordan and its capital,[2] Amman, have not escaped this trend.[2] In this study, I show how local food practices are affected by an urban centre's evolution, social divers-ification, and increasingly rapid access to a world network of trade and production, as well as by the profound changes introduced by globaliza-tion and resulting social and spatial transformations.

The Ammanian Food Model: Traditional Food versus Globalized Food

Amman has been the capital of the Hashemite Kingdom of Jordan since 1921. The city, once called Philadelphia, now has more than two million inhabitants of various ethnicities and religions and from different coun-tries. The old centre of Amman was al-Balad, the city's cradle and its storied heart. From there, the city spread into the nearby hills, or *jebels*. Although it was originally the political, religious, and economic core of the city, al-Balad is now exclusively a place of exchange between the cultures of the eastern and western parts of the city (Lavergne 2003). Amman is thus divided into two mentally and culturally distinct zones. The eastern zone is older, working-class, densely populated, has no tourism industry, and is the main destination for those taking part in the rural exodus and for refugees from the wars causing turmoil in the region. The western zone, built more recently, combines the residential, recreational, and service functions of a modern capital in which the process of globalization of trade is clearly underway. It is in this part of the city that big-box stores, restaurants serving foreign cuisines, shopping malls, fitness centres that specialize in weight loss, embassies, foreign cultural centres, and other institutions are concentrated. This spatial and social cleavage means that populations in the two parts of the city live side by side with diverging lifestyles — "'Americanization' or 'Westernization,' with all that these terms imply in terms of adherence to signs, immaterial symbols, and a consumer economy, on the one side, faithfulness to Eastern traditions and production of goods, on the other" (ibid., 106, our translation).

In Amman, three distinct groups have coexisted for a long time: peasants, Bedouins, and urban dwellers. When the kingdom was founded by King Abdullah I in 1921, different Bedouin tribes were living in the territory and following their ancient traditions. The new king, or *za'im,* privileged their customs, including food customs, over those of the peasant minority living mainly in the north part of the country, near the border with Syria. Even today, the kingdom's government endeavours to preserve Arab Bedouin customs and promote them as being the country's original traditions, while presenting itself as the standard-bearer of Western policy and culture. This policy may explain why emblematic Jordanian foods are linked to the Bedouin identity in the popular imagination. *Mansaf* and *sada* coffee are, respectively, the totem dish and beverage (Fischler 1995, 149) for Ammanians, reinforcing their food identity.[3] Mansaf, or Jordanian-style lamb, is a dish of mutton or goat meat cooked in a sauce made of *jamid,* a sort of curdled milk, accompanied by rice with almonds and grilled pine nuts. Sada coffee is prepared in traditional Bedouin style — that is, without sweetener or condiment of any sort, as the Arab name indicates. Mansaf and sada coffee are consumed during rites of passage in Jordanian society, such as engagements, marriages, and funerals.

Nevertheless, Ammanian cuisine,[4] or city cuisine, like all Jordanian cuisine, combines Bedouin[5] and peasant[6] cuisine and is based on seasonal agricultural products. The current urban cuisine is a mix of the two. The Ammanian diet is combined with Bilad ash-Sham[7] cuisine to form the culinary specificity of this geographic area. Bedouin dishes are reserved mainly for festive occasions, whereas peasant dishes are the daily fare.

Ammanians nevertheless show obvious signs of adapting to globalization in the food sphere. This adaptation is revealed quite clearly in the mass infatuation with fast food, the large number of restaurants serving foreign cuisines that are currently invading the capital, and the enormous consumption of carbonated beverages. This market is dominated by Pepsico, which was the first large foreign company to move into Jordan. It inundated the country with its Pepsi, 7Up, and Mirinda brands, to the point that these beverages dethroned the traditional coffee and tea, considered up to then the authentic beverages of Jordanian sociability. In addition, major agrofood retail franchises — such as Safeway, C-Town, and Place and, more recently, Cozmo and 7-Eleven — have built outlets in the western part of Amman. These modern, globalized stores sell ingredients for both local and international cuisine, including Asian cuisine, which is currently fashionable.

Foreign cuisine is deployed in Amman through the expansion of numerous ethnic restaurants — Indian, Chinese, Thai and, especially, Italian and Japanese — most of them situated in the western zone. The presence and success of Japanese restaurants is surprising, in fact, since the indigenous population is not interested in fish. Jordanians are big consumers of red meat, especially beef, as well as white meats, which are much less expensive. The effects of food globalization are also evident in the consumption of offal. In general, only the oldest people and residents of working-class neighbourhoods enjoy these products; everywhere else, they are clearly rejected. There is also a generalized concern with food safety that tends to reduce the quality of products to their sanitary dimension: the primary criterion of acceptability is that foods not be harmful to consumers' health.

Conclusion

In Amman, ancestral traditions related to Bedouin, peasant, and urban ways of life coexist with one another. The globalization process that affects these traditions is assessed and integrated in various ways, making the city an example of how new values, habits, and products from globalized markets are incorporated into different layers of society. What this study reveals is that in the context of a rapidly expanding urban centre, characterized by great spatial, social, and economic diversity, globalization, on the food level at least, is far from acting as a homogenizing factor. Rather, because of the social fracture between the eastern and western parts of the city, globalization provides impetus towards a powerful aspect of autonomy with regard to identitary food traditions, because the means, values, mentalities, and identities of the two sides are diametrically opposed.[8]

chapter 11

Food Globalization and Autonomy Strategies: The Case of Meat in Tunisia

Paula Durán Monfort

IN THIS STUDY, I analyze the effect of globalization on local food models, a phenomenon related to food acculturation (Millán 2000a).[1] This process has different effects on the various components of the food system. My evidence tends to prove that it is more difficult to change central foods than peripheral ones (Gracia Arnaiz 1997, 29-33). I first describe observable changes produced in Tunisian food-retailing spaces centred on meat, a product that has major social significance. I then look at strategies that social actors have developed in relation to this food and its local or global availability.[2]

Retail Spaces: Local Representation and Global Certification

In a country such as Tunisia, retail spaces such as the market and the supermarket are places that reproduce the symbolic dichotomy between the local and the global.[3]

The Market and the Placement of Local Meat

The market is the local retail space. Consumers perceive it as a place that is familiar to them, even if they find imported products there. At the market, animals are presented in two ways: alive or freshly killed or butchered. The animals that are marketed live are mainly small species such as poultry (chickens, turkeys, partridges, and so on). This arrangement not only offers potential customers freedom of choice with regard to the freshness and appearance of the product, but it also permits them to be present during the prescribed ritual.[4] Large animals such as cattle and lambs are offered for view by shoppers once they are sacrificed. To prove the freshness of the meat, certain parts of the animals, such as the head, the skin, and the tongue, are displayed and sometimes decorated conspicuously, such as beef nostrils ornamented with two large fresh red peppers. In this context, social representations of meat are built around the freshness and localization of the product (the provenance of the product and the processing or retail space), which guarantee that the ritual has been performed and allow for categorization of the meat as a food fit for consumption.

Supermarket, Superstore, Big-Box Store: The Discursive Certification of Global Meat

Traditional and neighbourhood retail and commercialization spaces are being transformed as the establishment of supermarkets and French franchise big-box stores (Champion, Géant, Carrefour) encourage the introduction and presence of food industrialization in local behaviours. The display of packaged and canned food products necessitates a discursive assertion of the values and signification of these products, whereas the value and signification of local foods are intrinsically associated with them when they are available at the market.[5] In this process, which induces a rupture between production and consumption, consumers' mistrust tends to increase. Thus, the food industry tries to reassure purchasers by providing information. The freshness of the processed product is attested to by the use of posters and by labels that certify that the packaged meat is that of an animal recently sacrificed: "To guarantee maximum freshness, the products are packaged and cut all day long," announces one poster.[6] A map of Tunisia showing the provenance of the meats on offer is also displayed. The caption reads, "Our meats are exclusively Tunisian." These messages are designed to reassure consumers about the origin of the food and its compliance with the required ritual, and thus to reduce the insecurity that the industrial process tends to provoke. Further, the value associated with "localism" requires the certification of *foreign* food products. For this reason, imported foods with animal-origin ingredients must be certified as fit for halal consumption.

The presence of food alterity is evident in how pork is handled in big-box stores. The selling of this symbolically soiled product requires that there be a separation, a sort of firewall, between it and obviously licit beef and lamb, so that the latter will not be "contaminated." "We assure you," a poster reads, "that the pork is cut in a different department with special utensils." Thus, the food industry certifies imported products as halal to encourage their reconciliation with the collective imaginary and the community's food model. Industrial foods produced locally do not need such discursive affirmation of the process, however, since the *localness* of the meat provides assurance that the ritual has been performed.

Local Safety and Industrial Uncertainty: Consumers' Representations, Discourses, and Strategies

Food Acquisition and Global Consumption

Various discourses refer to the acquisition, preparation, and consumption of global foods. Whereas many consumers select a particular food product for ease of supply, preparation, and consumption, some choose it because it confers a certain social status. This strategy of adapting to food industrialization and responding to transformations taking place in society is reflected in how foods are obtained:[7] "I shop at the Carrefour because everything is in the same place and because it is cheaper" (man, Tunis, fifty years old, university educated). Similarly, people choose industrial food dishes that save considerable time; hence the quickly expanding availability of ready-to-eat dishes, purchased especially by young people, such as sandwiches with sliced turkey, merguez sausage, or tuna, or sometimes shawarma, thinly sliced grilled meat served in bread with tomatoes and grilled onions, seasoned with *taratour,* sesame sauce. Industrial foods are introduced for times without ritual importance — that is, *peripheral* eating times.

Attraction and Social Valorization of Food Alterity

Foreign products are chosen — even though their price is triple that of products of local provenance — for the high social prestige that they offer their purchaser: the purchase and consumption of these products represents an elevation of social status conferred by food. The consumption of pork significantly reproduces this attraction. The discourse underlines the relatively foreign status of the product in comparison to common food practices: "It's for foreigners who live in Tunis," people say. However, there is a gap between discourses and practice, since imported ham and pepper sausage are quite desirable, especially among young men, because they symbolize food modernity. It is one way for them to distance themselves from local tradition.

Autonomy versus Globalization: Selection of Local Foods for Important Eating Occasions

Tunisian consumers balk at purchasing traditional products produced industrially, even if they are licit and certified. This is the case, for example, for the phyllo rolls called "Fatima's fingers" or frozen *briks,* precooked dishes such as *madfouna* (a dish made with spinach, lamb trotters, and meatballs), and *ojja* (a modest dish made with tomatoes, hot peppers, and eggs, sometimes supplemented with *qaddid* dried meat, merguez, or lamb brain). Nor will they buy frozen chopped meat, which they view as being designed for foreign consumers.

Consumers' selection of local foods constitutes a strategy of autonomy in the face of global alterity. For special social occasions,[8] local food products are used to make traditional dishes with high symbolic value, while conferring a high social status by strengthening the sense of social belonging and revalorizing culinary traditions: "Traditional foods require traditional treatment" (Goody 1995, 45).

Purchasing and Consuming the Global and the Local

Food tinkering[9] takes place in the daily diet, as industrialized foods are combined with local products. It is exceptional for global foods to be processed and inserted into festive occasions, because the foods consumed confer greater social valorization. Young people play the main role when this break is made. Thus, the activity of modern eaters must be seen as the expression of a tension between two antagonistic strategies: the trend towards homogenization and the defence of identities (De Labarre 2001).

Conclusion

Globalization does not affect all foods the same way. The process of cultural change and transculturation of foods is still in its initial phase, affecting peripheral aspects of the traditional food model. At present, elements that the globalized food model will shape are in the process of being excluded or included.

Global foods are not accepted at dining times and spaces in which culinary tradition is highlighted. Local foods are required to make dishes with high social status in the food regime. Local foods thus continue to occupy a central position in the community food identity, and their selection is a factor in the reproduction of autonomy that counters globalization.

PART 5

Cultural Autonomy: Languages and Education

Our focus on cultural autonomy continues in this section with an examination of interactions between globalization and three subjects associated with the cultural sphere: the fate of Arabic as a literary language, the teaching of English as a second or third language, and policies in the higher education sector.

In Chapter 12, François Zabbal notes that literary texts are inscribed within local histories marked strongly by form, style, and content. In the face of globalization, however, these local aspects of literary works become more difficult to sustain. Zabbal describes these threats through an examination of the rapidly changing situation of the Arabic novel over the last twenty years. Noting the pressures on Arab writers to publish their works in French or English rather than Arabic, he points out that Arab writers are less widely read in Arabic than are foreign authors translated into Arabic. When Arab authors write first in French or English, it is because they anticipate attracting more readers than if they had written in Arabic. Even more disturbing, perhaps, is that some Arabs prefer to read works by Arab authors in French or English rather than Arabic. All of these trends compromise cultural autonomy in Arab societies.

Mongi Bahloul follows up on Zabbal's study in Chapter 13 by discussing the role of English and the teaching of English as a foreign language in North Africa. He begins by observing that English has entered a complex linguistic landscape — a region in which classical Arabic, modern standardized Arabic, Berber, and French coexist in a state of perpetual change. The rapid ascent of the influence of English seems to be linked to the growth of programs for teaching English as a foreign language, in response to pressure from academic and government circles that are in the sway of globalizing processes led by the United States. The popularity of English as a second language has increased in recent years, and this change has triggered a fierce debate over the role of foreign languages in the region. Part of the debate centres on the fact that most North Africans consider English an instrument of recolonization and see the spectre of a new crusade in the Mediterranean region.

Our overview of issues in cultural autonomy ends with Houda Ben Hassen's comparative research on higher education in France and Tunisia in Chapter 14. Globalizing processes have a strong influence on higher education institutions because of their role in the promotion of cultural and economic development; their production of highly qualified "human capital"; their contributions to national policies that promote economic growth; their participation in the general competitiveness of a country; and their position as a fundamental pillar of civil society because of their instillation of basic citizenship values. Ben Hassen shows how France and Tunisia have responded differently to these pressures. She situates her analysis in the context of the General Agreement on Tariffs and Trade, which defines the rules for international trade in the higher education sector.

chapter 12

Globalized Literature and Autonomy: The Arabic Novel in the West

François Zabbal

LITERARY TEXTS ARE INSCRIBED in a local history marked strongly by form, style, and content. This is true of all works that take shape in a literary milieu, regardless of whether they are exposed to external influences. In other words, the roots of texts lie deep within the soil from which they draw their sustenance. After they are published, they continue to live and flourish in the medium that has nourished and supported them, since they need to be adopted, amplified, and distributed, in totality or in selected fragments, through their culture's complex and twisting history. Yet the old territorial order of literature seems to be threatened today. Many fear that a writing form without social attachments or a clear identity will soon sprout — a parasitic plant that will graft itself onto other bodies. Like a note on the Internet, the nationality of this writing form will be blurred without its content being disproportionately affected: its provenance will be unimportant, as long as its language enables it to be displayed on the addressee's screen. Nevertheless, globalization has aspects that creators have deemed positive, notably with regard to freedom of expression. Authors who are gagged, censored, or even banned in their own country are suddenly offered unlimited prospects. By escaping national constraints, they believe, their works will suddenly have access to a world stage, making them less vulnerable.

Over the last twenty years, Arabic novels have had a dazzling rise to international prominence that is difficult to comprehend fully. Beyond the enthusiasm or skepticism expressed by cultural stakeholders and observers of the literary scene, it is possible to see new features in the relationship between authors and their works, and between these works and the literary sphere.

Migration between Languages

Literary works have always had an ambiguous relationship with language. They are at once its laboratory and its custodian. At the same time, they "inhabit language," in the sense that they are realized through language. And yet writers retain the freedom to rearrange language, or even disrupt it to the point of creating their own. They may also separate from it to undertake migrations with unforeseen consequences. Many émigré authors have faced the choice of continuing to write in their original language or adopting that of their new country. Aleksandr Solzhenitsyn remained utterly faithful to Russian, but many authors, and not minor ones, made the leap: for instance, Vladimir Nabokov opted for English, Milan Kundera for French. Both expanded their readership as a result, but their decision was also motivated by the need to integrate into a new country and a literary milieu with which they felt that they were in step. They were then "naturalized." When the Czech literature prize was awarded to Kundera in 2007, thirty-two years after his forced exile, there was criticism in Prague about this choice.

"One does not inhabit a country, one inhabits a language," wrote Émile Cioran. This idea, which has become the slogan of the French-speaking world, may be understood less as a linguistic fraternity than as the enhancement of one language by multiple contributions. The encounter between an author and a language that is new to her or him may give rise to great creative productivity. We tend to forget that the United States and the countries of western Europe owe much in the fields of art and literature to the talent of émigrés from central Europe. The grafts from the old tree yielded a harvest of new and tasty fruit.

The European Family

These authors had to make the transition into a language that belonged to a vast group of European languages that had evolved in parallel, allowing for constant borrowings. For centuries, the Latin taught in universities had formed a common ground, a sort of amniotic fluid, that fostered the unity of Europe beyond national differences. The proximity of languages was also reinforced within the continent over the course of history when one language in a specific region was particularly vital — French, Italian, or German, for example. As artistic and literary works circulated, they contributed to the enrichment of a culture that could be called European.

A profound change is occurring in the status and position of the main language of exchange — which, today, is American English. In general, it is tempting to compare the global spread of this language to that of imperial languages of the past. The closest example that I can think of is French, which first became prominent in Europe as a language of culture and trade because of the political prestige of France's royalty and the spread of French arts and letters, notably in the eighteenth century. French was spread into non-European countries by the colonial undertaking and its underlying universalist ideology.

A world language is one that is open to the contributions of its speakers — under certain conditions, such as the decentralization of normative bodies that set linguistic uses. For instance, American English gradually broke away from the mother English language through borrowings from the idioms of indigenous and immigrant populations. Until recently, the immigrants, mostly European, and especially Anglo-Saxon, helped to keep American English within an ensemble that we could call, for convenience, Western. In recent decades, however, the massive influx of non-European immigrants, who bring totally different cultures and languages, has wrought a major change in American English — not only to its lexicon and syntax but also to its cultural dimension.

Globalized Language

Just as the West has split into two, giving birth to a second West — the United States — American English has followed a path that is no longer entwined with that of European languages. The United States is increasingly distinct with regard to culture and language. This distinction does not, however, account for the almost ritual denunciation of American cultural imperialism as being the agent of acculturation of entire populations and the alienating extension of a dominating idiom. In effect, American English has been attacked from within.

One observation about contemporary literature stands out. Compared to Europeans, Americans do not translate much. Keen observers such as

Edward Said have seen this as a sign of anti-Arab racism — although the ostracism, if indeed it is ostracism, concerns all foreign literatures. Scandinavians have just as much reason to complain about it, as do Germans and Koreans. In 1999, out of ten thousand novels and poetry collections published in the United States, only three hundred were translations. This number went beyond imbalance to asymmetry, because in 50 percent of translations published throughout the world, the source language was English. In contrast, only 6 percent were published with English as the target language. The conclusion drawn, of course, was that the United States was almost utterly deaf to other cultural realities. This idea was so shocking to Americans that, in the wake of 11 September 2001, literary translation companies were quickly formed to address what had become an intolerable deficit. The objective of the Words Without Borders foundation, for example, is to connect readers directly "to the hearts and minds of people beyond American shores" (Wong 2007, 3). In the fall of 2006, the foundation published its first anthology of previously unpublished works from Iran, Iraq, North Korea, Sudan, and Syria, *Literature from the "Axis of Evil"* (Mason, Felman, and Schnee 2006). The underlying motivation of the initiators of the project, one might posit, was to understand the mentality of these people who so hated America.

Why is there so little translation in countries such as the United States? This question is fundamental to projects supported by UNESCO, an organization that has made mutual knowledge of peoples a tool for promoting peace. But perhaps the question should be turned around: why *do* countries translate foreign texts, especially literary ones? For what is really surprising in the gap observed between Europe and the United States is the former's constant, or even growing, interest in foreign literature. Whereas Americans seem indifferent to the stories of the world, European countries tirelessly gather and translate them. In other words, it is Europe's appetite for translations, as modest as it might be, that should arouse our curiosity.

This appetite goes beyond the prosaic interest that prompts a country to acquire the knowledge that it lacks in order to pursue various types of research. For instance, the important drop in numbers of translations of American social science works in Europe raised eyebrows in France, where the government plays a major role in this field. In 1999, a group of well-known intellectuals and academics addressed an open letter to the government on the translation policy. Two figures were highlighted:

between 1990 and 1997, the number of copies sold per social sciences title had fallen by 40 percent; within this overall number, translations had fallen the most, by 50 percent. Even more serious was that fewer and fewer emerging works were being translated — proof, for the authors of the letter, of the disappearance of the cultural mediators that are the true conduits between cultures.

The European attraction to foreign literature is far from banal. *The Thousand and One Nights* was appropriated by Antoine Galland, who made the story into a universal masterpiece. In Marc Crépon's (2002, 2, our translation) view, there are three types of relationships with non-European cultures: exploitation, importation, and translation. "Translation, unlike importation, does not retain anything from the culture except its foreign nature, its escapist exoticism." It affects the society in which the translation is performed and "thus becomes the operation through which European cultures become foreign to themselves, by differentiating themselves from themselves." But, far from being negative, this "becom[ing] foreign to themselves" may be an opening to non-European communities living within Europe and, as a consequence, the invention of a new form of existence. The colonial memory may thus be a common platform that no one wants to relinquish, as well as a memory of empire that perpetuates the initial impetus towards the foreign.

Peregrinations of the Arabic Novel

The discussion above suggests that translation is related to appropriation. However, the literary field is unique in that it deeply involves the vision of both the Self and the Other. In other words, we do not translate literature because we need to be informed about the state of mind of another population or the level that it has achieved in arts and letters. In the ninth century, the Arabs were engaged in a colossal undertaking of translation of the Greek philosophical and scientific heritage, but they were loath to translate Greek poems and plays into Arabic. They turned instead to Indo-Persian literature, from which, in the end, *The Thousand and One Nights* came to us.

It is therefore useful to look at the motivations for translation from Arabic and then envisage the effects that it induces for the authors. I will look at three linguistic fields: French, English, and German. This is a complex process, since it results from the intersection between the vision of the Other under consideration and individual initiatives. Despite the absence of statistical series, a comparison of different experiences reveals significant trends. It should be kept in mind, however, that translation from Arabic is a recent and relatively modest phenomenon. Indeed, most of the literary works translated in Europe are American. After that, lagging far behind, are cultural areas whose attractiveness seems to depend on a great number of historical, cultural, and political factors. In France, for example, there was a vogue for Latin American literature, followed by increased interest in literature from central Europe at a time when the debate over the gulag was sketching out a fundamental change in perceptions of the socialist world.

Arabic literature is not a great literature; admittedly, it occupies a modest rank in world literature. Over the past half century, few Arabic books have been ranked as masterpieces. Several figures have emerged, but none have become as well known as Naguib Mahfouz.

Anglo-American Translations

Given that literary translation as a whole amounts to only 2 or 3 percent of English and American publishing, it is understandable that interest in Arabic literature is low. Between 1986 and 1992, only twenty-six works of contemporary Arabic fiction were translated and published by English and American publishers. Over the same period, sixty were translated in France. In the past fifty years, most Arabic literature in English translation has been published by niche publishers with small print runs and limited promotional means, such as Quartet Books and Saqi in England and Interlink, University of Texas Press, and Three Continents Press in the United States. However, the main publisher of English-language translations of contemporary Arabic literature is the American University in Cairo (AUC) Press, which has published almost all of Mahfouz's work, many other Egyptian novels and, for the last fifteen years, texts from other Arab countries. Eighty percent of this production is sold in Cairo, 15 percent in the United States, and 5 percent in England. It is a safe bet that as many Anglophone Arabs as non-Arabs have read Mahfouz's books.

The low level of distribution of this literature outside of Egypt must be placed within the specific context of American and English publishing. Unlike the readership in most European countries, that in the United States seems segmented: there is a clear separation between general readers and scholarly readers. However, the latter group is not negligible: it includes enough Anglophone universities throughout the world that the cost of publishing a book can be amortized through purchases of copies by university libraries alone. The demand for translated texts may come from educators, who are eager for anthologies and reference books. In the early 1970s, English-speaking professors of contemporary Arabic literature had access to some works for their courses. *The Days* by Taha Hussein and *Diary of a Country Prosecutor* by Tewfik al-Hakim were already available in both English and French.[1] Trevor Le Gassick had translated and published Naguib Mahfouz's *Zuqâq al-Midaq (Midaq Alley)* in Beirut in 1966, while Desmond Stewart had translated al-Sharqawi's *Al-Ard (Egyptian Earth)* and Ghanim's *Al-Rajul alladhi faqada zhillahu (The Man Who Lost His Shadow)*.

One collection of short stories, one poetry anthology (Badawi 1967), and one play, however, were far from being all of the reference tools needed for a better knowledge of contemporary Arabic literature. In the late 1970s, new energy was infused into the English translation of Arabic literature by the Palestinian poet Salma Khadra Jayyusi. An enterprising and tenacious woman, she managed to produce translations thanks to her ability to persuade patrons. She has numerous anthologies to her credit, including *Anthology of Modern Palestinian Literature* (1994), *Legacy of Muslim Spain* (2000), and *Modern Arabic Fiction* (2005), a volume almost a thousand pages long. Acting as co-translator and editor, she launched the Project for the Translation of Arabic after concluding an agreement with John Moore, the director of Columbia University Press. A commission of English, American, and Arab experts was formed to translate works of poetry and fiction. The first book, *Modern Arabic Poetry* (Jayyusi 1987), was a remarkable collection, the quality of which was unanimously praised. One reviewer described it as "the finest available translations of a literature now ripe for discovery" (Allen 1994, 166). Anthologies of fiction followed, then novels, such as those by Palestinians Émile Habibi (New York, 1982) and Sahar Khalifah (London, 1986), Egyptian Yusuf al-Qa'id (London, 1986), Saudi Hamza Bogary (Austin, 1991), Palestinian Ibrahim Nasrallah (New York, 1993), Syrian Hanna Mina (Austin, 1993), and Yemeni Zaid Muttee Dammaj (New York, 1994). A total of almost twenty works were produced in the project.

The proponents' desire to provide a geographic literary opening points to the "pedagogical" purpose of exposing novice readers and students to a field up to then inaccessible. This is not substantially different from the intention that has guided AUC Press since its creation in 1960.

Every year, it publishes eighty new titles in all subject areas, and its catalogue includes almost eight hundred works, with a total annual print run
of three hundred thousand books. Acting as an interface between the
Egyptian literary milieu and the Anglo-American publishing world,
AUC Press brought to Egypt standards and operating rules that had been
lacking in Arabic publishing. For instance, AUC Press holds Naguib
Mahfouz's copyright and has ended the pillaging of works by the Nobel
Prize-winning author by unscrupulous publishers who had marketed
tens of thousands of copies of his novels. In recent years, other Egyptian
writers added to its catalogue have assigned AUC Press their international
copyright, but most Egyptian writers today prefer to conclude agreements directly with their foreign publishers.

There was another reason for the increasing number of new requests
for English translations after 11 September 2001. The translator of al-
Aswany's novel *The Yacoubian Building,* which was adapted into a movie
presented by Egypt at the Oscars, feels that it is important to understand
the culture of a country that is being pushed to adopt political and economic reforms. This need for knowledge has provided the new support
for literary translation. For example, following a debate in *Harper's* about
the small number of Arabic works translated into English, an anonymous donor paid $730,000 to the PEN Club to fund translations and find
publishers. Ten projects have been completed. In 2004, the Association
of American Publishers offered $10,000 in assistance to encourage pub-
lishers to translate Arabic literary works.[2]

German Translations

German is in third place, after English and French, with regard to the
interest paid to Arabic literature. However, it is in German that thought
about the act of translation has advanced the furthest. The movement
began timidly with a small Zurich publisher, Lenos. Founded in 1970 by
Heidi Sommerer and Tom Terrer, Lenos was situated politically to the
left and published fiction and essays. In 1983, an Arabic literature professor, Hartmut Fähndrich, published with Lenos a book by the Palestinian
author Ghassan Kanafani. But things did not go much further until 1988,
when Naguib Mahfouz won the Nobel Prize. Arabic literature then
began to sell. Authors such as Emily Nasrallah and Hanan al-Shaykh had
already had some success in Germany — especially the latter, who rose
to prominence with *The Story of Zahra* (1980).

A number of translations followed, and Lenos became the principal publisher of contemporary Arabic literature in German. Because Fähndrich alone decided which novels to translate, the time came when his choices were criticized violently. At first ignored by Arabic authors, translation into German began to provoke their interest, and even became desirable. Germany instituted an increasingly aggressive cultural policy and began to host Arabic writers at conferences, festivals, and residencies. This effort proliferated after 11 September 2001 and reached a peak with the decision to make the Arab world host of the 2004 Frankfurt Book Fair. For the Germans, who expected so much, it was a real fiasco: debatable selection of invited authors, conventional speeches and, especially, a total absence of exchanges between Arabic and German writers.

Fähndrich was seen to be at fault mainly for ignoring the greats of Arabic literature in favour of authors of mid-level importance. Yet an examination of the list of authors published by Lenos reveals an eclecticism that is completely normal when the translation initiative is taken by a small, private firm. In an interview with Ahmed Hissou in 2001 (see the website quantART.de), Fähndrich maintained that his choice was based on consultation with numerous experts in Arab countries, to which he travelled frequently. After reading the novels that were recommended to him, he assessed their impact as a function of what he knew about German taste. On this question, the only detail that he supplied concerned the reception of the more or less lyrical style of Arab authors in general.

There was also competition from European circles, according to Fähndrich. More than ten years before, the launch of the Memories of the Mediterranean project, financed by the European Cultural Foundation, situated in Amsterdam, and published in seven languages, had introduced a form of cooperation aimed at planning out the list of works to translate. In reality, the project focused on autobiographical texts intended to reveal daily life in Arab countries to European readers. The rarity of the genre encouraged the project's developers to be elastic in their selections: included in the list, for example, was *Naphtalene* by the Iraqi writer Alia Mamdouh, whose country had no coastline on the Mediterranean Sea! Furthermore, the story, although autobiographical, was presented as fiction. Overall, the project's program was not notable for its clarity. Networks of relationships and chance played a large role in discoveries — a translation sent by a doctoral student or a fortuitous encounter with an author or a book. It was widely known that one of the

211

project's initiators had been alerted by the Paris bookstore Avicenne to *The Ostrich Egg* by Egyptian author Raouf Massad-Basta (Leonhardt Santini 2006, 129).

Behind the blame assigned to Fähndrich and other translators was another more serious accusation: their selections were ideological, even political, in nature; in other words, they were seeking to present to a European public an outdated Arab society and archaic mentalities.[3] For example, Mahfouz's novel *Adrift on the Nile (Thartharat fawqa al-Nîl)* was translated, according to the detractors, with the goal of depicting Cairo circles corrupted by the consumption of hashish. Muhammad Choukri's *For Bread Alone* received a favourable reception only because of its provocative and crude tone; Edwar al-Kharrat's works, because he was a Copt! Others also insinuated that the European publisher was seeking to promote "anti-Arab" literature, a thinly veiled attack on the prominence accorded to the author Ibrahim al-Koni, a Touareg from Libya to whom Egypt had refused to give its award for best novel a few years before.

The most violent attack against German translations was made at the translation forum organized in Cairo in 2000 by the Supreme Council of Culture. At this event, a certain Muhammad Jibril lambasted "the plot against our Arab civilization and culture" fomented in Germany, where Arabic masterpieces were translated by bad translators affiliated with an anti-Arab publishing house.[4] In contrast, books published by Arab publishers in France and the United States never received similar criticism, even when the choice and quality of the translations left much to be desired.

French Translations

French translation followed a path as twisting and complex as that of English translation, including a groundswell of momentum after the Nobel Prize was awarded to Naguib Mahfouz. Nevertheless, there had been previous initiatives — sporadic efforts by academics, then more systematic projects by publishers. The teaching of contemporary Arabic literature was almost nonexistent before the 1970s and never stimulated efforts at publishing. It was not until the first translations appeared that the interest of professors of classical "medieval" Arabic literature in modern works could begin to be gauged. André Miquel, who held the chair of Arabic literature at the Collège de France, translated poems by the Iraqi writer Badr Shaker al-Sayyab (1926-64), published in 1977.

During the same period, Miquel's colleague, Jacques Berque, got to know some contemporary Arab authors, whose work he cited or introduced here and there. But the state of scholarly knowledge was such that the section on the contemporary period in the survey of Arabic literature written by Jamal Eddine Bencheikh — future translator, with Miquel, of *The Thousand and One Nights* for the *Encyclopediae Universalis* — was unsatisfactory because the author was unaware of different currents, did not write about important authors, and highlighted minor writers.

In the late 1960s, the publication list was short. The two books by Tewfik al-Hakim and Taha Hussein that had been translated into English were translated into French, and Éditions du Seuil had published an anthology of Arabic literature (1964).[5] New impetus came from an independent activist publisher, Pierre Bernard, who belonged to the generation that had been marked by the war in Algeria and had close relations with the Front de libération nationale regime. His publishing house received constant financial support from Algiers in the form of orders of prepurchase copies. This disguised sponsorship ended in the late 1980s, and the publisher was forced to fold in 1992. When Bernard died, in 1995, his collection was put up for auction, and much of it was purchased by Actes Sud; the rest, composed of works on Muslim mysticism, went to Albin Michel.

From 1972, when he founded Éditions Sindbad, to 1992, Bernard published 160 titles covering all aspects of the Arab world and Islam, including academic studies and classic texts translated from Arabic and Persian, as well as political works related to current events. Even before 1970, however, he had included in his program works by authors such as Naguib Mahfouz. At a time when the old Orientalist publishing houses were having trouble adapting to the climate resulting from decolonization, Sindbad was held up as an alternative. Two Orientalists of the new school, the above-mentioned André Miquel and Jacques Berque, offered their support. In fact, except for political titles, the "general literature" houses were beating a discreet retreat from "Arab world and Islam" subjects. There were few books on Islam, for example, except for those on mysticism published by Le Seuil, which was directed in the 1980s by a convert to Islam and leading expert on Ibn 'Arabi, Michel Chodkiewicz. Le Seuil's publication in 1985 of *Zayni Barakat* by Gamal al-Ghitani, an Egyptian of the generation after Mahfouz, was therefore unprecedented. Other publishers made timid contributions in the 1970s and 1980s. One of them, Jean-Claude Lattès, created a collection in which he published a dozen titles with financial support from the Institut du monde arabe. He did not stray from the rule that Arabic literature needed grants in order to be published.

It fell to Éditions Actes Sud, which already specialized in foreign literatures, notably Nordic and American, to pioneer a policy of non-cloistered publication. The "Mondes arabes" collection was created in the early 1990s with a mandate to publish notable literary works. The idea of supplying French readers with an exhaustive panorama of Arabic literature respectful of the local classification of authors was dispensed with. In addition, Actes Sud undertook what the publisher still calls today a "real author-oriented policy," consisting of supporting and guiding authors while trying as much as possible to publish their works as they were completed. The first title published by Actes Sud raised eyebrows in Arabic cultural circles. Collection editor Yves Gonzalez-Quijano, a French academic who had lived in Cairo and Beirut, chose to begin with the work of Sonallah Ibrahim, an Egyptian Copt and former communist who had been imprisoned and who belonged, as did Ghitani, to the "sixties generation" that followed Mahfouz. Then came stories by Salim Barakat, a Syrian Kurdish poet and novelist who had affiliations with the Palestinians in Beirut and was a friend of the poet Mahmoud Darwich. Sonallah Ibrahim remained an "in-house author" whose works were featured in the publisher's promotional campaigns.

When Pierre Bernard died, the purchase of Sindbad by Actes Sud made the latter the biggest French publisher of works devoted to Islam and the Arab world. The "Mondes arabes" collection was maintained, but novels appeared under the Sindbad imprint, without the distinction between the two always being clear. Both were now directed by a former Asian-languages librarian from Syria, Farouk Mardam-Bey, who, although a cultivated and eclectic man, was not really an expert in Arabic literature. A pro-Palestine Liberation Organization militant and director of the *Revue des études palestiniennes* since its creation in 1981, he maintained a unanimist front and did not conceal the reasons for his literary choices, which he sometimes attributed to the publishing house's directors. In short, the networks and connections that framed his activity were presented as the editorial policy, and its logic totally escaped observers. "The Sindbad catalogue," he said, "brings together in a single collection 'The Arabic Library,' a series of classic works, and another collection devoted to contemporary literatures. The latter combines translations from the Arabic with works — novels, stories, and poems — written in French."[6]

Actes Sud and Sindbad were not the only publishers with translations; other generalist publishers sometimes ventured into the minefield of Arabic literature. The cost of translation, however, was prohibitively high for those that did not receive financial assistance. In the absence of private sponsorship, the only solution was to apply to the Centre national des lettres (CNL), a public organization that provided funding upon the recommendation of specialized commissions. The mechanism for awarding this assistance was completely transparent, and expressions of gratitude to the CNL were never missing from the acknowledgments pages of major publishers — proof that they did not like to take risks. Actes Sud continued to apply for funds, including for works by previously published authors.

Almost fifteen years after Mahfouz won his Nobel Prize, the balance sheet was impressive, although publishers did not supply detailed statistics. Twenty-six of Mahfouz's novels and stories had been published. Even without benefit of advertising, his works were well received, and many were reprinted in paperback, which meant initial print runs of more than five thousand copies. Along with Mahfouz, dozens of authors of various nationalities were translated into French, painting a portrait of contemporary Arabic literature that was the result of choices made by publishers and their respective degrees of influence in French publishing. Sometimes, this portrait was at odds with the image reflected in the Arab world by press organs, literary critics, teachers, and readers. This phenomenon is not unique to Arabic literature; for example, American writers who are highly regarded in France do not always have the same success in their own country. In the case that concerns us here, it was of little import that the publisher's preferences played in favour of one author to the detriment of another. However, we might legitimately wonder whether the publishing program was sometimes governed by concealed ideological preferences.

Globalized Reading

The interest in Arabic literature resulted in relatively average sales, although they were high compared to the volume of sales in Arab countries. When a novel is published in Egypt with a print run of 1,000 copies, it has the right to a first print run in France of more than 2,500 copies, and it will probably be reprinted in paperback as long as it "sells." When editions in other languages are added, the gap gets even wider; an Egyptian novelist, for example, may have more readers abroad than in her or his own country. Sometimes this imbalance reaches stupefying proportions, to the point that it throws the author's relationship with her or his readers into question. For instance, al-Aswany's *The Yacoubian Building* sold 150,000 copies in France in its first year of publication.

Writing for Whom?

A number of Arab observers recently sounded the alarm: "Today in our countries, a literature is being written that no one reads, or at least very few people read, in its original language. That such a statement is an exaggeration should not hide a simple reality: there are few Arab readers; put another way, readers who are interested in Arabic literature written in Arabic are few and far between."[7] In the view of the editorialist in *Al-Hayat,* Arab writers become known today in two ways: "Either they are translated into foreign languages, especially French, which is well received in countries that had been French protectorates and became francophone, or they pass away and their reputation builds over the years, or even decades, after their death." A similar lugubrious tone reigned at the Salon du livre arabe in Beirut several years ago: one publisher installed at the entrance a coffin intended to represent the Arab reader — or, rather, the reader of texts in Arabic, for, paradoxically, readers of French-language books produced by authors of Arab origin were generally more numerous than were readers of works published in Arabic. In Algeria, for example, books in foreign languages outsold those in Arabic, although the potential readership was majority Arabic-speaking.

The editorialist erred, however, when he stated that the passion for translation into French involved only French-speaking Arab countries, because it also involved English-speaking countries. It is all the rage in Egypt, a country whose French affinities stretch back to a distant past — the first half of the twentieth century. The reason is that France plays the role of sounding board for world literature. An Arab author might have success in Germany, but he still must be read in France to gain international recognition. Translation into French thus has a specific quality that is worth exploring. From the point of view of authors, there is an immense benefit to be drawn from broadening their readership.

The translation of their work into a foreign language gives them access to thousands of readers throughout the world, even though they are irremediably separated from those readers by language and culture.

The Literary Sphere

Not only has the readership changed, but there has also been an upheaval in the publishing process through which literary works transit. When their work is translated, authors enter a new part of the book business that is fundamentally different from the one they know, since Arab publishers bear no resemblance to their European counterparts. First, Arab publishers do not really have literary directors, as many public agencies, such as those in Egypt, have collection directors on their payroll. In many cases, the publisher is a glorified printer and, at best, has someone read the entire manuscript before printing it. The most conscientious ones may make stylistic or spelling corrections, but they would never have the submitted work edited properly. In other words, there is nothing equivalent to the long gestation period that a manuscript undergoes with a European publisher, by the end of which the book may be so transfigured that one wonders whether a ghostwriter had a hand in things. The only recourse open to Arab authors if they want constructive criticism is to circulate their manuscript among a small circle of friends before delivering it to an Arab publisher. Once the work is published, the press reviews will play a more important role in its assessment than will the sales figures, which are often uncertain.

Today, two new orientations seem to be emerging. The first is the formation of a virtual Arab milieu that transcends national borders. In the past, some avant-garde outposts took publishing in innovative directions and disseminated new currents of thinking through the Arab world. This development occurred in Cairo and Beirut, two capitals that continue to be important to cultural production mainly because of their seniority in the publishing field.

Globalization was already at work in the late 1970s and associated with the massive immigration of the Arabic intelligentsia to Europe. Most gravitated to large metropolises such as Paris and London. During the 1980s, some forty Arabic titles were published in France. This number fell after the 1991 Gulf War, but the torch was passed to London, where three titles with steady sales (*Al-Hayat, Ash-Sharq al-Awsat,* and *Al-Quds al-Arabi*) brought authors of different nationalities to the public eye in the cultural pages of newspapers. The Internet has reinforced this trend but in a limited way, since it is used mainly by political forums.

Contrasting with Arabic cultural promotion activities is the strong structure of Western institutions. Publishing has become an industry in which large companies dominate, and publishers have means of promotion and distribution that have nothing in common with the archaic efforts of Arabic publishers. There is no doubt that foreign publishers have become attractive in Arabic literary circles, not least because of the promise of important remuneration.

Literary Direction

The translations under consideration here are processes that stretch over long periods of time and involve operations that are completely unknown in Arabic publishing, which, traditionally, does not use author contracts. Transfers of rights often cover only one print run, and authors generally reserve the right to take back their text. Foreign publishers, in contrast, offer Arab authors long-term commitments, the terms of which they are often forced to negotiate in laborious English. Assisted by the translator and the collection director (sometimes the same person), the publisher will, it goes without saying, play the role of literary director, not hesitating to make changes to the text.

It would seem that publication in Arabic no longer represents the main phase in the appearance of a literary text, with its translation into foreign languages only a chance extension and, in any case, a secondary one. Now, an Arabic novel comes to life only if it is translated into a European language. This principle is confirmed through the proven sign of a book's durability, the ISBN — that is, its registration in international databases. Without publisher stock, up-to-date catalogues, or a national legal deposit (in Lebanon, a major book-publishing centre, this system has just been instituted, but it will take years to be fully implemented), works are, in a way, evanescent. One Lebanese author said, when he saw his first novel translated, "I am happy that it has come out in French, since it will now have an ISBN and be listed in the [US] Library of Congress."[8] A notable exception to this rule is the creation of Arabic editions in Europe, notably in England (Mustafa al-Rayess and Saqi Books) and Germany (al-Jamal), which has led to the introduction of international standards that continue to be absent in the vast majority of Arabic editions.

What should we think of a literature focused completely on foreign markets, whose very production is increasingly dictated by international opinion? In effect, we see the emergence of an inversion of priorities: authors write thinking of translation in advance; they write, in a way, only to be translated — into English, mainly, but also into French, the noble language of literature, and then into other European languages. These authors' literary existence thus becomes dependent on the success of their work in translation, which is not completely theirs. Far from being trivial, this trend is picking up steam, notably with eminent authors or those considered to be stars by their European publishers. In 2005, a novel was published in French that had not been published in Arabic: the most recent book by Nabil Naoum, an Egyptian author who had long lived abroad and who was not known in Egyptian literary circles. Of course, these circles cannot be seen as the only guarantee of the literary quality of works, and it was not the first time that Naoum had published in French only.

No doubt, this path describes a minority of cases today, but it is still significant. It is likely related to a trend that took off in the 1990s of having a shorter period between publication of a work in Arabic and its publication in French. *Zayni Barakat* by Gamal al-Ghitani and *Najmat Aughustus* by Sonallah Ibrahim, both published in Arabic in 1974, were published in French — the first in 1985, the second in 1987. Ghitani was forty years old at the time, and Ibrahim was fifty (Leonhardt Santini 2006, 168). Compared to their older colleagues, such as Taha Hussein and Tewfiq al-Hakim, made famous by translations when they were sixty, the gap was considerably shorter, attributable perhaps to the intensification of cultural contacts between Europe and the Arab world. A few years later, in 1991, Naoum published *Retour au temple* in French, with Actes Sud, even before the book came out in its original language (in Beirut in 1994).

The gap continued to shrink. *Passage au crépuscule* by Rachid el-Daif, a writer known in limited French circles in the late 1970s, was published by Actes Sud in 1992, six years after his book appeared in Arabic. *Learning English* came out in Beirut in 1998, and the translation, which began immediately, appeared in 2002. The acceleration was even clearer with those who became the fetish authors of Actes Sud. The first was Ibrahim, two of whose works, *Le procès* and *Cette odeur-là,* initiated the "Mondes arabes" collection in 1992, appearing in French some thirty years after the original in Arabic. Thereafter, his works were published at a steady pace. *Dhât,* published in Arabic in 1992, was published in France as *Les année de Zeth* in 1993. This scant one-year gap was maintained, as the publisher began to count on sales by Ibrahim, who had quickly become its star author — to the point that the launch of a new translation was scheduled as soon as the work was published in Arabic, or even as soon as Ibrahim announced that the manuscript was advancing. This approach meant that the delay usually allowed for editing had been done away with: a year was barely enough time to complete the translation.

The Palestinian poet Mahmoud Darwich was honoured the same way. *Au dernier soir sur cette terre* was published the same year, 1994, in Arabic and French, and there was a one-year gap between the two versions of *Pourquoi as-tu laissé le cheval à sa solitude?* (1995, 1996) and *Le lit de l'étrangère.* For the Gallimard edition, Darwich himself wrote the preface for his poetry collection. He had no need for an introduction; he was practically a French writer.

The Arab Cultural Field

The new course of literary translation can be attributed to accelerated trade, increasing frequency of travel, Arab immigration to Europe and, in general, the opening up of global currents for cultural production. Is not a work that passes the test of translation, in the end, one that has achieved a certain degree of universality? In reality, this assertion can be made only in the case of the first type of transfer, when the work, matured in its homeland, is disseminated abroad and gradually broadens its readership. Today, we are clearly seeing the displacement of literary recognition away from the society of origin — a displacement that cannot be performed without a disaggregation of the Arabic cultural field. By disaggregation, I mean a loss of the capacity to integrate cultural and artistic production into a network of multiple significations forming a collective memory, identity, and project.

Translation into Arabic

One cannot study literary translation without looking at exchanges in both directions. To be complete, the picture must include translation into Arabic. In this area, the situation is disastrous. The cry of alarm launched by the *Arab Human Development Report* in 2002,[9] denouncing the huge lag of Arab countries with regard to education, training, and culture, caused a salutary shakeup. The numbers were eloquent. With regard to translation into Arabic, for example, the report compared the five thousand works translated annually in Greece (population of just over 10 million) to the three hundred translated by all Arab countries combined (population almost 280 million).

In reaction to this report, and especially after 11 September 2001, translation programs started up, notably in Egypt. The Supreme Council of Culture, directed by Gaber Asfour, set up projects to translate notable works in political and social science. In the literary field, the idea was floated of listing one thousand notable works in the human patrimony and translating them into Arabic. This idea, devised by bureaucrats, strongly resembled the Masterpieces of Humanity program launched by UNESCO a half century before.

From a quantitative viewpoint, these figures do not measure the depth of the Arab cultural crisis. Other statistical series must be cross-referenced, notably those about Arabic books and their distribution. It is, of course, a difficult undertaking, given the secrecy in which Arab publishers shroud the figures for their print runs and distribution. The recent book by Frank Mermier (2005) on Lebanese publishing since the 1960s, unmethodical and vague, does not provide a credible overview. For instance, Mermier does not compare sales figures for Lebanese novels with the print runs of their French-language versions. His assessments — quite inaccurate, and some of them supplied by the authors themselves — reveal large gaps. Still, one might reasonably maintain that it has become common for translated authors to be read more in any single foreign language than in their own language.

Less widely read, and less well paid, at home, authors see their works emerge thanks to their colleagues who are "writer-journalists," a category that came to the fore in the last half century. In Lebanon, Ounsi El Hage, a member of the editorial board of the magazine *Chi'r*, took charge of the *An-Nahar* literary supplement in the 1960s. Today, all editors of the culture sections of Lebanese newspapers are writers who make a living not from their novels or poems but from their salaries as journalists. This change has given rise to a phenomenon that draws the attention of many foreign observers: the regular publication of stories in newspapers, as a means of disseminating literature — and as a means of paying the bills at the end of the month.

The translation into Arabic of world literature, and cultural products in general, is not in itself essential to mutual knowledge among peoples.

It does, however, open the path to fertile cultural interactions. Such interactions emerged in the 1950s and 1960s, when the need to build a vision of the world and find answers to questions posed by the evolution of societies that had become independent incited intellectual elites to seek solutions, ways of thinking, and methods in foreign bodies of work. The ideological current that may be called Marxist provided a privileged space within which elements of foreign thought could be integrated into a local mould. It was not the only one, but it imposed a monolithic grid for comprehending reality. Today, the apparent eclecticism of the movement for translation into Arabic is nothing but unbridled acculturation by societies that do not have the means to forge their own tools for comprehension and explanation.

Conclusion: Intralinguistic Translation

If the truth be told, there is not really an Arabic cultural field, in the sense of a common space in which concepts and methods are exchanged and debated. The reason for this absence is complex and has to do as much with educational institutions and cultural facilities as with a common ideology that governs ways of thinking. One aspect of the disintegration of the cultural field is particularly interesting to this discussion: intralinguistic translation, the translation from Arabic to Arabic.

Translating from Arabic to Arabic means circulating significations, images, and symbols horizontally within the same culture, without the external referent being an obligatory and constant transition to comprehension. More prosaically, it describes the position of the reader of an Arabic text who cannot understand it unless he or she mentally rereads it in French or English. This is the impression given by most of the essays written in Arabic today.

The comfort with intralinguistic translation results in a deep imbalance in the structure of reading. It is known that Arabs do not read much. It is also known that those who *do* read consume religious writings more than general works, especially literary ones. For example, this result emerged in Egypt, according to the only survey done to date, which was conducted in 2005 in five Arab countries: Egypt, Lebanon, Morocco, Saudi Arabia, and Tunisia (Next Page Foundation 2005). Unfortunately, there is no equivalent survey for preceding years or decades, so it is impossible to make comparisons. From the results presented, which do not seem totally reliable, what can be concluded is that more works are read in foreign languages than in Arabic. It is likely that the rule applies to literature, as the example of Algeria, discussed above, shows.

Thus, fewer people read Arab authors than foreign authors. Once their works are translated, Arab authors' foreign readers will be more numerous than will readers among their compatriots. Sometimes, Arabs will choose to read these authors in translation, and the authors will gain readership and prestige. Above all, they will become authors in the full sense of the term, with rights recognized by an internationally valid contract, which no state will be able to withdraw from them. Socially, their international recognition will provide them, in addition to prestige, with the qualification of their noble trade as writers. They will also be engaged in a creative process to which they are not accustomed, imposed by the expectations of the foreign publisher. But what will the Arab public say? Arab readers, having become transnational, will nevertheless play the role of early reader that Western readers will never completely replace. It is to be feared that Arab authors, in gaining the status of writer, may lose their soul by neglecting their public.

chapter 13   **The Use of English in North Africa: From Globalization to Autonomy**

Mongi Bahlou

THE LINGUISTIC SITUATION IN North Africa is complex. A classical Arabic language, a modern and standardized Arabic language, Berber, and French coexist in a region in a state of perpetual change. These languages have inspired significant political reforms and major changes, for example, in education. In recent years, the learning of English has been gaining ground regularly and surely, complicating even further a linguistic landscape that is already quite problematic. English has also sparked recent controversies over foreign languages and their catalyzing role, triggering a highly ideologically charged cultural debate.

One possible explanation for the rapidly increasing influence of English in North Africa is the creation of projects for developing English language teaching (ELT) in secondary schools and universities. Such projects have been welcomed by Western lobbies within universities and by government circles, but they have also provoked criticism among promoters of Arabization, especially among proponents of a francophone Tunisia. For a better understanding of this issue, it may be useful to examine the nature of the ELT development projects, identify their objectives, and then see how the ELT program fits into North African frameworks. An overview of the literature on the subject is thus necessary. I re-examine works by Robert Phillipson (1992), Braj B. Kachru (1987), and Joseph Bisong (1995), as well as other articles and specialized studies, such as Chris Kennedy's "The KELT ESP Project, Tunisia"

(1985b) and "A Brief Survey of ESP in Tunisia" (1985a) and R.M. Payne's "The Training of English Students at the Faculty of Letters, University of Tunis" (1985), to give a sense of an inquiry that is pertinent to North Africa.

A Love-Hate Relationship with English

Phillipson (1992) has pointed out that ELT is not a "neutral, apolitical" activity, as most people seem to think. In his view, this is a "racist" attitude adopted deliberately in order to favour a particular language over other languages that are perceived as having a lower status. He sees ELT aid projects as a devious way to export and disseminate Anglo-Saxon values under cover of a language-learning policy. His strong denunciation was provoked by an interesting disclosure published in the British Council's (1987-88) annual report, in which the executive director stated the real underlying motives for linguistic assistance programs: "The real black gold is not North Sea oil but the English language. It has long been at the root of our culture and is now fast becoming the global language of business and information. The challenge facing us is to *exploit it to the full*" (ibid., 49, emphasis added).

According to Phillipson, assistance projects have both economic and ideological goals. The funds that support these projects are considered good investments, since they export a pedagogical language to "under-emancipated" third world peoples. The same scenario applies to the activities of the United States Information Service (USIS), which is active in many world regions. Its large-scale involvement in linguistic policies in developing countries and the expectation that it places on Peace Corps contingents to implement ELT programs also express political and economic goals. In Phillipson's (1992, 49) view, the effectiveness of the audio-linguistic method can be explained only in terms of American power. It is understood that the greatest impact of the American linguistic policy is felt in countries that are economically weak and dependent on the international community. In terms of the struggle against neocolonialism, Phillipson identifies a close relationship between the ELT system and its function as an instrument of foreign and national policy after the colonial period, once again pointing a finger at the leaders of the ELT project.

The hidden connections between academics and politicians in the "dominant centre" were first noted by Edward Said in his survey work

225

Orientalism (1978). According to Said, Orientalism covers a broad range of hegemonic beliefs and practices through which a dominant group is able to shape a dominated group, with the support of the academic community playing a decisive role. He develops his argument by referring to a period after 1955, when, in his view, the West used the subject area of Asian studies as a national policy instrument aimed at newly independent countries in the postcolonial world, rather than as a tool for knowledge development (ibid., 275). The same thing could be said, I believe, about the interest in and development of American and British studies during the Cold War in communist and some non-aligned countries.

Kachru (1987) seems to have a less radical analysis than do Said and Phillipson of the relationship between countries of the "periphery" and English. In his view, hostile reactions towards the English language have done nothing to reduce its strength as the "language for all times" or a "universal language." English overrides narrow considerations of a power play between the "inner circle" and other less influential communities of the former British colonies, as well as other countries falling within what he calls the "extended circle," such as Japan and China. Even in places where anti-Western feeling runs high, there is consensus on the vital role of English as the language of international communications and trade programs (McArthur 1997). English is thus perceived as an essential asset for inhabitants of developing countries, as a valuable source of science, technology, and communications. The linguistic points of view emphasized by Phillipson are less relevant to Kachru's approach to the hegemony of English. Kachru places the accent on utility rather than ideology and considers linguistic development from a different angle.

The idea that English and ELT assistance programs have utilitarian goals is developed by Bisong (1995) in an article called "Language Choice and Cultural Imperialism: A Nigerian Perspective." Bisong also minimizes the ideological dimension associated with the dissemination of English and maintains that in countries in which English is a foreign language, it serves specific objectives as an international language of communication. In his view, the adoption and use of English on the global scale is a sign of submission to and compliance with the requirements of the centre, but they may be explained in pragmatic terms. English, he adds, is an important language, which "performs a useful function in a multilingual society and will continue to do so, since no nation can escape its history" (ibid., 131). As a result, English should not be considered the "imperial language." The reasons for learning it are more practical, with no connection to dominant-dominated relations or centre-periphery comparisons. Bisong seems to be saying that people, wherever they are, are now mature and sophisticated enough to know where their best interests lie. Language-training development projects are not imperialist instruments but part of bilateral and cooperation agreements between the centre and the periphery, to use Bisong's terms. This has been the attitude of most government bureaucrats and language planners in the three countries of North Africa for the last thirty-five years. It is in the interest of North Africans, Bisong emphasizes, to have the capacity to function with two or more codes in a situation of multi-lingualism. Below, I explore this issue, paying particular attention to the Tunisian ELT project (1983-95), which exemplifies similar projects implemented in Morocco and Algeria over the same period.

Globalization: The Main Stages of the ELT Project in Tunisia

Tunisia's joining the community of Francophone countries and the fundamentalist thrust of the late 1970s and 1980s did not keep Tunisians from embracing foreign languages such as English, Italian, German, Spanish, and even Russian. In this sense, all assistance from the centre countries was greatly appreciated, as it was often associated, in the minds of both bureaucrats and students, with studies abroad and the acquisition of what was perceived of as expensive equipment such as tape recorders, VCRs, and computers. As a consequence, the Tunisian government signed agreements with ELT aid organizations such as the Ford Foundation, Amideast, and the British Overseas Development Administration, with the goal of stimulating the learning and teaching of English throughout the country.

The Development Phase (1983-89)

In 1983, the British government began a project, based at the Institut Bourguiba des langues vivantes (IBLV) in Tunis, the main objective of which was to promote and develop the learning of English for vocational purposes in Tunisia (C. Kennedy 1985a). The project used ELT experts recruited by the British Council as a catalyst to achieve two goals during the development phase:

- setting up a forum within which English teachers could exchange ideas about ELT
- building an information network enabling teachers to be constantly updated, so that they could follow developments in their field on the national and international levels. (Richards 1989)

The strategies adopted to reach these objectives were the creation of a consulting service, an ELT newsletter, and a regular program of one-day seminars and workshops hosted in turn by the different universities, as well as annual (national) seminars in the country's main recognized ELT establishments. The events offered teachers an opportunity to start working in schools and experience new teaching techniques. Most teachers active in these fields were encouraged to apply for more advanced training in the United Kingdom. The institutions directly linked to the project were able to benefit from donations of books and other documentary materials.

The Consolidation Phase (1989-91)

Added to promotion and development of ELT standards in Tunisia during the project-consolidation phase was the objective of improving the status of EFL (English as a foreign language) teachers. New goals therefore had to be designed to establish English as an option in the curriculum at the master's and doctoral levels in Tunisian universities (Payne 1984). It was also thought that British ELT experts could act as consultants for English teachers dispensing training at the IBLV, with specific reference to the type of ELT course given (Payne 1983). British consultants could also offer (upon request) advice regarding sources of teacher-training programs at the École normale supérieure de Sousse (Payne 1985).

Broadening the Stage (1991-95)

In August 1991, the Tunisian ELT project received fresh impetus from the signing of an agreement between the Tunisian government and the Overseas Development Administration to create a second consultative unit for the south part of the country under the aegis of the Université de Sfax. The unit was a structure analogous to the one in Tunis, and it defined ten objectives:

1 Extend the ELT project's consulting services to the institutions of the Université de Sfax.
2 Contribute to the ELT information network by establishing regular relations with the local EFL teachers.
3 Set up an ELT resource centre at the Faculty of Literature and Human Sciences at the Université de Sfax capable of providing advice and support for all universities and vocational training institutions in southern Tunisia.
4 Encourage EFL teachers in southern Tunisia to participate in the project's seminar programs.
5 Encourage the editorial committee of the ELT newsletter to take responsibility for production and distribution of the newsletter at cost price.
6 Advise and support EFL teachers in program formulation (including selection and development of appropriate materials if needed).
7 Advise Tunisian English professors to choose other options for specialization in ELT fields in Tunisia or the United Kingdom.
8 Advise and support the directors of the English Department in the Faculty of Literature and Human Sciences in the design and improvement of courses.
9 Help the university in the south to formulate a training program for English teachers, including a vocational component.
10 Organize seminars and conferences on different aspects of the English language at regular intervals.

The British government and the Department of Higher Education in Tunisia were jointly involved in supplying the funds and logistics for implementation during the three major phases of this project. The model for the Tunisian ELT project and its extension to Sfax were also used in Algeria, in the form of an affiliated project, in both Constantine and Oran, and in Morocco, with the major project located in Rabat and branches in Marrakech and Casablanca.

Autonomy: The British Withdrawal and Its Repercussions for the ELT Situation in Tunisia

The Tunisian ELT project no doubt brought globalization to the country's door. It also resolved a certain number of problems and provided a remedy to the main gaps in the ELT system in Tunisia. For example, books in English were now more available in university libraries and research centres. There were certainly more possibilities for those teaching EFL and for graduates with a degree in English to apply to join a university in the United Kingdom. However, as Judith Kennedy (1985, 8, our translation) observes, "any change in a system may produce problems ... solving them may produce a greater change in the system than the original idea." As I describe below, in attempting to achieve a certain number of clear objectives, the Tunisian ELT project, assisted by Great Britain, created a series of supplementary objectives the reaching of which required another form of assistance by the British. Since this assistance was not guaranteed, the process led inevitably to a degree of autonomy and self-sufficiency.

The ELT Assistance Project: A Generator of Complex and Diffuse Needs

British education experts involved in the project organized seminars and sent Tunisians to Great Britain for graduate studies or to upgrade their training in specialized ELT areas. In its final phase, the project was extended to educational establishments and to EFL students in the central and southern parts of the country. This approach seems to have proved wrong those who thought that the British Council and the American Centre were exclusively serving the interests of people who were lucky enough to live in Tunis and its suburbs. The extension of the project in fact gave hope and status to a number of institutes that had been forgotten for many years. The introduction of various books and the bursaries awarded to "southern Tunisians" in the early 1990s were the best illustrations of the decentralizing current. At another level, interest in ELT was evidenced in the publication of six issues of the Tunisian ELT newsletter in Sfax, the organization of a number of seminars in locations outside of Tunis, and a constantly growing number of participants.

However, as activities developed and diversified, Tunisian academics, left to their own devices after the British withdrawal, found it difficult to respond to the growing demand for pedagogical assistance. Now that many teachers were aware of what was going on in the ELT field, they naturally became more demanding in terms of assistance, advice, and supervision for doctoral studies. It was precisely this part of the project that made things challenging and frustrating once it came to an end. Unlike other undertakings with well-defined and easily quantifiable goals, such as the preparation of a textbook or the setting up of a college, it was difficult to arrive at a definitive form with these types of programs because they had more complex and diffuse objectives. During the implementation process, further objectives were devised that were problematic to measure or evaluate concretely. For instance, the new developments generated by the project raised the need for more ELT consultants at the national level.

The Difficulty of the Project, or the Need for Autonomy

To start, several questions must be asked: How did Tunisian teachers of English and education directors react to the withdrawal of the British? Were they able to continue to work in the manner defined by their British counterparts, or did the project disintegrate? What became of the Tunisian ELT newsletter and the resource centres in Tunis and Sfax? It would be premature to give definitive answers to these questions, since the British advisers left only in 2003. However, it is useful to offer some reflections on the ELT situation in Tunisia during the period between 1995 and 2004.

Successes

The first important change that took place following the termination of the British assistance project was the organization of summer universities in Tunisia rather than Great Britain. This change was caused mainly by a drop in foreign aid to the Tunisian Department of Higher Education. For two weeks in September 1996, twenty-five Tunisian English teachers participated in the first summer session organized in the country. A look at the evaluation sheets filled out by participants after the sessions reveals a sense of unease and dissatisfaction about the result and the supervision, despite the contribution and support of two English-language experts from British universities. Nevertheless, the undertaking was considered a pioneering step towards autonomy in the ELT field.

Another important event took place in November 1996 at the Tunisian embassy in London — the ELT in Tunisia conference — during which some issues were examined regarding the teaching of English in Tunisia and the future prospects for the project. British professors who had given lectures in Tunisian universities were invited to be the keynote speakers.

It is encouraging to note that EFL teachers continued to participate in training programs, even if on an informal volunteer basis. Today, there are still attempts to help ELT instructors before they begin teaching (see the successive reforms to higher education during the period from 1996 to 2004 in issues of the *Journal Officiel de la République Tunisienne*). The new courses for graduates in education science at the IBLV were a great step forward. It is quite significant that this institute is where the Tunisian ELT project was born.

The third Maghreb ELT conference, held in Tunis in February 1997, provided an excellent opportunity for many students and teachers to demonstrate their knowledge of, and interest in, questions regarding ELT. However, most of the former English professors in the various colleges and institutes still clung to old methods and did not really teach English as a tool of international communication. This conference was a turning point in the training of the new generation, to the credit of the program designers and language planners. It should be noted that when it came to presentations and correspondence, it was often the younger, less-experienced teachers who showed more knowledge of ELT.

Another encouraging development in the post-British ELT assistance project was the growing popularity of the resource centres in Tunis and Sfax. There were a significant number of new members among freshly recruited high school English teachers and ELT research students from Tunisian universities. These small libraries were impressive places, the envy of many other African countries. A major concern today is to attract a group of young teachers to work in these centres. It is important, in my view, that the greatest number of people possible be involved in the operation of the two ELT resource centres and that dependence on American and British assistance be reduced. Although it is desirable and beneficial that Britons and Americans remain engaged to a certain extent through support, it is essential that the ELT centres in Tunisia and other countries in North Africa be sustained and financed, over the long term, by North Africans.

A further promising sign is the existence of projects involving professors from different faculties (such as faculties of medicine or management) working together. Their work on the design of materials, for example, is coordinated through ELT centres or English departments on a volunteer basis. A small but constantly growing number of Tunisians are also undertaking research that will certainly be beneficial to the future of ELT in Tunisia. Now that there is a core of expert supervisors in the field (even though their number is still limited), it should be possible to create a team of academics in the linguistics fields capable of helping

Tunisia make progress in the ELT field. There is British support for developing a program through study bursaries in British universities for Tunisians engaged in research in Tunisia. Even more encouraging in terms of the durability of the project is the work accomplished within the country.

The Failures

An unfortunate development in the years following the British withdrawal was the decision to recruit fewer and fewer university-qualified ELT teachers and to transfer secondary-school teachers into language departments. The result was that secondary-school ELT in the upper grades fell victim to the exodus of experienced teachers, while the teaching of English at the university level was being dispensed by a body of professors who possessed no qualification for teaching at that level. In the English Department at Sfax, for example, 90 percent of the teachers knew nothing about research because they were originally recruited as English teachers from the elementary- or secondary-school level and found themselves miraculously parachuted into university-level language institutes that were in constant expansion and popping up like mushrooms all over the country. There was a long hiatus between official declarations about the importance of English and the decisions about how teachers were recruited. Rather than cut away the dead wood in EFL institutes by evaluating the ELT programs and removing the teachers who performed poorly, the current policy seems, on the contrary, to encourage the exclusion of the best teachers. Ideally, a greater number of ELT teachers should be tenured at the elementary- and secondary-school levels. They should be rotated: develop ELT programs for several years, spend a year or two in an English department, upgrade their language knowledge, and finally return to their original school to provide better instruction.

It is important that ELT teachers throughout the country be able to work together to build their skills based on the progress achieved to date. However, excluding the efforts of employees at resource centres to maintain a certain degree of coordination among teachers in a single discipline, the lack of central coordination at the government department supporting English teaching throughout the country is surprising.

The well-established tradition of seminars and workshops throughout the country, as part of the old British system, is theoretically still in place. In reality, however, institutes now hesitate to supply the funds and provide the logistics necessary to run them. Those who work in the resource centres in Tunis and Sfax are responsible for coordinating tasks and publicizing events. However, enthusiasm and dedication alone are not sufficient to ensure that the work is done and the objectives are reached.

As expected (Bahloul and Seymour 1992), the Tunisian newsletter did not receive much attention in the post-ELT project period. There is no doubt that financial issues and rivalries were behind the decline of this information tool and, finally, its disappearance. Many ELT instructors considered this disappearance the final blow to the communication network. Similarly, the proceedings of the second and third Maghreb annual conferences were never published because the funds from institutes naturally went to projects perceived as truly related to universities (and not ELT).

The reason for this unfortunate situation is the low profile of ELT in a country in which Islamic fervour is surging and anti-Americanism is growing every day. This situation tends to affect several key aspects: the attitude of teachers assigned to ELT and their status; recognition of the qualifications resulting from ELT training, whether achieved in Tunisia or abroad; and the status of ELT as a subject in itself and as a subject in relation to other subjects. Curiously, the creation of a department for training ELT instructors (ironically, it was called Département pour l'enseignement de l'anglais de spécialité [Department for the teaching of English as a specialty]) did not help to raise the level of ELT. To the contrary, its creation strengthened prejudices against English and the people involved in teaching it; adding insult to injury, the first contingent of twenty-five graduates from the department are now on a job-waiting list and likely to remain there for a long time. There is no success model, in that the ELT project has contributed little to improving the state of affairs or the status of those who teach English on the national level. As a consequence, it is widely estimated that isolated efforts are a curse on the education system and may lead to new pitfalls for teaching ELT in Tunisian universities in years to come.

Conclusion

In a short article in the *IATEFL Newsletter,* Andy Seymour, the former director of the ELT project in Tunisia, gave a positive assessment: "In Tunisia, the end goals of studying English are often not seen clearly. The

English taught is for general purposes but is called ESP (Teaching English for Specific Purposes) whenever it is taught to students who are not specializing in language or arts" (Seymour 1994, 26, our translation). If this is the situation of ELT in Tunisia, after two decades of British control, it will be the duty of university teachers of English, as activists and planners of the promotion of the English language, to take things in hand (autonomy) and act as a truly professional organization representing the interests and serving the needs of the community of English teachers. We must meet the needs of newly qualified teachers, just as we must take into consideration all of the different ELT specialties.

One way of working for the health of Tunisia as a country, and in better compliance with its future objectives, is to think of the status of English and the teaching of English as a question of organization and development. The first objective is a clear presentation of the teaching mission that all concerned parties should adopt. Without this mission being defined, those who are involved in the process will never be able to direct their efforts towards a single goal. Second, the teaching of English requires a great deal of energy. Impetus will be created if the government department assures teachers of its support and its desire to solve their major problems. The appointment of a program coordinator would be a sign of goodwill on its part. Naturally, Tunisian English teachers would have to support the process. Third, there must be an official and fully recognized structure for the teaching of English in Tunisia (the department in its current form does not fulfill this criterion). The structure should confer official status on EFL practitioners and their activities. This change also implies regular and constructive contacts among the main entities engaged in the teaching process. Clearly, the degree of cooperation may either stimulate the development or, on the contrary, provoke the decline of the undertaking of English teaching. Fourth, the material and human resources available are not sufficient to resolve the problems of English language teaching in Tunisia. These factors are important, but they may be totally ineffective if the structure, energy, and mission are not well established. Even today, resources represent a minor difficulty for language teaching. Greater attention should be paid to other aspects of ELT in the Tunisian context — a good argument for greater autonomy in a context of globalization.

Looking at the overall picture, we may ask several more questions. First, why did the British decide to leave countries that had benefitted from British assistance with regard to ELT training programs? The answer is that the Overseas Development Administration placed more emphasis on European countries after the collapse of the Soviet Union. Thus, Romania, Bulgaria, and Slovenia became more important in British eyes than Tunisia, Algeria, and Morocco. With European Union assistance and the prospect of new members from the former communist bloc as priorities, the British ELT establishment let the countries situated on the south shore of the Mediterranean Sea drift beyond its purview.

Second, if English is the language of business and technology, what is the policy of the Tunisian government with regard to its development and promotion in the economic and educational sectors? In Tunisia, the linguistic policy is far from being coherent. It has always evolved according to the interests in play linking Tunisia to France and to Anglo-Saxon countries, the rivalries between proponents of French and English, and those pushing for a unilingual society completely disengaged from modernity. For example, if relations with France are going well and France is displaying unreserved support for the regime's policy, then the French language will profit from these aspects, and hours allocated to learning French will multiply at all levels of the education system. The need for French teachers will grow from day to day, and positions will be opened in most secondary schools to meet the demand. If, in contrast, tensions should arise at an untimely moment between France and Tunisia, the United States will take advantage. Rather than defending a specific policy on the matter, it will see English as the object of particular interest by the authorities, and its introduction as a compulsory subject at the elementary-school level will suddenly become a priority. This activity will mean the recruitment of a significant number of teachers at a moment's notice, without regard for the quality or merit of a program model, and with ELT courses being concocted on the fly.

In relation to autonomy, government policy has not been insensitive to the call by certain factions of Tunisian society for a greater emphasis on Arabic to the detriment, of course, of other languages. In recent years, the regime has Arabized the administration almost completely by excluding the use of French and English. While recognizing that English is the language of business and of the liberal market economy, the Tunisian government does not see the need to engage in its promotion. It is presumed, correctly or incorrectly, that such activities fall under the bailiwick of private companies and business circles. Many companies and multinationals operating in Tunisia have instituted ELT programs for their staff, but up to now the results have been meagre and have had little impact in terms of aptitude for communication in the workplace. As a consequence, many firms have given up the idea of continuing these programs, even though they have made mastery of English a prerequisite in their hiring policies. To respond to demand on the job market, many private language schools have introduced English as a top priority. Thus, people wishing to upgrade their skills to get a job must take English courses in these private institutes. Once again, because of improvisation and the presence of unqualified instructors, the experience of learning English has been an obvious failure up to now.

Why is translation becoming widespread in North Africa? Particularly in Tunisia, it is considered a syndrome of autonomy and an antidote to the virus of globalization. Local and international firms are realizing that learning a new language requires time, money, and constant exposure to the target language. Because these conditions are difficult to produce in the context of Tunisian ELT, it has become clear that translation of the global language (English) into Arabic or French will be useful in the short term. It will partly resolve companies' problems and at the same time enable Tunisians to retain a sense of dignity and pride in their own language.

Finally, why do other Arab countries — the United Arab Emirates, Bahrain, Qatar, and others — adopt a more positive approach towards English than do, say, Tunisia and Morocco? Unlike the Gulf States, in which English reigns supreme, the countries of North Africa have considerable linguistic diversity, ranging from Tamazight (the Berber language) to variants of Arabic, French, and English, the last sneaking onto the scene as an interloper. An engagement with English is a luxury not only for societal reasons but also because economic resources are limited in North Africa, whereas they are abundant in the Gulf. Perhaps more important is the sensitivity of the North African public to socio-linguistic issues, an aspect that does not exist in the Arab countries in the Gulf. Most North Africans consider English to be an instrument of recolonization, the spectre of a new crusade in the Mediterranean region. English has been politicized and, in the eyes of North African populations, is a facet of evil. Governments in North Africa are thus aware of the risk of protests that may rise from the street if they were to show undue enthusiasm for the promotion of English in the region. Such promotion could occur only to the detriment of other local languages that are so cherished and appreciated by their users in Tunisia, Algeria, and Morocco.

chapter 14　　　　　**Globalization, Autonomy, and Higher Education: The French and Tunisian Cases**

Houda Ben Hassen

GLOBALIZATION, THE MAJOR PHENOMENON of the last decade, is in the process of changing the landscape of our planet, generating profound, rapid, and complex transformations that are not limited to production and trade but extend to cultural and social specificities that affect the quality of life of all individuals. Globalization tends to standardize the lifestyles of all people, no matter where they live.

In advocating economic liberalism, the international institutions that are globalization's promoters — mainly the World Trade Organization (WTO), the World Bank, and the International Monetary Fund (IMF) — are pressing to reduce the state's role by disengaging it from a sector that has been protected up to now: education. The General Agreement on Services and the World Trade Organization agreements signed in 1994 apply to a series of sectors to be liberalized, including education. Many countries are currently committed to the path to liberalization and the gradual and irreversible deregulation of their education systems, including higher education. Throughout the world, this policy shift is causing profound changes connected to the growth in demand for training, the spread of education to all social classes, the diversification of subjects taught, the creation of new channels for vocational orientation, and exponential increases in the cost for high-quality training.

In this chapter, I first analyze the effects of globalization on higher education in two Mediterranean countries with different levels of development: France and Tunisia. I have chosen to look at the higher education sector for the following reasons:

1 Higher education represents the final and key phase of an investment in human capital the goals of which, within nations, are promotion of knowledge and economic and cultural development.
2 Higher education institutions are considered places for knowledge "production" and for training highly qualified individuals.
3 Higher education institutions play a vital role in job-creation strategies and growth policies based on the environment for human capital and exploitation of knowledge. Today, knowledge and intelligence represent new comparative advantages among countries, strengthened and accelerated by globalization. The international trade in high-technology, value-added goods and services has constantly increased since the late 1970s, at the expense of the trade in natural resources and cheap labour.[1]
4 Higher education thus becomes a criterion for competitiveness among countries: the most attractive universities are those that stand out for the quality of training and the credibility and value of the degrees that they dispense. This is why, following the meeting in Lisbon in 2007, the European Union committed itself to becoming "the most competitive ... knowledge-based society in the world" by 2010 (European University Association 2007).
5 Higher education is a fundamental pillar in the construction of a civil society because it instills in individuals the values of citizenship and respect for democracy, human rights, and cultural diversity.

In higher education, the effects induced by globalization have led to numerous changes not only to how educational institutions are both funded and organized but also, more fundamentally, to their vocation. By accelerating trade, notably in services, globalization has reinforced the internationalization of universities, thus promoting student mobility. It has also shifted the objectives of higher education institutions towards the greater employability of graduates, which implies training focused more on market needs, to the detriment of research. Finally, it has developed a corporate culture based on competition and profitability within higher education institutions.

Second, I will show how globalization affects the autonomy of the three main stakeholders in higher education: students, teachers, and trustee organizations (the state, educational institutions, and so on). In the particular context of higher education, autonomy is equated with academic freedom, independence of scientific research, respect for state governance in the planning and implementation of educational policies, preservation of individual specificities of identity (cultural, religious, social, linguistic, and so on), and tolerance for cultural and intellectual diversity. These principles are essential to preserving the traditional vocation and fundamental mission of higher education, as defined by UNESCO.[2] Thus, autonomy is linked closely to material independence and free financial management. Yet one of the most notable effects of globalization resides in the supranational power, often exorbitant, accorded to international financial institutions. This power results from the following factors:

- The globalization of higher education emanates from texts formulated during multilateral WTO negotiations. In theory, decisions are made on the basis of the incontestably democratic rule "one member, one vote." But in practice, negotiations and consensus prevail. Needless to say, the most advanced countries (United States, European Union, Australia, Canada, Japan) have the final say in decisions.
- Developed and developing countries do not have comparable infrastructure or the financial means to deal with the growing demand for knowledge and training or to implement effectively and efficiently the reforms "adopted."
- Political and social structures — which are significantly related to the development stage of the countries under consideration — have varying degrees of influence on the reforms to be adopted, their implementation, and their evaluation. This depends essentially on the country's respect or lack of respect for democracy and individual freedoms, as well as the intellectual capacities of citizens and their awareness of the factors that could interfere with their autonomy.

For all of these reasons, and because the field of study of this project is limited to the Mediterranean region, I have used two models: that of a developed country, France, and that of a developing country, Tunisia.

In both cases, the higher education system has been subjected to reforms designed to align it with new norms imposed, directly or indirectly, by globalization. Beyond their development gap, these two countries were chosen because of the historical connections that tie them. The Tunisian educational system was designed based on the French model and evolved for more than a decade in close collaboration with French institutions and the French educational framework. Today, there is a large Tunisian student population in France, and Tunisian universities have engaged a large number of Tunisian professors who graduated from French universities. Furthermore, the traditions of cultural and commercial trade are facilitated by the fact that the majority of Tunisians currently speak French. The higher education system in Tunisia is thus, to a certain extent, a mirror image of the French system.

The Liberalization Framework: The General Agreement on Trade in Services (GATS)

The objective of the GATS is to liberalize international trade in services, including those in education, by encouraging deregulation, privatization, and the development of markets. During the GATS negotiations held under the aegis of the WTO (2000-5), the liberalization of educational services was encouraged, if not demanded, by the countries considered to be the top suppliers of education services, especially higher education, including the United States, Australia, New Zealand, and England (see Brouillette and Fortin [2004, 46-48]). Article I.3(b) and (c) stipulate that "any service in any sector" should be liberalized — in this case, those supplied "on a commercial basis" or "in competition with one or more service suppliers," "except services supplied in the exercise of governmental authority." By this definition, the article applies to education services, particularly higher education, from the moment that a student chooses to pursue university studies within a public or private educational establishment and pays for these services.

To implement the liberalization process for education services, the WTO subdivides these services into five categories:

- preschool and elementary school
- secondary school with two cycles and different vocational-training paths
- higher education, in all forms
- adult education
- other education-related services.

In the case of higher education, the GATS defines different modes of trade in services to be chosen by the countries that have decided to engage in the process:[3]

- transborder services through new information technologies (distance education, for example)
- services to foreigners (hosting foreign students)
- a commercial presence abroad — that is, the establishment of an institution offering educational services in a foreign country (university franchises)
- individuals offering services in a foreign country.

Negotiations on the trade in educational services lasted from 2000 to 2005. During the first two years, the signatory countries were asked to formulate their positions regarding the category of education service to liberalize, the mode of trade chosen, the nature of obstacles to be removed, and the limitations to be imposed on application of the GATS. These countries were then invited to bring their positions to the table and negotiate their total or partial application.[4] Although liberalization of education services, particularly those in higher education, was not obligatory, several developed countries made their positions known, and a number of developing countries expressed — willy-nilly — their desire to open their higher education systems by choosing at least one form of trade.

Although the EU is a signatory to the GATS, it has not taken a position on liberalization of the European educational system. Most member states were reluctant because of the prospect of having the project rejected by the public. Nevertheless, the EU's commitment to the process of liberalization is an incentive to member states, "which does not eliminate the threat but contains it, at least for the moment" (Laval and Weber 2003, 6, our translation).

It must be noted, however, that the countries of western Europe are expressing more reservations about the opening and privatization of their higher education systems than are the countries of eastern Europe, which, concerned with modernization and palliating funding difficulties, have chosen to privatize their institutions. France has shown its reluctance by being among the last European countries — if not the last — protecting its systems from the wave of privatization. This attitude is justified by cultural and political factors related to the concept of the republican state, which is well anchored in French public opinion and a non-negligible determinant of political decision making.

Although Tunisia was among the first developing countries to join the WTO, it has not expressed a formal commitment in this area, notwithstanding successive reform projects dictated by the missions of international financial institutions. Some of the recommendations made by these institutions, however, have already been implemented.

Higher Education in France

The main reforms made to the French higher education system originated in the declaration by the EU ministers of education (June 1999). The declaration gave rise to the Bologna Process, the objective of which is to create an open European space of higher education based on the following principles:

1 The promotion of mobility among students, teachers, researchers, and administrative staff, with the goal of formulating comparable methodology criteria and aiming for convergence and transparency of degrees. A number of instruments to this end have been instituted, including the following:

- the adoption of a flexible degree system in which the training period is based on the North American 3-5-8 model: three years for a licence (or bachelor's degree), five years of credits for a master's degree, and eight years for a doctorate (LMD)
- the adoption (starting in 2005) of easily readable and comparable degrees through a short description attached to the degree called a diploma supplement.

2 Promotion of graduates' employability by the creation of short training programs based on the competencies required by a profession to satisfy demand in labour markets.

3 Promotion of the European dimension, notably in study programs, and cooperation among countries with regard to quality evaluation.

4 Development of the competitiveness of higher education in the EU countries in order to attract more foreign students. The objectives of this approach are to make higher education in the region profitable and to strengthen the competitiveness of the European economy through the diversification of "exportable" services.

5 Finally, attaining the objective of "becoming the most competitive ... knowledge-based economy in the world, capable of sustainable growth ... and greater social cohesion" by 2010 (European University Association 2007).

Aware of the North American influence on this model, the developers of the Bologna Process tried to promote certain European specificities. In France, the higher education system faced upheaval because of the combination of three reforms:

1 The LMD reform, which, after 2005, was adopted by almost 80 percent of French universities.
2 The modernization of universities reform, formerly called the autonomy statute, which delegated to universities the responsibility for organizing themselves, notably with regard to pedagogy and choice of professors. Also on the agenda was increasing universities' financial autonomy by encouraging them to seek non-government funding, although most of their money continued to come from the public purse. Like the LMD reform, the modernization of universities pushes them to professionalize the training supply and raise the employability of graduates through a greater opening to the world of business and adjusting to the training needs of local firms according to the regional specificities of the job market.
3 The reform of the status of university staff, begun in the early 1980s (which saw the teaching load increased by half), which called for the contractualization of university staff and gave university presidents more power in "individual negotiations" of contracts. Also, and along the same lines, a parliamentary report written with a view towards austerity claimed that "contractualization and decentralization should lead to a drop in state personnel. Using contractual employment, permanent civil servants may also be asked to trade a lifetime employment guarantee for more attractive salaries."[5]

The most notable fact was that the LMD system used in North American and Anglo-Saxon countries was never imposed. Rather, it was willingly undertaken by the EU countries, and then by France, in order to align themselves with the standards applied in the countries that were leaders in innovation, scientific research, and quality of education. This choice was further justified by several factors: the acceleration of globalization; increased exchanges among university institutions all over the world (student mobility, exchanges of professors and researchers, and so on); university franchises, a strategy used by well-known universities, most of them Anglo-Saxon; and the development of information and communications technologies, which overcame the obstacles of borders and distances. The correlation between adoption of these successive reforms in France and the influence of the neoliberal ideology that drove them was often denounced by both the different stakeholders in higher education and the French press and public opinion. The consequences of the reforms helped to generalize the typically French cleavage between universities and the *grandes écoles,* and they affected graduates from these two types of institutions by marginalizing degrees from the former in comparison to those from the latter. French grandes écoles dispense different kinds of professional training and are known for their rigorous selection of applicants. They therefore draw the elite among French holders of bachelor's degrees who have completed their preparatory studies. Most of these students are from well-off families and have parents who are senior civil servants or in the liberal professions.[6] Compared to their colleagues in universities, students in the grandes écoles also benefit from better supervision, better material conditions, a quality of services allowing for more favourable working conditions, solid opportunities for graduates,[7] and even remuneration for the years of study at some schools (although, as a general rule, studies at these schools are more rigorous than those at university).[8] This split between universities and grandes écoles severely punishes candidates from disadvantaged social classes by excluding them from the best jobs, thus reproducing and even aggravating social disparities.

Similarly, adoption of the LMD reform and the university-modernization statute gave rise to the fear of a distinction between universities that were best placed in their cultural, economic, and social environment and, consequently, better endowed financially and "second zone" institutions, which do not always have as advantageous an environment. Indeed, the university-modernization statute, which encourages universities to open themselves up to the private sector by seeking funds and adjusting the curriculum to market needs, has been severely criticized for having subordinated higher education to the private sector by distancing it from its "historically constituted" primary mission of "autonomous production of knowledge and individuals' critical training" (de Montlibert 2004, 22, our translation). This subordination has been denounced as generating negative consequences with regard to both the profiles of students and the development of research and knowledge. On the one hand, the orientation of university training towards professional positions deprives candidates of the type of high-end training of knowledge that enables them to enhance their general culture, sharpen their critical faculties, and become better prepared for participating in political, social, and cultural life. On the other hand, the rise in the number of professional courses of study, accompanied by larger student bodies, is not compensated for by sufficient means to ensure a certain quality of education, a satisfactory supervisory framework, easy access to new technologies, and so on.[9] Supplementary sources of funding must be found through university-business partnerships, the development of continuous education, apprenticeships, and contracts with external economic stakeholders that offer funding for research activities. This mixture of funding sources is increasingly encouraged by the French government, with the support of international organizations. The content of training offered, the means provided to universities, and the prestige of their diplomas depend more and more on local economic stakeholders. The gap can thus be closed only as universities subordinate themselves further to the private sector. This approach contradicts the essential mission of higher education, which is to benefit students and society as a whole.

When curricula are designed first and foremost to respond to the needs of the market, higher education becomes more and more utilitarian, and universities are exhorted to develop applied research and focus on short-term profitability. Some even speak of a "regionalization of the training supply," alluding to the influence of the local economic environment on "the choice of research themes, how best to respond to the demands of local stakeholders, to the detriment of the university's scientific autonomy" (Abélard 2003, 5, our translation). In the current liberalized economic context, economic interests prevail over other objectives, such as human and social development. For students, the result is reduced freedom of choice, since they are pushed towards professional courses of study instead of the human sciences, which offer few or no career paths. This kind of streaming negatively affects their autonomy — a synonym for freedom, or material or intellectual independence.[10] And yet one of the major roles of higher education is to develop the creativity of young people and to instill in them the values of citizenship, democracy, and tolerance for cultural, religious, and social diversity. This is what constitutes the autonomy of individuals so that they remain unchanged within the external difference through which they express themselves.

The gradual subordination of universities and scientific research to the world of business and the local economic environment tends to create another gap between "poles of excellence," which are well endowed to support research and development, and university colleges, in which students' academic horizons are limited. This gap is made even wider because the "best institutions" grab the "best students," leading to the denationalization of degrees by gradually replacing the logic of the academic discipline, which had guaranteed the equal value of French national degrees, with that of the institution. This trend is likely to punish student populations from disadvantaged social classes, in the sense that their chances of gaining access to a renowned university are increasingly slim.

Furthermore, successive reforms affecting the status of university staff have been heavily criticized, including opposition to the integration of new "managerial" methods and the system of contracting out jobs. Contracts are seen as synonymous with insecurity and precariousness, whereas job security is considered the primary requirement for ensuring the growth of knowledge and know-how. Other consequences of these reforms are also under fire, such as one-semester courses imposed by the LMD reform and an increase in the workload of teachers to the detriment of their research activities, which means a gradual deterioration of their working conditions and remuneration. The frequent recourse, for budgetary reasons, to temporary teachers to fill pedagogical or didactic positions to the detriment of specialization positions will inevitably affect the employment of young researchers and doctoral students, the rate of effective supervision of students in their specialties, and the quality of teaching, especially in the "small universities," which to all intents and purposes are dependent on the state.

This policy of progressive disengagement by the state found its initial formulation in a statement by the European Commission and the Organisation for Economic Co-operation and Development (OECD):

If operating expenditure is trimmed, the quantity of service should not be reduced, even if the quality has to suffer. For example, operating credits for schools or universities may be reduced, but it would be dangerous to restrict the number of students. Families

247

will react violently if children are refused admission, but not to a gradual reduction in the quality of the education given, and the school can progressively and for particular purposes obtain a contribution from the families, or eliminate a given activity. This should be done case by case, in one school but not in the neighbouring establishment, so that any general discontent of the population is avoided." (Morrisson 1996, 5)

In short, this is how the educational system is to be privatized and subjected to the logic of the market. The successive reforms, deemed to impede the progress of French universities, testify to the domination of a "single way of thinking" that is the basis of the globalization process.

The degradation of academics' working conditions and unattractive job offers to candidates who excel in their subject areas have led to the "brain drain" that is stripping the French economy of part of its human potential and essentially benefitting the receiving countries — the United States primary among them — which do not have to pay the initial cost for training and investment. The overall regional and global trends in the expatriation of researchers and highly qualified personnel show that the wealthiest countries enjoy the fruits of the investment in human capital made by less wealthy and advanced countries. As this phenomenon becomes more pronounced, it is causing irreparable damage to less-advanced countries, to the detriment of their political and economic autonomy.

Higher Education in Tunisia

Because of its geographic proximity to Europe and its history as a French protectorate, Tunisia has continued to maintain close relations with France through commercial, cultural, and human exchanges. When the European Economic Community was created, Tunisia opted for a strategy of opening and trade in order to be more than a bit player in the expansion of international trade and global economic growth. In the higher education sector, most exchange programs take place with France in the form of cooperation projects, co-supervision, and the rapid movement of Tunisian students, researchers, and teachers towards France. By choosing opening and integration with the European space, Tunisia has also sought to align its higher education system with international standards for objectives and structure.

As a developing country, Tunisia incurred public debt in the 1980s, which had an effect on the public sector, including education and higher education. The repercussions of the Structural Adjustment Programs were felt in higher education through budgetary austerity measures[11] that weighed heavily on the facilities of higher education institutions, scientific research, the rate of supervision, and the quality of para-university performance. The recourse to indebtedness opened the path to interference by international financial institutions in education policies, to the detriment of the country's autonomy. This situation led to a series of reforms, some of which have already been implemented.[12] Among them were the following:

1 an increase in registration fees and fees for para-university services
2 an increase in the weekly workload of teachers
3 the use of secondary-school teachers[13]
4 the creation of a category of academics devoted exclusively to teaching
5 the separation of higher education from scientific research
6 the achievement of a "pedagogical minimum of failures"
7 an increase in the number of, and funding for, short educational programs
8 a reduction in staff in literary and human sciences programs
9 the privatization of and/or encouragement of private investment in higher education
10 the decentralization and evaluation of university institutions.

The implementation of these recommendations, combined with an explosion in student numbers, led to a continuous drop in the quality of education in Tunisia. The exponential growth in demand for training and higher education would require considerable means in order to guarantee high-quality education. The number of institutions had to rise, effective supervision had to be ensured, and new technologies had to be integrated, the costs of which were even higher because student bodies were constantly evolving. Although the number of universities kept pace with the growth of student numbers, the essential problem remained.

Whereas adoption of the World Bank directives explains the theory of the higher education system in Tunisia, a number of inseparable factors explain it in fact. Some are related to the lack of funding for infrastructure, equipment, and research; others are related to the change in structure of the teaching staff and the degradation of their working conditions, as well as the gradual deterioration of studying conditions in unwelcoming institutions and the increased privatization of para-university services.

The World Bank missions recommended privatization of both teaching and para-university services.[14] In 1995, registration fees, long symbolically low, suddenly increased[15] — generating revenues necessary for developing the privatization of education.[16] The share of the state budget devoted to higher education stagnated at around 4 percent (4.20 percent in 1984-85, compared to 4.08 percent in 2002-3), while the number of students multiplied by 7.5 (the nineteen-to-twenty-four-year-old age class to which these students belonged grew from 5 percent of the total population in 1984-85 to 26 percent in 2002-3). As a proportion of GDP, the budget devoted to higher education remained relatively stable (1.13 percent in 1984, compared to 1.28 percent in 2002). Expenditures per student therefore dropped from 2,500 dinars in 1987 to 1,380 current dinars in 2002. The changes in these indicators — an increase in the number of students in higher education coupled with a reduction in public funding — penalized students from low-income classes and exacerbated discrimination and ruptures between social classes. In fact, one of the most notable effects of globalization in less-advanced countries has been a widening gap between the wealthy, with more and more advantages, and the poor, who suffer more.

The effects of the reforms in higher education did not spare the teaching corps. With the age of professors starting to trend downwards in the early 1990s, faculty structures underwent a radical change, as illustrated by the drop in the proportion of corps A teachers (senior lecturers and professors) among total teachers, and the steady growth in the proportion of corps B teachers (assistants and assistant professors). This structural change was accentuated by the increasingly frequent use of technicians and teachers from secondary schools,[17] who occupied pedagogical and didactic positions and not specialties. This trend explains, to a point, the drop in pedagogical level and the decline in the value and credibility of Tunisian degrees. Since 2000, increased teaching loads and supervision duties have interfered with research. The degradation in teachers' working and research conditions, the deterioration of their purchasing power, their marginalization in collective negotiations, and their lack of certain political and union freedoms and scientific autonomy not only devalue their status as academics, but they also put their position as people with rights into question.

Implementation of the World Bank recommendations, which was accompanied, starting in the 2005-6 academic year, with the LMD reform, triggered the proliferation of short programs that minimized the cost of training, thus responding to "national priorities" and to the requirements of the economy with regard to employment. Despite its pragmatic scope, this system requires refinement, since there is no assurance that the economic fabric is capable of absorbing all of the growing number of work-ready graduates. Furthermore, the funding of professional training sacrifices the areas of literature and human sciences, now abandoned because they produce "bad bachelor's degrees." The marginalization of non-scientific disciplines, which are incompatible with national priorities, will end up creating a "two-speed" educational system. In the light of the close link between a society's autonomy and its material independence, the effects of globalization on the autonomy of the higher education system are obviously more important in developing countries, such as Tunisia, than in more advanced countries. Tunisia did not formally engage in the liberalization of its higher education system, but the influence of neoliberal ideology on education and teaching policies is very perceptible, to the point that the country has openly opted for "priority axes," limiting scientific research within universities considerably and thus accentuating Tunisia's dependence.

Perspectives for the Future

Although France and Tunisia have delayed their full engagement in the process of liberalization in the education sector, they cannot escape the wave of liberalization. For France, it is just a matter of time. In Tunisia, a good number of GATS provisions are being applied and testify to a measured disengagement by the state. The GATS provisions do not take into consideration "the specificity of public services, which, since they were initiated, have been a means of attaining the objective of equality" (Rivals 2003, 1, our translation). The ultimate objective of the GATS is to suppress not-for-profit public services and subject those that are competitive to market logic. Further, the GATS considers grants to be obstacles to free competition and forbids states from allocating grants to services engaged in the process of liberalization. The intention of the GATS provisions is thus to make the market for educational services of signatory countries, including higher education services, open and accessible to all suppliers of these services, national or foreign, and these suppliers must be treated on an equal footing with regard to grants or for any other measure.

The pre-eminence of GATT rules over national laws is a frightening prospect, for once the higher education system is ruled by market logic, academics will be considered "production factors" and, thus, will be paid at their "marginal productivity." If this is acceptable with regard to encouraging academics to expand their scientific research, contributing more to the sustainable development of their society, the state still has a role to play in the promotion of research through grants and funding of the necessary infrastructure.

It must be remembered that the reforms underlying the normalization of university courses and degrees bring students to the centre of the system by giving them the advantage of mobility and diversification of disciplines, thus potential opportunities. But any coin has its flip side, and this one brings up the spectre of mass production of insecure employees and "cosmopolitan citizens" deprived of a proper identity. Thus, it is important to underline a paradoxical effect generated by globalization. Although this process is supposed to strengthen the mobility of students and researchers and accelerate the dissemination of knowledge globally through new information and communications technologies, the material and regulatory restrictions on the mobility of students from the South to the North are multiplying. This analysis of higher education shows that the vision of globalization as generating more democracy, freedom of choice, free blossoming of individuals, and reconciliation between North and South must be revised when it involves sectors that have historically fallen exclusively within the aegis of the state and that cannot be subjected to market logic without economic and social repercussions.

PART 6

Globalization and Autonomy: The Economic Question

The final section of the book begins with Lotfi Bouzaïane's general review of the development of state economies in the Mediterranean region. In Chapter 15, Bouzaïane observes that the region's economies profited from a period of unprecedented growth during the 1990s and the early 2000s. He describes the growing influence of globalization over the last fifty years and evaluates its contribution to this period of expansion. However, he notes, economic disparities between Northern and Southern countries in the region remain persistent and high. Standards of living, measured by per capita income, are five times higher in the North than in the South. With the exception of Libya, none of the Southern countries has a per capita income close to that of the less-well-off Northern countries. The chapter ends with an assessment of the prospects for change in these inequalities over the medium term.

The subsequent chapters, more detailed and localized, help to complete the picture of persistent economic inequalities between North and South and the strategies formulated to reverse these trends. In Chapter 16, Rim Ben Ayed Mouelhi conducts a systematic analysis of the strategic behaviours of economic and political stakeholders on both sides of the Mediterranean Sea in order to evaluate the potential of their interactions to strengthen or weaken countries' capacity to seize the opportunities offered by globalization. The analysis reveals the predominance of Northern stakeholders and the need for Southern countries to sacrifice part of their autonomy to build alliances with their counterparts to the North while reforming their own social structures. In Chapter 17, Samouel Béji extends the analysis to an examination of the changes that have taken place in the region's financial and banking systems. In both the North and the South, states have lost considerable autonomy in this area. At the same time, the transnational firms in the wealthy EU countries have grown more autonomous and are increasingly active on global markets. In Chapter 18, Jihen Malek contributes to a better comprehension of the factors affecting economic autonomy by examining industrial policy. She shows how the focus of industrial policy instruments has shifted in response to globalization and to research and development, science, and innovation. The move away from traditional industrial policy instruments places the Southern countries at a disadvantage, since their capacity for scientific and techno-logical development is significantly more modest than is that of the more developed EU states.

Nizard Jouini's analysis, in Chapter 19, reflects research on regional integration accords, discussed in Chapter 2, and on the role of stakeholders in civil society, discussed in Chapter 16. Jouini demonstrates that globalization has caused civil society stakeholders to participate more fully in economic integration policies and, as a result, to become signatories to accords. Because of the greater contribution by civil society, these accords are better able to address the social effects of economic integration and interdependence. Cities in Southern states, however, still suffer the effects of political restrictions on civil society stakeholders and, sometimes, the absence of freedom. As a consequence, the accords rarely give rise to expressions of concern about globalization and its negative effects in these countries.

This part of the book finishes with an exploration of another area of possible growth in the South: outsourcing. In Chapter 20, Fatma Sarraj indicates that although conditions seem favourable, outsourcing remains embryonic in the southern Mediterranean compared to the Asian countries of India and China. Despite their geographic distance, these countries are more competitive. Pushing the analysis further, Sarraj suggests that Southern states that invest in modernizing their infrastructure, public services, and transportation and communications networks and offer an advantageous fiscal environment will be in a better position to profit from the possibilities of outsourcing.

chapter 15

The Economics of Globalization and Autonomy in the Mediterranean Region

Lotfi Bouzaïane

THE MEDITERRANEAN REGION, as a geopolitical entity, has seen a remarkable revitalization since the mid-1990s. Europe, the Maghreb, and the Middle East are recognized in international bodies, but the Mediterranean region is at the heart of major issues such as the environment,[1] economic cooperation, immigration, and security, and it has become a subject of interest to researchers in political and social sciences.[2] In the 1990s, following the launching of Euro-Mediterranean integration projects, the Mediterranean region, which bridges geographic disparities and diverse populations, began to attract the attention of economists (see Chapter 19, this volume).

In this chapter, I propose an economic explanation for the revival of the Mediterranean region within the current globalization process. I will show that the paradoxes and limitations that globalization imposes on the region are simply expressions of a desire for autonomy by the countries concerned. I will then take a look at the long-term future of this region, which is torn between globalization and autonomy.[3]

The Globalization Process in the Mediterranean Region

The integration of Mediterranean countries with globalization is not recent, but it gained momentum in the 1990s through a series of institutional events, such as the creation of the World Trade Organization (WTO), and geopolitical and technological developments.[4] In addition, a dialectical movement strengthened the globalization process in the region, while broadening its geo-economic area. I discuss these two aspects by tracing the evolution of the globalization process and the way in which it expanded and defined the Mediterranean space.

The 1940s to the 1970s: Early Stages of Globalization

Integration of Mediterranean countries into the globalization process began after the Second World War. Some of the countries in the region were among the first signatories to the Havana Charter of 1948, through which the International Trade Organization was created. Although the organization's charter was signed by fifty-three states, it was not ratified by any member country, owing, notably, to pressure from the Republican majority in the US Congress, which opposed Democratic president Harry Truman. Instead, the General Agreement on Tariffs and Trade (GATT) was created. Enhanced a number of times, it governed international trade for almost a half century, until 1994. The Southern countries in the Mediterranean region, formerly colonies or protectorates, signed the agreement after they freed themselves from foreign domination. The desire to integrate into the world market was thus an essential aspect of the economic policies of newly independent countries.[5] The goal was to broaden the national component of the market economy that, under colonization, had been integrated into the system of the metropolis. This integration was especially notable in relation to food production, which was essentially agricultural and artisanal in nature. Agricultural reforms and development plans were quickly implemented by the new governments in Southern countries, with the support of international financial institutions, in order to integrate all sectors into the market economy, replace independent work with salaried work, and modernize production systems with a view to improving productivity. In Northern countries, the postwar period was marked by the contribution of the Marshall Plan to the reconstruction of Europe, designed to guarantee the continent a secure position in international trade.

The East-West rivalry overshadowed the widespread advance of trade relations in Mediterranean countries. The socialist political economies in some Southern countries concealed a broadening of the market economy and integration into the world economy. Giving priority to import substitution, these countries tried to use market mechanisms to generate as much surplus as possible in order to fund projects for mechanization, infrastructure construction, and industrialization. The game of alliances — for some countries with the Western bloc, for others with the Soviet bloc, or by creating competition between the two — allowed for access to international funding by lending a liberal or socialist tint, depending on the circumstance, to the economic policy followed.[6] In any case, the elements essential to a market economy were gradually instituted, leading to intensification of foreign trade. There was, however, one major difference between Northern and Southern countries with regard to integration with the world economy. In Northern countries, the state was simply the supervisor of market mechanisms (the exception was France, where a large public sector oversaw production, controlled exchange rates, and controlled the prices of numerous products).[7] In contrast, except for Libya, Lebanon, and Israel, all Southern countries had administered economies with price, investment, and exchange controls, as well as a large public sector.[8]

The paths taken by the countries in the Mediterranean region were dictated by the opportunity offered by their proximity to one or the other of the Cold War centres, whose separation was symbolized by the Berlin Wall. Each of these countries felt free to create the economic policy that served its interests and social legitimacy and to administer its economy by technopolitical categories to manage tensions and ensure social redistribution. To the extent that productivity increases were linked to generalization of the market economy and the availability of foreign funding, such nuances in economic policy expressed a form of autonomy in relation to the requirements of the world market, without throwing the integration process itself into question. Industrial policies were formulated with the aim of strengthening this autonomy (see Chapter 18, this volume).

The 1980s: A Turning Point

In the mid-1980s, there was a decisive turning point in the globalization process, which matured a decade later. The pace of globalization accelerated in the Mediterranean region. First, the Soviet Union lost impetus, which had an impact on the possibilities for funding and foreign exchange alternatives, and it then collapsed, which dashed the hopes of the countries in the region for any form of autonomous market economy.[9] During the decade, data-processing capacities improved, thanks to the revolution in information and communications technologies.[10] These two factors, combined with the limitations of economic policies for administered markets, forced countries in the region to adopt a set of liberal economic reforms.[11]

After the fall of the Berlin Wall, the unification of Europe accelerated and spread to countries of the former socialist bloc. The information and communications technologies (ICT) revolution enabled certain Northern countries, such as Ireland and Finland, to expedite their economic growth. Because advances in ICT changed the notion of geographic distance, the proximity of the Mediterranean shoreline countries, which had favoured intraregional trade, ceased to be a decisive factor.[12] The trade space thus expanded to include more distant zones.

In this context, the creation of the WTO accelerated globalization with two major innovations.[13] The first was the requirement of reciprocity of privileged customs status. In the Mediterranean zone, the Southern countries, which had benefitted from duty-free exports to the European Union since the 1970s, had to accept the formation of a free trade area to be able to continue to have this advantage.[14] This change forced Southern countries to open up their foreign trade with the EU. The second innovation concerned the replacement of the principle of voluntary participation with the principle of consensus. In other words, a country no longer had a choice about adopting the rules: they were now imposed on all member countries, except when an enforcement measure made an exception to the rule. The new system was thus more restrictive and contributed to the acceleration of globalization. However, countries that in the past had been content not to adopt a clause, without negotiation, were now encouraged to participate in the formulation of international accords. This encouraged the formation of alliances within the cogs of the WTO among countries as distant from one another as India, Brazil, South Africa, and Egypt, which gave any new agreement concluded within the WTO a more confirmed global dimension.

New Frontiers for the Mediterranean Region

The creation of the WTO and its operating terms, the development of ICT, and the changed geopolitical situation engaged the Mediterranean region in a new dynamic at the beginning of the twenty-first century. Integration into the international market took on a more globalized dimension. The region was extended farther north and east, from the Scandinavian countries to the edges of the Sahara Desert, from the Atlantic

Ocean to the borders of Iran and Russia. In other words, the economic space of the Mediterranean region expanded beyond its geographic territory.

The levers of economic autonomy that had been represented by sector-based industrialization and social redistribution policies, exercised through the mechanisms of an administered market — particularly in the South — were replaced by others. The notion of competitiveness now became the pillar of economic policy. The ability of an economy to preserve and win market share involved profiting from a market segment that gave it a form of autonomy and the means to conduct its own domestic policy, owing to the loss of industrial policy intervention on prices. The long march towards globalization, begun in the mid-1940s, was thus accelerated, a half century later, in a broadened Mediterranean space, as the globalization movement in the region was revitalized in a context weighted with expectations and paradoxes.

Paradoxes and Economic Limitations of Globalization in the Mediterranean Region

For all of the reasons mentioned above, with the new phase of globalization, the Mediterranean region has become an entity with strong interactions, along with a number of heterogeneities that give rise to numerous paradoxes.

Commonalities

For the southern Mediterranean region, geopolitical and economic factors offer one aspect of its connection to the north side of the sea, as more than two-thirds of Southern countries' trade is with Northern countries. Trade became more diversified over the last decade but concerned mainly subzones of the expanded European Union.[15] Geopolitics is also a factor in the integration among Southern countries, whose populations, most of them Arab and Muslim, remain sensitive to the Arabic nationalism of the 1950s, reprised by Islamism since the 1980s. Among the Northern countries, the economic factor is essential in terms of the incorporation of new EU member countries, but it does not greatly affect the EU's attitude towards the rest of the Mediterranean region, given that most of its economic trade is conducted with the rest of the world.[16] The geopolitical factor remains a central concern for the EU countries in relation to their Eastern and Southern neighbours.[17] Subscribing to globalization is nevertheless a principle shared by all countries in the region, even if their positions diverge with regard to pace of integration, choice of priorities, and emphasis on issues such as agreements on agricultural liberalization.[18] This is a true paradox in view of the social costs, the upheavals, and the questioning of particular interests generated by globalization. The paradox is explained by the effects induced by the first wave of globalization (1940-90), which enabled countries in the region to adopt consumption styles and production technologies that had become almost universal, although local production continued to persist and develop. Globalization also offered an opportunity for increased mobility and restructuring, which gave population segments access to these new consumption styles.[19] New socio-professional categories associated with the business world began to supplant the technocratic bureaucracy of the period of public administration of markets. The argument that integration into the world economy would have a positive impact on economic well-being was a constant leitmotif in official discourses, supported by the catchphrase of general liberalization of foreign trade, especially imports, more in relation to consumption than production. Nor did Europe escape the attraction of the North American consumption model, which it assimilated so well that it disseminated it in its turn to Southern countries and elsewhere.[20]

Remaining Economic Disparities

The Mediterranean region remains clearly divided in terms of standard of living, with a per capita income often five times higher in the North than in the South. With the exception of Libya, no Southern country has a per capita income close to that of the least well-off countries in the North (see Figure 15.1). Although economic growth is more rapid in the South, it is not rapid enough to enable Southern countries to catch up with Northern countries in a reasonable time horizon. Only a radical transformation of institutions in the South and a much higher volume of foreign investment than the current level would make more rapid growth possible. Through the gradual suppression of customs barriers and a reallocation of resources to economic activities, globalization, in the sense of liberalization of foreign trade, will lead to better use of the resources available in each country. This will be a function of comparative advantages and the higher efficiency of production units in response to the

Figure 15.1   Long-term persistence of income disparities per inhabitant

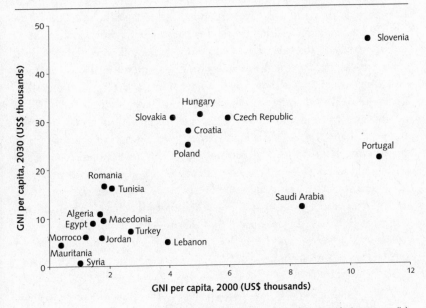

Note: Gross national income (GNI) is in constant $US dollars (at purchasing power parity).
Source: World Bank data for 2000 and author's projection for 2030, taking account of changes to parity in purchasing power.

greater competitive threat that will affect these countries' markets, both upstream and downstream.

A number of studies circulating in Southern countries in the mid-1990s determined that there had been gains in terms of well-being owing to the creation of free trade areas and the liberalization of foreign trade. These gains were estimated at an equivalent of two or three points of economic growth.[21] Although this represents, in some cases, one or more additional half years of growth, it is not enough, on its own, to ensure economic catching up. This dichotomy would in principle favour mobility of factors — capital and labour — in a way that would ensure, theoretically, a closing of the gap in living standards. In the Mediterranean region, such mobility has yet to become reality.

Capital and foreign-investment flows are still weak, given the unfavourable competitive position of Southern countries compared to other world zones (see Chapter 20 by Fatma Sarraj, this volume). When it comes to labour, the situation is similar. Differences in standards of living produce a great pull towards the North for unemployed or relatively poorly employed workers in the South. The demand for labour in the European Union involves, in particular, the manual construction and related trades, basic health care, and even jobs with more sophisticated qualifications in the education and computer sectors.[22] Without a clear immigration policy, the European countries practise a discriminatory sawtooth policy, sometimes proceeding case by case. This kind of policy gives rise to illegal immigration flows towards the North, which leaves observers perplexed about the simultaneity of such a phenomenon with the new phase of globalization.[23] Without neglecting the critical immigration threshold attained by communities from the Southern countries, which supposedly has a negative effect on the general well-being of Northern societies, this issue nonetheless poses a limit on the extension of a globalization process. It is presumed that globalization will be accompanied by mobility of production factors — both capital and labour.

Obstacles to Globalization

In the countries of the Mediterranean region, globalization will no doubt help to improve standards of living through the introduction of greater economic efficiency.[24] However, the substantial reduction in the development gap between Northern and Southern countries is countered by the limited mobility of factors. The mobility of capital is circumscribed by the slow development of institutions in Southern states, which wish to preserve control over the functioning of their economy — a form of affirmation of autonomy.[25] Mobility of labour is impeded largely by Northern countries concerned with preserving domestic social assets, another form of affirmation of autonomy in relation to the potential implications of globalization. All of these factors reduce globalization to a single dimension: liberalization of trade in goods and services.

Another limitation on globalization in the region is linked to rent-generating natural resources. David Ricardo (1995) was one of the first economists to show that rent on natural resources subsists in the capitalist system and is formed according to the same market laws. Liberalization thus does not eliminate this type of rent, which returns to the owner, except that there are no economic laws that explain how the natural resources are used. The market may explain or contribute to the formation of the prices for these resources, but it cannot determine who will benefit from the resulting rent. The appropriation of natural resources thus remains in the political domain, and globalization does not offer conciliatory solutions with regard to appropriation of the rent, which explains why the temptation to capture it will continue both despite and because of globalization.[26] Such rent is also why globalization will continue to be a source of tension between social groups both domestically and on the international level.

Historically, the expansion of markets within a country was accompanied by different arrangements for the appropriation of natural resources. The fiscal regime, or collective appropriation, made it possible to reconcile liberalization to a point, based on private property and the sharing of rents. On the international scale, such solutions are not easily imaginable.[27] In the Mediterranean region, many countries have come into conflict over the use of natural resources. In the twentieth century, imperialist intruders were interested in appropriating the resources of conquered countries. In the current stage of globalization, the geographic distribution of natural resources, notably water and hydrocarbons, has transformed the Mediterranean region into a site of sharp tensions that may degenerate. Or, on the contrary, they may evolve towards a peaceful partnership, although such an evolution would be outside of the immediate process of globalization.

No one is unaware that the Mediterranean region has a serious shortage of freshwater. In the North, the water is of poor quality due to industrial and urban pollution; in the South, there is insufficient water to meet the needs of irrigation and of industrial and domestic use (see Figure 15.2). In addition, water resources are often distant from where the water is treated. Conflicts over preservation of water quality and water use are still latent, limited, or localized. Many of the conflicts in the Middle East and Sudan, however, may be attributed to the use and control of water. In Europe, frictions are beginning to arise over pollution of river water. Future economic development of the Mediterranean countries will increase the pressure on water use, exacerbating the conflicts related to it.

The region is rich in hydrocarbon resources, but the distribution of these resources and of their allocation and use is uneven from country to country (see Figure 15.3). In general, the available energy resources surpass the needs of Southern countries, and the variability in allocation among these countries is great. Libya, for example, an oil power, has for three decades practised a fairly aggressive policy towards its neighbours. The reason for the occupation of Kuwait by Iraq and for the ensuing first

Figure 15.2   Average allocation of fresh water in Mediterranean countries, 2003

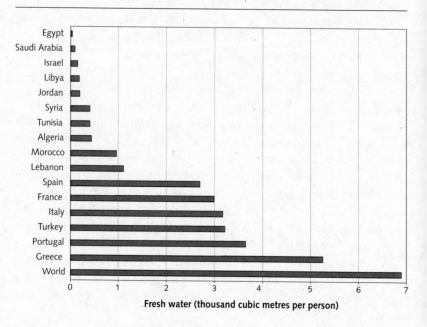

Fresh water (thousand cubic metres per person)

Source: World Bank, World Development Indicators, http://web.worldbank.org/, accessed August 2006.

Gulf War was control of petroleum resources. In today's situation of full globalization, the entire region east of the Mediterranean Sea is destabilized by the occupation of Iraq, a country with rich oil resources. Alternative energy supply is also an important element. For example, Europe is dependent on natural gas from Russia, with all of the geopolitical complications that this generates. Although the question of water is an essentially intra-Mediterranean problem, that of hydrocarbons places the region within an international context.

Globalization is not dissociated from this situation, in that liberalization of international trade pushes all economies to become more competitive. The cost of natural resources is an important element in the competitiveness of factors, giving rise to hypersensitivity about energy issues as globalization advances.[28] There is in fact another form of autonomy in play: the countries with energy resources exert it by determining the supply of hydrocarbons on the world market. Meanwhile, energy-consuming countries seek to assure themselves of energy supply under

Figure 15.3   Net energy imports as percentage of domestic use per country, 2003

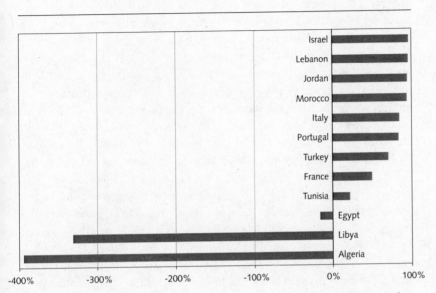

Source: World Bank, World Development Indicators, http://web.worldbank.org/, accessed August 2006.

conditions that preserve the competitiveness of their products and do not threaten their economic autonomy.[29]

To summarize, the limitations and paradoxes that attend globalization in the Mediterranean region, with their implications for autonomy, mean that the region is at a historic turning point. Borders pushed to new extremities and populations increasingly sensitive to economic fractures sit alongside blockages or tensions affecting the mobility of production factors and the appropriation and sharing of natural resources. The path is thus open to international interference in the region, which may further reconfigure its geo-economic contours by making globalization more important in an extra-economic sense.

A Plural Mediterranean Region: Long-Term Prospects

The globalization process is not yet completed in the Mediterranean region. It began in the second half of the twentieth century and has leapt ahead in the last decade. According to its proponents, it will homogenize economic development and replace political conflicts with economic partnership and fair competition.[30] The process will be completed only when all of the mechanisms making it possible for these promises to be fulfilled are implemented. From an economic point of view, the global- ization agenda is full. The areas of agricultural liberalization and trade in services are still being debated, and formulation of the modalities of pro- tection of intellectual property rights is underway. Pollution rights and social dumping, among other subjects, are still on the drawing board. Nevertheless, the future of globalization in the Mediterranean region will depend on the lifting of blockages on the mobility of factors and management of the ownership of natural resources. The closing of gaps in per capita income levels and the peaceful coexistence of countries in the region will depend on these kinds of changes. Obstacles to the progress of globalization in the Mediterranean region are closely linked to a search for macroeconomic autonomy that is not yet affecting adher- ence to the process itself. The persistence of these obstacles, however, will reduce most commitments to lip service and the claim of autonomy to social and ideological demands.

Determinants of Globalization and Autonomy in the Mediterranean Region

Prospective analysis is an approach that explores the possible futures for a given system in light of the significant trends and ruptures that mark its development.[31] Future scenarios are formulated based on a reasoned choice of hypotheses involving the possible evolution of these ruptures, including the variables representative of the system under study. The Mediterranean region is presented as a complex system with a certain number of economic parameters with which its integration into the globalization process can be assessed. Once the system's portrait has been completed, it becomes possible to envisage its overall evolution in rela- tion to globalization, its impact on countries in the region, and its impli- cations for autonomy. The system's variables are classified in terms of their reciprocal influences and dependencies so that coherent future scenarios can be constructed.

To simplify the analysis, I have chosen the following aggregated rep- resentative variables:

1   the disparity in living standards in the region
2   the management of tensions over natural resources in the region
3   the mobility of production factors between North and South
4   extra-Mediterranean interference in the region
5   opposition to governance and societal models
6   ideological differences among political currents
7   the progress of globalization in the region
8   manifestations of autonomy in the region.

The first three variables, which are discussed above, are strongly linked to the economic dimension of globalization. The fourth variable was mentioned during discussion of the issue of management of natural resources and will be captured through its link to the economic dimension of globalization.

The variables on governance models and ideologies are included in this representation to illustrate, in part, the non-economic dimension of globalization. Unlike the first wave of globalization (1945-95), the current wave has seen the rise of Muslim fundamentalism (in the South), a revival of nationalism (in the North), and other ideological and political movements that are heterogeneous and indicative of a view opposed to liberal globalization and that propose governance and societal models quite distant from the model of liberal democracy. Variables 7 and 8 refer to the progress of globalization and to the type of autonomy demanded by countries that have subscribed to it and are not opposed to the process out of hand. The combination of these two variables gives a picture of the nature of globalization and the forms of autonomy that accompany it. I wonder, in particular, whether forms of social autonomy, non-economic in nature, might supplant forms of economic autonomy.

Economy, Ideology, and Societal Models

The variables in this system are in the reciprocal relations of dependence and influence. Examining these relations for pairs of variables and applying the appropriate techniques, they can be prioritized according to their influence or dependence on the system as a whole. Table 15.1 shows the influence and dependence relations used for this analysis. The variables are represented in rows and columns. The rows represent the influences; the columns, the dependencies. For each row, each cell has a value of 1 or 0,

Table 15.1   Influences and dependencies of variables in the future dynamic in the Mediterranean region

No.	Variable	Number								Total influence
		1	2	3	4	5	6	7	8	
1	The disparity in living standards in the region	0	1	1	0	1	1	0	1	5
2	The management of tensions over natural resources in the region	1	0	1	1	0	0	0	1	4
3	The mobility of production factors between North and South	1	0	0	0	1	0	1	0	3
4	Extra-Mediterranean interference in the region	0	1	1	0	0	1	1	1	5
5	Opposition to governance and societal models	0	1	1	1	0	1	0	1	5
6	Ideological differences among political currents	0	0	1	1	1	0	1	1	5
7	The progress of globalization in the region	1	0	0	1	0	0	0	1	3
8	Manifestations of autonomy in the region	0	1	1	0	0	1	1	0	4
	Total dependence	3	4	6	4	3	4	4	6	34

depending on whether the variable in that row is considered to have an influence on the variable in the corresponding column. This is a direct influence, not related to the other variables in the table. The value 1 is given in each case that the influence is deemed important. The cells on the diagonal have the value 0 by convention. For prioritization that also takes account of indirect effects (the fact that one variable might act on another through a third variable in the system), we use matrix-by-matrix multiplication. Figure 15.4 offers a picture of all variables with direct and indirect effects after application of matrix-by-matrix multiplication on Table 15.1.[32]

A prioritization of variables shows that disparities in living standards (Variable 1) and allocation and management of natural resources (Variable 2) are the least dependent on the rest of the variables in the system. In other words, the future of globalization in the Mediterranean region will depend on these variables, rather than influencing them. This is, of course, the point made above, but placed here in a system that also takes account of non-economic factors. Mobility of factors (Variable 3) and extra-Mediterranean interference in the region's geopolitical affairs (Variable 4) are influenced by income disparities and management of

Figure 15.4   Variables for the future of globalization and autonomy in the Mediterranean region (rated according to influence and dependence)

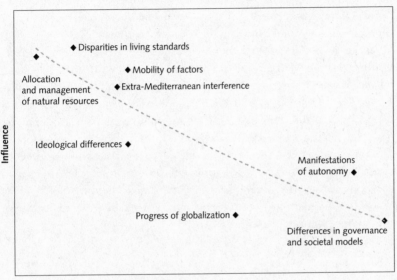

Note: In this figure, dependence increases from left to right, and influence increases from bottom to top. Following the curve from left to right, we go from variables with strong influence and weak dependence to variables with weak influence and strong dependence.

natural resources. The rest of the system depends on all of these variables. Ideological differences (Variable 6) are dependent on the system's economic variables and on extra-Mediterranean interference, although it should be noted that the ideological differences are enduring and may potentially influence the economic variables. By its position in this representation, ideology plays the role of transmission line between the economic and geopolitical variables and the rest of the variables in the system.

The progress of globalization (Variable 7) and forms of autonomy (Variable 8) are strongly dependent on economic variables, geopolitics, and ideology. Opposition to governance and societal models (Variable 5) appears to be the most dependent dimension in the system. In my model, all other variables accentuate or attenuate opposition to the societal model and not the reverse.

This model allows us to envisage different scenarios for the future. What is important is that the keys to differentiating the scenarios are economic and geopolitical. The ideological dimension, which is the most widely publicized in the media because of the rise in power of fundamentalist movements, is important, but not in the top position. Opposition to societal models is even less influential.

In conclusion, it should be noted that the lengthy process of globalization has put the Mediterranean region at the mercy of economic stakes related to the importance of its natural resources and its economic disparities. Its borders have expanded to new areas beyond the traditional geographic Mediterranean region. The ongoing globalization process has accelerated since the mid-1990s and is highlighting manifestations of economic autonomy. However, as globalization runs up against economic and geo-economic problems that it cannot solve because of its own dynamic, ideological divergences favouring new manifestations of autonomy will be accentuated. Opposition to societal models and governance is once again on the agenda.

Editor's Note: The last sentence now appears prescient in light of the Arab social rebellions that began in Tunisia in December 2010 and have continued in several North African countries in 2011.

chapter 16

Globalization and Autonomy in the Mediterranean Region: The Roles of the Main Stakeholders

Rim Ben Ayed Mouelhi

THE CHANGES INDUCED BY multilateral accords and by new conditions generated by globalization have had a major effect on the Mediterranean region. Globalization is defined here as liberalization of trade and financial exchanges, deregulation of markets, dismantlement of duty protection, offshoring, free circulation of people, and the impact of these phenomena on political and cultural life. Many countries in the region have committed to implementing vast trade-liberalization programs as part of the World Trade Organization (WTO) multilateral system, mainly through bilateral cooperation accords with their main trading partner, the European Union (EU). For instance, bilateral free trade agreements with the EU were signed in 1995 by Morocco and Tunisia, soon followed by Algeria, Egypt, Lebanon, and Syria. These agreements covered aspects linked to financial, cultural, and political cooperation, but trade liberalization was the most important component. In South-South relations, the Arab countries relaunched the free trade program, broadened to the Arab world, in 1997, but no real advance in execution of this program has been observed since then.

In the current state of affairs, it would be inaccurate to speak of the Mediterranean region as a globalized space. Trade among Southern countries is weak, while the dependence of these countries on those north of the Mediterranean Sea is growing. The EU's balance of trade with countries in the southern Mediterranean region is relatively equalized, whereas that of Southern countries with the EU is totally negative. Furthermore, although the EU is the top investor in the eleven Southern countries in terms of foreign direct investment, this amount represents only 6 percent of its total investments, well below the proportion devoted to the countries of South America (top destination, 20 percent in 1996) and Asia (16 percent). Finally, migratory flows are being increasingly subjected to limitations and controls. All of these factors show that despite geographic proximity, the degree of integration of Northern countries with the economies of Southern countries in the Mediterranean region remains very low in comparison with the United States' integration with Latin America or Japan's with the countries of Southeast Asia.

In this chapter, I consider it a given that globalization is a measurable and dynamic process. In terms of economic, social, and political opening, this process is still at a very low level in the Mediterranean region. Why? Is there resistance or opposition to a vision of opening up to the world? How will things evolve in the future? How far will globalization advance in the Mediterranean region over the next thirty or forty years? It is my hypothesis that the possible futures for globalization in the Mediterranean region will depend on significant, entrenched trends as well as on whether individuals will have compatible or contradictory visions and what their priorities and power relations are. It is true that developments in technology, transportation, and production processes play a fundamental role in globalization. But globalization is also a result of power relations and the political strategies formulated by different stakeholders to influence its course. These stakeholders are "connected and engaged in perpetual negotiations; together, they produce governance in the Mediterranean region" (Schwamm 2003, 3, our translation).

Because they involve trade, production, investment, and financing relations, globalization and regional integration both influence and activate a number of economic, political, and social stakeholders: states, civil society organizations, firms, various associations, non-governmental organizations (NGOs), and others. These stakeholders are engaged in a wide range of activities and interventions and may have diverging or converging objectives with regard to numerous issues. They may be antagonistic towards globalization if it goes against their interests. Some support the process of opening in the Mediterranean region and seek to strengthen and accelerate it to protect themselves from globalization, among other things, by creating regional autonomous spaces. Others try to resist globalization by impeding the march towards greater opening or propose alternatives for various reasons, among them defence and preservation of individual or institutional autonomy. For a given stakeholder, the strengthening of globalization in the Mediterranean region may threaten certain of its objectives and promote others. Such stakeholders support the expansion or withdrawal of the process depending on whether it advances or jeopardizes their priorities. The final situation will depend on the hierarchy of stakeholders and their power relations, priorities, attitudes towards globalization, and alliance or conflict strategies.

In this chapter, I do the following:

- reveal the major stakes involved in the opening and globalization phenomena in the Mediterranean region
- identify the main stakeholders or groups of stakeholders that may influence the course of events and shape the globalization process in the region
- analyze the play of stakeholders by determining their situation, the threats that they face, the objectives that they might have, their attitudes towards globalization and autonomy, and the strategies that they may envisage to strengthen or impede globalization
- analyze the possible interactions among the different stakeholders' strategies by looking at existing or potential conflicts or alliances.

Once the stakeholders' power relations and priorities are brought to light, I assess whether, in general, the project to strengthen globalization is being endorsed or resisted. For this, I use the approach proposed by Michel Godet for analysis of the play of stakeholders in a given system, which consists of four steps: identifying the major stakes in the system, identifying the stakeholders, establishing a hierarchy of stakeholders, and establishing their positioning in relation to a number of objectives. These steps are based on quantitative techniques and on collective reflection sessions during workshops.

The Stakes of Globalization in the Mediterranean Region

In the Mediterranean region, as elsewhere, globalization makes winners and losers; it creates opportunities and is rich in promise, but it is also a real threat. Here, I shall try to highlight the major stakes and key questions for the future of globalization in the Mediterranean region, in relation to which the stakeholders will position themselves.

Rim Ben Ayed Mouelhi

For the region's Northern countries, and even more for its Southern countries, Mediterranean integration is a means of protection against globalization. It is a particular form of search for autonomous spaces. The organization of trading blocs creates a protectionist or preferential space in opposition to an accelerated dismantling of borders. For the North, it involves coping with the increasing influence in the world economy of regional groupings such as NAFTA, comprising the United States, Canada, and Mexico. On the south side of the Mediterranean Sea, countries no longer have a choice: a new economic division of the world is emerging (North America, Europe, and East and Southeast Asia) and, to continue developing, they must integrate with one or another grouping. For the Maghreb countries, integration with the EU seems to be the only option likely to help them open up and actively insert themselves into the global economy (Benlahcen Tlemçani and Tahi 2002).

In a context of competition between the United States and Europe for control of the south shore of the Mediterranean Sea, the EU must be able to share with these countries its concept of globalization by influencing the course of events. If it does not, the United States will impose its own game rules. In effect, the Mediterranean region is a strategic space for the United States, especially because of its hydrocarbon resources. Thus, the capacity of the United States to influence global economic regulation is a major issue for the EU.

The Mediterranean region is an area into which an ageing European economy, whose businesses need a "new frontier" with markets in continuous growth, can be extended. European firms want to be in a position to respond to increasing demand for high-value-added goods. Europe must therefore develop an ambitious neighbourhood policy and extend it throughout the Euro-Mediterranean zone. For Southern countries, access to technology and the closing of the digital divide, especially through a greater opening to the North, remain major issues. The influx of foreign direct investment through stronger integration with Europe is one way to modernize the economies of Southern countries, because it offers on-the-job apprenticeships, technological transfers, job creation, and other benefits. Regional integration is thus a reservoir of growth for both North and South, and it holds out prospects for increased economic expansion through economies of scale, regional specialization, advantages in allotment of production factors, and more effective use of productive resources owing to increased competition. Global-scale problems (environment, migration, natural resources, quality of life, and so on) cannot be resolved by unilateral policy. Initiatives at the regional and global scales are thus more and more necessary, and cooperation between Northern and Southern countries will be indispensable.

The Mediterranean region is also a major security concern for Europe.[1] For the North, free trade and integration with the South constitute a strategy for reducing the risk of conflicts provoked by "economic frustration." Northern countries are aware that their security is closely linked to the stability of Southern countries. For Southern countries, consolidating the current reforms and creating a development-oriented economic and social environment remain the priorities. Opening is also a political means of increasing the degree of democracy. Globalization offers these countries opportunities for development on the condition that their institutional structures are strong. The EU has a great deal of influence on the political decision makers in the South who are committed to accelerating economic, social and, especially, political reforms. Such changes would offer the partnership a sound base and a chance to endure.

One risk of a greater opening and generalized liberalization for the Southern countries is that they would be confined to production of low-value-added goods, with little technological content, using a poorly qualified labour force. For the North, in contrast, there is the risk of seeing certain activities disappear because of offshoring. This would have consequences for employment in the territory, causing new forms of poverty and an increase in social inequalities. Further, there is a risk of loss of autonomy, since globalization speeds the pace of transfer of power from a national level to a supranational one through international and regional institutions.

Globalization — through the cultural diversity that it instigates, the information that it circulates, and the consumption standards that it disseminates — results in the spread of a planetary culture. However, there is also a risk of erosion of national cultural identities. The creation of a heterogeneous grouping and the diversity around the Mediterranean Sea may give rise to conflicts flowing from acculturation. Finally, for Southern countries, changes that may lead to total integration are situated at the level of political systems: uncontrolled democratization could lead to unpredictable upheavals.

The Stakeholders

The main groups to consider in the governance of the Mediterranean system were identified by a working group. To simplify representation of the complex system in the Mediterranean region, I limited myself to the most active stakeholders in the globalization process, and I grouped them together when necessary. Below, I describe the different stakeholders chosen for my analysis and their objectives, priorities, and means of action.

The State (Nstate)/(Sstate)

Up to now, states have been most interested in preserving national sovereignty and social cohesion. Privatization of the economy and constraints on the state's prerogatives are two significant trends that are likely to be reinforced in coming years in the Mediterranean region, as everywhere else. On the international level, the state's functions of management and regulation will be reduced and transferred to associations and NGOs. An increase in social needs, combined with a lack of state resources, will mean that states will no longer be able to assume their regulatory function on their own. States are gradually disengaging from the productive sphere in order to limit themselves to national defence, maintaining public order, and judicial matters. In short, states are facing issues related to the loss of power, authority, legitimacy, and autonomy. This crisis in the nation-state is particularly a sensitive issue in the Mediterranean region: in the North, countries such as France have a strong centralist tradition; in the South, most countries are ruled by authoritarian regimes in which the state clings to its sovereignty and continues to act as a patron, though less and less effectively.

It should be noted that states are heterogeneous in terms of power and performance. States north of the Mediterranean Sea are strong and effective, while those to the south are weak and ineffective. Thus, Southern and Northern states, despite certain convergences on issues, may have different positions with regard to a given objective. For these reasons, the "state" stakeholder has been split into two groups: Southern states (Sstate) and Northern states (Nstate) in the analysis of stakeholders' play below.

Businesses (Nbus)/(Sbus)

Businesses are essential to development, job creation, promotion of economic and social reforms, and gradual liberalization. The opening and intensification of competition have strengthened the role of firms in the race to global competitiveness and market conquests. Faced with the need to remain competitive, businesses seek to create wealth, not jobs, and to accumulate profits. This means that costs are high; national-size businesses will look to subcontracting or offshoring and will try to invest in countries with the fewest restrictions in terms of labour laws and social conventions. Increasingly, products and services will be developed in different countries, and labour and skills at a good quality-price ratio will be sought. One priority for businesses is to find high-quality skills and efficient partners to satisfy customers' scheduling and quality requirements. Businesses therefore become "global stakeholders whose decisions and behaviours often seem to be exempt from any national consideration to the point that they impose their own law on national political leaders" (Schwamm 2003, 4, our translation). Several authors have expressed the fear that the future global economy will be managed exclusively under the influence of stakeholders with private interests, such as multinational businesses.

Stronger Mediterranean integration would give Southern businesses lower-cost access to the vast Northern market, as well as to cheaper materials, equipment, and technology. But at the same time, they would face stiffer competition from Northern businesses, which would have access to a new and growing market and possibilities to produce at a lower cost. Southern businesses (Sbus) will be distinguished from Northern businesses (Nbus) in the analysis of the stakeholders' play.

The Media (Nmedia/Smedia)

The various broadcast media are information and communications organizations. They have the power to influence the way people live and think. They report on and possibly encourage reforms, but they are also capable of distorting reality and spreading disinformation. Their activity is mainly commercial. In Northern democratic systems, the media are fully independent and exercise their influence as makers of public opinion. In contrast, the media in the South (Smedia) operate in an environment in which freedom of expression is relatively controlled; they are distinguished from the Northern media (Nmedia) in the analysis of Mediterranean stakeholders' actions.

Civil Society

Civil society is composed of individual groups or private communities that voluntarily join together on a local, national, or international scale for non-profit purposes: unions, NGOs, associations, elites, religious and ethnic groups, and sometimes even political parties. Included in this category are also pressure groups that "seek to influence those who exercise power and to better buttress their demands and mobilize resources, citizens' associations, and interest groups" (Séguin, Maheu, and Vaillancourt 1995, 108, our translation). In short, "Civil society exists when voluntary associations, of any sort, deliberately seek to have an influence on certain social rules" (Scholte 2002, 213, our translation).

My analysis will encompass the following components of civil society: non-governmental organizations, elites, religious groups, and political parties.

Non-governmental Organizations (NNGO/SNGO)

Non-governmental organizations proliferate, especially in high-revenue Northern countries. Their activities extend into various fields, and they are often perceived as reflecting citizens' interests better than do political parties. In Southern countries, they are perceived as offering citizens a gateway to access public life in the absence of political opposition. All over the world, the role of states is shrinking while that of these non-state stakeholders is growing.

Non-governmental organizations are of different sizes and have various operational styles, objectives, and fields of intervention. They are involved in the delivery of services that directly benefit local communities (linked to development, jobs, health, or the environment) and/or in political activism. In Southern countries, associations and NGOs are often under the supervision of the state, which they reinforce in various ways (Ben Néfissa 2004). Many Southern associations are authorized by the government rather than created by charter, and the state thus has full power to control them. Up to now, international NGOs have financed local Southern associations to a large extent, but partnerships are increasingly developing around common objectives. Southern NGOs have tended to team up with Northern NGOs to gain more resources, recognition, and rights.

Non-governmental organizations are solicited more and more to participate in international summits and conferences as representatives of their respective countries' civil societies. International organizations want to establish contacts with local NGOs (especially in the South) and develop effective partnerships, as these NGOs are thought to be more likely to have an impact on target communities and to mobilize sources of international funding (Chiffoleau 2004). International agencies are increasingly recognizing the NGOs' role as deliverers of social services and promoters of good governance. Their main means of action include petitions, lobbying, civil resistance, communications, information exchanges, awareness-raising efforts, organization of international meetings, demonstrations and confrontations, and boycotts. Southern NGOs (SNGO) will be distinguished from Northern NGOs (NNGO) in the Mediterranean region in the analysis of stakeholders' actions.

Unions (Nunion/Sunion)

Union activists demand that globalization include a social dimension and that fundamental rights decreed by the International Labour Organization be integrated in a binding manner into agreements concluded under the aegis of the World Trade Organization (freedom of union association, freedom of collective negotiation, abolition of all forms of forced labour, effective suppression of child labour, elimination of all forms of discrimination, and other issues).[2] Their demands deal mainly with purchasing power, salaries, and job security. On the north side of the Mediterranean Sea, preservation of the European social model is a priority for unionists. Social security, solidarity, and access to health care are core values of the European social tradition. The unions bring considerable pressure to bear with regard to the integration of a social dimension into the globalization process by establishing alliances with NGOs to attain specific objectives. They can also ensure that multinational corporations improve working conditions and provide a significant counterweight to transnational businesses. Their activism and actions may limit the margin of control of national and international stakeholders.

Whereas in Northern countries, the unions are able to impose economic and social changes, in Southern countries these organizations are either withdrawing or clearly a state appendage. In the South, civil society, including unions, is the "natural extension of the state ... and an inseparable part of imposing its wishes and will" (Fouad, Refat, and Morcos 2004, 157, our translation). The unions in the North are distinguished from Southern unions in the analysis of stakeholders' play.

Exchanges and cooperation between Northern and Southern union organizations are expanding. Means of common action may be defined through such exchanges, as embodied in the Euromed Union Forum. Among the forum's priorities are recognition of skills (similar salaries for similar qualifications) and the fight against job insecurity.

Elites

Elites are "ensemble[s] of social groups that dominate society through their influence, prestige, wealth, and economic, cultural, or political power" (Chaussinard 1986, 110, our translation). They often stand out for their education and high level of culture, and they seek to make their mark in the public space.[3] Their political participation might be union-related, associative, partisan, or in opposition to the existing regime. They are concerned with key development issues such as freedom, democracy, respect for the environment, fair trade, justice, and human rights.

In the democratic systems north of the Mediterranean Sea, elites have long played an important role by expressing their opinions through free, developed media outlets. Governments and the public are attentive to their discourses and willing to be influenced by them. In the authoritarian systems in the South, elites have been manipulated by the government to appear to be its complement. More and more, the elites in the South are demanding freedom of expression and disseminating their ideas through new information technologies. Their influence will grow in the future. Their opinions reflect shared positions regarding stronger Mediterranean integration and the demands for autonomy. Some support this opening, while others oppose it. Some are proponents of autonomy, while others reject it. However, they have certain general objectives in common: human rights, democratization, workers' rights, protection of disadvantaged groups, and so on. With different means of communications and action to make their ideas known, the Northern elites (Nelite) are distinguished from the Southern elites (Selite) as stakeholders.

Religious Groups (religethn)

These are religious groups, often organized on the regional level, that are opposed to freedom of individual choice. In Southern countries, these groups militate against the Westernization of societies for ideological or religious reasons. Religious parties, more or less active in the South, seek to become a political force and accede to power. With information technologies, individuals sharing the same beliefs and values are able to mobilize and attract sympathizers without regard for distances. These groups are fighting for autonomy and political independence. Their activities have been kept under control by the existing regimes. The likelihood that they will accede to power and transform these countries into religious republics is low at the moment. Northern countries, however, are leery about the rise of radical Islamism, for example.

Political Parties (Npartypow/Spartypow, Nopp/Sopp)

These stakeholders are motivated by the search for power. They influence governance by exercising legislative power and therefore play an important political role in consolidating democracy. Political parties, in power or in opposition, provide oversight and guidance and seek to recover or gain supporters and bolster their legitimacy. They demand to participate in every step of the decision-making process, and their ultimate objective is to come to power. Parties in power do not face the same constraints or have the same objectives as opposition parties, and the two are in continual conflict. In the South, opposition parties are reduced in most cases to individualities — a few well-identified opposition icons. Unlike in Northern countries, there are no organized opposition movements in Southern countries, and the party in power may be confused with the state. In my analysis of stakeholders' play, I distinguish parties in power in the South (Spartypow), parties in power in the North (Npartypow), opposition parties in the South (Sopp), and opposition parties in the North (Nopp).

To summarize, north of the Mediterranean Sea, civil society forms a dynamic, autonomous, and increasingly powerful fabric. It influences political choices and may counteract all state hegemony, including decisions by international agencies. In the South, civil society stakeholders do not form a sufficiently dense and strong fabric, and their ability to make political and social changes is limited at present. This is likely to change as awareness grows that the state does not have the capacity to assume all responsibilities (Al Sayyid Said 2004) and the democratization process becomes more active. Furthermore, the different groups making up civil society north and south of the Mediterranean Sea are attempting to form links with one another to promote an alternative model based on democracy, justice, and autonomy. Stronger connections among these different civil society stakeholders (both national and international) may help to shape the governance system in the Mediterranean region. These groupings no longer seek permission from states to deploy their solidarity strategies (Milani 2004). The rapid development of an information society in the North and, to a lesser extent, in the South will expand their role. In short, civil societies in the North and the South have different capacities for intervention, means of action, and power relations, despite a convergence in terms of their objectives.

Individuals in the North and the South (Nind/Sind)

In this chapter, the individual is considered the basic unit. Individuals have the power to react to different projects in the Mediterranean region through their right to vote, independent of whether they belong to an organized civil society group. Individuals' common objectives and interests are well-being (standard of living and quality of life), personal fulfillment and the preservation of identity (autonomy factor), and access to cultural diversity.

Expansion of trade and the lowering of customs tariffs have induced a drop in consumer prices. Individuals in both the North and the South, as consumers, have benefitted from adjustments to domestic and foreign prices and unfettered access to different goods, and their well-being will improve (over the long term, after an adjustment period) through increased purchasing power. However, the continued disengagement of the state from the social sphere and the reduction in state transfers because of globalization and opening could negatively affect the well-being of individuals, especially the most disadvantaged. Individuals in the North (Nind) are distinguished from those in the South (Sind) given their different reactions to certain issues related to Mediterranean integration and the search for autonomy. For Southern consumers who tend to "follow the leader," the greater opening makes Western consumer products and habits more accessible. The trend towards standardization of consumer behaviours through the dissemination of dominant cultural models and the propagation of Western values has been rejected by some in the South (extremist religious groups or political parties). For these

Southern communities, accelerated integration would lead to greater ease of movement for individuals despite the strengthening in the North of a diametrically opposed policy.

In the North, some communities, many of them sensitive to extreme-right ideologies, are reluctant to encourage a policy of opening towards their Southern neighbours. They are calling for stricter border controls. These communities want to preserve the benefits that they have acquired in terms of social coverage, pensions, and public services.

International Organizations (IO)

International organizations are responsible for regulating the international system, ensuring international financial stability, and monitoring countries' compliance with international standards and regulations. They advocate greater flexibility, greater liberalization, state disengagement, and a market economy. These institutions have become dominant stakeholders in the world economy. "Not only countries seeking their help but also those seeking their 'seal of approval' so that they can better access international markets must follow their economic prescriptions, prescriptions which reflect their free market ideologies and theories" (Stiglitz 2002, 18). The countries that are members of these institutions generally have power proportional to the size of their respective economies. As a consequence, the institutions are often directed and controlled by the wealthiest industrial countries (by tacit agreement, the International Monetary Fund is led by a European, while the World Bank is led by an American), which, in turn, are dominated by the interests of large commercial and financial firms. They have a level of autonomy that enables them to make the voices of societies heard and to impose limits on overspending by certain countries through international conventions, treaties, and agreements.

Among these organizations, the WTO is the globalization stakeholder par excellence. It is a virtual world government, controlling market regulation and international trade. Its fields of intervention are broadening as liberalization expands. "The WTO is in the process of stripping countries and citizens to the minimal attributes of sovereignty" (Khor 1997, 9, our translation). Its main mission is to impose harmonious commercial development that benefits everyone.

Table 16.1 Main objectives

No.	Description	Abbreviation
1	Have global influence	influ
2	Have access to technology	tech acc
3	Seek spaces for expansion, opportunities	expansion
4	Deal with threats to security	sec threat
5	Establish peace and stability in the Mediterranean region	peace stab
6	Manage migratory flows	migra flow
7	Consolidate reforms and accelerate democratization in the South	dem reform
8	Competitiveness	competitiv
9	Increase well-being, living standard and quality	wellbeing
10	Preserve identity	identity
11	Access to cultural diversity	diversity
12	Fight poverty and insecurity	pov insec
13	Strengthen globalization	glob stren
14	Westernization	westerniz
15	Maintain domestic and international macro stability	macr stab
16	Preserve national sovereignty and state supremacy	nat sov
17	Exercise power and authority	pow auth
18	Job development, growth, and creation	job grow
19	Benefit from Northern financial support	fin support
20	Attract FDI	FDI

The Stakeholders' Interactions: Interpretation of the Results of the MACTOR Method

After I identified the main issues and stakeholders involved in globalization in the Mediterranean region, I drew up a preliminary list of objectives. The definitive list of objectives (see Table 16.1) was finalized during workshops and brainstorming sessions that brought together a pluridisciplinary group of GERIM (Groupe d'études et de recherches interdisciplinaires sur la Méditerranée) researchers. The Mediterranean stakeholders were then positioned in relation to these objectives according to whether they were in favour, against, or indifferent. This enabled me to identify the key questions and objectives that will affect the future rules of the globalization game in the Mediterranean region.

The objectives may be grouped in three general areas:

- searching for and preserving autonomy (community, individual, institutional): 10, 11, 14, 16, 17
- active integration with globalization: 1, 2, 3, 4, 5, 6, 8, 13, 19, 20
- general interest and defence of universal values: 6, 7, 9, 12, 15, 18.

Assessment of the Stakeholders' Power Relations

The MACTOR method, developed by Michel Godet and introduced in 1990, is appropriate for this type of analysis on the play of stakeholders. The method seeks to visualize the alliances and conflicts among stakeholders around a group of objectives, taking their power relations into account (Hatem 1993).

Once the stakeholders were identified and presented,[4] I evaluated their power relations by measuring the capacity of each to influence each of the others. To do this, I constructed a matrix of direct influences in order to assess the influences and dependences between each couple of stakeholders. The matrix was filled by a group of multidisciplinary experts belonging to the GERIM research group using the principle of the MACTOR method.

The matrix reveals power relations. The sums of influence entered in the rows and columns show the degree of influence and the degree of dependence of each stakeholder. These results may be represented on a chart that offers a visualization of relative positions and allows a typology of the stakeholders to be made — a hierarchy of the current state of globalization in the Mediterranean region (see Figure 16.1).

This chart can be broken down into four quadrants that represent four types of stakeholders.

- *Dominant stakeholders:* situated in the northwest quadrant of the chart, these stakeholders have a strong influence but are not influenced by others. In this group are the following Northern stakeholders: opposition parties, media, elites, NGOs, parties in power, unions, and states. International organizations are also in this group.
- *Dominated stakeholders:* situated in the southeast quadrant of the chart, they are strongly influenced by the other stakeholders but exert no influence themselves. In this group are the following Southern stakeholders: NGOs, elites, businesses, opposition parties, individuals, and media. In particular, individuals in the South have an influence equal to 0 but a high level of dependence.

Figure 16.1   Influences and dependences among actors

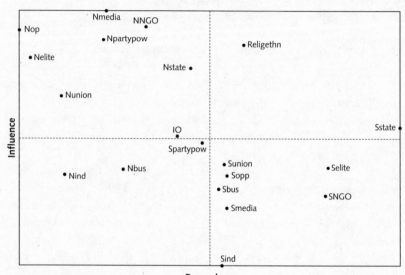

Dependence

- *Intermediary stakeholders:* situated in the northeast quadrant, they are both very influential and highly dependent. In this group are Southern states and religious and ethnic groups. They have the means to act on the system but are subjected to the influence of other stakeholders, and so they may encourage or impede the globalization process in the Mediterranean region. They should be watched closely.
- *Autonomous stakeholders:* situated in the southwest quadrant, they are both weakly influential and weakly dependent. In this group are Northern individuals and Northern businesses.

To have a synthetic idea of each stakeholder's degree of influence and dependence, I consider the parameter of power relations. This coefficient is higher when the degree of influence is high and the degree of dependence is low for a given stakeholder. When it is over 1 (the average), the stakeholder has great access to the means to take action to complete its projects and missions and expresses a strong capacity to impose its priorities.

Figure 16.2   Histogram of MIDI power relations

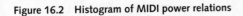

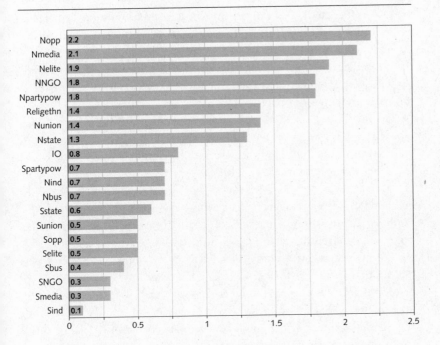

Opposition parties in the North have the strongest power relations. They have a strong capacity to impose their priorities with almost no degree of dependence. They are classified well above Northern states in terms of power relations. Because they are not constrained by responsibilities of governing and because their principal strategy is to oppose the policies of the party in power, they are often able to question the government's projects and structures. They influence the party in power's decisions and even block some of its plans. They also denounce the undemocratic practices of Southern states and criticize Northern governments' rapprochements with Southern governments in the name of democratic principles and human rights. In a democratic environment, their main courses of action are discourse, lobbying, and appealing to the electorate. The failure of the European constitution bill was a good illustration of effective opposition in the North. Opposition parties are thus key stakeholders in the evolution of globalization in the Mediterranean region because, depending on their interests, they may strengthen or block globalization in the region. The evolution of the globalization process in the Mediterranean region will depend heavily on their plans and priorities, which should be monitored closely. If a large part of the opposition in the North is against globalization, the process is at high risk for pullback. If the opposite is true, it will have every chance of advancing. For example, extreme-right parties are intractably opposed to the free circulation of people.

The media in the North also have a great capacity to influence the globalization process in the Mediterranean region. In Northern democratic systems, the media are characterized by a high degree of independence. They are organs through which the opinions of the opposition, the elites, and the parties in power express opinion. In the South, stakeholders — elites, and, incidentally, governments, parties in power, and opposition parties — are, in the absence of free and diversified media outlets, very attentive to the media in the North. Acting as outlets for Southern opposition opinion, Northern media outlets sometimes denounce the absence of democracy and the burgeoning injustice in Southern countries. They are able to reorient certain decisions to favour better governance in the South, a condition necessary for stronger globalization in the Mediterranean region. Southern governments are always careful to present to their Western allies the image of states that are, if not democratic, at least on the path to democratization. The media are also able to shape public perceptions in the North of Southern regimes and their populations negatively (or positively), and to threaten or encourage any project for rapprochement between South and North. The Northern media have a very strong capacity to influence, mainly through discourses and ideas. They activate individuals and public opinion and are capable of influencing states' decisions and guiding their choices.

In the North, the withdrawal of the state and the greater role taken by non-state stakeholders has pushed NGOs to the foreground. International agencies increasingly recognize NGOs as promoters of good governance. Through their activism, political demands, and the influence that they exert on NGOs and civil society in the South, Northern NGOs may encourage the acceleration or retardation of globalization. Most stakeholders recognize that NGOs' actions regarding major aspects of globalization will not soon weaken and thus seek to establish communication mechanisms with them. Media coverage of NGOs' actions and activism has no doubt strengthened their role. In passing, we should note the very poor ranking of Southern NGOs in terms of power relations. They are simply an appendage to the state apparatus and are stripped of any domestic influence. As a consequence, they have very little influence on the future of the Mediterranean region.

One unexpected result, however, cropped up in this analysis: religious groups hold significant power, making them more influential than Northern states. They are typically transversal, transborder stakeholders — in essence, globalized. They are growing in importance. Their main means of action are discourse, ideology, transfers and financing, lobbying and, sometimes, violence. The rapid development of an information society has expanded the role of these groups, which are very heterogeneous in their movements and priorities, ranging from a struggle against globalization, especially its cultural aspect (in the South), to propagation of Western values (in the North).

International organizations have average power relations, greater than those of Southern stakeholders but weak in the Mediterranean context and compared to Northern stakeholders. In other words, their capacity to make the rules of the game that Mediterranean stakeholders must play remains below that of Northern stakeholders. International organizations are dominated by the commercial and financial interests of Northern countries, which, actively participating in negotiations under their aegis, are able to block or advance tariff dismantlement and multilateralism. They are also capable of weakening or strengthening the multilateral system.

Southern stakeholders have unfavourable power relations with the other stakeholders and are dominated completely. This is particularly evident for Southern individuals, who are deprived of all power and means of action. It is important to note that Northern individuals have power relations that are average but clearly stronger than those of Southern individuals. In the North, individuals are active socially; although subjected to influences, they have the capacity to act on the course of events, which makes governments attentive and sensitive to their opinion. In the South, in contrast, governments do not follow and are little affected by public opinion. In the current state of affairs, Southern individuals are not yet representative agents. Their reactions are not sufficiently mediatized, and they therefore cannot be placed on the same level as Northern individuals.

Given the globalization process in the Mediterranean region and in this game, the results confirm in general the significance of Northern stakeholders, to which we must add religious groups. This is an additional indicator of the persistent domination of the North over the South. Globalization, far from attenuating this domination, seems to reinforce it. These results reflect quite well the models of governance north and south of the Mediterranean Sea. In the North, the state is sensitive to and influenced by the components of society (opposition parties, elites, NGOs, media, and so on). The governance model is characterized by a dense social fabric and shared power, within which different stakeholders express themselves and participation is the rule. In the South, where governments are authoritarian, the state dominates the workings of the economy and the population as a whole. It benefits from favourable power relations with different components of society. Independent and impervious to influences, it is the master of the domestic game. The party in power makes the rules of the political game and has comparative advantages resulting from its close relationship with the state apparatus. Despite this domestic supremacy, Southern states are seeing their importance fade in the context of globalization.

Positioning of Stakeholders on the Objectives: Identification of Key Questions for the Future of Globalization in the Mediterranean Region

The positioning matrix for stakeholders on objectives shows the degree of involvement of each stakeholder in all objectives. To make this estimate, we take the sum line by line (stakeholder by stakeholder). The most involved stakeholders — those most committed to the game and concerned with a large number of objectives — are Northern states, Southern states, international organizations, individuals in the North and the South, and parties in power in the North. In general, they are heavily engaged in the globalization process in the Mediterranean region. The least involved stakeholders are Northern elites, Southern and Northern businesses, and the Southern media (see Figure 16.3).

Figure 16.3 presents the degree of involvement of stakeholders with various objectives and shows the extent of strong and weak positions for each objective. There is consensus on most objectives and little confrontation among stakeholders. Because there is almost no opposition of interest, little conflict is possible, and so there is convergence. This result may be explained by the fact that the objectives are expressed in the

Figure 16.3   Histogram of stakeholders' involvement on 2MAO objectives, 2007

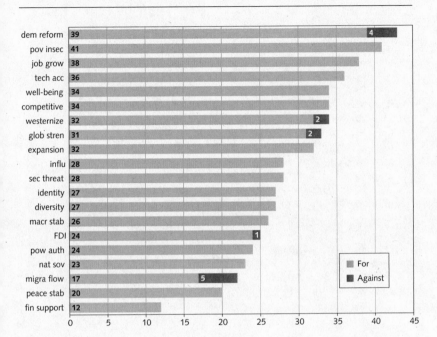

form of objectives of collective interest to which few stakeholders are opposed. The objectives of democratization, fighting poverty, development and growth, competitiveness, and access to technology and globalization concern a large number of stakeholders and would be decisive for the evolution of globalization in the Mediterranean region. The objectives of searching for financial support, peace and stability, limiting migratory flows, and preserving sovereignty involve a limited number of stakeholders.

If, in addition to the number of stakeholders concerned with each objective, we take account of their respective power relations, we can deduce the stakeholders' degree of mobilization for each objective. It is not enough that a stakeholder be concerned with or involved in one or more objectives; its means of action and the level of real power to mobilize on the different objectives must also be considered (see Figure 16.4).

The most mobilized stakeholders, those at the heart of the game (the most involved, but also with the strongest power relations) are in the

Figure 16.4   Histogram of stakeholders' mobilization on 3MAO objectives

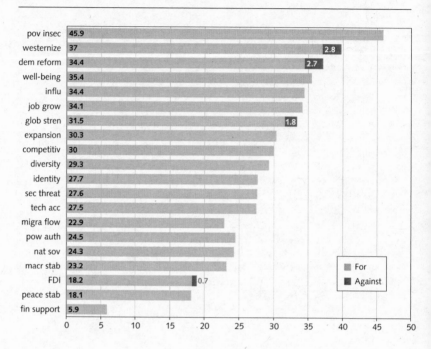

North: states, opposition parties, parties in power, NGOs, unions, international organizations, and religious groups. The least mobilized stakeholders are in the South: individuals, media, businesses, NGOs, elites, and unions. Some of these stakeholders are very involved in the game but do not have enough power; they are weakly mobilized. For example, individuals, states, and parties in power in the South, despite a high degree of involvement, are not very mobilized because they have few means and little power to act.

The objectives of fighting poverty, Westernization, democratization, and having an influence on the international scene, among others, are the most mobilizing objectives (they involve a large number of stakeholders actively) and quite consensual. The stakeholders mobilized for these objectives are in favour of them, and their commitment to realizing them is quite firm. These are key issues for the future of the Mediterranean region, and it is thus possible to imagine cooperation strategies and alliances among stakeholders aimed at reaching these objectives.

The objective related to access to technology involves mainly Southern stakeholders, which are in an unfavourable power relationship. This finding means that mobilization for this objective is weak. In contrast, the objectives of searching for financial support, peace and stability, foreign direct investment, and sovereignty have almost no mobilizing effect on the stakeholders. The stakeholders are strongly mobilized on objectives of collective interest: fighting poverty, democratization, development and growth, well-being, expansion, opening, and globalization. Northern stakeholders have inherited a strong social tradition, and their attachment to high social standards, development issues, and fighting poverty is strong.

Democratization of the South is a strongly mobilizing objective for Northern NGOs, international organizations, media, opposition parties, and states and, to a lesser extent, Southern stakeholders. These last, which often have access to neither political representation nor free expression, are not mobilized. The Northern countries have the firm conviction that their model is *the* model of reference, and a success, and they are trying to apply it. At the same time, Northern stakeholders seek to propagate and highlight Western values, cultures, and lifestyles. Moreover, Southern states that are not opposed to Westernization consider it a rampart against the threat of fundamentalist Islam. Southern stakeholders in general are not opposed to Westernization when it means access to the Western consumption model, unless it profits religious groups. In short, Westernization is a consensual and mobilizing objective.

The objective of strengthening globalization mobilizes, particularly in the North, the following stakeholders: the media, states, NGOs, parties in power, and opposition parties. This result shows that Northern stakeholders do not fear a greater opening to Southern countries; they even demand it. In comparison to Southern countries, those in the North are economically, socially, and politically advanced and want to profit fully from all of the possibilities offered by a more open Mediterranean space. The kind of globalization that worries them, rather, is that represented by powers such as the United States and the emerging Asian countries.

The objective of having influence particularly mobilizes the media, states, NGOs, elites, and parties in power in the North. These stakeholders seek to shape global events, and a broader opening in the Mediterranean can only strengthen their impact. The media are expanding their broadcasting reach and increasing their market share through this opening. For Northern states and parties in power, there is a need to deal

293

with the increasingly threatening influence in the world economy of regional groupings such as NAFTA. The strengthening of globalization in the Mediterranean region is a good response to this issue. In this regard, the free trade agreement between Morocco and the United States may be perceived by the Europeans as an American threat to their interests in the region.

Questions of identity, cultural diversity, the quest for power and authority, and sovereignty, all arising from the autonomy sphere, are relegated to the background, with an average level of mobilization. They concern only a few stakeholders, do not give rise to particular conflicts, and do not constitute key issues for the system, although they are frequently brought up. The question of identity mobilizes religious groups, in particular, and the question of sovereignty concerns states and parties in power in the North. In the Mediterranean context, loss of autonomy is not a fear for the Northern stakeholders, which are confident about the superiority of their model and know that they are dominant in the region. In contrast, they are suspicious about American and Asian models. Southern stakeholders fear a loss of autonomy but, in the absence of other prospects for sustained development and growth, they have no alternative but to accept the opening in the Mediterranean region by imitating as best they can the model of the Northern countries, even if it means, in exchange, losing autonomy.

Colonization and immigration have played a large role in the cultural integration of Southern and Northern countries. This result is therefore not really a new fact. Currently, there is growing awareness in Southern countries of the need to defend their identity and promote it to their own populations, although this need is not a battlefield or key question. Up to now, the South has profited from the cultural opening, avoiding such entrenched positions as the systematic rejection of all new cultures resulting from globalization. In Algeria, for example, some have felt that singing in French is a sign of returning to the colonizer's culture and of domination by Western culture, but this belief has not kept *ray* music from achieving popularity in the country.

The question of migratory flows mobilizes states and opposition parties in the North an average amount. For these stakeholders, the priority is to manage these flows in order to select for qualified labour rather than limiting migratory flows absolutely. The South is a reservoir of labour for an ageing North with a shrinking working-age population. Contrary to the official discourse, businesses in the North are not seeking to limit

Table 16.2 Degree of mobilization around objectives by stakeholder

BMAO	influ	tech acc	expansion	sec threat	peace stab	migra flow	dem reform	competitiv	wellbeing	identity	diversity	pov insec	glob streng	westerniz	macr stab	nat sov	pow auth	job grow	fin support	FDI	Mobilization
Nstate	4.0	2.7	4.0	5.3	4.0	4.0	2.7	2.7	4.0	1.3	2.7	4.0	4.0	5.3	4.0	4.0	4.0	4.0	0.0	2.7	69.3
Sstate	0.6	1.8	2.5	1.8	0.0	0.6	1.2	1.8	1.2	0.6	0.0	1.8	0.6	1.2	1.8	1.2	2.5	2.5	1.2	1.8	27.0
Nbus	1.3	2.0	2.0	1.3	0.0	-0.7	0.7	2.6	0.0	0.0	0.0	0.0	2.0	0.0	2.0	0.0	1.3	1.3	0.0	-0.7	17.6
Sbus	0.0	1.2	1.2	0.8	0.0	0.0	0.4	1.6	0.0	0.0	0.0	0.0	-0.4	0.0	0.4	0.0	0.0	0.8	0.8	0.8	8.4
Nopp	2.2	0.0	0.0	4.4	0.0	4.4	2.2	0.0	6.6	2.2	4.4	6.6	2.2	4.4	2.2	4.4	6.6	6.6	0.0	0.0	59.3
Sopp	0.0	0.0	0.0	0.5	0.0	0.0	2.0	0.0	1.0	1.0	0.5	1.0	0.5	0.5	0.5	1.0	1.5	1.0	0.0	0.5	11.6
Npartypow	3.6	0.0	0.0	3.6	0.0	5.4	1.8	1.8	5.4	3.6	3.6	5.4	3.6	5.4	3.6	5.4	0.0	3.6	0.0	3.6	59.7
Spartypow	0.7	2.2	0.7	1.5	0.0	0.0	-1.5	0.7	0.7	1.5	0.0	2.2	0.7	0.7	0.7	2.2	2.2	1.5	0.7	2.2	22.7
Nmedia	6.2	4.1	6.2	0.0	0.0	0.0	4.1	8.2	0.0	4.1	4.1	2.1	4.1	6.2	0.0	0.0	0.0	0.0	0.0	0.0	49.4
Smedia	0.9	0.6	0.9	0.0	0.0	0.9	0.9	0.9	0.0	0.6	0.9	0.0	0.3	0.6	0.0	0.0	0.0	0.0	0.0	0.0	6.4
Nelite	3.8	1.9	0.0	0.0	0.0	1.9	1.9	0.0	3.8	3.8	3.8	3.8	1.9	3.8	0.0	1.9	0.0	0.0	0.0	0.0	30.2
Selite	0.5	0.9	0.5	0.5	0.0	-0.5	1.8	4.2	0.9	0.9	1.4	0.5	0.9	0.9	2.8	1.4	0.5	0.5	0.0	1.4	10.4
Nunion	1.4	1.4	1.4	1.4	2.8	4.2	1.4	4.2	2.8	0.0	1.4	2.8	-1.4	0.0	1.1	0.0	0.0	2.8	0.5	1.6	34.6
Sunion	0.0	1.6	0.5	0.0	1.1	0.0	1.1	2.2	1.1	0.5	0.0	1.1	0.0	0.0	0.0	0.0	0.5	1.6	0.5	1.6	14.8
religethn	2.8	2.8	4.2	0.0	1.4	-1.4	2.8	0.0	1.4	5.7	0.0	4.2	2.8	-2.8	0.0	0.0	4.2	1.4	1.8	0.0	38.2
NNGO	3.6	0.0	3.6	1.8	3.6	1.8	5.4	0.0	1.8	0.0	3.6	5.4	3.6	3.6	0.0	0.0	0.0	0.6	1.8	0.0	41.7
SNGO	0.3	0.3	0.6	0.3	0.0	0.3	1.2	0.0	0.6	0.3	0.6	0.9	0.9	0.3	0.0	0.0	0.0	0.6	0.6	0.3	8.2
IO	2.5	1.7	2.5	2.5	2.5	0.0	2.5	2.5	1.7	0.0	0.8	2.5	2.5	2.5	2.5	2.2	1.7	2.5	0.0	1.7	35.0
Nind	0.0	2.2	0.0	2.5	2.2	0.0	1.4	0.7	2.2	1.4	1.4	1.4	0.7	1.4	1.4	2.2	0.0	1.4	0.0	1.4	26.0
Sind	0.0	0.2	0.0	0.1	0.2	-0.1	0.1	0.1	0.2	0.1	0.1	0.1	0.1	0.1	0.1	0.1	0.0	0.2	0.2	0.1	2.2
Number of agreements	34.4	27.5	30.3	27.6	18.1	22.9	34.4	30.0	35.4	27.7	29.3	45.9	31.5	37.0	23.2	24.3	24.5	34.1	5.9	18.2	
Number of disagreements	0.0	0.0	0.0	0.0	0.0	-2.6	-2.7	0.0	0.0	0.0	0.0	0.0	-1.8	-2.8	0.0	0.0	0.0	0.0	0.0	-0.7	
Degree of mobilization	34.4	27.5	30.3	27.6	18.1	25.5	37.1	30.0	35.4	27.7	29.3	45.9	33.3	39.9	23.2	24.3	24.5	34.1	5.9	18.8	

migratory flows; they are more interested in profiting from low-cost labour.

Conclusion

In this chapter, I have shown that globalization in the Mediterranean region makes as many losers as winners and that the rules of the game are largely defined by the powers of the moment. The game of stakeholders in the Mediterranean region thus reveals power relations that favour Northern stakeholders and a general convergence of interests, which point to accelerated globalization in the Mediterranean region. The dominant stakeholders in the North know that it is in their interest to have greater opening, in terms of strategic influence, areas for expansion, and prospects for growth. They are also well aware of their position of strength and their superiority in the Mediterranean region. The question of loss of autonomy does not seem to constitute a major threat to them. Southern stakeholders, for lack of a viable alternative, would be ready to negotiate, sacrificing part of their autonomy for more development and growth.

The future of globalization in the Mediterranean thus depends largely on the decisions and strategic choices of stakeholders in the North. It is under their impetus that the process will continue or stagnate since they have the leading strategic role in the region. Southern stakeholders, deprived of most power of influence, may act indirectly by making the necessary changes and reforms within their countries. They may first unite with a view to advancing reforms and preparing for a greater opening. They may also form alliances with Northern stakeholders in order to further the globalization process. A favourable economic situation in the South (advances in reforms and restructurings) and subscribing to the project of stronger globalization (and also reinforced South-South regional integration) would be necessary to involve the North and enable it to profit from geographic proximity. The prospects for strengthening globalization are still conditioned by the level of development and the strategic choices of Southern countries, for which subscribing to this movement will contribute to the achievement of common objectives.

The future of the globalization process in the Mediterranean region nevertheless remains an open question. The stakeholders may take different paths, and a number of scenarios are possible:

- Rapid globalization, with an economic and political rapprochement of the two shores under the impetus of the North, may be explored. The South, taking its model from the North, which has proved itself by its performance, will seek to catch up by aligning itself with the most productive practices on the economic level and the most democratic ones on the political level. The Southern stakeholders may opt for transition to a more effective model that is capable of capturing technological transfers, reaffirming the anchoring of their development within the Euro-Mediterranean zone. These are planned scenarios involving cooperation in regard to development poles, common policies, migratory flows, socio-cultural developments, and Southern reforms. The intervention and voluntarism of Northern stakeholders will be decisive, but changes in the South would be necessary to achieve this type of scenario.

- Globalization that is impeded or slowed by a lack of willingness by Northern stakeholders to conclude new agreements. Or globalization may be held back by Southern stakeholders that are not interested in catching up or strengthening their internal governance. On the one hand would be a North that does not seek to collaborate with the South because it is preoccupied with its internal problems and the construction of Europe; on the other, a South left to itself, enclosed within its borders, impervious to any reforms. In the long term, this positioning will lead to an identitary disengagement and anti-Western reactions that will broaden the gap between the North and the South.

chapter 17

The Challenge of Financial Globalization in Countries South of the Mediterranean Basin

Samouel Béji

THE END OF THE Cold War and the collapse of the Soviet bloc consecrated the supremacy of the "liberal" American model over communist doctrine. Classically inspired liberal ideas were propagated throughout the world in all fields, but particularly in the economic sector. For instance, governance models were standardized to be based on and support the doctrine of the sacrosanct "market economy," promoted during and after the Cold War by the proselytes of liberalism. This doctrine stipulates that the market is the only institution likely to ensure the most efficient allocation of resources. The spread of market "culture," what we call globalization today, is none other than an attempt to achieve political and economic unity in the world, to create a perfectly homogeneous entity governed by the rules of the market economy.

It was thus completely predictable that once financial systems were recognized as important in the growth process, they became prime targets for the change required by globalization. They were to be permeated with liberal directives so that they would march in lockstep to the tune of globalization. In this context, international financial institutions (IFIs) — in this case the International Monetary Fund (IMF) and the World Bank — played a preponderant role in promoting globalization and, more specifically, the ideas of liberal finance. In the late 1970s, the United States and Great Britain inspired other countries to implement reform policies based on liberalization and deregulation. These policies were applied to two key areas: the labour market and the financial system

(Plihon 2003, 24). States have seen their autonomy with regard to decision making and the formulation of appropriate public policies considerably eroded by globalization. Even developed countries have concerns, but the nature of the loss of autonomy is different in these countries than it is in developing countries.

In this chapter, I focus on how globalization is changing the operation and organization of financial systems. I explore collective and individual conceptions of autonomy and the financial and institutional characteristics of countries south of the Mediterranean Sea. I show how the apprehension of globalization differs from country to country. My goal is to understand the impact of financial globalization on the perception of autonomy, both collective and individual, for developed and developing countries.

The countries south of the Mediterranean Basin have been no exception to the globalization rule. In the late 1980s, they embarked on Structural Adjustment Programs (SAPs) under the impetus of the IFIs. Structural adjustment plans are "standard" financial policies, intended to get all developing countries on board the globalization train, which is conducted by the United States and rolls on the track of propagation of the market model. In the first part of this chapter, I examine a study on the effects of SAPs on the financial systems of all these countries in order to establish a typology of the countries concerned. In the second part, I describe the dangers that these countries must be on the lookout for in relation to loss of autonomy if they devote themselves whole-heartedly to international financial integration with no run-up or prerequisites. I give my view on the general question that this chapter asks about these countries' apprehension of financial globalization and address two other issues that are just as important: how the autonomy of developed countries has been affected by financial globalization and how their perception differs from that of developing countries, among them the countries that are the subject of this study.

Modernization of Financial Systems in Countries South of the Mediterranean Basin

Over the last two decades, the governments of countries south of the Mediterranean have engaged in programs to upgrade and restructure their financial systems. Their goal was to create the ideal conditions for expansion and development of their financial markets for more active participation and a more important role in the economy. This policy also aimed, over the long term, to liberalize the financial system completely by opening the capital account. The attempts at restructuring were conducted under the aegis of the IFIs, which made their loans and assistance conditional on compliance with the rules governing all market economies. The reforms were carried out to different degrees and with varying amplitudes. Below, I give a brief description of the levels of financial development by sector for all of the countries in the region.

Financial Deepening

Financial deepening is a technical term that designates the degree of "financialization" of the economy and provides information on the size of the financial system. In other words, it is a measure of the use of financial instruments and their diversity in an economy; the more financial savings instruments an economy has, the less hoarding there is and the more developed the financial system is considered to be. According to this criterion, Jordan benefits from a broad and "deepened" financial sector, since its rate of financialization is the highest in the region. Other countries, including Tunisia, Morocco, Egypt, and Syria, have also improved in this regard — that is, there has been increased access to services offered by the financial sector in these countries.

The Banking Financial Sector

The financial systems in the selected countries are bank-dominated. This term means that the banking systems are omnipotent in relation to capital markets in the region, although their penetration in national economies varies significantly as a function of the volume of assets in the respective banking system. For example, the share of banking assets is more than 250 percent of GDP in Lebanon, whereas it is below 50 percent of the GDP in Algeria. Lebanon is an exception in the region because it has the most highly developed banking system. Jordan has a ratio of banking assets to GDP of about 200 percent. Algeria's rate of bank penetration is the lowest in the region, and Tunisia's is still considered insufficient in relation to the country's economic potential. Although inadequate in many respects, banks finance more production in these countries than do financial markets. The new wave of financialization of the economy favours financial disintermediation, to the detriment of classic financial intermediation. In this sense, it is commendable that the IFIs' prescription calls for the banking system to act in concert with the logic of primacy of financial markets, rather than continuing to preserve its traditional mission of financial intermediation. Nevertheless, the role of banks remains preponderant in these countries. In my view, this structure provides a basis upon which the countries in the region could build more developed financial systems in their own way.

The Non-banking Financial Sector

In the 1990s, the countries south of the Mediterranean Basin began to reform their financial markets. The pace and extent of these reforms differed from country to country. The reforms affected mainly the banking sector, given the important position that this sector occupies in these countries' economies. This slow pace of reform contributed to the relatively slow development of capital markets. In fact, the financial markets in the countries concerned are generally underdeveloped and suffer from a lack of financial innovation and a narrow palette of choices of financial products. This configuration does not offer the opportunities for diversifying the risks incurred by financial investment or for efficient and optimal use of the economy's financial resources. The volume of transactions is insufficient, and bond markets are dominated by a state presence. Insurance companies, pension funds, and investment mutual funds remained limited and underdeveloped.

In the light of this study, we may build a general categorization of the countries according to their degree of financial development. Here, financial development is likened to financial opening and integration into the globalized financial sphere. The notion of financial development related to financial opening is, however, contested, since a developed financial system, according to the criteria of IFIs and international lenders, is a system that has totally liberalized its capital account, and in which access to banking and financial markets is free to non-residents. This perception of financial development is erroneous, even unfair. It does not take account of the specificities of countries and of the political and institutional contexts in which they are situated. For example, the countries under analysis have among the highest savings rates.[1] Why would these countries be interested in opening their financial systems to foreign participation unless it is to provoke an influx of short-term speculative funds seeking to profit from the differential in interest rates, which will cause instability in securities prices and fluctuations that generate crises?

I have established a classification of countries according to the state of development and modernization of their financial systems on the basis of previous analyses (see Table 17.1). There are a number of explanations for the specific nature of the financial systems in the region. Political and economic instability, caused partially by the difficult security situation in the region, is one of the most important reasons. These risks are illustrated by the low sovereign risk rating (the risk that a country will refuse to meet its financial obligations) assigned to countries in the region.

Other relevant factors also reveal the reality of the region's financial systems. The slow development of the financial and banking sectors is partly attributable to the existence of other sources of financing for the economy. For example, for several countries (Algeria and Libya, notably) revenues from exports of oil and natural gas have limited the development of the banking sector, since these revenues constitute the main sources of economic-development financing in these countries.

The quality of bank and business governance is another important explanatory factor for the development level of financial systems in the region. Experts with the IMF believe that state interventionism and a lack of competition not only do not encourage banking innovations but also limit the aptitude of the financial system to find and fund the best investment opportunities. A weak judicial apparatus makes it difficult to strengthen the rights of creditors, and this weakness discourages bank financing, since bankers cannot use statutory means to bring lawsuits against insolvent clients. Regulation and oversight of the banking sector in the region have not risen to international standards, leading to increased risk to savers in terms of bank quality and performance.

Although the quality of the judicial and legal apparatus is considered to be adequate and relevant, the negative view of state interventionism

Table 17.1 Ranking of countries according to development of the financial system

High level	Medium level	Low level
Israel	Algeria	Libya
Jordan	Egypt	Syria
	Morocco	
Lebanon	Tunisia	
	Turkey	

must be tempered in the operation of banks, especially in the countries under consideration. Recourse to market mechanisms alone does not ensure the most efficient allocation of financial resources in these countries, where market imperfections are caused by an institutional and legal shortfall that engenders a lack of transparency, which is needed for proper operation of markets. State intervention is therefore legitimate in these instances; furthermore, at the beginning of a development process, the state must protect existing systems in order to better oversee banks and financial markets and ensure that they operate properly. We can look back at many European countries (such as France and Italy) that followed this plan from the end of the Second World War up to the 1970s. This strategy ultimately proved to be profitable, since countries such as France achieved economic performances unequalled from then to the present, owing to the protection of their financial systems.

For my study on the evolution and trends of financial systems in the region, I used a technical tool known as the Feldstein-Horioka test[2] to measure the degree of integration of the countries' financial systems into the financial globalization of countries in the region. The test is used to analyze the relationship between investment and domestic savings for a group of countries by calculating the proportion of investment coming from domestic savings. If this proportion is very high (tending towards 1), it means that the financial system is hermetic and that investments are financed only by citizens' accumulated savings. If, however, this proportion is low (tending towards 0), it means that investments receive little financing from domestic savings and a large proportion from foreign savings. These savings can be captured only if the financial system is open and turned outwards.

The results of this study confirm the observation on the situation of the region's countries' financial systems. Using a sample of twenty-one countries, including the group of countries south of the basin and other industrialized countries that are very active on international financial markets (the United States, France, Japan, Great Britain, and others), I found that, overall, domestic savings contributed to 60 percent of investments. In addition, taking into consideration only countries other than Southern countries — that is, only industrialized countries — I found that the proportion drops to 45 percent. This finding means that, in those countries, only 45 percent of investments are financed by domestic savings, while the rest is financed by foreign investors participating in their financial markets. We may therefore surmise that the countries south of the Mediterranean Basin have financial markets that are not open enough to foreign operators, and that they have some reluctance, if not fear, about opening their markets. It also means that indirect financing via financial markets is not as widespread as in industrialized countries. This difference goes hand in hand with the results of the above analysis of the development of the different segments of financial systems.

Again, this result attests not to a delay in development of financial systems but to a rather legitimate prudence. One of the drawbacks of this type of test is that it gives a snapshot of the situation but does not take account of the possible gradual progress towards the opening of financial markets. It is completely normal that the countries under consideration are not as open as developed countries, given that most of them are following a gradual path to opening.

Financial Globalization and the Risk of Loss of Autonomy

Financialization of the economy is supported by a rise in the decision-making power of markets. As we know, the Washington Consensus is based mainly on the idea that the state's power to intervene in economic operations must be as limited as possible. This power is to be given to the markets, which will ensure the best possible operation of the economy, given its resources. This vision of economic organization offers markets considerable margin of manoeuvre, to the detriment of that of governments. Some authors think that the ransom of financial globalization is in fact the relative impotence of governments to react to the caprices and mood swings of markets in general, and financial markets in particular, owing to the growing financialization of the economy. The state suffers the loss of collective autonomy, whereas individual autonomy, characterized by markets and the main actors on these markets, profits. The field of possible public choices is clearly limited, to the point that there may now be a certain "tyranny of financial markets" (Bourguinat 1995, 49, our translation). These new constraints take two forms: self-fulfilling crises and loss of autonomous public policies.

Self-Fulfilling Crises

Unlike crises in fundamentals, which are linked to imbalances and maladjustments inherent to the real economy, self-fulfilling crises are the product of hedges made by a certain number of stakeholders. These hedges cause the market to follow certain trends rather than others, leading to crises that provoke instability. One example of crises in fundamentals are those caused by trade imbalances, which often pose serious political and moral challenges. One form of self-fulfilling crisis is caused by a huge supply of hedge funds, the circulation of which is facilitated by international financial deregulation and is likely to trigger a fortuitous crisis. When the actors in a market know in advance that by continuing to adopt a particular attitude they will move the exchange rate in the direction that they want so that they can make a profit, a crisis may occur. In effect, increased density of speculative behaviours and higher amounts put into play would lead to market "tyranny" and keep the authorities from impeding hedges (Bourguinat 1995, 53). Regulatory institutions will be forced to follow the market trends imposed by the play of actors (or, rather, speculators) without being able to interfere and thus find themselves prisoners of the game of market rules.

The Loss of Autonomy of Public Policies

The growth in supply of funds and the mobility of portfolios have had a direct impact on the effectiveness of monetary and budgetary policies. It is obvious that financial globalization has affected the autonomy of formulating monetary policy because it is more and more difficult to distinguish financial assets from monetary assets, if we take account of the criterion of liquidity. Traditionally, monetary institutions targeted monetary aggregates as a way to control liquidity to meet the needs of the economy — to avoid either inflation or insufficient liquidity to "lubricate" transactions. With deregulation, which facilitates mobility of portfolios, financial assets have become more and more liquid, which makes the task of monetary authorities more difficult when they want to implement their own policies as a function of the economy's needs.

It must be mentioned that international financial deregulation has the merit of relaxing budgetary constraints. This outcome is far from detrimental during economic recessions, which are characterized by a deterioration in budgetary resources. Nevertheless, national interest rate hikes have a weak effect on domestic indebtedness when agents have the possibility of replacing domestic assets with foreign assets, which occurs when financial markets are strongly integrated.

This analysis shows that, just like businesses, states are subjected to the logic of financial globalization, which, moreover, provokes competition among governments for access to financing. This increased competition creates potential bargains for international high-finance stakeholders such as institutional investors (pension funds, mutual funds, and insurance companies), which can impose their will on governments as they have already done on businesses. The crises in the European monetary system in 1993 and in emerging countries during the 1990s (Argentina, Brazil, Mexico, South Korea, and others) showed that governments do not have the means to withstand a lack of confidence in the credibility of their policies. This weakness illustrates governments' loss of autonomy in the context of globalized finance. Fiscal policies have also become more difficult to implement as, under the impetus of financial globalization, taxpayers and businesses find more opportunities and possibilities for refraining from paying taxes, thus lowering their tax burden.

The problems posed by fluctuations of capital and the loss of autonomy in formulating macroeconomic policies are more serious for Southern than for Northern countries. The debt crisis in the early 1980s and the subsequent loss of political autonomy are an illustration of the catastrophic consequences of fluctuations in capital flows. The power of international financial markets to undermine the political autonomy of Southern governments was illustrated dramatically by the crisis in the Mexican peso in 1994, attributable to the loss of investor confidence in international financial markets (Helleiner 1999, 145).

Some authors have noted that as soon as governments' authority and autonomy decline, new non-state entities emerge and take over financial markets by substituting themselves for governments. Sinclair (1994, 462) shows that security-rating agencies have "new" power to determine the objectives of macroeconomic policies. In his view, these agencies demonstrate the increased influence of what he calls "sovereignty-free actors" in the formulation of policies and the erosion of the traditional political order. Thomas Friedman developed the same point of view with regard to Moody's Investors Services, which, in his opinion, caused the crisis in the Mexican peso by under-quoting Mexican bonds and public debt securities: "You could almost say that we live again in a two-superpower world. There is the US and there is Moody's. The US can destroy a country by leveling it with bombs. Moody's can destroy a country by downgrading its bonds" (quoted in Helleiner 1999, 146).

The Nature of the Loss of Autonomy in Developed Countries

One might gather from the above analysis that developed countries (those of the European Union and North America, notably) have a fairly ambiguous relationship with financial globalization. On the one hand, they sacrifice their collective autonomy, which is state autonomy and the symbol of national sovereignty, to individual autonomy. On the other hand, the individual autonomy gained by multinational firms broadens states' margin of manoeuvre to seek financing on integrated international financial markets and to define in this light which public strategies and economic policies to pursue. It is a situation in which power is being transferred from the state to firms, which indirectly dictate the steps that the state will take. In developed countries, the state is confronted with a double loss of autonomy. The first is caused by its integration into the financial globalization movement and its corollary of loss of collective autonomy in relation to the ability to formulate adequate economic policies. The second is caused as collective autonomy is replaced by the individual autonomy of large international firms, which dictate, via sometimes illicit connections, the steps that the state will take.

Loss of Autonomy in the Mediterranean Countries

The results of the Feldstein-Horioka test show that a large share of the domestic investment of southern Mediterranean countries (60 percent) is explained by domestic savings, which attests to relative financial closing in relation to international capital flows. But does this explanation mean that there is a gap to be made up or delayed financial development? Certainly not. If we compare the situation of developed countries with that of southern Mediterranean countries, we find that the former have sacrificed, to a certain extent, their decision-making autonomy to the profit of private entities that are multinational firms. This approach is not the case in the southern Mediterranean region, where governments are interested in not ceding collective autonomy to individual autonomy for two reasons. The first is that they do not have adequate economic structures to both deal with and become integrated with financial globalization. These countries do not have economic entities that are large and solid enough — resembling European multinationals — to take advantage of an eventual concession of collective autonomy to individual autonomy. The second is of a political and institutional order, since the inadequacy of the legal and institutional environment in the countries deprives them of the possibility of becoming financially integrated without incurring a real risk of crisis (Béji 2007). To benefit from the opening and liberalization of financial transactions among countries, financial systems must be strengthened by a sufficiently developed legal and institutional infrastructure. Specifically, economies that do not have a legal system that guarantees property rights or the application of contracts between entities entering a financial agreement suffer in general from a weak incentive to make loans and establish financial transactions.

Conclusion

The idea of using autonomy to ward off the globalization movement is different in developed countries than in developing countries. For the former, the collective autonomy defended by states has given way to individual autonomy for large firms. These firms' relationships with financial globalization are not unambiguous, since they are economic entities that are both subjected to its influence and condition its functioning. Developed countries must determine whether it is to their advantage to renounce part of their collective autonomy so that multinational firms may benefit from increased individual autonomy. For the countries south of the Mediterranean Basin, the problem is a different one. Since these countries do not have to arbitrate between collective and individual autonomy, they have to determine how long they will continue to protect their collective autonomy.

Appendix: The Feldstein-Horioka Test

The test consists of studying the relationship between domestic savings and domestic investment. This relationship has been used to measure international capital mobility.

$$\frac{I}{Y} = \alpha + \beta \, \frac{S}{Y} + \varepsilon$$

With: I = domestic investment; Y = GDP, S = national savings

Estimates by generalized least squares (GLS) for all countries:

Coefficients: GLS

Panels: heteroscedastic

Correlation: No autocorrelation

Estimated covariances: 19	Number of observations: 401
Estimated autocorrelations: 0	Number of groups: 19
Estimated coefficients: 2	Observations per group: Minimum: 4
	Average: 21.10526
	Maximum: 23

Log likelihood: 980,1594   Wald chi2(1): 628.43

Prob > chi2 : 0.0000

Investment	Coefficient	Std. error	Z	P>Z	[95% conf. interval]	
Savings	0.6074386	.0242311	25.07	0.000	.5599466	0.6549307
Constant	9.384461	.5396359	17.39	0.000	.8326794	10.44213

Estimate in panel data (countries other than Southern Mediterranean countries):

Fixed effects, regression (within)

R^2: within: 0.3505	Number of observations: 225
between: 0.7667	Number of groups: 10
overall: 0.6221	Observations per group: Minimum: 21
	Average: 22.5
	Maximum: 23

corr (u_i, Xb): 0.3769 $F(1,214)$: 115.49

Prob > F: 0.0000

Investment	Coefficient	Std. error	t	P>t	[95% conf. interval]	
Savings	0.459993	.0428035	10.75	0.000	0.3756226	0.5443634
Constant	11.98655	.8971286	13.36	0.000	10.2182100	13.7548900

sigma_u: 1.6082326

sigma_e: 1.6408211

rho: 0.48997085 (fraction of variance due to u_i)

F test that all $u\_i = 0$: $F(9,214) = 18.10$

Prob > $F = 0.0000$

The countries studied:

Developed countries: Belgium, Canada, France, Germany, Great Britain, Italy, Japan, Portugal, Spain, United States.

Southern Mediterranean countries: Algeria, Egypt, Israel, Jordan, Lebanon, Libya, Morocco, Syria, Tunisia, Turkey.

chapter 18 **Industrial Policy in the Mediterranean Region and Capacities for Autonomy in a Context of Globalization**

Jihen Malek

GLOBALIZATION HAS RELAUNCHED THE debate on the relevance of industrial policy. On the one hand, the international economic context in the industrial sector is in a state of constant change under the influence of globalization processes, which is creating regional blocs, new emerging countries, trade-liberalization agreements, the dismantlement of preferential accords, ecological threats, and many other factors that states must face. On the other hand, it has become more and more difficult for governments to define and apply measures to stakeholders whose activities are no longer circumscribed by national territories, and whose industrial systems are increasingly integrated with the world economy. In the Mediterranean region, factors that have weighed heavily on the dynamic of the Euro-Mediterranean process include the expansion of the European Union, the persistence of regional conflicts, the creation and strengthening of the World Trade Organization, and a greater opening to world trade by China, a country that now provides the greatest competition for Mediterranean industries in their main market, Europe.

Up to the mid-1990s, nation-states, particularly in the Mediterranean region, used industrial policy for economic and social regulation. They were able to intervene in and administer markets in ways that served their respective purposes. The only limitations were the intrinsic efficiency and the means of financing such policies. Starting in the mid-1990s, international commitments required these states to renounce, more or less rapidly, a number of the instruments at the core of the industrial policies that enabled them to make differential allocations of resources on a sector-by-sector basis.

My objective in this chapter is to describe how globalization has changed states' industrial policies and practices and reduced their collective autonomy. I also describe how industrial policies have been rethought in ways that give states new ways to orient their economies, thus restoring some of their autonomy, or granting them a new form of autonomy. The chapter is in two parts. In the first part, I analyze the evolution of the concept and content of industrial policy under the sway of globalization by comparing two types of industrial policy: "direct" policy, compatible with the pre-globalization period, and "indirect" policy, compatible with globalization. In the second part, I analyze the industrial policies undertaken by a sample of Mediterranean countries.

The Content of Industrial Policy and Globalization

Government interventions in industry developed at different rates and under different conditions in various countries. Yves Morvan (1983, 20, our translation) proposes one of the most general definitions of industrial policy, which encompasses the widest possible range of modalities and implications: "A group of decisions affecting the overall conditions under which agents conduct their activities; the objective is better distribution of factors and regulation of changes in profit rates." Such decisions target objectives and mobilize instruments, the two elements that define the content and categories of industrial policy.

Of course, the objectives of industrial policy vary depending on different countries' situations, problems, and needs, which are, in turn, affected by structural and situational changes. Nevertheless, it is possible to summarize in general terms the objectives that have prevailed during the periods before and after globalization. Globalization accelerated in the mid-1990s with the advent of the World Trade Organization, though its first signs appeared before that decade. For convenience, I will place the point of separation between the two periods at the beginning of the 1990s. In the years immediately following the Second World War, the needs and constraints of reconstruction in war-torn countries gave priority to objectives such as creating infrastructure and protecting national industry. Later, with the liberalization of trade and capital movements, growing interpenetration of markets, and acceleration of technological innovations, more and more structural adaptations were encouraged to favour technological innovation and restructuring of the entire industrial sector.

During both periods, industrial policy provided a framework generally favourable to industrial firms by directing both the relative share of various branches of industrial activity and the technological choices of various producers. Policy makers sought to strengthen the effectiveness of the entire production system. At the same time, these policies tried to respond to concerns about making the adaptations gradual, taking into account both regional balance and geographic fit in given locations, while limiting national dependence on foreign countries. These kinds of trade-offs are inevitable in the industrial development sector. To accomplish all of these tasks, industrial policy used a wide range of instruments.

There are many typologies of industrial policies. I borrow a distinction used by a number of authors, including Morvan (1983), Brousseau (1995), and Cohen and Lorenzi (2000), that differentiates between direct and indirect industrial policy measures. Indeed, the globalization process has thrown into question the possibilities for recourse to direct and targeted industrial policy measures: grants, takeovers, specific protectionist barriers, public commissions, and other measures that refer to industrial nationalization, the management of public utilities, sector-based restructuring policies, and certain aspects of regulatory policy. These have become less and less easy to apply, leaving room for only a few traditional measures: monetary and trade environment policies, energy and infrastructure policies, policies favouring small- and medium-sized enterprises, and policies regarding public markets.

Industrial policies are increasingly tending to converge across countries in response to economic globalization. Global industry is going through a wave of profound changes linked to the technological revolution in electronics and computers, cultural developments in corporate organization, and changes in consumer needs. Furthermore, competition from Asia is growing, and economic cycles have ever-wider swings. All of these changes are occurring simultaneously with a movement towards liberalism and the dismantlement of anti-competition mechanisms, materialized by the creation of free trade zones, integrated economic spaces, deregulation, and other factors.

Thus, there is a trend towards indirect environmental measures (taxes, territorial development, and so on) that may be targeted to specific areas (research and development assistance, competition regulation, and so on). These measures are related essentially to policies for control of technological systems and innovation capacities; to policies related to knowledge development, skills, and learning capacities; and to policies guaranteeing international representation of national industrial interests.

Having discussed the question of industrial policy, how it is changing and how it is being questioned in the context of globalization, a distinction can be established between measures taken during the pre-globalization period and those taken post-globalization. Table 18.1 summarizes the differences in the content of industrial policies in terms of instruments used in each of the two periods. The table uses as sources different reports by the Organisation for Economic Co-operation and Development (OECD) concerning industrial practices.

Beyond the distinction between direct and indirect measures, these measures represent the different forms that industrial policy instruments take. The main ones are fiscal (fiscal benefits and incentives), financial (financing and credit), administrative (the creation of state agencies, organizations, and institutions, or industrial promotion funds), contractual (plans, programs, and agreements established between the state and

Table 18.1 Content of industrial policies, pre-globalization and post-globalization

Industrial policy measures	
Pre-globalization	Post-globalization
Measures supporting public corporations, public markets, and nationalized firms	Deregulation measures and competition policies (privatization and others)
Sectoral measures	Measures supporting public R&D
Measures supporting infrastructure	Measures supporting public-private collaboration and technology-distribution networks: corporate–university–public research agency
Measures supporting education and training	
Measures supporting physical investment	Measures supporting sectoral innovation networks
Measures concerning regional development	Measures supporting research and development and innovation in SMEs
Measures to promote exports	
Measures supporting international investments	Measures supporting regional innovation
Measures supporting SMEs	Measures supporting innovative technological firms and innovation in the private sector
Environmental-protection and energy measures	Measures supporting science and technology human resources
Services-supply measures	Measures to attract FDI
	Institutional measures

certain sectors, or between the state and firms), and substitution (the state substitutes itself for private firms in the industrial sector). Another line of demarcation between the two models is the transition from industrial to technological policy. I discuss this aspect in my review of the experiences of a sample of Mediterranean countries, which shows the changes in instruments country by country and from period to period.

Industrial Policies and Autonomy

Industrial policy is subjected to the realities of the national economy. It is formulated within a system of constraints and exposed to different random events, which influence the strategic choices and means used to apply the policy. Being able to describe the industrial policy instruments of certain countries is thus of great interest. The sample of countries studied in this chapter is composed of France and Spain, countries belonging to the European Union, and Tunisia, a developing country. Although this analysis is not historical in nature, it involves some detours into the past for a better understanding of the choices made during the pre- and post-globalization periods. It is difficult to give a precise date for the change of period, as there was no obvious transition to globalization common to all countries in the sample. However, the changes related to globalization that had the most significant effect on industrial policies took place in the 1990s: the emergence of a number of new technologies, liberalization of trade, and institutional collaborations.

Adopting the definition of autonomy given by De Bandt (1983, 40, our translation), the "degree of freedom available to the government to define an industrial policy," we may examine the degree of autonomy of industrial policy in a sample of Mediterranean countries. Within the framework of globalization, how was a new form of autonomy created by making a transition from an industrial policy to a technological policy?

France and Spain

In France, a number of industrial policy phases have succeeded one another since 1945, with each corresponding to a specific strategy for strengthening the productive system. During the period 1945-65, French industrial policy was aimed at ensuring reconstruction, then expansion, supported by public corporations and a few private groups working in basic industry. In the 1960s and 1970s, industrial policy was character-ized by the implementation of major technological programs and a policy of concentration, mergers, and restructuring aimed at creating national champions. A major change took place in the 1980s and early 1990s, when industrial policy was shifted towards encouraging and promoting innovation, research and development, assistance to small- and medium-sized enterprises (SMEs), and alignment with European Community legislation.

Better distribution of technological innovations in the production system, assistance to innovative firms, and the promotion of SMEs were the new industrial policy orientations in the 1990s. Then, in the 2000s, French industrial policy turned mainly to supporting research and de-velopment and corporate innovation and the promotion of science and technology human resources by increasing the number of scientists and researchers, reforming universities and public research agencies, imple-menting measures to encourage entrepreneurship and growth of SMEs, and developing technological cooperation and dissemination networks.

In Spain, the orientation of industrial policy in the 1940s and 1950s was determined by the need to reconstruct the economy and protect national production. Then, in the 1960s, measures were formulated to encourage modernization of industry, improvement of infrastructure, gradual trade liberalization, foreign investment, mergers and concentra-tions, regional development, plans and programs for basic sectors, and development and modernization of SMEs. In the 1970s, incentives were given for deepening concentrations, mergers, and partnerships. Measures and special programs in specific sectors (energy, metallurgy, capital goods, transportation equipment, chemical industry) were applied. The presence of public corporations, encouragement of foreign investment, and promotion of an industrial policy for regional development were also part of the Spanish industrial policy. At the same time, measures aiming to develop vocational training in industry were implemented, as were a research and development policy to promote industrial expansion and an anti-pollution policy.

In the 1990s, industrial policy measures were aimed at accelerating the alignment of the Spanish economy with that of the most advanced European partners. An industrial strategy was established to stimulate competitiveness; this strategy involved strengthening traditional indus-trial sectors and restructuring public corporations so that they could function in compliance with market criteria. Stimulus packages for business services were applied to strengthen productivity and product differentiation and to promote better industrial design, especially among SMEs. Improvements to the technological infrastructure, the development and dissemination of new production technologies, the encouragement of economies of scale, and the internationalization of Spanish firms through expansion or cooperation agreements were priorities during this period. Finally, improved technical and management training and the establishment of statutes and measures in the areas of industrial promotion, safety, and quality were important parts of the industrial policy.

In the early 2000s, Spanish industrial policy aimed to develop the corporate science and technology system, improve the competitiveness of firms, and focus action on citizen services. There were also concerns with social welfare; with the creation of knowledge through public research and development expenditures oriented towards information and communications technologies, biotechnologies, and nanotechnologies; with incentives for strengthening cooperation among firms, universities, and other public research agencies; with reinforcement of research in public research agencies and with university reforms; and with support for corporate research and development and innovation. Finally, scientific and technological human resources were promoted through a strategy of developing scientific and technical personnel and encouraging research and development and innovation in the private sector.

Although clear differences exist between France and Spain in terms of industrial policy, there is growing convergence regarding a certain number of measures around various forms of technological policies. Since 1945, and despite what seem to be similarities at first glance, the two countries have faced different challenges and taken different paths, which only now are beginning to converge.

Tunisia

The Tunisian state began to implement industrial policies when it became independent in 1956. The first concern was to build basic industrial channels and national companies and to develop several basic industries. Then, during the 1970s and 1980s, as private initiatives were stimulated and exporting industries and extra-territorial industrialization were developed, new institutions were created to promote the industrial sector, education, skill building, and foreign direct investment. In the 1990s, Tunisian industrial policy was marked by the privatization of state corporations. Measures were adopted concerning investment in high technology and industries with an exporting vocation, assisting SMEs, promoting exports, encouraging training and education, and attracting foreign direct investment. Although little attention was paid during the first decades following independence, scientific research evolved significantly after the early 1990s with the creation of technology parks and new industrial zones, the upgrading of firms, and the setting up of business incubators.

In the 2000s, industrial policy was based on encouraging applied research, the promotion of research and innovation, and the creation of businesses. An attempt was made to strengthen the partnership between the research sector and industrial firms, develop information and communications technologies, encourage public investment in infrastructure and scientific facilities, and assist innovating firms in agrofood, textiles, and clothing. In an attempt to make the best of globalization, Tunisia deployed considerable efforts to develop the organizational and institutional infrastructure of the research and development sector and to improve incentives for technological investments.

Changes in Industrial Policy to Preserve Autonomy

Table 18.2 summarizes the measures that the countries studied used during the pre- and post-globalization periods. (For countries south of the Mediterranean Sea, the comparison is limited to Tunisia because of the availability of data.) This comparison confirms what has been stated above. The transition from the pre-globalization period to the post-globalization period is marked by a change in the content of industrial policies in two essential ways: first, the renunciation of direct measures; second, the use of measures to support technological development.

Conclusion

The above analysis and the synthetic table that summarizes it clearly show the transition from industrial policies that characterized pre-globalization to policies targeting technology and research and development in the post-globalization period. With the liberalization of trade and capital movements, growing interpenetration of markets,

Table 18.2 Changes to the content of industrial policies

Measure	Pre-globalization			Post-globalization		
	France	Spain	Tunisia	France	Spain	Tunisia
Measures supporting public corporations, public markets, and nationalized firms	X	X	X			
Sectorial measures	X	X	X			
Measures supporting infrastructure	X	X	X			
Measures supporting education and training	X	X	X			
Measures supporting physical investment	X	X				X
Measures concerning regional development	X	X				X
Measures to promote exports	X	X	X			
Measures supporting international investments	X	X				
Measures supporting the creation of SMEs	X	X				X
Deregulation measures and competition policies	X	X				X
Environmental-protection and energy measures	X	X		X	X	X
Services-supply measures	X	X				X
Measures supporting public R&D	X			X	X	X
Measures supporting public-private collaboration and technology-distribution networks: corporate–university–public research agency	X	X				
Measures supporting sectorial innovation networks				X	X	
Measures to stimulate R&D and innovation in SMEs				X	X	X
Measures supporting regional innovation	X				X	X
Measures supporting innovative technological firms and innovation in the private sector				X	X	
Measures supporting science and technology human resources				X	X	X
Measures to attract FDI		X	X	X		X
Institutional measures	X	X	X	X	X	X

Note: "X" in a cell indicates that the measure concerned was put into practice in the corresponding country for the period.

acceleration of technological innovations, and other phenomena accompanying rapid growth, a different policy framework appeared. All measures, in both the North and the South, targeted research and development and technological innovation. A number of countries set explicit objectives for public research and development expenditures that evidenced the growing awareness of links between research and development and innovation and economic growth, as well as more concerted efforts to have scientific and technical policy serve economic goals. In many countries, interactions between public research agencies and the private sector underwent major reforms. Most countries sought to strengthen relations between science and industry by encouraging technological transfers between public research entities and the private sector. Emphasis was also placed on supporting corporate research and development and innovation through indirect financing by replacing grants and direct loans with upgrades to the educational system so that it could respond to the needs of the economic system. Skill development became integral to maintaining the educational system as a link between innovation policy and employment policy.

This situation means that the question of autonomy is posed in a new light and does not have the same significance as it did during the pre-globalization period. Globalization has challenged only some of the so-called traditional forms of public action and has created, on the other hand, new measures to complement this process. The development of measures to promote a knowledge economy, influenced by changes in the source of corporate competitiveness and nations' competitive advantages, shows the imperative of new industrial policies. As Table 18.2 shows, different countries have shifted traditional industrial policies towards technological policies that recognize the key role of innovation. In fact, this development is noted in OECD studies that emphasize the point at which industrial policies are called upon to change, under competitive conditions and with a new distribution of stakeholders.

In the post-globalization context, industrial policies are encouraging a new kind of autonomy. Measures include better quality of public research and education (increase in and reorientation of public research and development expenditures, reforms of universities and public research agencies, development of cooperation among public research agencies); promotion of research and development and business innovation in the private sector (protection of intellectual property, promotion of entrepreneurship); strengthening of cooperation and networking among innovation organizations (improved quality of interaction among firms, research institutions, and governmental agencies; growth in inter-sector mobility, development of clusters and of regional innovation); and the stimulation of science and technology human resources (growth in numbers of engineers and scientists, training of knowledge workers).

Globalization has partially challenged the autonomy built by trad-itional industrial policies, which must not only adapt to the new context but also anticipate changes that are driving major transformations in the extent and form of autonomy. Furthermore, a new industrial develop-ment agenda for the Mediterranean Basin is emerging: the Northern countries are investing more and more in high-value-added activities, with active innovation policies. The Southern countries would like a policy of technological catch-up. As a consequence, a gap is forming between Northern and Southern countries, and simple technological transfers are less and less easy, as Southern countries need to increase specific skills and technologies.

Although each country has a different industrial policy, all are facing the same challenge: an in-depth recasting of industrial policy measures in favour of technological policy. We may therefore say that globaliza-tion has disrupted industrial policies by depriving them of direct inter-vention measures, essentially because of international agreements that govern integration into extra-national economic markets. However, countries have not given up their industrial policies. On the contrary, industrial policy has been reconstructed around a new axis: technological development. Thus, states have tried to preserve a form of autonomy in relation to the effects of the international market. Northern countries changed more rapidly and earlier than did Southern countries, which have taken the same path but belatedly, while trying to let go of trad-itional policies only gradually. Beyond these differences, globalization is in the process of standardizing not only the operating procedures of the trade zone but also the means of regulating it and specifying the auton-omy of participating countries.

Thus, globalization imposes neither passive subjection to, nor simple withdrawal from, industrial policies; rather, these policies must be up-dated and redeployed to create the conditions for an effective techno-logical policy capable of controlling the effects of globalization. The transition from direct to indirect intervention reduces the possibilities for using industrial policy to regulate employment and incomes and, thus, social transfers. These will no longer be possible except through direct transfers by social funds and grants. The transition to taking action regarding technology, instead of industrial structure, is forcing states and populations to subscribe to a competitive model, with all of its consequences for standards in the labour market.

chapter 19

The South Mediterranean Countries and Economic Opening: The State of Affairs

Nizard Jouini

IN THIS CHAPTER, I address the following questions: What have South Mediterranean countries accomplished on the institutional level to consolidate their economic partnership with North Mediterranean countries? Is there interdependence between South Mediterranean countries and the rest of the world, and if there is, to what degree? What is the new situation in terms of convergence between less and more advanced economies? What are the interactions between regional integration in the Mediterranean and the overarching process of globalization? What is the impact on individual and collective autonomy in South Mediterranean countries?

The term *globalization* is defined here as the growth of trade and exchange in an open international economic system that is integrated and borderless. This definition corresponds to what has been observed in recent decades: remarkable growth in trade and exchange, which has affected traditional international trade in goods and services, currency swaps, capital movements, technological transfers, and international migrations and flows of information and ideas.

Developing countries' participation in world production continues to grow. The major challenge for these countries has been to take advantage of the new global system to achieve sustained growth and reach convergence with more advanced countries. Many developing countries have chosen a gradual approach to adapting to the new order imposed by globalization. These countries aim for regional integration, which they see as facilitating their insertion into the world economy. The Euro-Mediterranean Partnership project (formerly known as the Barcelona Process) takes into consideration two other aspects in addition to, and as important as, the economic: the political and the social aspects. The project also affords an opportunity to establish civil society participation. This policy does not have an impact north of the Mediterranean Sea, where civil society has existed for a long time. In contrast, for civil societies in the South, the project is important to the development of associations at both the local and international levels. Exchanges of ideas, financing, networking capacity, and the creation of political spaces are the factors on which civil societies in the South are counting the most. The question of civil society is thus linked to that of economic integration.

In the first section of this chapter, I describe the evolution of the institutional framework allowing for integration into the global market. The second section deals with levels of interdependence and an analysis of convergence between the less and more advanced countries in the region. In the third section, I explore the relationship between integration (using the Barcelona Process as an example) and development of civil society in the Mediterranean region. Finally, I offer some conclusions.

Integration through the Institutional Framework

The South Mediterranean countries tend to integrate regionally in order to achieve global-level integration. Indeed, these countries are weaving a fabric of agreements facilitating North-South integration, South-South integration, and integration between Southern countries and the rest of the world. However, the Euro-Mediterranean Partnership is the most important agreement in terms of trade and the one on which the Southern countries are counting the most to catch up to the more advanced countries.

North-South Integration: The Barcelona Process

The Barcelona Process resulted in cooperation agreements among all Mediterranean region countries and was aimed at creating a free trade zone in the region by 2010. The Euro-Mediterranean Partnership is intended to provoke changes within the institutional apparatuses that regulate economic and social life in these countries with the goal of integrating them into the global market.

Development in Southern countries was an effect of the unilateral opening of the European Union (EU) market to exports of several products manufactured by third countries. For instance, in the 1970s, cooperation between the EU and the South Mediterranean countries was based on trade preferences that encouraged duty-free access to European markets for these countries' industrial products. At the same time, third countries were allowed to continue to protect their own markets with customs barriers. It was an asymmetrical situation. The new agreements signalled a return to symmetry in trade policies, accompanied by financial support for institutional reforms (fiscal policy, financial liberalization, and so on).

The evolution of North-South trade integration, materialized by bilateral accords between individual South Mediterranean countries and the EU, was gradual and varied depending on whether the subject of the agreement was industry, agriculture, services, or finance. The industrial sector was the best prepared and, as a consequence, the first to benefit from the agreements. As Table 19.1 shows, industrial association accords have been in effect with Tunisia since 1996 (applied early) and should be completed in 2008. For Morocco, an agreement came into effect in March 2000, and industrial free trade should be completed in 2010. Trade between the EU and Israel in industrial products is already liberalized;

Table 19.1 Geographic scope of partnership agreements showing progress in negotiations

Progress in negotiations (trade section)	Conclusion of negotiations	Signature of agreement	Entry into effect
Tunisia	June 1995	July 1995	March 1998*
Israel	September 1995	November 1995	June 2000
Morocco	November 1996	February 1996	July 1997
Palestine	December 1996	February 1997	July 1997
Jordan	April 1997	November 1997	May 2002
Egypt	June 1999	June 2001	June 2004
Lebanon	January 2002	June 2002	March 2003
Algeria	December 2001	April 2002	In process of ratification
Syria†	Underway	Not yet	Not yet

* Early application as of January 1996.
† Negotiations have ended, and the Council is still studying the possibility of signature.

for this country, the early signature of the agreement reflects a success in terms of specialization.

In the context of price liberalization, the Barcelona agreements made a special case for agricultural products, and the plan called for renegotiation three years after the agreements came into effect. For the trade in services, there was neither an established nor specific negotiations. All parties agreed to respect their obligations to the World Trade Organization (WTO). In the case of Algeria, the engagement of EU commitments under the General Agreement on Tariffs and Trade was planned in return for granting the country (not a WTO member) the most-favoured-nation clause and a reciprocal non-discrimination clause (covering both the most-favoured-nation clause and national treatment) for maritime transport services.

South-South Integration

Integration among the South Mediterranean countries is the key to raising the potential for generating economic benefits for the entire Southern region. Integration creates economies of scale that would compensate for the narrowness of each respective market and encourage investment flows into the region. The efforts made to promote integration among the Southern countries have drawn interest thanks to the Barcelona Process, which has led to the signing of a series of regional accords among South Mediterranean countries. A review of the accords among North and South Mediterranean countries reveals the existence of two groups. Countries in the first group are looking to improve their level of integration into the South Mediterranean region. In this group, accords have been concluded among Tunisia, Morocco, Egypt, and Jordan, on the one hand, and among Egypt, Jordan, Syria, and Lebanon, on the other hand. Generally, these accords exclude basic agricultural products and aim for gradual liberalization of trade in industrial products.[1] Countries in the second group have a very low level of integration. In this group, integration via bilateral accords is weak, mainly because of political or economic conditions. For example, Algeria has signed only one free trade agreement, with Jordan. Similarly, Israel has been excluded for political reasons and has only one bilateral agreement, with Turkey.[2] Finally, Turkey, given its customs union with Europe, offers preferential tariffs to other countries in an attempt to obtain concessions in return.

The Arab countries on the south shore of the Mediterranean Sea and the countries of the Arab Maghreb are involved, respectively, in the Greater Arab Free Trade Area (GAFTA),[3] which came into effect in 1998, and the Arab Maghreb Union (AMU). The GAFTA agreement provides for a full dismantling of tariffs on industrial products over ten years and a schedule for agricultural products. However, the scope of this agreement is limited because of non-tariff-related obstacles and incomplete application. Implementation of the AMU is dependent on the political context.

Finally, the Agadir Agreement is a regional accord signed by Tunisia, Morocco, Egypt, and Jordan. This agreement, signed in 2004, is a significant step towards accelerating the integration of Southern countries. In fact, it provided, in principle, for total dismantlement of barriers to trading industrial goods as of 6 July 2006. The difference between Agadir and the other agreements is that it brings together the countries most economically ready to integrate into the European market, which favours economies of scale and a higher degree of foreign direct investment (FDI). The Agadir Agreement includes a number of incentives, particularly the elimination of non-tariff obstacles (dealing with quotas, constraints, techniques, management rules, and other issues), although it does not interfere with the other Euro-Mediterranean agreements that provide for suppression of non-tariff barriers.

Southern Countries and the World Trade Organization

The Mediterranean countries (both North and South) are trying to reconcile regional integration and global integration. The World Trade Organization is in the foreground of the global economic integration process. The WTO currently has 150 member countries. Cyprus, Egypt, Israel, Malta, Morocco, Tunisia, and Turkey joined in 1995; Jordan, in 2000. Other countries, such as Algeria, Lebanon, and Libya, have observer status and are planning to join. Syria and the Palestinian Authority are not participants.

The multilateral dimension of trade liberalization has resulted, for the Mediterranean countries, in a reduction in protectionist obstacles, especially those of a non-tariff nature. Despite this progress, the current average (unweighted) import tariff is still much higher than the average tariff in developing countries. Nonetheless, joining the WTO has necessitated a massive adjustment of national legislation in each country with regard to trade, in order to comply with the new multilateral obligations. The most critical sectors, requiring the adoption of a new regime, have concerned suppression of authorization to import, anti-dumping measures, and legislation on safeguarding imports.

Interdependence and Convergence

Measurement of the economic interdependence between the Southern countries and the rest of the world gives an idea of these countries' degree of integration into the global market. On the economic level, the impact of globalization is difficult to discern, as it is manifested in changes in international flows of information, technological transfers, trade effects, specialization, FDI, and global capital flows. It is thus synonymous with growth in international trade and exchange in an integrated international economic system.

The Mediterranean region brings together countries that are at different stages of development. On the north shore of the sea are developed European countries with globalized and internationalized economies linked to other economies. On the south shore are developing countries that tend to be less open to the outside but are taking small steps towards integration into the global market via the north shore countries that are EU members (on average, more than half of these countries' trade is conducted with the EU; almost 5 percent with partner countries; and about 40 percent with the rest of the world).

The economies of the South Mediterranean countries are linked to the rest of the world, including the North Mediterranean region, through a small part of their economic activity. Only the trade in goods and services[4] has been somewhat liberalized; mobility of capital and labour has not been affected. Even at the level of goods, trade involves mainly industrial products. Trade in agricultural products has barely begun. The South Mediterranean region is not always able to present itself as an attractive zone for capital flows (FDI and financial flows). It harvested only 0.7 percent of global FDI in 2000. In fact, FDI flows for these countries vary from 4 percent (for countries such as Tunisia, Israel, and Jordan) to 1 percent (for countries such as Morocco, Egypt, and Lebanon). Integration of financial capital in the Mediterranean region is practically nonexistent.

In my research, I measured the changes in interdependence among Mediterranean economies using an index calculated on the base of four indicators. The method of calculating the index is to make a single average from four normalized indicators.[5] Taking account of the availability of data, I chose the following indicators:

- imports and exports of goods and services as percentage of GDP
- revenues of factors received as percentage of GDP
- FDI flows as percentage of GDP
- variations in the terms of trade.

Table 19.2 shows the change in the integration index for the sample over time. Changes in the index of the entire sample of ten countries, on the basis of the four indicators chosen, show that, on average, the region is in the process of achieving deeper integration into the global economy.

The evolution of interdependence (on the basis of the above four indicators) among the countries in the sample reflects both economies already integrated into the global market and economies that are not yet integrated. As a consequence, it is of interest to isolate the group of developing countries (South Mediterranean countries) to gain insight into the evolution of their integration into the world market. Using the above method, I calculated the average common factor for Southern and Northern countries.[6] Figure 19.1 illustrates the two curves.

The Southern Mediterranean countries are increasingly interdependent with the rest of the world. This interdependence is at a low level compared to Northern Mediterranean countries, but it is growing more rapidly, which means that the two curves are converging. However, the nature of Southern countries' increased interdependence with the rest of the world is different in two ways from that of Northern countries. The first difference is the low level of interdependence of South Mediterranean economies. The second is that interdependence is related more to imports than exports.

South Mediterranean countries are interested in benefitting from new opportunities for growth through different economic channels (technology, market size, FDI, and others) to help the region catch up to developments in the North. Tests on the possibility of Southern countries' convergence with Northern countries, however, show that the former will never be able to catch up with the latter.[7]

Table 19.2 Changes in integration index, by country and year

Country	1990	1991	1992	1993	1994	1995	1996	1997	1998	1999	2000	2001
France	36.0	39.0	44.8	46.5	37.8	53.0	53.5	51.0	61.3	65.5	53.8	46.8
Italy	40.0	40.3	41.5	45.5	43.0	43.3	51.0	50.3	53.5	56.3	30.0	47.5
Portugal	45.8	44.5	36.3	36.5	35.5	42.0	34.5	36.8	42.5	38.8	45.0	47.8
Spain	29.8	32.8	48.8	27.5	26.8	41.3	50.3	51.0	48.3	38.8	46.8	55.0
Morocco	30.0	24.5	47.5	27.8	34.3	16.8	38.3	42.0	34.5	46.5	40.0	61.5
Tunisia	39.8	28.5	42.8	43.5	43.0	35.5	35.0	39.0	42.0	37.8	44.8	41.8
Turkey	25.3	26.8	17.3	35.5	29.3	29.8	28.5	28.3	29.0	27.5	20.0	36.0
Egypt	30.0	39.8	36.5	28.0	31.0	23.0	29.5	30.3	19.8	27.8	27.8	27.3
Israel	42.0	52.5	41.5	51.0	34.0	24.0	38.0	45.3	46.8	54.0	59.0	57.8
Jordan	26.3	15.8	15.0	12.0	18.0	6.0	17.5	30.0	26.5	22.3	39.5	19.0
Total sample	34.5	34.4	37.2	35.4	33.3	31.5	37.6	40.4	40.4	41.5	40.7	44.0

Note: see note 5 on page 329, for details on the calculation of the index.

Figure 19.1 Comparison of evolution of the integration of North Mediterranean and South Mediterranean countries into globalization

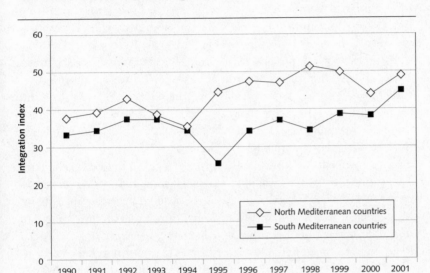

There are three homogeneous groups in the Mediterranean region. The first is composed of Cyprus, Israel, and the European countries in the region. All of these countries are converging towards the European average. The second group is composed of Tunisia, Egypt, Morocco, and Turkey; these countries are achieving relative catch-up with the European average. The gap in per capita income from the European average varies by country. Finally, the third group is composed of countries that diverge: Algeria, Syria, Greece, and Jordan.[8]

Opening and Development of Civil Society in South Mediterranean Countries

The South Mediterranean countries have agreed on a number of regional and bilateral accords aimed at development and NGO participation. Nongovernmental organizations have recorded the weakest growth rates in the Southern countries (see Table 19.3).

The number of inhabitants per NGO indicates that the situation has deteriorated for civil society associations in South Mediterranean countries. With the exception of Lebanon, the changes in number of inhabitants per NGO in these countries between 1993 and 2003 were not auspicious. That is why the Barcelona Process represents an opportunity for civil societies in these countries to open to the outside world while benefitting from material and immaterial resources. The agreements contain promises with regard to social development. The Barcelona Accord is expected to create political space, provide financial means, and favour greater interconnection between these networks and those in Northern countries.

By definition, civil society tries to represent the collective values and aspirations of citizens and social groups through independent, voluntary action. As a consequence, it needs a political space within which to legitimize its intervention, represent groups, or influence the direction of certain agreements or policies concerning the general interest. The Barcelona agreements have created this political space in the Mediterranean region through the integration of clauses calling for development of an independent civil society. According to the European Commission, there cannot be development without civil society participation. In its social program, the Barcelona Process emphasizes the need for civil society to participate in the Euro-Mediterranean Partnership and strengthens decentralized cooperation instruments in order to favour exchanges among different development actors.

The Barcelona agreements offer a forum for cooperation among all Mediterranean countries. One aim of this partnership is to stimulate changes in the institutional apparatuses that regulate economic and social life in these countries so that they can be integrated into the global market. Furthermore, the European Commission and other European bodies have constantly emphasized the need for civil society to participate in the establishment of relations among partner countries. The various actions decided on in the context of the partnership include meetings, exchanges of experiences, and contacts among the participants in Mediterranean civil society.

In addition to programs designed to develop civil society in partner countries, the European Commission funds bilateral and regional projects emanating from civil society in specific sectors. Civil society organizations in the Mediterranean region are able to establish relations through the Euro-Mediterranean Civil Forum. The Euro-Mediterranean Study Commission and the Euro-Mediterranean Forum of Economic Institutes bring together twenty-seven institutions from partner countries in the areas of foreign policy, economics, and security. Colloquia are organized every six months under the aegis of the European Economic and Social Committee. Independent of civil society organizations, other groups, such as elected representatives, find spaces of cooperation with Euro-Mediterranean institutions.

In general, civil society — and NGOs in particular — can represent the interests of groups that have been harmed, which makes its presence desirable and desired in international organizations. The founding clauses of the WTO emphasize cooperation and consultations with NGOs (Shamsie 2000). In October 1996, a number of measures were taken by the General Council of the WTO with regard to data supplied by the NGOs and the organization of colloquia on subjects concerning civil society.[9] In the context of the regional accord among Arab countries, a special department was created for engagement with civil society. The project allows for organization of consultations with civil society, in collaboration with ministerial councils. Some consultations have taken place within different councils, such as the Social Affairs Council, the Environmental Council, and the Information and Communications Council, but both the number and the influence of these consultations have been insufficient.

The European Commission's new neighbourhood policy gave rise to a program called the European Initiative for Democracy and Human Rights to promote and support social issues in third countries. The program makes available €100 million each year to accomplish two objectives:

- the development and consolidation of democracy and the rule of law — respect for human rights and fundamental freedoms (Chapter B7-701 of the initiative)
- support the activities of international criminal tribunals and the International Criminal Court (Chapter B7-702).

In fact, civil society and NGOs received a negligible amount of money out of the total funding for third countries by the European Union. Unlike the economic and political spheres, civil society received only 3 percent of total funding in five countries in 2005-6.

Conclusion: Impact on Autonomy

In this chapter, I have assessed a decade of opening and its impact on the Mediterranean region's homogeneity. When studying autonomy, it is necessary to distinguish the economic side of the Barcelona Process from its social side, which also has economic implications. In addition, within the economic part of the agreement, we must distinguish between the institutional aspect linked to the signed agreements, on the one hand, and the level of effective exchange conveyed by interdependence with the rest of the world, on the other hand. Autonomy may be captured at the level of individuals, at the local level, or at the collective level — that is, that of an individual country or a group of countries in the South Mediterranean region. The table below shows the different degrees of

Table 19.3   Changes in number of international NGOs by country in the Mediterranean region, 1993-2003

Country	Number of secretariats[1]		Inhabitants per secretariat[2] (thousands)		Change 2003/1993	
	1993	2003	1993	2003	(1)[3]	(2)[4]
Turkey	15	40	3,333	1,667	2.7	0.5
Belgium	1,484	1,855	7	6	1.3	0.8
Cyprus	6	17	118	45	2.8	0.4
France	1,334	1,405	43	43	1.1	1.0
Greece	38	94	270	112	2.5	0.4
Italy	412	544	139	106	1.3	0.8
Spain	131	301	303	133	2.3	0.4
Lebanon	13	33	250	111	2.5	0.4
Libya	14	4	313	1,429	0.3	4.6
Morocco	17	17	1,429	2,000	1.0	1.4
Syria	15	9	909	2,000	0.6	2.2
Tunisia	27	31	313	313	1.1	1.0
Israel	71	98	99	96	1.4	1.0
Total sample	3,577	4,448	80	73	1.2	0.9

1   The convergence test applied below detects the exact list of non-convergent countries.
2   In the interpretation of the cases of France and Belgium, account must be taken of the fact that these countries are the seat of, respectively, the European Parliament and the European Commission. The presence of these bodies is conducive to the creation of international NGOs in these countries.
3   Number of secretariats (2003/1993).
4   Inhabitants per secretariat (2003/1993).

Source: Union of International Associations, Yearbook of international organisations: Guide to civil society networks (2003, 2004).

autonomy by type of agreement (see Table 19.4). There is a distinction between individual autonomy on the local level and autonomy on the collective level — that is, South Mediterranean countries grouped together or individually.

In South Mediterranean countries, agreements are negotiated and established by official authorities to the exclusion of civil society. As Table 19.4 shows, signing the agreement alone has few implications for the autonomy of individuals, as they do not voice an opinion regarding the agreement. In general, individuals do not participate in the formulation of accords, even through civil society organizations (except in exceptional circumstances), as is the case in South Mediterranean countries. In contrast, on the governmental level, the signature of accords conveys a certain sense of belonging to a regional group. South Mediterranean countries have signed many accords, but they do not necessarily reflect the pattern of exchanges in the region. For example, the Maghreb countries are the most important trading partners for Tunisia, and yet, in proportion to their number, they have signed fewer bilateral and regional accords with Tunisia than with Arab countries. The stakes in these accords thus go beyond economics alone.

The real level of trade has an economic effect on individuals and the collectivity. As a consequence, there is a direct impact not only on the wealth of countries but also on the purchasing power of individuals at the local level. Individuals, as heads of firms or as consumers, are interested in lower prices, diversity of products, suppression of indirect and direct customs barriers, and similar issues. When it comes to collective autonomy, it is clear that the higher the level of interdependence with the economies of developed countries, the better the country's integration into its neighbourhood and with the world. Finally, the social aspect is very important, because it grants more autonomy to individuals and

Table 19.4 Types of autonomy and aspects of the agreement

Type of autonomy	Institutional aspect of the agreement	Trade and interdependence	Social aspect of the agreement
Individual autonomy	0	XX	XXX
Collective autonomy	XX	XXX	0

0: no correlation; X: weak correlation; XX: intermediate correlation; XXX: strong correlation governments. Accords that integrate the social aspect, such as the Barcelona agreements, make it possible to limit the perverse effects of free trade on individuals and allow for a better sharing of wealth on the local level and among countries.

Economic performance is often opposed to concepts of equity, equality, or social protection, which essentially constitute expenditures. As a consequence, the introduction of a social component into certain agreements seeks to balance economic benefits among the parties and, mainly, to preserve the interest of individuals on the local level. These individuals, as consumers, producers, or members of civil society, thus become more autonomous economically and can influence the path of accords through civil society pressure groups.

chapter 20   **The Mediterranean and Outsourcing**

Fatma Sarraj

IN THIS CHAPTER, I analyze the relationship between globalization and outsourcing in the Mediterranean region.[1] A specific conception of autonomy is implicit here regarding the Mediterranean space following the realignment of activities associated with globalization-induced outsourcing. This chapter is in three parts. In the first part, I discuss the relationship between globalization, outsourcing, and autonomy. The second part lists the countries of the region in terms of their attractiveness as locations for delocalization and outsourcing activities. In the third part, I explain, through transaction costs (the decisive factor in implementation of delocalized activities), the mitigated performance of the Mediterranean region with regard to outsourcing.

Globalization, Outsourcing, and Regional Autonomy

Here, globalization is defined as the growing interdependence of economic activities, expressed by rising integration of national economies into the global market. According to economic theory, free trade eliminates commercial barriers and integrates markets, stimulates competition and efficient allocation of production, and lowers transaction costs, while favouring a relocalization of economic activities. Globalization is thus conveyed by changes to commercial structures following delocalization of production by multinationals[2] made possible by intra-branch exchanges.

In this context, multinational firms stand out as major stakeholders in liberalization and market integration, and they are responsible for two-thirds of international trade. Their expansion has led to flexible production networks that promote an international division of labour (Trigo 2003). These networks are a mix of subsidiaries and sub-subsidiaries (ownership relationship), as well as local firms under contract (coordination relationship) that are seeking integration into the delocalized production process through complementarity. Activities are distributed according to the potential of the host country in terms of comparative advantages for each production operation. The spatial dispersal of fragments of the production process into different countries is one of the economic manifestations of the globalization of production.

Robert Feenstra and Gordon Hanson (1996) dubbed this mode of production "outsourcing," which they define as a new production model adopted by multinational firms in which services and production activities are performed abroad and then combined with those performed in the firm's original country. Generally likened to subcontracting applied to a wider field — notably, services — outsourcing is done either in the home country or in a foreign host country. In the latter case, it is likened to vertical delocalization of production.

Through outsourcing, firms seek to profit from national, regional, and international differences in costs of production factors, especially salaries and raw materials. But the cost is not the only reason, because a large number of firms have become involved with delocalization to gain access to certain skills and to improve the quality of services supplied. Thus firms consider not only the criteria of competitiveness and prices but also the standard of quality.

Globalization stimulates outsourcing, which is one of its most visible manifestations. It is thus not surprising that the use of outsourcing is expanding spectacularly in both quantitative and qualitative terms. The global market for externalization of production processes, or business process outsourcing (BPO), has reached a value of $100 billion.[3] In Europe, BPO was evaluated at €25 billion, or 4.5 percent of estimated growth for the BPO market in 2004. By 2007, this figure had reached €33 billion. The development of this new organizational choice was not limited to standard tasks and operations; it also concerned high-value-added operations and services. In the first quarter of 2005, 456 services contracts were let, a 5 percent increase over the same period in 2004.[4]

Specifically, outsourcing of information technologies, computer management, and software development rose constantly in 2002 and 2003.[5] In effect, the share of facility management in computer services worldwide rose from 22.8 per cent in 2002 to 23.8 percent in 2003. In Europe, the increase was 1.7 percent over the same period.[6] For the United States, the Forrester Research Center estimated that outsourcing of these operations would reach 99 percent by 2008. The United States and Europe outsourced these types of operations to different countries. India was ranked as the top destination for outsourcing, which grew to 30.5 percent of its exports, mainly in software and services. Revenues reached $12.5 billion for the fiscal year ending 31 March 2003, and 85 percent of the exports went to the United States.

With outsourcing, a number of production segments escape the control of a particular community, which thus loses one of the levers of autonomous economic policy. Outsourcing can, however, reconstruct autonomy at a cross-border regional level if a region, in this case the Mediterranean region, is able to contain delocalizations in its geopolitical space or attract them from other regions. The tearing of the fabric of intraregional relations, woven over decades of trade through geographic and cultural proximity, and now put to the test by globalization, may be stopped. Through the networks that it develops, outsourcing also allows the region as a whole to preserve its economic integration, or at least to preserve a significant influence in the global economy. The countries of the region will therefore benefit from the likelihood of greater economic autonomy.

The more outsourcing is developed in the region, the more intense are the economic integration and the social and political consequences. This economic boost gives the extra-national regional entity a certain degree of autonomy in relation to the rest of the world. All countries that have had their control over the productive fabric reduced following outsourcing have regained such control to one degree or another on the regional level.

Outsourcing promoted by globalization may be both a threat to a country's economic autonomy and a vector for re-energizing activities by making new means available to communities. For the countries of origin, outsourcing is a choice that increases economic competitiveness and raises the potential for productivity by freeing resources that had previously been devoted to activities that were less competitive. For host countries, generally developing countries, outsourcing is a means of reducing unemployment, stimulating foreign trade, lowering the deficit in balance of payments, and encouraging a growth dynamic. Channelled by foreign direct investment (FDI), outsourcing is a source of financing that does not generate debt and favours the creation of sites of technological and scientific innovation.

Let us now see how the Mediterranean region is in the process of retaining its globalization-related delocalization activities and attracting other activities. The cross-border redefinition of networking by multinational firms in the Mediterranean region will enable the region, particularly its southern part, to find a new source of extra-national autonomy.

Outsourcing in the Mediterranean Region

A close examination of the structure of exports by product, according to the share of finished goods exported in relation to the total of exports and the share of intermediate goods imported in relation to all imports, shows whether there is a trend towards outsourcing in a country. This approximation, adopted by Feenstra and Hanson (1996), which assesses the scope of outsourcing by all exports of intermediate goods, confirms that there has indeed been a fragmentation in the production process that features an action of procurement from foreign sources, or outsourcing.

There are two steps to measuring outsourcing and its scope. The first consists of calculating the share of intermediate products imported in relation to all imports. This ratio shows whether countries are strongly or weakly engaged in fragmentation operations. The second step involves an evaluation of the share of exports of finished products in relation to all exports. This ratio reveals whether there is outsourcing of processing and assembly, which presumes procurement of components. This measurement method has certain limitations, because the indicator in question tells us little about the outsourcing that takes place when a subsidiary is installed — that is, when outsourcing is likened to delocalization, approximated in a number of studies by FDI. This shows the importance of limiting strategic FDI undertaken by multinationals in the context of contracts or partnership or subcontracting agreements.

At this level, it is important to know the position of Mediterranean countries in the chain of fragmentation of production processes in relation to the EU, on the one hand, and to countries in the rest of the world, on the other hand. This information shows the degree of dependence of the Mediterranean countries on these other regions. A high level of frag-mentation of the production chain would be the expression of a high volume of trade based essentially on intermediate goods. On the basis of my analysis, I consider that the more trade between two countries is based on intermediate and semi-finished goods, the higher the chance that the countries in question will develop industrial and other kinds of assembly operations.

For Tunisia, Morocco, Turkey, and Egypt, the share of imports of intermediate goods is 60 percent. This level is significant in that it shows that these four countries are fully engaged in the game of fragmentation with the EU. Lebanon is strengthening its ties with the EU to a lesser extent, whereas Jordan is disengaging from the EU and strengthening its position in the production chain in relation to the rest of the world. Israel, which is more highly developed than the other Mediterranean countries, is integrating with the logic of vertical production at the rate of 39 percent with the rest of the world and 38 percent with the EU.

When we look at the share of exports by category in total exports, we note that the Mediterranean region is taking part in the fragmentation of production on the international scale, as certain countries are increasing their share of imported intermediate goods.[7] Over the same period, there has been an increase in exports of finished goods, indicating that pro-cessing, assembly, or outsourcing is very likely.

Proving that outsourcing in fact exists in the region leads us to exam-ine the nature of FDI in the region (the objective of the second step of analysis). The geographic distribution of FDI in the region, in both quantitative and qualitative terms, for 2004 is as follows: 53 percent for production projects (creation, expansion, and delocalization); 24 percent for financial partnerships, joint ventures, and purchase of assets; and 23 percent for commercial projects. Analysis by destination of subregion and country of destination distinguishes three blocs: the Machrek, the Maghreb, and other countries (Israel and Turkey). In 2003, these three blocs received, respectively, 19 percent, 55 percent, and 28 percent of FDI. In 2004, these rates changed, respectively, to 25 percent, 51 percent, and 24 percent of all FDI.[8]

In Algeria and Syria, there is a trend towards take-off. Algeria led the Mediterranean Economic Development Area (MEDA) in terms of FDI in 2004, especially in the energy sector. It also attracted major projects in sectors other than petroleum and natural gas, such as Castel centrales électriques (France). Similarly, the pharmaceutical sector (estimated at

€700 million per year, 80 percent of which is imported) benefitted from numerous investments: construction of a laboratory in Oran for the Spanish firm Asac Pharma and creation of a subsidiary of the French group Harmattan.

Lebanon, Egypt, and Jordan are similar in this respect. Lebanon has achieved a remarkable position in computer and Internet consulting and in research and development. This development has overshadowed its position in industrial production, except in the agrofood industry. Jordan, in a complex geopolitical context, draws an important share of FDI from one year to the next from emerging countries such as India and China, but also from Tunisia, often of a diversified nature.[9] There are also cigarette-manufacturing and agrofood projects, mass distribution, and services. Egypt quintupled its FDI flow from 2003 to 2004, specifically through basic industry projects (energy, chemistry, cement), a trend that is growing in the food-distribution sector and telecommunications. Turkey considers itself an outsourcing heavyweight. In 2004, it attracted thirteen automobile projects (from Ford, Renault, Bosch, Honda, Hyundai, and Isuzu), three aeronautics projects, eight agrofood projects, and four pharmaceutical projects.

Other countries, including Israel, Malta, and Cyprus, have shown their capacity to attract top-drawer projects. For Israel, there were seven software projects and three high-technology electronics projects, three biotechnology and medical research projects, and four consulting projects. Malta had projects relating to generic drugs and services. Cyprus concentrated on services and research and development and made its international vocation known (business centres, representation offices).

In terms of which businesses invested in the region, the automobile and energy sectors had the greatest concentration of investors (Renault, Hyundai, Bosch, British Gas, and so on). Some groups made three or more investments in the region: Accor, eight projects; Orascom and Renault, seven; British Gas and Lafarge, five; China National Petroleum, four; Sun, Cisco, IBM, Majid Al Futtaim, and Siemens, three. Turkey, traditionally favourable to the automobile industry, benefitted the most from this sector (thirteen projects), followed by Morocco with eight projects, Tunisia with three automobile cable projects, and Algeria, where Michelin resumed its investment.

The European and American industries traditionally present in these sectors are receiving more and more competition from Japanese and other Asian rivals who have invested more than the Americans in recent years. In Turkey, Toyota, Honda, and Isuzu have an increasing presence in the automobile sector. The sector that is most dynamic in the region is telecommunications. Six projects involve mobile telephony (new licences, investments in expansions, new networks, and purchases), and fourteen call centres were opened in 2004 — the majority in Morocco, but the largest one in Tunisia.

There was strong expansion in the software sector — materials and consulting — which accounted for 61 percent of all FDI in 2004. This growth confirms an orientation towards high-value-added activities and demonstrates the outsourcing trends in services. For example, Israel (top rank) claims to have the highest concentration of young companies in the world, on par with Silicon Valley. The volume of investments in this sector is €62 million (Sisco).

Overall, the Mediterranean region is trying to encourage the creation of more of these projects, notably by developing scientific parks and technocities. For instance, Tunisia decided to build one new technocity per year for ten years. The Tunisian Ministry of Economics estimated that this would create jobs and generate an annual business volume of €13.5 billion in the foreign-trade zones devoted to new information and communications technologies (Jaffrin and de Saint-Laurent 2005).

Textiles represent the top export for Turkey, Morocco, and Tunisia. This industry is considered vital for the Mediterranean countries, since it provides 50 percent of manufacturing exports from the MEDA region to the EU. Foreign direct investment in the textile sector dropped by about half in 2004 as the Multifibre Arrangement wound down. Today, the region finds itself confined to subcontracting, a precarious activity. Turkey, which was the leader in textile production in the Mediterranean region, no longer receives foreign investment in this sector. The same is true for Syria and Egypt, countries in which cotton provides jobs for 15 percent of the employed population. Morocco, which became less competitive in the textile sector in the early 1990s, lost about twenty thousand jobs.

In general, the Mediterranean region seems to receive outsourcing-type FDI. This trend is also found in the changes in export and import structures in the region's countries. Outsourcing in the region is still in its infancy and depends strongly on two variables: the strategies of multinationals and the attractiveness of the territories.

A survey conducted on the image of the region revealed that it was not attractive enough to draw potential investments. Foreign direct investment

343

is concentrated in the textile sector, with a gradual increase in the electronic sector and in parts and components for automobile companies. In other words, the region is not as attractive as the countries of Asia, notably China and India. Despite the geographic distance and cultural differences of Asian countries, they represent a threat to the Mediterranean countries, notably with the ending of the Multifibre Arrangement in January 2005. The central and eastern European countries do not represent as strong a threat, because the nature of outsourcing found there is more of the substitution type.

The Mediterranean region is doing well in the era of delocalization, but it is still embryonic in terms of outsourcing in comparison with the experience of Asian countries and, to a lesser extent, central and eastern European countries, which offer much more attractive conditions. For the latter, complementary outsourcing is the best fit for their attractiveness conditions. In fact, the conditions for subcontracting low-value-added activities are not sufficient to attract subcontracting of services or outsourcing of high-value-added activities. Such outsourcing requires more than competitiveness in terms of factor endowment — it also requires competitiveness linked to quality of organization. For classic subcontracting to develop into high-value-added outsourcing activities, there must be, in addition to an abundance of favourably priced factor endowments, the presence of competitiveness linked to quality of organization, as measured by the evolution of transaction costs. Outsourcing is no longer a simple trade relationship generated by advantages in factor endowments; it is also an organizational choice based on lowering transaction costs.

Transaction Costs and the Future of Outsourcing in the Mediterranean Region

Under globalization, the lowering of transaction costs around the world has favoured the development of outsourcing specifically in services and high-value-added operations. How has this situation played out in the more limited framework of the Mediterranean countries?

My analysis of outsourcing trends — or, more specifically, offshore delocalization — in the region has shown that the movement has been slow to develop, and I found an explanation for this trend in the region's weak attractiveness. I presumed that this variable is fluid, which offers the countries concerned the possibility of an internal dynamic that, by offering political incentives, may change their ability to capture more FDI outsourcing. Because transaction costs form one of the decisive components of attractiveness, I evaluate these factors below to gauge their effects on outsourcing in the region.

An analysis of the evolution of transaction costs in the region involves examining changes in legal infrastructure and communications networks. We assume that an adequate legal infrastructure is an indispensable aspect of attractiveness. The choice of the second indicator is justified by the fact that a reliable, well-developed communications network encourages trade relations. The combination of these two indicators has an influence on the evolution of transaction costs, which in their turn have an impact on the development of outsourcing in the region. By the legal infrastructure of a country, I mean the laws and institutions that reflect a desire to attract FDI by highlighting an advantage in terms of attractiveness. All countries in the region have tried to strengthen their legal infrastructures to boost their attractiveness and remove obstacles to investment. With regard to communications networks, countries in the Mediterranean region have implemented various policies in order to stimulate a more open and dynamic economy by having a telecommunications sector that allows opening to markets. Almost everywhere, mobile telephony licences have been granted, through competitive bids, to major international operators. This step triggered a communications explosion throughout the region, as well as the rapid appropriation of new communications tools by populations.

For a closer look at the communications infrastructure in the region, I used two indexes. The first is the density of fax machines per one thousand inhabitants in each country. The second is the waiting time to receive a telephone line. By both measures, Israel is clearly ranked at the top, with a communications infrastructure comparable to that of the countries of Europe. Next comes Morocco, with a well-performing network and a highly developed structure, particularly for mobile telephones.

In Tunisia, the trend has strengthened in recent years, especially with the entry of a new national operator that has stimulated competition, which has induced an improvement in the price and quality of services offered. The information and communications technologies sector has been growing since 1997 thanks to the volume of investments (which has tripled since the reference year of 1997) in this sector and to the

345

creation of the Parc technologique des télécommunications, which offers a climate propitious to high-value-added services, particularly software development.

In Lebanon, the telecommunications system is sophisticated. The country has a completely operational electrical network, a new international airport, expanded and renovated port facilities, and an ambitious roadwork program. Lebanon therefore has one of the best communications infrastructures in the region. The development of transportation infrastructure by integration of new information and communications technologies marks a push towards improving infrastructure in general, as well as a means of communicating with neighbouring countries. The result will be improved attractiveness of the region, which will encourage FDI inflow. It is obvious that a lack of communications infrastructure causes the flight of FDI in general and of subcontracting networks in particular. These require oversight and coordination that perform well in space and over time.

The telephony infrastructure exists, but access to certain specific services is difficult. The costs of telephone communications are still slightly higher than in Europe. Monopoly structures in some countries influence the price of goods, but waves of reform seem to be well underway.

The Internet is working well in Israel, Morocco, Tunisia, Malta, Jordan, and Lebanon. Egypt and Turkey are progressing in this sector. Only Syria is still behind. The Internet offers the firms dispersed through the region the ability to work online. It should be noted that in Tunisia, Israel, Lebanon, Malta, and Morocco, administrative formalities are carried out more and more by electronic means. In Morocco, the development of information technologies, notably the Internet, began in 1995. The equipment rate in societies that are connected indicates that the vast majority of them are Internet users, once their firms have reached a certain market size. The quality of development offered by firms that provide Internet services meets the highest international standards.

Overall, remarkable efforts at modernization have been made in infrastructure, utilities, and transportation and telecommunications systems. Tax systems are being adapted to market economies. All of these transformations are leading to the emergence of a regional grouping poised to profit from trade stimulated by a general drop in transaction costs caused by the opening of economies to the world market. The opening of economies to trade and the interdependence of international relations have pushed countries to harmonize their legal structures and create better means of communications. The market is young and burgeoning, especially in sectors such as Internet and telecommunications, which investors cannot ignore. In this regard, the prospects for Turkey, Tunisia, Morocco, and Israel are seen as the most promising. Proximity with Europe is a certain advantage, but this proximity is perceived in cultural rather than logistical terms, since transportation and visas play in favour of competitors from the central and eastern European countries.

Conclusion

The countries of the Mediterranean region are participating in the fragmentation of production activities through an increase in their imports of intermediate goods and their exports of finished goods. An examination of the nature of FDI made in the Mediterranean Basin, especially offshore FDI, proves that the countries of the region are attracting subcontracting projects. The region is evolving with globalization and progressing beyond simple processing and assembly activities (textiles, automobiles) to performing high-value-added service activities (electronics, telecommunications, software development, computer components, consulting, and even research and development).

Despite the existence of conditions deemed favourable to outsourcing in the Mediterranean region, however, this activity remains embryonic compared to outsourcing in the countries of Asia (India, China), which, despite their geographic distance, are more competitive. The problem with the Mediterranean region is related not only to the market but also to economic agents' capacity to adapt and the quality of organization in these countries. The quality of organization depends essentially on the evolution of transaction costs. In the past, firms opted to internalize operations to avoid going through the market, which engendered transaction costs that were considered high. Today, in contrast, firms are opting to externalize their operations through the market, because the transaction costs on the market have dropped under the effect of globalization. Currently, remarkable efforts at modernization of infrastructure, utilities, and transportation and telecommunications systems have been achieved. Similarly, legislation and tax laws have formed a climate propitious to trade in the region. The prospects for Turkey, Tunisia, Morocco, and Israel are perceived as the most promising, especially in sectors such as Internet and telecommunications, which are young, developing markets.

The proximity of the Mediterranean region to the countries of Europe is an asset for stimulating outsourcing exchanges, whereas technological transfers contribute to the development of human capital necessary to develop organizational competitiveness. This capacity, in turn, is a prerequisite if the countries of the region are to take advantage of outsourcing activities. If the Mediterranean region remains preoccupied with the simple factorial endowment of production that is judged more competitive, outsourcing firms will restrict themselves to subcontracts limited to low-value-added activities. The development of more profitable outsourcing — that is, outsourcing of high-value-added and highly specialized value-added activities — requires that the Mediterranean region make more effort to improve the quality of its organization, which will involve progress both in communications structures and in the legal structures of the region's institutions. The region may then be able to strengthen its economic weight in the world, and each country in the region will have an opportunity to draw on this strength to reconstruct its collective autonomy.

EPILOGUE

chapter 21

Globalization and Autonomy: The Individual in the Maghreb

Interview with Dr. Hashmi Dhaoui

As conceived in the psychoanalytic framework, the individual's autonomy consists not in the elimination of the unconscious, but in the establishment of a different relationship between the conscious and the unconscious. The subject of autonomy thus arises as an active and lucid jurisdiction, making possible a policy of freedom based on individual responsibility.

— Cornelius Castoriadis, *The Imaginary Institution of Society*
(our translation)

WE FELT THAT IT would be pertinent to ask Dr. Hashmi Dhaoui about the dimension of the individual in Islamic Arabic culture in the new context of globalization. Dr. Dhaoui is a psychiatrist and psychoanalyst who has written three books about Islam and the condition of the individual in the Maghreb.[1]

Y. Essid: As you know, the book in which this interview will appear concerns globalization and autonomy in the Mediterranean region. Because you are a psychiatrist and psychoanalyst, practising in a country on the south shore of the Mediterranean Sea, I would like to discuss with you a very specific character: the Arab individual in the Maghreb and the East Mediterranean region. By *individual,* I do not mean the person who comes in for a consultation, but an individual who is representative of a community or society, and who today is prey to complex anxieties.

We shall use psychoanalysis as an instrument for interpretation of the current state of affairs in this region. This interview is placed at the end of the book because people who have read the contributions to this volume will have a better idea of many of the questions that we must address.

Before starting the interview, let us introduce our protagonists. First, there is the new context of globalization, in a region full of contrasts, disparities, and inequalities. The north shore of the Mediterranean Sea is composed of prosperous countries with democratic governments and populations that enjoy high standards of living, formidable social protection systems, and cultures in step with postmodernity. On the south shore of the Mediterranean Sea are countries that, although they are not totally detached historically and economically from Europe, are going through a critical period in their evolution. In these countries, society is trying to decide (a euphemism so that we do not speak of schizophrenia) to what it should subscribe or belong: the political entity that constitutes it as a state, the cultural arena that it shares with the rest of the Arab world, or the Islamic community to which it belongs as a matter of sentiment. Does this very contrasting map of the Mediterranean region strike you as correct?

H. Dhaoui: Yes, it does. Although globalization continues to be irreversibly implemented in countries on the south shore of the Mediterranean Sea, individuals in these countries are not changing anything about the way they behave, which means that they continue to relate to both the conscious dimension and, especially, the collective unconscious, composed of personal learning and collective content, which acts subliminally. Carl Jung defined the collective unconscious as archetypal data, not specific to individuals, gathered through the prodigious heritage of humanity's evolution. In effect, the content of the collective unconscious is ordered around archetypes; Jung defined it as "the old, primitive and analogic way of thinking still alive in our dreams that reconstitutes ancient ancestral images." Thus, the self is formed of the sum of the personal unconscious and the common inheritance of humanity. In contrast, the ego is structured by mimicry. And so, it is as if there is a conflict between these structures — self and ego — within individuals in South Mediterranean countries. This schema is quite universal, but among us it is characterized by opposition between modernity and tradition. For instance, the most prominent heritage in this part of the world is formed of

Islam and Arabic culture. Islam plays a role in the formulation of the religious dimension and the positioning of the subject with regard to sin. Being Arab acts as a group of moral values and social virtues that are inscribed in a communitarian framework. But we must never forget the region's opening to the West, which leads to a sort of schizophrenia.

Furthermore, our society has a specific structure. This is the family, which operates according to a very clear separation between the parent role and the teacher role, leading to multiple objects for identification, since the child is raised by a number of people. The result of this upbringing is an individual who, to function harmoniously, must constantly deal with the demands of the group. The group's opinions and wishes provide the individual with continual stimulation, awakening her or his self and leading her or him to place the community ideal before self-realization. We thus see pseudo-independence within dependence, since the group's demands, and thus its stimulation, must be satisfied for the individual to accede to a degree of autonomy. This dependence means that individuals can do nothing but cloister themselves within the traditional register, which rejects all those who identify with modernity. The modern individual risks being seen by the majority as disrespectful of the community, or even provocative. This marginalizing and guilt-inducing behaviour is not harmonious with the individual's self.

Y. Essid: The individuals who make up Mediterranean Arab society must also be viewed on three different dimensions. First, they are challenged by universal — or, we might say, global — questions, such as principles related to the constitutional state, destruction of the environment, wars and violence, Islamic fundamentalism, technological progress, and mass communications. Second, they face questions of a regional order, such as Arab nationalism, through the Israel-Arab conflict or the Euro-Mediterranean project. Finally, they are confronted with purely national questions, such as the authoritarian nature of political regimes, poor governance, absence of citizenship, and economic and social underdevelopment. All of these dimensions will affect their relationships with the political, social, and religious spheres.

What would you say, as a psychiatrist, about the personality of Arab individuals who come to consult you to ease their emotional suffering?

H. Dhaoui: In relation to what you are saying, it is understandable that I am more and more frequently confronted with pathologies caused by an inner conflict. It is a conflict related to the sense of guilt generated by the denial of one or another of these two registers. Indeed, I often see, when treating people from the Maghreb — especially those who have access to Western lifestyles — a functioning belonging to a collective unconscious in the traditional register, on the one hand, and belonging to the ego and to acquired knowledge in the register of modernity, on the other hand. This double functioning causes inner conflict, which leads to decompensation.

This result would explain, on a macroscopic level, why one part of our society chooses to deny everything that might emanate from modernity by privileging the collective unconscious, while the other part privileges the ego and, thus, the person who has identified with the Western ideal. A reconciliation must be sought between aspiring to modernity and re-specting tradition; this reconciliation will lead to the achievement of a certain postmodernity through Jungian individuation, which corresponds to self-realization, as the individual learns to distinguish herself or himself from the sense of belonging to the community by becoming aware of the interrelational system that links the subject's ego to her or his unconscious. This is the direct path to creating an interrelationship between the individual and the environment. It is the role of psycho-analysis as a therapeutic mode to encourage the ego to recognize the desires of the unconscious, so that the ego can then decide consciously whether it is appropriate to satisfy these desires.

Y. Essid: Let us look at how globalization affects the three dimensions mentioned above.

- On the global level, every country in the world is experiencing accelerated integration into what is called the liberal market economy — in other words, globalization. This integration is expressed, among other things, in Southern countries' increasing dependence on the North. The same material and cultural products are now circulating among regions with very different living standards and cultural traditions, leading to a general standardization of modes of consumption. Such a situation inevitably has repercussions for the populations of Arab countries, which are already greatly torn be-tween tradition and modernity, East and West, and are seduced by the call of religion, subjected to the weight of the past, beset by poverty, facing a difficult future, and so on.

- Globalization accelerates attempts to create regional groupings, such as the Maghreb union and the Euro-Mediterranean Partnership project.
- On the national level, globalization puts at risk the interests of producers who are poorly prepared for global competition and have benefitted up to now from protection by their states. On a political level, it reduces states' sovereignty, not only with regard to the choice of their economic model — privatization, gradual disengagement by the state from sectors up to now safeguarded, such as education and health — but also by necessary interference in their affairs with regard to the application of democratic principles and respect for fundamental human rights.

Do you feel that the Arab individual, who is being pulled in three different ways by these three dimensions, is capable of dealing with this reality?

H. Dhaoui: The denial of all contributions by Western modernity has caused a spectacular regression among Arab Muslims. This regression has taken place at a libidinal level along the same paths as those taken by the Muslim world throughout its history. It has reawakened unconscious material that is recognized in the collective memory and that is turned to nostalgically. It is opposed to the progress signified by life moving forward over time, by adaptation to requirements posed by living conditions in today's world — that is, globalization. As the Muslim world integrates into globalization, it is revealing all its problems.

In its regression, the Muslim world has lost its vital energy. It has returned to its starting point, the original site of archetypal possibilities, which for the Muslim world are the first three centuries of its life, nostalgically valorized within our collective unconscious. The loss of the libido established in its past renders the Muslim world moribund, or at least gravely ill, and this effect is expressed by its inferiority complex. The shadow of what the Arab Muslim world once was is expressed today through the compensation mechanism of a sense of omnipotence, which is found among Islamist ideologues. This is a death-dealing form of functioning, which we must oppose by the symbolic sacrifice of this nostalgia in order to release vital energy. This is how we may transform this regression into progress and integration into the history that we Muslims left behind six centuries ago. It is from this imaginary position that the ego will have to make the sacrifice, so that it is reborn as something other than subject. Thus, the Arab Muslim world must accept the sacrifice of the myth of omnipotence and choose between life and death — between resurrection and annihilation. It is at the level of our psyche and our collective unconscious that this desire must operate to ensure our self-regulation.

Y. Essid: Let us now look at autonomy. The idea of autonomy, taken here in the etymological sense of the term, is the premise that the individual is the source of the law and of its history. Speaking of the autonomy of the Arab individual, we have a tendency, given our Western culture and our bookish references, to speak of the individual defined by the Enlightenment as having an inherent value independent of her or his belonging to a community. That is, individuals have value not because they belong to a community but, on the contrary, because they are capable of tearing themselves away from their community. In the traditional and religious context of the Arab world, the law is always imposed on the individual, who is attached to traditions, religion, and family. This is heteronomy rather than autonomy. We would have expected to see national independence lead to the emergence of a free Arab individual who has acquired the capacity to transcend her or his community, the space of the clan, tribe, or village, historical tradition, and to establish herself or himself, thus, as a source of entitlement. Such persons would then be capable of positioning themselves as individuals with a value independent of their roots in a tradition, a language, a culture ... Given all of these contradictions, can we speak of a regressive functioning being experienced by populations in the Mediterranean Arab world?

H. Dhaoui: Before answering you, I cannot help wonder about a few things. The first is whether the individuals in this region are capable of modernity. To the definition given by Mohamed Arkoun, "the critique through reason of everything that reason produces," I would add, "on condition that personal freedoms are respected." But when we look at the state of Arab countries, from Morocco to Jordan, the picture is quite disappointing. Since independence, Arab regimes have seen the installation of charismatic leaders, the figure of the *za'îm,* who is in fact the only free individual. He is often symbolically associated with the father of the nation, the paterfamilias, the head of the family — the basis of our communitarian society, in which individual responsibility is totally diluted.

This situation forms individuals who must perpetually act in harmony to cope with the requirements of the group; the group's opinions and hopes are continual stimulations for individuals, awakening their selves by allowing the community ideal to come before self-realization. Jung (1988, 116) expresses it as "the abdication of the self for the good of the collective corresponding to a social ideal: it is even seen as a virtue and a duty to society."

In our societies, individuals embody a hierarchy according to their degree of belonging. First come the members of the family, according to the religious precept that "relatives are the most worthy of the good." Then come the inhabitants of the neighbourhood, the village, the region, the country, the Arab or African nation. This is a sort of independence within dependence, for we must always take account of the demands of the immediate group and its stimulations to accede to some degree of autonomy, although we must not try to find the path to individuation. In other words, people realize their individuality while satisfying the social ideal behind a mimetic and identity-based persona — a persona, according to Jung, that does not enjoy any true reality but is simply the formation of a compromise between the individual and society. Thus, the Arab individual is no longer inscribed in the traditional register that rejects modernity — a behaviour that is in contradiction with her or his self. This is what we are seeing more and more in consultations: a pathology attributable to an internal conflict over a sense of guilt generated by the denial of one of the two registers.

In fact, this is what led me to change over to Jungian analysis after having been a Freudian. According to Freudian psychoanalysis, individuals no longer have the freedom to act once they integrate the principle of reality, in which the social environment imposes its law. Furthermore, if they refuse to submit and act according to their impulses, the law of society is imposed on them through internment. Jung developed a more humanistic approach. He proposed a model that allows the individual to escape the constant grasp of the community. It asks individuals to take account of the needs of the people around them, of their personal unconscious associated with the heritage of humanity forming what Jung calls the self; it also encourages them to seek autonomy, represented by the persona of the subject of identity and mimetic origin. Jung calls this positioning of the individual in relation to her or his personal desires and the requirements of the community "individuation." This model is very exaggerated in the South Mediterranean countries; in the Arab world, it leads to the dilution of individual responsibility as a result of the type of education followed, even undergone, by the individual. It is the authoritarian transmission of a cultural heritage, creating in the subject a dependence on the group in a relational, heteronomic, intra-familial system. This type of education slows the individual's evolution, which is likely to regress even after psychological maturation. In effect, in an authoritarian education, the individual applies orders in the presence of the teacher. Individuals internalize taboos and may reach maturation with an ethical and moral superego, but then the collective community, which remains highly operational in our societies, stifles these individuals, diluting their responsibility within the collective responsibility of group intervention in the individual space. This stifling causes regression in the form of an escape phenomenon that is expressed by assaults on the public and common space by irresponsible individuals. The communitarian collective psychologically imposes its law on the individual, who, in reaction, physically assaults the public and common space. This is what led Jung to state, "The stronger is the collective regulation of men, the greater is the individual immorality."

Y. Essid: The West built its prosperity with Protestantism as the path to wealth; Asia drew on Confucianism; could Islam be inspired by its ethic to build its future, at a time when capitalism is triumphing and considered to be the only avenue?

H. Dhaoui: If prosperity is related to Protestantism in the West and Confucianism in Asia, Islam has an ethic that may enable it to reconstruct itself. I refer first to a poem by one of the four founders of the theological-legal schools in Islam, Muhammad Ibn Idris al-Shafi'i (767-820), founder of Sufism, who was known for his tendency to reconcile and compromise among the different doctrinal currents. In one of his programmatic poems, he uses beautiful metaphors to highlight work, among them "The lion can catch its prey only when it leaves its lair" and "The arrow can reach the target only if it leaves the bow." Furthermore, Islam has nothing against capitalism; I would go so far as to say that merchant capital contributed more to Muslim conquests than did religious fervour, but that is another story. Islam has also strongly encouraged social solidarity by requiring payment of the *zakat,* an income tax that was made the third pillar of the new faith. Thus, the system encourages profit and capital accumulation, although it includes safeguards to ensure social justice. It is completely normal for a universal religion to set out a socio-economic system that is capable of easily adapting to globalization. The problem is, rather, with political regimes ... Moreover, Maghreb workers are fully as hard-working as Polish or Chinese workers; we may simply consider the reputation and dynamism of Maghreb workers labouring in Western countries, where they assume a responsibility that is not diluted in the collective responsibility.

Y. Essid: Before addressing globalization, let's look at history. It would be interesting to address the case of the individual in the Maghreb at different times in history and through various aspects of personality: social, cultural, and economic structures.

H. Dhaoui: First is the pre-colonial period, when individuality was embedded in the community fabric — clan, tribe, village, and so on. The individual did not make the law. The religion was the source of law and provided the connection among individuals in a single community.

With colonization, the reference systems for the Arab individual, community identity, and religious identity were shaken, as were the traditional economic structures. Let's think of urbanization: it was mainly in the cities that the process of individuation was affirmed with the dislocation of cells of community life and the opening of modern social spaces, in which a large number of people found new economic attachments based on responsibility for themselves. School attendance also had this effect, to the extent that the French colonizer opened access for individuals to modern rationality, giving rise to a third reference system that used the secularization of political life — nationalism — as a lever. Although it was stated in the context of the national liberation movement and considered a revolutionary act, nationalism was not able to change the basis of the individuality of Arab people and remained external to them. Their individuality, still embedded in the community and the religious fabric, was unable to break free of the space of the clan, the tribe, and the village, which continued to support them.

Y. Essid: Did independence bring modernization or modernity?

H. Dhaoui: Independence was based on a modern state that was the guardian of the national fact. The nation stood out as the primary reference.

This was also the period of modernity and rejection of tradition. The idea behind modernity is that individualism means progress and emancipation from religion and different forms of heteronomy. There was a partial rupture with the sacred and the traditional world of the past, as well as a partial opening to the notions of modernity and universality, among the Westernized elite, but all to the exclusive advantage of the patrimonial state: absence of democracy, dictatorship by a single party, charismatic leader taking the role of a father figure who overlooked all itineraries in which individual consciences were stalked by the unknown, the uncertainty of the future, the growing anonymity of society, the vertiginous diversity of the world. As autonomous socio-economic actors, Arab individuals are still unstable, psychologically and mentally dependent. They are commanded to assume responsibility for their daily life but without assuming any responsibility in the city. They still do not make the law. They are not yet masters of their destiny, even though they have managed to liberate themselves from the colonizer. They are not even citizens. So, how can they be conceived as autonomous, the source of entitlement, acting on and having full authority over their fate?

Y. Essid: This new situation facing Arab-Muslim society accentuates the transition towards globalization, the dissolution of the great ideological truths, disaffection with pan-Arabism, rejection of institutional Islam, skepticism about utopian discourse and the edification of great leaders, adherence to mass consumerism, and the omnipresence of mass media. Can we thus talk of a "destabilization" of the Arab person's ego, characterized by a withdrawal inward or by the emergence of an individual who has no beliefs?

H. Dhaoui: Starting in the 1970s, the process of affirming individual autonomy accelerated to the point that the models and norms of the global market penetrated throughout society, the ascendancy of the father weakened, and the state lost its means of ideological mobilization. Society then became split between those who were comfortable on the path to integration into the new environment and those who were the victims of this integration. The latter tended to reject not only the nation-state but also the very notion of the nation — a collective space of identification based on the anonymous equality of all individuals — and wanted to restore pre-eminence to the family and the faith as essential reference points of community life that would return the individual to imperfect autonomy. Proponents of this view had a conception of culture as rooted in *asâla, turâth,* and other communities. The former chose the lay and democratic option and proposed to perfect the individual's autonomy by trying to bring her or him to completion through citizenship. This side did not win out, for, to do so, it would have been necessary:

1 for there to be within the masses a current of thought that dared to praise the individual
2 for the social role played by the modern individual to move beyond the limitations of intellectual work, bureaucracy, and the liberal professions to occupy a decisive niche in production (and this would achieve globalization by reducing the state's sovereignty and involvement in the economic sector)
3 for a new global environment to support, politically and economically, these internal changes.

But how can Southern societies be mobilized today, outside of the influence of fundamentalism? How can they be put on the path to democracy without correcting the current disparities arising from the laws of the market? What becomes of the fact that the autonomy of the individual in the South has now become a planetary stake that goes beyond the strict framework of the national state?

Y. Essid: This time, autonomy and freedom are gained at the expense of other freedoms, to which contact with goods is systematically preferred.

H. Dhaoui: This institutional form perceives social life and solidarities as burdens, even archaisms. The market establishes a separation between individuals in the form of a space of freedom and mutual autonomy dominated by objects. Society has no hold over individuals and only ratifies individual choices. The economic sphere is becoming disembodied from the obligations that society bears at all times, be they political or moral. The trade relationship destroys traditional links of dependence and solidarity and replaces them with a world of goods. In the Maghreb, there is a context of simultaneous globalization and re-Islamization, and the individual tends to be affirmed through adherence to a virtual Islam that has escaped the control of any institution or organization. This type of individual autonomy challenges collective engagement as the necessary connection to the relationship with the sacred — the central dogma of Islamism.

Y. Essid: Following this historical overview, my question is whether, in spite of everything, globalization will free Arab individuals from their straitjacket, give them an awareness of freedom and responsibility, and leave them the choice to act.

H. Dhaoui: Globalization may provide the opportunity to wake up and take revolutionary action against ignorance and the established order in our societies. This would be an act of modernity. What is modernity, if not a valorization of the individual who becomes capable of leaving the path of her or his fellow citizens — of making, whenever necessary, a clean slate of tradition — in order to establish a new order based on the rationality shared by all? Now is the time for self-examination. It is in this context that one may propose psychoanalysis as a modern therapy for such a state of affairs. Psychoanalysis is an exploration of the individual's past in order to make her or him aware of all her or his buried complexes. It helps us to recognize our faults so that we can better overcome them. Thus, our uneasiness will no longer be projected onto others, as we will know that we alone are responsible for what happens to us and for our future. It is the only rampart against fatalism, the only means of climbing to the level of responsibility with regard to our present situation.

Abbreviations

AMU	Arab Maghreb Union
AUC	American University in Cairo
BPO	business process outsourcing
CGEM	Confédération générale des entrepreneurs marocains
EEC	European Economic Community
EFL	English as a foreign language
ELT	English language teaching
EU	European Union
EMP	Euro-Mediterranean Process
FTA	free trade area
FDI	foreign direct investment
GATS	General Agreement on Trade in Services
GATT	General Agreement on Tariffs and Trade
GAFTA	Greater Arab Free Trade Agreement
HDI	human development indicator
IBLV	Institut Bourguiba des langues vivantes
ICT	information and communications technologies
IFI	international financial institution
IMF	International Monetary Fund
MEDA	Mediterranean Economic Development Area

MENA	Middle East and North Africa
MNF	multinational firm
MTC	Mediterranean third countries
NMS	New Member States (of the European Union)
OECD	Organisation for Economic Co-operation and Development
SAP	Structural Adjustment Program
SME	small- and medium-sized enterprises
UMA	Union du Maghreb arabe
UNDP	United Nations Development Programme
WB	World Bank
WTO	World Trade Organization

Notes and Acknowledgments

Introduction

1 "The cultural enables the imposition of the political. It shows the true nature of the infatuation with the Mediterranean. This is the source of the ideological function of the contemporary Mediterranean" (Ruel 1991, 8, our translation).

2 "The fact that preference is given to the free trade agreements rather than to other forms of integration (bilateral projects) suggests that the efforts at integration are less part of a regional defensive strategy but constitute, rather, an attempt to deepen competitiveness in order to attack the global market and fall within the liberalization strategy instigated in the 1990s" (Nicolas 1997, 295, our translation).

Chapter 1: Globalization, Governance, and Autonomy

1 When the former French prime minister Lionel Jospin was urged to oppose layoffs by beneficiary firms, he declared, "I can do nothing about it!"

2 On his foreign trips to China, India, South Africa, Angola, and elsewhere, the French president systematically takes along a delegation of entrepreneurs and business people seeking contracts.

3 Or "crony capitalism" (Deblock 2002, 7).

4 This contestation was popularized by the famous "Polish plumber" slogan.

5 Of France's GDP, 25 percent is exported.

6 This observation has been made by all of the human-rights organizations, as well as by the UN and the European Parliament.

7 Ibn Khaldūn discusses this in detail in his *Prolegomena*. In the present volume, see the chapter by Olivia Orozco.

8 In fact, in many countries, the nation-state is expressed appropriately only on certain occasions, such as sports events, when citizens support the national team playing against other nations.

9 Evidence of this is the assistance received by families from their members' working abroad.
10 With the exception of certain basic necessities, which remained subsidized in most countries.
11 This is already the case in Syria. Libya and Egypt are tempted to follow its example.
12 An example is the bloody repression of the riots in Casablanca in 1965. The fact that the offence of expressing an opinion was punished with torture and long-term imprisonment earned this period the nickname "the years of lead."

Chapter 2: Globalization, Autonomy, and the Euro-Mediterranean Space

1 In the multilateral negotiations at the World Trade Organization (WTO) ministerial conference in Cancún, certain developing countries revealed, for the first time, a combative attitude; they made demands and were clearly opposed to decisions made generally against their wishes. Countries on three different continents — India, Brazil, and South Africa — decided to defend their right to development.
2 In this respect, in particular, geopolitics is distinct from economics (mainly with regard to quantification of the effects of free trade), because in many cases it is used to justify integration schemes that either are refuted by economics or have ambiguous effects.
3 In this essay, we make a distinction between autonomy and sovereignty. We consider sovereignty to be the collective autonomy to make political decisions. Autonomy is defined in the broader sense of the capacity to make decisions and undertake actions in political, economic, financial, and other spheres.
4 These were the twelve partners on the south shore of the Mediterranean: Algeria, Cypress, Egypt, Israel, Jordan, Lebanon, Malta, Morocco, the Palestinian Authority, Syria, Tunisia, and Turkey.
5 At the Stuttgart conference in 1999, senior civil servants from the countries in the region started to formulate a Euro-Mediterranean Charter for Peace and Stability, but adoption of the charter fell victim to the political and military tensions in the Middle East (Commission européenne 2000).
6 The Mediterranean partners were Algeria, Egypt, Israel, Jordan, Lebanon, Morocco, Syria, Tunisia, and Turkey. Neither Mauritania nor Libya took part in the Barcelona Process, but they have been observers at the ministerial conferences since 1999.
7 These figures were calculated on the basis of values expressed in billions of dollars of GDP in 2003. In PPP $ billion, the EU-15 contributes to 30 percent of world wealth and to 90 percent of regional wealth. On the other hand, the twenty-two partner southern and eastern Mediterranean countries (the nine Mediterranean partner countries plus Mauritania, Libya, and the Palestinian Territory, plus the NMS-10) contribute to less than 4 percent of the world GDP and less than 10 percent of the regional GDP.
8 Between 1995 and 2003, Egypt, Israel, Jordan, Lebanon, and Syria, the countries of the southeast Mediterranean, saw a slower rate of growth of both their exports to and their imports from Europe (Femise 2005).
9 The human development indicator is defined in paragraph 2.26 of the 2005 report as a "composite index that measures a country's average achievements in three basic aspects of human development: health, knowledge, and a decent standard of living. Health is measured by life expectancy at birth; knowledge is measured by a combination of the adult literacy rate and the combined primary, secondary, and tertiary gross enrolment ratio; and standard of living by GDP per capita (PPP US$)."

10 According to the data of the United Nations Conference on Trade and Development for the countries of central and eastern Europe and EUROSTAT for the Mediterranean countries, the EU-15 invests $833 per inhabitant in the countries of central and eastern Europe and $110 per inhabitant in the Mediterranean countries, while American FDI is only $152 per inhabitant in the former and $49 per inhabitant in the latter (Beckouche et al. 2004).

11 In the latter case, it should be noted that the United States is playing on the field of a third global pole, that of Asia.

12 The Femise report (2005) uses the term *soft integration,* but it seems to us that the term *shallow* better conveys the reality of the relationship between the EU and the Mediterranean partners, because the word *soft* presumes the implementation of an evolutionary process that, in the end, may lead to deep integration, unlike the premise for the new "neighbourhood" policy proposed to the Mediterranean partners.

Chapter 3: '*Asabīyya*, Market, and Society

I would like to thank William Coleman, Yassine Essid, Yván Martín, and Frank Foley for their useful comments.

1 I have sought to understand how 'asabīyya engenders a particular redistribution mechanism that determines the "victims and beneficiaries" of a given social system. New forms of 'asabīyya may appear among groups that benefit less from the new rules introduced by globalization or may provide a rallying point for social groups whose old privileges are threatened as new forms of distribution and social-exchange relations are instituted. Although it induces a positive aspect and a sense of belonging, 'asabīyya may also serve negative, reactionary, or exclusionary social projects.

In the same way that tribal or Bedouin communities resisted or coexisted on the margins of the dynasty as described by Ibn Khaldūn, 'asabīyya today may take on reactionary forms such as resistance identities, to use the term coined by Castells (1999, 6). The new 'asabīyya, powerful after the fall of the dynasty, was extended in the form of new identitary projects, which had the goal of establishing a new social order. Hidden among Islamist groups in different countries in the Mediterranean region is a certain movement towards participation in the democratic game and adaptations to lead to more global projects. These movements seem to reflect a transition from "resistance identities" towards "project identities," from a defensive 'asabīyya of the local group towards a community 'asabīyya, active, evolved, and with a vision for change. The results, however, remain indeterminate. Such reactions and movements may create a sub-society or a sub-economy, or they may create alternative forms of social organization that defy the globalization model. Finally, they may simply be desperate reactions to the transformation of society, similar to those that Polanyi observed in the second quarter of the twentieth century.

See the first texts, dating from 1879 and 1899, by A. Von Kremer and L. Gumplowicz, who translated '*asabīyya* as "a kind of race-cohesion" (Simon 2002, 34).

2 Before him, although expressing a different point of view, theoreticians of Arab nationalism such as Sāti' al-Husrī (1961) had already developed this idea (Simon 2002, 38).

3 See also Stiglitz's preface to Polanyi (2001) and Howard-Hassmann (2005).

4 Castells (1998, 89), like Polanyi, explains the reactions against globalization in local communities by analyzing the effects of the "great transformation" on modern societies.

367

5   For more research on Ibn Khaldūn, see Simon (2002, 11-80).

6   See Carleton Coon (1958), discussed in Anderson (1984).

7   See, among many others, Katsiaficas (1999).

8   *Imaginary* in the definition of Cornelius Castoriadis, as used by Hannoum: "Incessant and essentially determined creation (social-historical and psychic) of figures, forms/images ... What we call 'reality' and 'rationality' are its products" (Hannoum 2003, 63).

9   For a comparison of Ibn Khaldūn and Tönnies, see Spickard (2001). A similar analysis of the taxonomy of societies is found in Lewis Henry Morgan's *Ancient Society* (1877), which had a major impact on the development of anthropological studies; see Lenski (1994).

10 In the early nineteenth century, S. de Sacy had translated and published some parts of the *Muqaddimah* and then other philological research and historical studies of the text. For a review of Orientalist and non-Orientalist studies produced as a result, see Simon (2002). Abdelmajid Hannoum (2003, 67n29) leans explicitly towards the thesis that Durkheim had read Ibn Khaldūn and drew on some of his concepts. He bases this conclusion on the fact that one of Durkheim's doctoral candidates was none other than Taha Huseyn (1889-1973), whose thesis was a study of Ibn Khaldūn's work. However, in 1917, the year of Huseyn's thesis examination and of Durkheim's death, Durkheim's book *De la division du travail social* (1893) had already been published, thus excluding the possibility of Huseyn's exclusive influence on Durkheim.

11 Simon cites several studies, which prove the lack of a scientific basis for a division between "uncivilized-nomadic-Arabs" and "sedentary-civilized Berbers," by showing that the majority of tribes combined the two forms (Simon 2002, 51).

12 See Hannoum's (2003) illustration of the current transformation implied by de Slane's translation of the term.

13 On Ibn Khaldūn's terminology, see the thesis by Kamil Ayad, published in 1930 and cited in Simon (2002). See also Gabrieli (1930).

14 "In fact, al-Mahdi's rise was not due only to his ancestry going back to Fatima (the daughter of the Prophet). His followers were the Hargha and the Masmūda, because of their clan spirit (*'asabīyya*) and because he deeply shared this spirit" (Ibn Khaldūn 1967, 40, our translation).

15 Ibn Khaldūn speaks of two things that give the tribe strength and pride, "lineage and a sense of the group" (*nasabihi wa 'asabīyyatihi*), thus introducing a first distinction between 'asabīyya and direct ancestry (the former term establishing a more direct reference to blood ties, *arhāmihim wa qurabā'ihim*).

16 "Compassion and affection for one's blood relations and relatives exist in human nature as something God put into the hearts of men. It makes for mutual support and aid, and increases the fear felt by the enemy" (Ibn Khaldūn 1969, 98).

17 Labica (1968, 216, our translation) emphasizes how Ibn Khaldūn used the term to apply to people of the Book as being "peoples of *'açabiyya*."

18 De Slane used more than twenty-two different translations (Simon 2002).

19 The theory of orthodox religious history considers Muhammad's message as having replaced early tribal solidarity in the time of polytheism and ignorance (*Jāhilīya*) with belonging to Islam alone (Gabrieli 1930, 491 and 512).

20 Rosenthal (in Ibn Khaldūn 1958, lxxxviii-lxxxix, our translation) states that the concept was closer to *'isābah* and the Qur'anic term *'usbah*, "both meaning 'group,'" in a more general sense and not always necessarily linked to blood ties; Anderson (1984, 119-20) agrees that the concept is based on this identity and that it is endowed with the essential quality of mobilizing groups to action.

21 Katsiaficas (1999, 53) introduced an identitary or nationalist character to this social cement, following the example of Gellner, who spoke to him about "nationalism."

22 Ibn Khaldūn uses five terms with different linguistic roots: al-ijtimā', al-tamaddun, al-hadāra, al-t'annus and, especially, al-'umrān (Saadé 1966). My conception of the term civilization is broader than the meaning that Ibn Khaldūn gives to the words hadāra and 'umrān. Hadāra is related to the sedentary way of life or social organization, while 'umrān refers more generally to the social group or, probably, the culture. For the translation of the term ummah as "religious or historical community" and jīl as "generation" rather than "race," as used in colonial discourse, see Hannoum (2003, 75-80).

23 The monarchs of the dynasty become known for their refinement (kays). In the French translation, V. Monteil translates kays as "cunning" and, later, as "refinement." "With this, the dynasty is strengthened, sovereigns succeed each other at its head, they rival each other for cunning (kays), and they lose the secret of Bedouinsm (sirr al-badâwa) and its simplicity, the Bedouin qualities of moderation and restraint. The royal power appears, with its despotism and its sedentary culture, carried towards refinement" (Ibn Khaldūn 1967, 435, our translation).

24 In the French translation, this distinction does not appear: Dignitaries adopt habits of "'sophistication' (ta hadhluq). Drowning in comfort and luxury, their habits and needs become diversified" (Ibn Khaldūn 1967, 435, our translation).

25 Speaking of the superiority of guardians or riches and fortunes in Plato's ideal state, Ibn Rushd (1966, 150) adds, "You can see this clearly in communities which grow up among the desert-dwellers [al-barârî], nomads and poor men who quickly subdue peaceful, wealthy communities, as did the king of the Arabs to the king of Persia."

26 See Gabrieli's (1930, 479 and 487) analysis of the transition from 'asabīyya as "esprit de corps" or "partisan spirit" to a second form of 'asabīyya, articulated through alliances and "clientelism." It is on this second form that Simon's (2002, 47) analysis is based.

27 "It is because the patron-client relationship creates a contact on the same order as a common ancestry" (Khaldūn 1967, 200, our translation). Ibn Khaldūn (ibid., 133) does not, however, mention the patron-client dichotomy but rather the relationship that is established with the client.

28 Castells (1998, 88, our translation) refers to "building refuges."

29 Once again, I am drawing a parallel with the terminology used by Castells.

30 This is a broader version of the "promise or reality of wealth" with which capitalism traps the individual in Gellner's (1981, 93) vision.

31 Once again, a series of arrangements that Polanyi termed a premodern market embedded in cultural and social forms of control.

32 Castells (1998, 396) posited that the new identity of purpose would arise from contemporary identities of resistance.

Chapter 4: Transmission of Texts and Globalization of Knowledge

1 Between the twelfth and fifteenth centuries, the powerful orders of Calatrava, Santiago, and Alcántara were pre-eminent in Spanish history as military and political forces. In the fourteenth century, their military vocation was transformed into an institution that was both political and religious. Their main mission was to conquer Spain back from Islam (Gerbet 1994, 254).

2 A Romance language, Castilian was one of the local languages on the Iberian Peninsula that were not descended from Latin; Catalonian and Aragonese are other examples. There was, however, a desire to make Castlilian the language of all of the kingdoms.

3 On the *Biblia de Alba,* see Paz y Melia (1922); the volume accompanying the facsimile published by Schonfield (1992); and Fellous (2001).

4 See Prologue, fol. 14v, *Biblia* I (Paz y Melia 1922, 19, our translation): "This is why, very great Lord, the path that I have chosen for this translation, through divine grace and that of the Lord, the Reverend Master Arias, and the Reverend Master Johan de Çamora, Brother of the order of preachers, is to harmonize as much as possible Jerome's translation with the Hebrew as if it were a single text, sometimes moving parts forward and sometimes back, so that the gloss is very correct. And where I cannot harmonize them, I shall follow the Hebrew, conforming thus to Jerome's recommendation ... This is why I ask for mercy from those who will see this translation and the commentaries related to the text, that they be inclined to judge kindly the good intention [that moves me]. And if they find something good in the translation or commentary of this book, I confess that it was stolen and taken from crumbs [that I was able to gather] from the great hall [the library] and the [work] table of said reverend angel of God, your bother in blood and imperial lineage, Master Arias."

5 His Christian name refers to the apostle Paul, previously Saul of Tarsus. Converts often adopted an apostle's name, a very Christian name, or the name of their patron when they were baptized. Pablo de Santa Maria had not inconsiderable influence with the ecclesiastics and in the court circles of Juan I. He was responsible for important diplomatic missions, such as the one to discuss the financial arrangements that sealed the reconciliation between the Trastámara of Castile and the Lancasters of Portugal. He showed his first inclination for conversion in 1390-91, but it has not been possible to determine whether the conversion took place during the riots of 1391. His conversion led to that of many other Jewish intellectuals (Rucquoi 1993, 216-25).

6 In his letter, the Great Master wishes Moses Arragel glory; he uses the word *honnra,* which means esteem and respect. A stronger term than the word *honour (honor),* it is equivalent to *gloria.* Prologue, fol. 1v-2r (Paz y Melia 1922, 26); Fellous (2001, 23).

7 See, notably, chaps. 2, 3, and 15 in Paz y Melia (1922, 2-4, 13) (fol. 3ra-4ra, 10va-11rb).

8 See the description of the miniatures in the prologue in Schonfield (1992, 35-146), particularly in the chapter "Catalogue raisonné of the Miniatures" (79-80), and Fellous (2001, 70-74, 77, 86).

9 The *s*'s are extended into the interlinear space, the cedilla is placed far beneath the letter and is a smaller module, and the downstroke of the *h* descends into the interlinear space in a leftward curve (Canellas 1966, 116-77, pl. lxxvi). The writing in this manuscript is similar to that in ms. 10289 in the Biblioteca Nacional de Madrid, which is the translation into Castilian by Pedro de Toledo of *The Guide for the Perplexed.*

10 The copies of the *Proverbios Morales* are conserved, respectively, at the Biblioteca Nacional de Madrid (ms 9216), the convent library at San Lorenzo del Escorial (ms b iv. 21), the Real Academia de España (R.M. 73), and Cambridge University Library (Add. 3355). There is a critical edition of this work (Sem Tob de Carrion [Ciceri] 1998); see the introduction, 13-18. The *Book of the Kuzari* is conserved at the Biblioteca Nacional de Madrid under manuscript number 17812 and has been published — *Yehudah Halevi, Book of the Kuzari* (Lazare 1990) — and published in facsimile (Yehudà Halevi 1996): *El Cuzari, Edicion facsimil del Ms. 17812 (s. XV) de la Biblioteca Nacional,* Madrid, 1996. *The Guide for the Perplexed* is in the Biblioteca Nacional de Madrid, ms 10289. My analysis of these manuscripts will be published at a later date.

11 Pulgar, among other members of the high nobility, was one of the patrons of new translations or copies of literary and sacred works.

12 In 1422, a Franciscan monk began to translate the *Postilla super totam Bibliam* by Nicolas de Lyre, upon the request of Alonso de Guzmán (Biblioteca Nacional de Madrid, ms KK-3-8).

13 Haggadoth are prayer ritual books reserved for use during the festival of Passover (Pessah), commemorating the Jews' exodus from Egypt. The Sarajevo Haggadah, conserved at the National Museum of Sarajevo, in Bosnia-Herzegovina, is in Italo-Gothic style, which was prevalent in Catalonia at the time, and resembles the 1343 manuscript *Crónicas de Jaime II* (University Library, Barcelona). It contains three coats of arms that confirm that it is originally from Aragon (Narkiss 1969, pl. 10, 60-61). See the complete facsimile edition with analysis of the manuscript ([Werber] 1999).

14 *Biblia de Alba*, prologue, fol. 12r (our translation) (Paz y Melia 1922, 110).

15 This is manuscript 12793 conserved at the Biblioteca Nacional de Madrid; the two illustrations are in folios 35vb and 36r (Bordona 1930, 304, notice 776; Fellous 2001, 286 ill. 177-78, 287-89).

16 Narkiss (1969, 74-75); Oxford, Bodleian Library, MS, Kennicott I.

17 Paris, BnF, Hebrew 15; Sad-Rajna and Fellous (1994, 127-36, notice 53).

Chapter 5: Islam

Translator's note: I used the following Qur'an translation: Ali, Abdullah Yusuf, *The Qur'an: Translation,* 13th ed. (Elmhurst, NY: Tahrike Tarsile Qur'an, 2004).

1 In spite of the intrinsically globalized nature of certain economic sectors, economies remain in the hands of respective national actors. Describing the case of the offshore economy in Tunisia, Béatrice Hibou (2006, 198, our translation) states that it "is fully part of a national economy that remains, despite adjustments and successive liberalization programs, strongly protectionist, and thus also easier to monitor and normalize. Paraphrasing Janet Roitman and Gérard Roso, one might say that the country encourages 'offshoring' in order to remain national."

2 Some debates present globalization as a threat to culture and to languages; they lose sight of the fact that local practices may coexist with and even benefit from the globalization process. In this study, I show that local communities use globalization to strengthen their local practices. For example, the communities of Chiapas have adopted new communications technologies to strengthen local specificity, notably in the educational sphere. This shows that traditional and modern practices may coexist in local communities that take advantage of globalization by treating it as an opportunity rather than as a threat.

3 "The globalization of religions over the last several centuries has, in general, been induced by extra-religious causes" (Thual 2003, 189, our translation).

4 It is for this reason that I propose the notion of internationality in the title of this chapter, for it indicates what might become of the field of globalized religion.

5 It is the religious duty of all Muslims, according to the Qur'an, to commend what is decent and condemn what is reprehensible (al-'amr bi l-ma'rûf wa l-nahy 'an l-munkar). Long disused, this injunction was revived and institutionalized in the Muslim world by the Saudi regime through a governmental agency created in 1979 (1400 h.), called hay'at al-'amr bi l-ma'rûf wa l-nahy 'an al-munkar, the mission of which is to ensure that public morals comply with the religious standards of Islam. This repressive and severe apparatus is constantly denounced by various human rights organizations. On the evolution of this Qur'anic injunction in the history of Islam, see the monumental work by Michael Cook (2001).

6 Except in Turkey, where the principle of laïcité is inscribed in the Constitution.

7 *Marabout,* from the Arabian *murabit,* "a soldier living on the border in a *ribat* (fort) and devoting himself to both jihad and exercises of piety." Today, the term designates chiefs of fraternal societies who gather their disciples in monasteries called *zawiyahs.* This movement is called maraboutism (Sourdel and Sourdel 2004).

8 "On African soil, Asian Islam lost its universalist power. In other words, it was cleansed of its holy fury and became diversified and compartmentalized into local observances. North African maraboutism had, in some way, imposed a departmental and cantonal reform on extreme Semitic monotheism" (Berque 1957, 5, our translation).

9 "Although they did not form a distinct clergy, the ulama nevertheless played an essential role in traditional Muslim society. They controlled institutions judged vital at the time: worship (direction of prayer and preaching); education, on which they held a virtual monopoly; the direction of minds (the mufti had to accommodate problems of all types, which varied depending on the place and the circumstances, to the intangible prescriptions of religious law); and, finally, the religious justice of the *qadi,* who had jurisdiction over everything dealing with personal status and actual affairs of religion — an immense domain with poorly defined borders" (Chérif 1980, 590, our translation).

10 Notably by followers of Wahhabism, a political and religious movement founded by jurist Muhammad Ibn Abd al-Wahhab (1703-92). A pact, referred to as the Pact of Najd, was concluded between al-Wahhab and the al-Sa'ud family — it is still in force — to bring to Arabia a strict form of Islam that would ban Sufism and all forms of worship of the dead or saints associated with polytheism.

11 Any practice or idea considered not to comply with the norms of early Islam.

12 "The mosques, sites of worship, teaching, and social life, are often paired with a varied grouping of fraternal societies, sometimes rivalling ones, that allow heterogeneous elements to be managed from one country — or even region — to another ... The strength of the fraternal society system resides in its deterritorialization, as the fraternal societies are structured in a network and not based in a defined territory" (Thual 2003, 192, our translation).

13 Piece of fabric that covers the entire body with a screen woven in at eye level.

14 The most common name for the "Islamic" scarf that covers the hair, front and back of the neck, and shoulders.

15 Persian word for a piece of fabric, often black in colour, that covers the entire body except the face, hands, and feet.

16 Veil covering the entire body except the eyes.

17 The khimar covers the head and chest but leaves the face uncovered.

18 Long jacket worn with a veil that covers the face.

19 Traditional Tunisian women's veil, made of white cotton, fine wool, or silk, that covers the entire body.

20 Qur'an, 3:83: "All creatures in the heavens and on earth have, willingly or unwillingly, bowed to His Will" (see Ali 2004, 36).

21 Al-Azhar, a mosque-university in Cairo, was founded by the Fatimids in 973. A symbol of Sunni orthodoxy and of the official Islam of the Egyptian state, it enjoys international renown and is still the favoured destination for Asian and African students. For a millennium, it was the authority with regard to fatwas, responding to solicitations from religious bodies in both Muslim and non-Muslim countries, which gave it a transnational dimension.

22 Erected around 730, the Al-Zaytuna Mosque is the main mosque in Tunis and the largest one after the Kairouan Mosque. In addition to being a religious building, in the twelfth

century it became an institute of higher education, which it remained until the modernist reorganization of the education sector by Khaïr-Eddine, at the time grand vizier of Sadok Bey, by decree on 12 January 1875. Al-Zaytuna College, which dispensed a traditional, essentially religious education known as Zeitounian, went through a second reform in 1958, the De Biesse reform, which resulted in the expulsion of 850 *mudarri* teachers.

23 "In the exercise of their institutionalized function of guardian of this text, the ulama tended to reproduce it, comment upon it, or hold it up as sacred, unchanged, and un-changeable. With the accumulation of commentaries, access to the text was more and more mediatized, and its comprehension was filtered through a specialized teacher who provided access to the 'caste' of those who 'know the meaning.' The commentaries and interpretations thus had the effect, contrary to their stated objective of interpretation, of removing the original text from common comprehension and restricting knowledge of it to a determined group, the scholars, who were self-defined as 'the only ones who can understand.' The text thus became an instrument of authority and a means of regulating access to this authority, and its revelation was therefore controlled and transformed into a potential means of social control. The mastery of the law by the ulama gave them the power to legitimize the entire social system and, at the same time, to codify the main relationships uniting individuals and establishing models of behaviour" (Dupret 1999, 169-70, our translation).

24 "This specificity put them in a position of very particular autonomy with regard to the political power, which did not have the authority to act in the name of God directly and without mediation" (Kepel 1985, 430, our translation).

25 Their positions in all respects were generally conservative. "When it came to thought, they were content to be imitators. On the social level, they were fierce defenders of order and the existing economic and social system; on the political level, they were allies or defenders of all established power (as bad as it was, it was preferable to 'anarchy')" (Chérif 1980, 592, our translation).

26 "Although it enjoyed a certain hegemony, Al-Azhar was subjected to strong controls by the Egyptian state starting in the 1960s. These controls helped to 'demystify' the institu-tion, making it one pillar among others in the official religious field" (Orelli 2002, 121, our translation).

27 Decrees of 29 March 1956 and 1 October 1958. The goal was to "gradually eliminate all old forms of teaching ... [that are] inappropriate, hybrid, or obsolete" (speech made by Habib Bourguiba in Tunis, 15 October 1959, our translation).

28 One example is the production *Hadhra* by Fadhel Jazîrî (Universal Musique, 2001). This is a spectacular hybrid staging of liturgical songs adapted to popular tastes and perfectly in phase with the infatuation of a segment of the Tunisian middle class, which was up-rooted and in identitary crisis, with "Sufi" music.

29 An Egyptian author considered one of the greatest Arab thinkers of the twentieth cen-tury. Hussein (1889-1973) was Egyptian minister of education in 1950. His work *Fî al-shi'r aljâhilî* (On pre-Islamic poetry) drew fierce attacks from the religious establishment.

30 Khalid Muhammad Khalid (1920-96) was a progressive Egyptian intellectual who wrote about social change in the Arab world. He was made famous by the publication in 1950 of a book titled *Min hunâ nabda'* (From here we start), in which he described the dangers to Egyptian and Arab society of the creation of a theocratic state. His work was censored by the issuing of the Al-Azhar fatwa, but the judiciary later authorized its distribution.

31 An Egyptian author and reformer, educated at Al-Azhar University and Oxford, Ali 'Abd al-Raziq (1888-1966) is known mainly for his controversial book *Al-islam wa 'usul al-hukm*

(Islam and the source of political authority), published in 1925, in which he defines the position of Islam in relation to the principle of the caliphate and points out that organization of a Muslim state is of a purely temporal order, since the Prophet of Islam had never himself organized a government.

32 Kacem Amine (1863-1908), an Egyptian jurist, man of letters, and reformer, who received his education in France, was a proponent of the principles of freedom and progress founded on an Arab-Islamic culture. In a series of articles, he denounced the ills of Egyptian society, but he was known mainly for his leadership in the struggle for emancipation of Muslim women through his book *Al-mar'a al-jadîda* (The new woman), in which he discusses the veil, polygamy, and divorce.

33 Sheik Muhammad Mitwalli al-Sha'rawi, born in 1911, was a great man of letters who graduated from Al-Azhar in 1940 and taught in various Egyptian cities before going to Saudi Arabia in 1950 to teach theology at Um Al-Qura University. In 1963, he was appointed a director of Al-Azhar University; from 1976 to 1978, he was minister of religious endowments. He wrote a number of works, including an exegesis of the Qur'an.

34 Trained at Al-Azhar, Mohammed al-Ghazali al-Saqqa (1917-96) was a member of the Muslim Brotherhood in the 1940s, embraced socialist ideas in the 1950s, and returned to a more traditionalist, but still militant, approach to Islam in the 1970s. During the 1980s, he became a television personality while he was acting as rector of the Emir Abdelkader University of Islamic Sciences in Constantine, Algeria.

35 An Egyptian, Sheik Abdul Hamid Kishk (1933-96) graduated from the Faculty of Theology at Al-Azhar despite going blind at a young age. Appointed a mosque imam, he used his position as a platform to denounce social and political conditions in the country, for which he was imprisoned for two years. After he was released, in 1968, his inflammatory sermons were followed for ten years by large crowds, recorded on audio- and video-cassettes, and widely distributed throughout the Arab world.

36 Educated at Al-Azhar, Yusuf Al-Qaradawi (born in 1926) was imprisoned a number of times because of his affiliation with the Muslim Brotherhood when Gamal Abdel Nasser was president of Egypt. He is considered by his many disciples to be a moderate conservative, while others see him as a dangerous Islamist. He gained worldwide visibility through the Al-Jazeera television program *Sharia and Life*. A religious scholar proselyte born in Egypt, he founded the European Council for Fatwa and Research in 1997, with the assistance of the transnational Federation of Islamic Organizations in Europe. The council aims to offer a religious reference for European Muslims and to be an interlocutor with governments and civil society with regard to the organization of Muslim worship in Europe.

37 Qur'an 11:6. A number of fatwas have been issued by religious leaders on the legality of contraception. The first, issued in 1937 by Sheik Abd Al-Majid Salem, authorized the faithful to practise contraception and to use abortion if the life of a pregnant woman was in danger. Moreover, political leaders imposed birth-control programs. A declaration was signed in 1966 by nineteen heads of state, six of them Muslim (from Iran, Jordan, Malaysia, Morocco, Tunisia, and the United Arab Republic). "From the monarchy to the republic, from King Farouk, the first to take the precaution of passing the message of moderate demographic growth through the channel of Islamic dignitaries, to President Mubarak, who recently proclaimed that population growth was 'engulfing all reform efforts,' the official credo was, with a few nuances, identical" (Courbage 1994, 214, our translation).

38 Nasr Hamid Abu Zayd was an assistant professor of Islamic studies at the University of Cairo. He wrote a number of articles and books on Qur'anic exegesis and other subjects

related to religion, using new methods of textual analysis. His work provoked fierce criticism by both official Islam and Islamists. His books were proclaimed heretical, and he was declared an apostate in 1995, which, under sharia, annulled his marriage to Ibtihal Yuonis, his Muslim wife, and made him subject to public condemnation, as it was the duty of all Muslims to apply this law. He had no choice but to go into exile. About this affair, see Bâlz (1997) and Abou Zeid (1999).

39 Except that "the acts that they consider free and autonomous are in fact 'the result of a mechanism of constraints that preceded their intention and within which 'and in relation to which they take a position'" (Tersigni 2005, 51, our translation).

40 "In diaspora, globalization strengthens two forms of distancing: one from the culture of origin and the other from societies into which diasporas have chosen to integrate. It is while this choice is being made that the autonomy of diasporas is founded" (Saint-Blancat 2001, 82, our translation).

41 Abul-A'la al-Maududi (1903-79) was born in India. A self-taught religious scholar, journalist, and writer, he founded the Islamist movement Jamaat-e-Islami, with the goal of establishing a truly Islamic state and society in Pakistan, in the 1940s. He finally immigrated to that country in 1947. Al-Maududi's writings and political activities exerted a major influence on Islamist movements, including in the Arab world.

42 The grandson of Hassan al-Banna, founder of the Muslim Brotherhood movement, Ramadan was active in the political debates concerning the Islamic scarf, notably in France. He has written a number of books on Islam in the West, among them *Les Musulmans d'Occident et l'avenir de l'islam* (2002) and *Islam, le face à face des civilisations* (2005).

43 Young Egyptian preacher, star of a popular talk show broadcast on satellite channels called *kalâm mina l-qalb* (Words from the depths of the heart), and now the host of an official website: http://www.amrkhaled.net/ (see Haenni 2002).

44 This opinion was, in principle, simply a consultative document, the value of which resided solely in the moral authority of the mufti who issued it. It had no legislative or executive nature, but it might serve as a foundation for the *qadi* when he handed out his sentence. It was, in a way, the instrument that allowed Muslim normativity to adapt to changing reality (see Tyan 1965).

45 In Egypt, the Dar al-Ifta', the "fatwa committee," was created in the late nineteenth century. The 1961 reform gave rise to the Lajnat al-Fatwa, the fatwa commission, which is seconded by the Majma' al–Buhuth al-Islamiyya, the Institute of Islamic Research (Orelli 2002).

46 Although the main function of the Majelis [Assembly] Ulema Indonesia (MUI) was to support and, in some cases, justify the government's programs and policies, some fatwas, such as those dealing with the breeding of frogs and rabbits for consumption, were controversial, and certain Muslims denounced the MUI, saying that it was seeking to legitimize government policies rather than see to the common good (Hosen 2004).

47 "Tantawi therefore brought a profane competency as a full member into the sacred domain of the divine law" (Orelli 2002, 112, our translation).

48 This is exemplified in an interview with Bernard Saules, president of the National Union of Football Referees, speaking of the early retirement of the Swedish referee Anders Frisk following death threats made against him by supporters of the Chelsea Club in England: "There are refereeing errors every weekend and on every playing field in the world," he said, "but it must not be forgotten that Mr. Frisk's early retirement took place following the 'fatwa' declared against him by José Mourinho, the Chelsea coach" (*Le Monde,* 18 April 2005).

49 Promulgating fatwas has become the main activity of self-proclaimed preachers. Today, certain European countries (through their Muslim communities) are issuing counter-fatwas to frustrate and contest the monopoly of Islamist groups. For example, on the first anniversary of the Madrid attack, the secretary-general of the Islamic Commission of Spain, Mansur Escudero, issued a fatwa declaring that Osama bin Laden had contravened the precepts of Islam by supporting those attacks (Radio-Canada 2005).

50 According to statistics from 2007, fifty fatwas per day were issued on Islamic websites. The Islamonline website alone broadcasts thirty-five fatwas per day and had a bank of 644,000 fatwas in 2007!

51 According to Houweydî (2007), there are more than five thousand satellite television channels in the world, 325 of which are Arab, and about fifteen totally Islamic. In 2007, there were more than 260,000 Islamic websites.

52 Wâ'il Lotfî, "Tasrîh dînî bi mumârasat al-jins," *Rose al-Youssef,* 28 June 2007.

Chapter 6: Muslim Women in the Mediterranean Region

1 In Egypt, more than 450,000 people went on the Umrah pilgrimage in 2006 alone.

2 "The orientation of human capital towards a search for low labour costs led to an increase in the female population active in the labour market from the mid-1970s to the threshold of 2000: from 18.5% to 23.4% for Egypt, from 20.9% to 27.77% for Morocco, from 14.1% to 25.39% for Tunisia" (CAWTAR 2001, 16, our translation).

3 In much of the First Epistle to the Corinthians, St. Paul answers questions raised by the congregation about marriage, the wearing of the veil by women in church, the Christian way of celebrating the Lord's meal, and spiritual donations.

4 Qur'an, sura 24:31, 33:53, and 59.

5 The texts of Islamic jurisprudence are saturated with this. There are dozens, if not hundreds, of these authors; among the most famous are al-Ghazali, Ibn al-Jawzi, and Ibn Koutayba.

6 It is interesting to compare this idea to certain consultations by Saudi sheiks such as Ibn Al Baz: "Even at home, women are ordered to remain veiled so as not to be seen by the angels, or they shall be the cause of *fitna* [seduction provoking discord]." Another, Sheik al-Aythamine, said, "The woman's garb must fall to cover her feet; it must even drag on the ground so that it erases the traces of her steps on the sand, because these traces may provoke a man's sexual desire" (Riffaat 2003, 178 and 180, our translation).

Chapter 7: Local Tunisian Music and Globalization

1 Malouf has become the typical traditional Tunisian music.

2 Mohamad Abdel Wahab (1900-91): famous singer, composer, lutist, and actor. He is considered one of the main architects of the revival of Arabic music.

3 The riqq or *reqq,* called *târ* in the Maghreb, is a percussion instrument with ten pairs of small cymbals.

4 The nay is a reed flute that is very popular in the Middle East and the Maghreb.

5 *Maqam* (plural, *maqamat*) designates the organization of scales of unique melodic paths, obeying mathematical and aesthetic rules. Each system of intervals and paths has its own name — *Hidjaz, Huseynî, Bayatî,* and others — and a specific colour and feeling. Compositions based on maqamat form the basis of urban "scholarly" music, as opposed to "popular" music.

6 Hanine y Son Cubano was formed in 1999. On their self-titled album (Elefrecords Mosaic Music, 2005), "the marriage of Arabic singing and Cuban rhythms is surprisingly natural. Surprising? Not really, when we consider that a number of titles were originally Cuban songs adapted into Arabic. The producer of the album *Hanine y Son Cubano*, Michel Elefteriades, had the interesting idea of taking these songs in the opposite direction and re-Cubanizing them. Perhaps we owe the partial success of the album to this underlying kinship. Partial, because although the result of this Arabic-Cuban encounter never sounds artificial, the concept sometimes seems to take over from the production, which could have been more subtle!" (Roul n.d., our translation).

7 "*Tarab* is ecstasy, the deepest possible emotional response to music, and generating *tarab* is the musicians' overriding goal" (Eyre n.d., our translation).

8 Farid el-Atrach (1915-74): writer, composer, performer, and lute virtuoso, born in Syria, naturalized Egyptian. One of the great masters of Arabic music, a long-time rival of Abdel Wahab, he played in 31 films and had 350 songs in his repertoire.

9 A percussion instrument widespread in the Maghreb and the Middle East. It is a goblet-shaped drum made of terra cotta or ceramic with a membrane of fish skin. Today, it is more commonly made of aluminum with a plastic membrane and adjustable screws to improve its resonance.

10 Rodolphe, Baron d'Erlanger (1872-1932): painter and musicologist born in France and naturalized British. He moved to Tunisia, where he had a palace built according to Andalusian architectural standards; he named it Ennajma Ezzahra (Star of Venus). He surrounded himself with musicians, learned about qanun, and took an interest in Arabic musical treatises of the Middle Ages. His work on and interest in music were so import-ant that King Farouk I asked him to organize the first Congress of Arabic Music. D'Erlanger worked on this project with the help of Tunisian and Middle Eastern musi-cians, as well as with Baron Carra de Vaux. Unfortunately, his poor health made it im-possible for him to go to Cairo for the congress, and he died in Tunis on 29 October 1932. With his contributors, he produced six books, the first being published during his life-time and the last in 1959. His palace now houses the Centre des musiques arabes et méditerranéennes.

11 The term *mezoued* is derived from the Arabic word *mizwij,* which means "double." This wind instrument is composed of a double chanter terminating in two cow horns, and a goatskin bag. The bag, which serves as a bellows, is activated by the player's arm, so that he can breathe while producing a sound that is continuous and sharp. The chanters, made of reed, are decorated in red, have five or six holes, and are tuned in unison. This instru-ment is related to the *zukra.*

12 Oum Kalthoum (1904-75): undoubtedly the greatest Arab singer of the twentieth cen-tury, nicknamed, justly, the "Star of the East," Kawkab al-Sharq.

13 There is no longer a Tunisian, Egyptian, or Qatari audience, but an Arab audience. Similarly, there are no longer singers of one or another nationality, but Arab stars.

14 *Daf(f)/def(f)/duf(f)/douf(f)*: Arab percussion instrument. At first glance, the daff looks like a riq. However, the riq has a much narrower edge and also has small cymbals, which the daff does not always have. These days, there is a tendency, when the daff is compared to its close cousin, to call the riq a *daff alsaghîr* or "small daff." The riq is an instrument of great virtuosity with bright sounds, one of the main drivers of the takht. It is thus a profane musical instrument, whereas the daff, which has a dull tone, is used more fre-quently to accompany religious songs. In Morocco, some daffs have a square or triangu-lar shape.

15 Bouzouki *(buzuq/buzukee/bozuk/bouzouq):* Greece, Turkey, Kurdistan, Syria, Lebanon, Egypt. The bouzouki probably has its origins in a Turkish instrument such as the *saz*. It has a small, deep, oval sound box with a long fretted neck and metal strings. The instrument is tuned in a tempered mode, and it therefore cannot play microtonal ranges. It has four double strings. It was originally used as a solo instrument by immigrants to Syria and Lebanon. Instruments related to the Turkish bouzouki are the *cura* (three strings), the *ebaglama* (six strings), the *asik sasi* (nine strings), and the *meydan sasi* (twelve strings).

16 Gombri: a stringed instrument measuring 109 centimetres in length. Its neck and sound box are made of wood, and the sound box is cylindrical and covered with goatskin. The wooden bridge is called a *rakez*. The three melodic strings made of gut are stretched by leather bands on the sound box. Behind the bridge is a metallic plate containing rings to amplify the rhythm *(chanchana)* (Houaïda n.d.).

17 The quarter-tone maqam is rarely used now. Out of almost one hundred listed maqamat, only three are currently used: *nahawand* (minor), *'ajam* (major), and *kord*. Only four- and two-beat time signatures are used (essentially, *wihda* + *nisf wihda*).

Chapter 8: Globalization and Food Autonomy in the Mediterranean Region

1 In English, just one word designates this food category, while in Spanish there are three: *verduras, legumbres, hortalizas;* in Arabic, there is also just one term, *judar.*

2 "It is possible to establish that the giving and trading of food weaves a network of relations as important and irreducible as that determined by matrimonial exchange" (De Garine 1991, 1495, our translation).

3 "Comer y beber conlleva una apropiación inalienable, una privatización total de recursos indispensables que otros podrían pretender" (Millán 1997, 223).

4 Even if "la agricultura está convirtiéndose en una actividad de localización precaria y revisable" (Bérard and Marchenay 2005, 33).

5 Festival of sacrifice of a sheep.

6 These are eggs produced by chickens raised in an industrial operation. The chickens are grown in a space with an area equivalent to a DIN A4 sheet of paper, which forces them to be immobile. They are fattened until they are forty-two days old, at which point they are slaughtered.

Chapter 9: The Fuentes de Ebro Sweet Onion

1 In December 2005, it had 4,230 residents.

2 Mercazaragoza and Mercabarna are the largest wholesale markets in these two regions and their areas of influence, respectively.

3 A designation of origin (according to EU Regulation 2081/92) is used to designate an agricultural or food product originally from a region, a specific location or, in exceptional cases, a country. The characteristics and qualities flow fundamentally or exclusively from the geographic environment, human and natural factors included. Production and processing must take place within the determined geographic zone.

Chapter 10: Globalization of Food Practices in Amman

1 "La cuina personal, la domèstica, la local, la comarcal, la regional, la nacional, àdhuc la internacional, es veuen afectades per la globalització" (Millán 2000a).

2 Palestinians, Syrians, Iraqis, and Lebanese have arrived in and appropriated Amman, as-similating Ammanian food culture and contributing culinary traits from their respective original geographic areas. Abu-Odeh (1999) distinguishes Transjordanians, who lived in Jordan before the country was created; Palestinians, who live in Palestine; and Jordanians, who hold Jordanian passports. These distinctions are fundamental to an understanding of Jordanian society today.

3 "Un cierto número de indicadores gustativos afirma una identidad alimentaria y delimita muy vigorosamente la pertenencia culinaria a un territorio determinado" (Contrearas 1993, 13).

4 For a definition of *cuisine*, see Fischler (1995, 34).

5 "The Bedouin subsists on cereals and milk products ... Cereals, mainly wheat, are taken with every meal, often in the form of bread and *burghul*, cracked wheat. Unleavened bread is baked daily and eaten fresh. Burghul is boiled and eaten as a complete meal, sometimes with butter or yogurt. Bread, however, still constitutes the bulk of the average Bedouin diet" (Abu Jaber, Gharaibeh, and Hill 1987, 68, our translation).

6 Among peasant dishes are *maqloube*, made with rice, chicken, eggplant, and/or cauli-flower, to which potato is added; *musajjan*, large breads abundantly garnished with onion, olive oil, chicken, and sumac and then baked; *mulukhiya*, a soup usually served with rice; and *kubbe*, a type of wheat semolina ball stuffed with chopped meat. Some of these dishes represent the Palestinian or Syrian identity rather than the Transjordanian identity.

7 This is the ancient Ottoman province that encompassed Jordan, Syria, Lebanon, and Palestine. Although divided by French and British colonization, which made them polit-ically separate states, these countries remain strongly united culturally and socially.

8 In Lavergne's (2003) view, although it seems logical that the inhabitants of western Amman would ignore those of eastern Amman, it is not clear that the inhabitants of eastern Amman feel any envy for those in western Amman, where the values are so dif-ferent from their own.

Chapter 11: Food Globalization and Autonomy Strategies

1 "Food models are socio-technical and symbolic ensembles that connect human groups to their environment, form a foundation for their identity, and institute an internal social differentiation process" (Poulain 2002, 25, our translation).

2 Four factors that determine or condition the selection of foods are related to the process of buying it: (1) its availability in the retail outlet, which is influenced by the consumer's socio-economic position; (2) the social representation, that is, the symbolism that the food has in the context of the society and the culture that generates this group of signifi-cations; (3) the social status and role that the selected food has in the model of food affilia-tion; and (4) the consumer's social status and role (including when the food was chosen and when it is eaten).

3 For more details, see Durán Monfort (2005).

4 I am referring to meat declared *halal* when the animal sacrifice is made according to Islamic prescriptions: "Pronouncing the name of God is central to this ritual. After turning the head of the sheep towards *Ka'aba*, the sacrificer pronounces the *tasmiya* phrases: in the name of God *bismillah*, the *takbir*; God is the greatest *allahu akbar*; and the permission to remove the soul *subhana man hallalaka li-l dhabîh*" (Kanafani-Zahar 2000, 150, our translation).

5 Advertising by major transnational food companies introduces the symbolism of the local into the collective imaginary to encourage consumption of industrial products.

6 These posters appear mainly in big-box stores such as Carrefour and Géant. In this case, the text is from a poster displayed at Carrefour.

7 The food behaviour of Tunisians has changed because of the professionalization of women and transformations in housing modes. This has made the production of traditional dishes more complicated than it was when women's role as mother and homemaker gave the time needed to prepare food. Traditional utensils are becoming harder to find, and modern utensils are not appropriate.

8 Sundays and festival days, especially meals breaking the fast during the month of Ramadan or during Eid al-Adha (festival of the sacrifice of the lamb), both occasions for family reunions.

9 A term used by Joan Lacomba (2001) (our translation).

Chapter 12: Globalized Literature and Autonomy

1 *Al-Ayyâm* (London 1932; Cairo 1943) and *Yawmiyyât nâ'ib fi al-aryâf* (London 1947).
2 Associated Press, 5 February 2005.
3 Samir Jiryis, *Al-Hayat,* 4 December 2004.
4 Ibid.
5 A second volume edited by Anouar Abdel-Malek was published in 1978.
6 Interview in *Le Monde des Livres,* 27 April 2006 (our translation).
7 Rabi' Jaber, *Al-Hayat,* 27 April 2005 (our translation).
8 Comment made to the author.
9 Published by the United Nations Development Programme. Other reports have followed, including the 2004 report on "knowledge societies."

Chapter 14: Globalization, Autonomy, and Higher Education

1 The World Development Report for 1998-99 concluded, "Today's most technologically advanced economies are truly knowledge-based ... creating millions of knowledge-related jobs in an array of disciplines that have merged overnight" (World Bank 1999, 16).

2 See *World Declaration on Higher Education for the Twenty-First Century: Vision and Action* and *Framework for Priority Action for Change and Development in Higher Education,* adopted by the World Conference on Higher Education under the aegis of UNESCO in 1998, http://www.unesco.org/education/educprog/wche/declaration_eng.htm.

3 Classification on the basis of article I of the GATS.
4 GATS, article 1.3.
5 France, National Assembly, *Rapport d'information, le contrôle des dépenses publiques et l'amélioration des performances de l'État, dossier législatif,* no. 765, 2 April 2003, http://www.assemblee-nationale.fr/12/rap-info/i0765.asp.

6 "The statistics show that the children of senior civil servants and professors represent almost 50 percent of students in the preparatory classes for grandes écoles, compared to 7 percent for sons of workers, while the latter represent more than 37 percent of children in their age class ... For example, most of the students admitted to the major competitions such as those for the École Normale Supérieure or the École Polytechnique come from ten preparatory schools. Taking this to the point of absurdity, one could no doubt establish that the majority of students in the most important French grandes écoles started their education in one or two hundred preschool classes!" (Attali et al. 1998, 20, our translation).

7 Statistics show that the proportion of graduates from the grandes écoles who are unemployed is clearly lower than is that of graduates from university master's and doctoral programs.

8 From one to four times as rigorous, depending on the "rank" of the university and the type of training in the respective grande école; see Attali (2008).

9 In a book written by a group of researchers, professers, consultants, and administrators, titled *Pour une pédagogie universitaire de qualité* (Leclercq 1998, 16-18, our translation), quality indicators for training institutions were given by experts working in the Belgian experience context, and high among them were "the means that the organization has and that it judges essential to reach the objectives pursued," "the autonomy that the organization has to adapt its educational program, both on the pedagogical level and in the design of programs," "the administrative, pedagogical, organizational, and financial constraints weighing on the organization or felt as such by it," and "the means developed so that the education dispensed encourages the learning of autonomy, creativity, and communication."

10 In an article subtitled "Recettes pour une université plus mercantile," the Abélard group (2003, 8-9, our translation) offers an eloquent example, that of Université de Limoges — considered "average" among French universities — in which courses of study are "grounded within other disciplines." For instance, a master's degree in human sciences with three disciplines — "history, geography, sociology" has been transferred into a master's degree with a "blurred discipline": "territories, powers, cultures, and patrimonies." The authors of the article question the usefulness and value of such a degree "in the face of other master's degrees from other (better-ranked) establishments, which directly display the disciplines."

11 The United Nations Development Programme's report on human development for 1992 (PNUD 1992) notes that "the net transfer of resources to wealthy countries is accelerating as the IMF is beginning to require the repayment of its loans. Between 1986 and 1990, $31.5 billion was transferred to the IMF alone, a sum representing about 22 percent of capital outflow from the South and East to the North" (our translation).

12 Recommendations of the World Bank (1998). The World Bank's report identifies some of the obstacles faced by the higher education sector in Tunisia, in the context of an economy in transformation.

13 On this question, but for teaching of English, see the chapter by Mongi Bahloul in this volume.

14 In 2006, more than 40 percent of the dormitory capacity at universities was privately run.

15 In their report, the World Bank (1998) experts advocated the "best scenario" of setting registration fees at 570 Tunisian dinars.

16 According to the Department of Higher Research, Scientific Research, and Technology in 2006, there were twenty-two private universities (compared to eighteen in 2005), with more than 2,200 Tunisian and more than 3,000 foreign students.

17 Secondary-school teachers are not supposed to do research, whereas high-quality higher education cannot be disconnected from scientific research.

Chapter 15: The Economics of Globalization and Autonomy in the Mediterranean Region

1 Plan Bleu (http://www.planbleu.org) is a good example of a long-term project to study threats to the Mediterranean region's environment.

2   Since antiquity, the Mediterranean region has been a space of trade relations and of confrontation between regional powers. This was also the case during both world wars.

3   In this chapter, the North-South binomial refers to the countries situated on either side of the Mediterranean Sea. Taking the economic realities of these countries into account, Turkey is considered a Southern country and Israel a Northern country.

4   The Mediterranean region has seen various eras of intense political and economic integration. Modern integration is part of a much broader process that tends to homogenize different dimensions of the social and economic life of countries in the region. Today, globalization is a process of partnership or voluntary alignment. No unifying model attempted in the Mediterranean has succeeded in reconciling the political, social, and economic differences in the region.

5   The independence movement began in the mid-1950s in Morocco (1956) and continued until the early 1960s. Algeria was the last country to obtain independence, in 1962.

6   For example, the question of funding for the Great Dam on the Nile River drew Egypt into the group of countries close to the Soviet bloc. Given the refusal by the World Bank, seen as an institution controlled by the United States, to fund the Aswan Dam, Egypt turned to the Soviet Union to find the funding it needed for the project.

7   In France, the price of a baguette, the most popular style of bread, was liberalized only in the early 1990s.

8   In Libya, the government began to take over direct management of the economy in 1969, when the regime changed, and this trend was exacerbated after the first increase in the price of oil in the early 1970s.

9   For decades, the countries and allies of the Soviet bloc had offered developing countries, including the countries south of the Mediterranean Sea, the possibility of product-for-product trade.

10 The significance of the availability of economic information and data on different countries during the 1980s in the dissemination of economic liberalization models has not yet been fully studied. It can be said, however, that the data available to the signatories to the WTO accords are better formulated than were the fragments of information that the negotiators of the Havana Accord attempted to gather (see the GATT archives, digitized by the library of Stanford University [http://gatt.stanford.edu/page/home]).

11 In general, the incentive system in administered markets was considered less effective than that in a liberalized market system. The idea that an administered economy favoured workers over consumers was borne out in various difficulties with the stabilization of Southern economies and slowed growth in Northern countries.

12 Industrial subcontracting, which developed between Northern and Southern countries from the 1970s to the 1990s, spread to other regions, particularly Asia, in the form of outsourcing (see Chapter 20 by Fatma Sarraj, this volume). The ease of communicating orders, fabrication models, and data through ICT was an important aspect of this evolution.

13 It is worth noting that the founding of the WTO in a Mediterranean country, Morocco, revived the old International Trade Organization project, stillborn in an American country forty-three years before.

14 The free trade areas (FTAs) concern trade in industrial products. The implementation of an FTA is generally programmed for a decade.

15 For example, there was greater tourist flow from the new eastern European members of the EU to Southern countries. Tourism is one of the largest sectors of services exports (about one-third) by Southern countries.

16 Foreign trade by European countries with southern Mediterranean countries represents less than 5 percent of their international trade. This is why the EU does not show much interest in the Southern countries. Nevertheless, a number of initiatives have been created to support development in the South. There have even been attempts to find an economic justification for a more vigorous economic development policy in the South, arising from the idea that the market potential of the South could serve as a lever for the economic revival of the North, and could even provoke some additional economic growth (Pastré and Chevalier 2003).

17 The two most important issues for the EU in its relations with its Southern neighbours are security and control of migratory flows. The broadening of the EU to eastern European countries was motivated largely by the desire to strengthen its borders with Russia and remove the zone from Russian influence.

18 See Chapter 16 by Rim Mouelhi in this volume on the perception of globalization by stakeholders and elites and on the major nuances that affect their relationship without truly throwing it into question. In the agricultural sector, some European countries, France chief among them, have long dragged their feet about giving up major grants accorded to their agriculture sector and liberalizing foreign trade. Some Southern countries, such as Egypt, fear the effects of liberalization on essential crops such as cereals and industrial crops such as cotton.

19 The opening of the first Carrefour store in Tunisia was a major event. An unprecedented traffic jam blocked traffic around the new big-box store for several hours. However, Tunisians had been accustomed for some time to seeing the products sold in the new point of sale on the local market.

20 The case of big-box supermarkets is typical.

21 This is a single gain in level of gross domestic product spread over the long term.

22 A recent study on labour needs in France established that there is a risk of labour shortages in these fields (Chardon and Estrade 2007).

23 Similar to what takes place on the border between Mexico and the United States, the Mediterranean region has become the theatre for a revolving-door chase between immigrants and border-control authorities. The immigrants, some of them from sub-Saharan countries and others from Maghreb countries, are finding riskier and riskier ways to cross the Mediterranean Sea, putting their lives in danger. According to some sources, there have been more than twenty shipwrecks per week.

24 Of course, this does not exclude certain social costs and questions about specific interests.

25 The chapter by Abdeljabbar Bsaies in this volume (Chapter 1) discusses this question in depth. We may recall how Southern countries often declare their commitment to institutional reform projects that are suggested to them by international institutions while demanding the right to run these programs at their own pace, often for legitimate reasons.

26 Ricardo (1995) maintains in fact that rent charges will continue to exist because of capitalism and that they are not linked to the feudal nature of the old regime.

27 In some cases of cross-border mineral deposits, international accords have settled the question of appropriation. Examples include accords between Tunisia and Algeria concerning exploitation of underground water in the Sahara and accords between Tunisia and Libya concerning exploitation of offshore oil deposits.

28 The energy content in industrial production is 10 percent on average.

29 Energy prices also have an effect on the cost of living and thus on salary levels and purchasing power, which amplifies their role in the competitiveness of production factors.
30 It must be noted that this is one of the few regions in which, following a war that involved
   all of the countries except Switzerland and a few micro-states, as well as a long period of
   colonization, peaceful relations were established among the former belligerents.
31 Here, I adopt an approach to prospective analysis popularized by Michel Godet, particularly in his work *Manuel de prospective stratégique* (1997).
32 Prioritization techniques make it possible to construct a synthesis of proposed presumed
   relations between pairs of variables. I take account here of the direct and indirect effects.
   These techniques do not make it possible to synthesize my hypothesis on dependence and
   influence relations between pairs of variables. This hypothesis reflects what is most commonly observed in the literature. It does offer, however, a more complete view of the
   system as a whole, in light of the synthesis resulting from the use of the techniques.

Chapter 16: Globalization and Autonomy in the Mediterranean Region

1 The Mediterranean region is "the EU's southern border, along which it must have a presence to manage migratory flows, combat the possible spread of international terrorism,
   and encourage a development policy heavily dependent on cooperation in order to fight
   various illegal activities" (Prodi 2002, 3, our translation).
2 International delegation of unions to the WTO summit in Doha, November 2001.
3 Here, I define *elite* in the intellectual sense of the term.
4 Following long debates in GERIM working and discussion groups.

Chapter 17: The Challenge of Financial Globalization in Countries South of the Mediterranean Basin

1 The savings rates were 26 percent, 25.54 percent, and 21.6 percent, respectively, in Jordan,
   Morocco, and Tunisia in 2002, compared to 14.66 percent and 14.56 percent, respectively,
   for Great Britain and the United States for that year (World Bank statistics, 2002).
2 The details of this study are provided in the Appendix.

Chapter 19: The South Mediterranean Countries and Economic Opening

I would like to thank Professor Abdeljabbar Bsaies, Lotfi Bouzaïane, and Yassine Essid for
their comments, which had a great influence on this chapter. I alone am responsible for the
ideas and results contained within it.

1 Immediate tariff dismantlement, gradual tariff dismantlement, negative lists.
2 Israel also has sector-based agreements with Egypt and Jordan concerning the textile
   sector, signed in 2004.
3 These countries are Egypt, Jordan, Lebanon, Libya, Morocco, Syria, and Tunisia. The
   Palestinian Authority ratified the agreement but has not yet applied it.
4 Services remain dependent on the WTO Agreement.
5 Variables are normalized using the equation $Yit = (xit-min)/(max-min)$, where Yit is the
   value of the normalized indicator, and xit represents data relative to the indicators. *Min*
   and *max* represent, respectively, the minimum and maximum values in the sample.

6 The Southern countries are Morocco, Tunisia, Turkey, Egypt, Israel, and Jordan. The Northern countries are France, Italy, Portugal, and Spain.

7 Author's working notes on catching-up among Mediterranean countries.

8 The convergence test applied below reveals exactly which countries are non-convergent.

9 The participation and influence of civil society in this regard remain limited.

Chapter 20: The Mediterranean and Outsourcing

1 Outsourcing should not be confused with facility management. Outsourcing is defined as subcontracting on a larger scale (from one link in the production chain to providing a service). In this context, outsourcing is subcontracting applied to a broader field of production and the supply of a good or a component of a good to the corporate department globally attached to the production system (for example, after-sales, marketing, communications).

2 "A firm is considered multinational if it possesses at least one production unit abroad" (Mucchielli 1998, 5, our translation).

3 Gratner Centre, figures published on Journal Du Net, "JDN solutions," 17 July 2005, http://www.journaldunet.com.

4 Source: Data Monitor, BPO and IT services in the world in the first quarter of 2005.

5 The total French expenditure in facility management was €4.35 billion in 2004, a rise of 8.6 percent over 2002. See the International Data Center (IDC) website.

6 See the IDC website: Poids de l'infogérance sur les services informatiques.

7 For Tunisia, Morocco, and Turkey, over 60 percent of all goods exported are finished goods. For Israel, the share of exports of intermediate goods is constantly growing and has exceeded 70 percent with the rest of the world. Algeria is still dependent on its natural resources, and Libya, initially an exporter of finished goods, is beginning to see a new trend towards intermediate goods. Egypt is in the same situation.

8 MIPO (Mediterranean Investment Project Observatory), 2003-4, "Destination sub-region for FDI projects by number of projects."

9 See Appendix 3, "Index des entreprises ayant investi dans MEDA depuis deux ans," in Jaffrin and Saint-Laurent (2005, 71-72).

Chapter 21: Epilogue

1 *Pour une psychanalyse maghrébine* (Paris: L'Harmattan, 1999); *L'Amour en islam* (Paris: L'Harmattan, 2001); with Gérard Haddad, *Musulmans contre l'islam* (Paris: Éd. du Cerf, 2006).

Works Cited

Abélard (collective). 2003. La transformation néolibérale de l'université: Recettes pour une université plus mercantile. In *Universitas Calamitatum: Le livre noir des réformes universitaires*, 1-31. Broissieux: Éditions du Croquant (coll. savoir/agir).

Abou Zeid, Nasr. 1999. *Critique du discours religieux*. Paris: Sindbad-Actes Sud.

Abu Jaber, Kamel S., A. Fawzi Gharaibeh, and Allen Hill. 1987. *The Badia of Jordan: The process of change*. Amman: Publications of the University of Jordan.

Abu-Odeh, Adnan. 1999. *Jordanians, Palestinians and the Hashemite Kingdom in the Middle East peace process*. Washington, DC: United States Institute of Peace Press.

Allen, Roger. 1994. PROTA: The Project for the Translation of Arabic. *Middle East Studies Association Bulletin* 28 (2): 165-68.

Al-qâhira wal hijâb (Cairo and the veil). 2006. *Al-Sharq al-Awsat* (London-based newspaper), 24 November.

Al-Qurtubî. 1978. *Al-Jâmi' li Ahkâm al-Qur'ân*. Vol. 7. Beirut: Édition Dâr Iyhâ' al-Turâth.

Al-Sayyâb, Badr Shaker. 1977. *Le golfe et le fleuve*. Trans. André Miquel. Paris: Sindbad.

Al Sayyid Said, Muhammad. 2004. Culture de la relation entre le civil et le politique dans les ONG. In *ONG et gouvernance dans le monde arabe,* ed. S. Ben Néfissa, N. Abd al-Fattah, S. Hanafi, and C. Milani, 65-79. Paris and Cairo: Karthala and Cedej (coll. Kalam).

Ali, Yusuf. 2004. *The meaning of the Holy Quran*. Beltsville, MD: Amana Publications.

Anderson, Jon W. 1984. Conjuring with Ibn Khaldun: From an anthropological point of view. In *Ibn Khaldun and Islamic ideology*, ed. Bruce B. Lawrence, 111-21. Leiden: E.J. Brill.

Appadurai, Arjun. 1996. *Modernity at large: Cultural dimensions of globalization*. Minneapolis: University of Minnesota Press.

Aristotle. 1999. *Politics*. Trans. Jowett Benjamin. Kitchener: Batoche Books.

Arkoun, Mohammed. 1998. L'islam actuel devant la tradition et la mondialisation. In *Islam et changement social*, ed. Mondher Kilani, 1-29. Lausanne: Payot.

Attali, Jacques, et al. 1998. *Pour un modèle européen d'enseignement supérieur*. http://guilde. jeunes-chercheurs.org/Reflexions/Documents/1998-attali.pdf.

—, ed. 2008. *Rapport de la Commission pour la libération de la croissance française.* http://www.liberationdelacroissance.fr/files/rapports/rapportCLCF.pdf.

Badawi, Muhammad Mustafa, ed. 1967. *A critical introduction to modern Arabic poetry.* Cambridge: Cambridge University Press.

Baer, Yitzhak. 1998. *Historia de los judíos en la España cristiana.* Barcelona: Riopiedras.

Bahloul, M., and Andy Seymour. 1992. Project sustainability: A case study of the Tunisia, ESP project. *ELT Management* 8: 2-6.

Bâlz, Kilian. 1997. Submitting faith to judicial scrutiny through the family trial: The Abû Zayd case. *Die Welt des Islams* 37 (2): 135-55.

Beck, Ulrich. 2002. *Qué es la globalización? Falacias del globalismo, respuestas a la globalización.* Barcelona: Paidós estado y sociedad.

Beckouche, Pierre, Yann Richard, Delphine Digout, and Pascal Lamy. 2004. *Atlas d'une nouvelle Europe: L'Europe élargie et ses voisins — Russie, Proche Orient, Maghreb.* Paris: Éditions Autrement.

Béji, Samouel. 2007. Ouverture financière et développement financier dans la région du bassin sud de la Méditerranée: Approche institutionnelle et calcul de seuils de développement. Paper presented at a workshop at Université Paris XIII, France, 14 January.

Ben Abdelkader, Fahmi, and Daniel Labaronne. 2006. Gouvernance, libertés et spécificités institutionnelles des MENA dans le contexte économique mondial: Analyse à partir d'une approche multidimensionnelle. RSCAS No. 2006/02, Robert Schuman Center for Advanced Studies, European Union Institute Working Papers.

Benlahcen Tlemçani, Mohamed, and Sofiane Tahi. 2002. Maghreb/UE: Pour une nouvelle intégration économique. Paper presented at the International Conference on Trade, Currency Unions, and Economic Integration, Toronto, 17-20 May.

Ben Néfissa, Sarah. 2004. Introduction. In *ONG et gouvernance dans le monde arabe,* ed. S. Ben Néfissa, N. Abd al-Fattah, S. Hanafi, and C. Milani, 11-25. Paris and Cairo: Karthala and Cedej (coll. Kalam).

Bérard, L., and P. Marchenay. 2005. Sobre los productos de la tierra en las cocinas de carácter local: Algunas observaciones sobre la herencia compartida y la denominación. In *Sabores del mediterráneo: Aportaciones para promover un patrimonio alimentario común,* ed. J. Contreras, A. Riera, and F.X. Medina, 222-31. Barcelona: Institut Europeu de la Mediterránia.

Berque, Jacques. 1957. Quelques problèmes de l'Islam maghrébin. *Archives des sciences sociales des religions* 3 (1): 3-20.

Bisong, Joseph. 1995. Language choice and cultural imperialism: A Nigerian perspective. *ELT Journal* 49 (2): 122-32.

Bonner, Michael. 2005. Poverty and economics in the Qur'an. *Journal of Interdisciplinary History* 35 (3): 391-406.

Bordona, Dominguez. 1930. *La miniatura española.* Vol. 2. Barcelona: Firenze, Pantheon.

Bourdieu, Pierre. 2000. *Les structures sociales de l'economie.* Paris: Seuil.

Bourgüinat, Henri. 1995. *La tyrannie des marchés: Essai sur l'économie virtuelle.* Paris: Economica.

Boyer, Robert. 1978. Les salaires en longue période. *Économie et Statistique* 103: 25-57.

Brasseul, Jacques. 2004. Le déclin du monde musulman à partir du moyen âge: Une revue des explications. *Régions et Développement* 19: 20-54.

Brouillette, Véronique, and Nicole Fortin. 2004. *La mondialisation néolibérale et l'enseignement supérieur.* CSQ Communications, January. http://cbcsq.qc.net/sites/1673/documents/secteurs/d11373 (accessed 22 September 2008).

Brousseau, Éric. 1995. Les apports de l'analyse économique des contrats à la mise en oeuvre des politiques industrielles. *Revue d'économie industrielle* 71: 181-98.

Canellas, Angel. 1966. *Exempla scriptorum latinorum, pars altera*. Vienna: Caesaraugustae.

Castells, Manuel. 1998. *La era de la informacion: Economia, sociedad y cultura*. Vol. 2, *El poder de la identidad*. Madrid: Alianza Editorial.

—. 1999. *Le pouvoir de l'identité*. Paris: Fayard.

Castillo, Monique. 2001. Les droits de l'homme entre cosmopolitisme et mondialisation. Working document, Department of Philosophy, Université de Poitiers. http://www.sha.univ-poitiers.fr/philosophie/.

Castoriadis, Cornelius. 1975. *L'institution imaginaire de la société*. Paris: Seuil.

—. 1987. *The imaginary institution of society*. Translated by Kathleen Blamey. Cambridge, MA: MIT Press.

Castro, Americo. 1984. *España en su Historia: Cristianos, Moros y Judios*. Critical edition. Barcelona: America Castro.

Catusse, Myriam. 2002. Actores privados, acción pública: La patronal y la política en Marruecos. In *La sociedad civil en Marruecos*, 160-85. Barcelona: Icaria.

CAWTAR (Center of Arab Women for Training and Research). 2001. *The Arab women development report: Globalization and gender— Economic participation of Arab women*. Tunis: CAWTAR.

Chardon, Olivier, and Marc-Antoine Estrade. 2007. *Les métiers en 2015*. Report of the group Prospective des métiers et qualifications, France, January. http://www.strategie.gouv.fr/ (accessed 3 July 2008).

Chaussinard, Guy. 1986. Élites. In *Dictionnaire des sciences historiques*, ed. André Bruguiére, 110-13. Paris: Presses universitaires de France.

Chérif, Mohamed Hédi. 1980. Hommes de religion et pouvoir dans la Tunisie de l'époque moderne. *Annales: Histoire, Sciences Sociales* 35 (3): 580-97.

Chevallier, Dominique. 1997. Harmonie des peuples méditerranéens? *Politique étrangère* 62 (3): 399-413.

Chiffoleau, Sylvia. 2004. La place des ONG dans la réforme du système de santé en Égypte. In *ONG et gouvernance dans le monde arabe*, ed. S. Ben Néfissa, N. Abd al-Fattah, S. Hanafi, and C. Milani, 271-83. Paris and Cairo: Karthala and Cedej (coll. Kalam).

Chkir, Hafidha. 2000. *Le statut des femmes entre les textes et les resistances: Le cas de la Tunisie*. Tunis: Chama.

Claret, Andreu. 2004. Prologue: La complexité de la société marocaine. In *La société civile au Maroc*, ed. Maria-Angels Roque, 12-20. Paris: Publisud.

Cohen, Elie, and Jean-Hervé Lorenzi. 2000. *Politiques industrielles pour l'Europe*. Paris: La documentation française.

Commission européenne. 2000. *Le processus de Barcelone: Cinq ans après 1995-2000*. Luxembourg: Office des publications officielles des Communautés européennes.

—. 2005. *Dixième anniversaire du Partenariat Euro-méditerranéen: Un programme de travail pour relever les défis des cinq prochaines années*. Communication de la Commission au Conseil et au Parlement européen. http://www.humanrights-observatory.net/revista3/Barcelona1.pdf.

Contrearas, Jésus. 1993. *Antropología de la alimentación*. Madrid: Eudema.

Cook, Michael. 2001. *Commanding right and forbidding wrong in Islamic thought*. Cambridge: Cambridge University Press.

Coulomb, Pierre, and Florence Jacquet. 1994. Les relations CEE-Maghreb, deux années cruciales: 1986 et 1996. In *Crise et transitions des politiques agricoles en Méditerrannée*, ed. A.M. Jouve, 21-42. Montpellier: CIHEM-IAMM.

Courbage, Youssef. 1994. L'imprévisible fécondité égyptienne. *Population* 49 (1): 212-22.

Crépon, Marc. 2002. Mémoires d'empire (exploitations, importations, traductions). *Trans-européennes* 22: 1-25.

De Bandt, Jacques. 1983. La politique industrielle: Réponse de l'État-nation à la crise? *Revue d'économie industrielle* 23: 36-56.

Deblock, Christian. 2002. Du mercantilisme au compétitivisme: Le retour du refoulé. *Cahiers de recherche 02-03 — CEIM.* Publication of the Groupe de recherche sur l'intégration continentale, Université du Québec à Montréal, September. http://www.er.uqam.ca/nobel/ieim/IMG/pdf/Refoule.pdf.

De Garine, I. 1991. Les modes alimentaires: Histoire de l'alimentation et des manières de table. In *Histoire des moeurs.* Vol. 1, *Les coordonnées de l'homme et la culture matérielle,* ed. Jean Poirier, 1447-627. Paris: Gallimard (coll. Pléiade).

De Labarre, Matthiey. 2001. *Modernidad y alimentación: Hacia una aculturación culinaria? Quaderns de la Mediterrània.* Barcelona: Institut Català de la Mediterrània d'Estudis i Cooperació.

De Montlibert, Christian. 2004. *Savoir à vendre: L'enseignement supérieur et la recherche en danger.* Paris: Éditions Raisons d'agir.

Denoeux, Guilain. 2004. Promouvoir la démocratie et la gouvernance dans les pays arabes: Les options stratégiques des bailleurs de fonds. In *ONG et gouvernance dans le monde arabe,* ed. S. Ben Néfissa, N. Abd al-Fattah, S. Hanafi, and C. Milani, 60-75. Paris and Cairo: Karthala and Cedej (coll. Kalam).

Dieckoff, Alain. 2000. *La nation dans tous ses états: L'identité nationale en question.* Paris: Flammarion.

Duby, Georges, and Michèle Perrot. 1991. *Histoire des femmes.* Vol. 1. Paris: Plon.

Dupin, Henri, J.L. Cuq, M.I. Malewiak, C. Leynaud-Rouaud, and A.M. Berthier, eds. 1997. *La alimentación humana.* Barcelona: Bellaterra.

Dupret, Baudouin. 1999. L'historicité de la norme: Du positivisme de l'islamologie juridique à l'anthropologie de la norme islamique. *Annales: Histoire, Sciences Sociales* 54 (1): 169-96.

Durán Monfort, Paula. 2005. Selección alimentaria: Disponibilidad y representación social del alimento — La carne *halal* y los espacios de distribución en el área mediterránea. *Revista de Trabajo Social y Salud* 51: 211-38.

El-Cheikh, Nadia M. 1997. Describing the Other to get at the Self: Byzantine women in Arabic sources (8th-11th centuries). *Journal of the Economic and Social History of the Orient* 40 (2): 239-45.

Enriquez, Eugène. 2000. Démocratie, capitalisme et développement en Europe occidentale. In *Développer par la démocratie,* ed. Sophia Mappa, 81-120. Paris: Karthala.

Espeitx Bernat, E. 1999. Producción, distribución y consumo de los productos de la tierra: El caso de Cataluña. In *Alimentación y cultura: Actas del Congreso Internacional, 1998, Museo Nacional de Antropología, España,* vol. 2, by Congreso Internacional de Alimentación y Cultura, 781-96. Huesca: La Val de Onsera.

European University Association. 2007. *Lisbon Declaration.* Brussels: European University Association.

Eyre, Banning. n.d. Book review of *Making music in the Arab world: The culture and artistry of Tarab,* by A.J. Racy. Afropop Worldwide. http://www.afropop.org/multi/feature/ID/312/Tarab:+Making+Music+in+the+Arab+World (accessed 29 August 2008).

Farb, Peter, George J. Armelagos, and William Desmond. 1985. *Anthropologie des coutumes alimentaires.* Paris: Denoël.

Feenstra, Robert C., and Gordon H. Hanson. 1996. Globalization, outsourcing and wage inequality. National Bureau of Economic Research (NBER) Working Paper No. 5424, January. http://www.nber.org/papers/w5424.pdf?new_window=1.

Fellous, Sonia. 2001. *Tolède, 1422-1433: La Bible de Moïse Arragel de Guadalajara — Quand un rabbin interprète la Bible pour des chrétiens.* Paris: Somogy.

Femise (Forum Euro-Méditerranéen des Institutions en Sciences Économiques). 2005. *Le partenariat euro-méditerranéen, 10 ans près Barcelone: Acquis et perspectives.* Edited by S. Radwan and J.-L. Reiffers. http://www.femise.org/PDF/Femise_T2005fr.pdf.

—. 2006. *Rapport du Femise 2006 sur le partenariat euro-méditerranéen: Analyses et propositions du Forum Euro-Méditerranéen des Instituts Économiques.* Ed. S. Radwan and J.-L. Reiffers. http://www.femise.org/PDF/Femise_A2006fr.pdf.

Fischler, Claude. 1995. *El (h)omnívoro: El gusto, la cocina y el cuerpo.* Barcelona: Anagrama. Original French version titled *L'homnivore* (Paris: Odile Jacob, 1990).

Fitouri, Chedly. 1983. *Biculturalisme, bilinguisme et éducation.* Paris: Delachaux et Niestlé.

Fouad, Viviane, Nadia Refat, and Samir Morcos. 2004. De l'inertie au mouvement. In *ONG et gouvernance dans le monde arabe,* ed. S. Ben Néfissa, N. Abd al-Fattah, S. Hanafi, and C. Milani, 110-25. Paris and Cairo: Karthala and Cedej (coll. Kalam).

Gabrieli, Francesco. 1930. Il concetto della 'Asabiyyah nel pensiero storico ei Ibn Khaldûn. In *Atti Della R. Academia delle Scienze Di Torino, Classe Di Scienze Morali, Storiche E Filologiche,* 473-512. Turin: Stamperia Editoriale Rattero.

Geertz, Clifford. 1987. *The interpretation of cultures.* New York: Basic Books.

Gellner, Ernest. 1981. Cohesion and identity: The Maghreb from Ibn Khaldun to Emile Durkheim. In *Muslim Society,* ed. Ernest Gellner, 86-98. London: Cambridge University Press.

George, Susan. 1999. *A short history of neoliberalism.* Global Policy Forum. http://www.globalpolicy.org/globaliz/econ/histneol.htm (accessed 22 July 2008).

Gerbet, Marie-Claude. 1994. *Les noblesses espagnoles au Moyen Âge, XIe-XVe siècle.* Paris: Armand Colin.

Godet, Michel. 1997. *Manuel de prospective stratégique.* 2 vols. Paris: Dunod.

Goldzihedr, Ignaz. 2003. *Les sources de l'Islam.* Preface by Rémi Brague. Paris: Desclée De Brouwer.

Goody, Jack. 1995. *Cocina, cuisine y clase: Estudio de sociología comparada.* Barcelona: Gedisa.

Gracia Arnaiz, Mabel. 1997. *La transformación de la cultura alimentaria: Cambios y permanencias en un contexto urbano (Barcelona, 1960-1990).* Madrid: Ministerio de Educación, Cultura y Deportes.

Gutwirth, Eleazar. 2003. Le Sefer Yuhasin (Livre des Généalogies) et la période tunisienne d'Abraham Zacut. In *Juifs et Musulmans en Tunisie,* ed. S. Fellous, 93-101. Paris: Somogy.

Habermas, Jürgen. 1996. *Between facts and norms: Contributions to a discourse theory of law and democracy.* Trans. William Rehg. Cambridge, MA: MIT Press.

Haenni, Patrick. 2002. Au-delà du repli identitaire ... Les nouveaux prêcheurs égyptiens et la modernisation paradoxale de l'islam. Analysis for Religioscope, November. http://www.religioscope.com/pdf/precheurs.pdf.

—. 2005. *L'islam de marché: L'autre révolution conservatrice.* Paris: Seuil.

Hagège, Claude. 2003. Le multilinguisme dans la sphère judéo-tunisienne. In *Juifs et Musulmans en Tunisie,* ed. S. Fellous, 115-37. Paris: Somogy.

Hannoum, Abdelmajid. 2003. Translation and the colonial imaginary: Ibn Khaldûn, orientalist. *History and Theory: Studies in the Philosophy of History* 42 (1): 61-81.

Hatem, Fabrice. 1993. *La prospective, pratique et méthodes.* Paris: Economica.

Hayek, F. August. 2007. *Droit, législation et liberté.* Paris: Presses universitaires de France.

Helleiner, Eric. 1999. Sovereignty, territoriality and the globalization of finance. In *States and sovereignty in the global economy,* ed. D.A. Smith, D.J. Solinger, and S.C. Topik, 138-57. London: Routledge.

Hervieu-Léger, Danièle. 2001. Crise de l'universel et planétarisation culturelle: Les paradoxes de la mondialisation religieuse. In *La globalisation du religieux,* ed. Jean-Pierre Bastian, Françoise Champion, and Kathy Rousselet, 87-96. Paris: L'Harmattan.

Hibou, Béatrice. 2003. Le partenariat en réanimation bureaucratique. *Critique Internationale* 18: 117-28.

—. 2006. *La force de l'obéissance: Économie politique de la répression en Tunisie.* Paris: La Découverte.

Hosen, Nadirsyah. 2004. Behind the scenes: Fatwas of Majelis Ulama Indonesia (1975-1998). *Journal of Islamic Studies* 15 (2): 147-79.

Houaïda. n.d. Les cordophones: Souvenirs et imaginaire Le gombri. Museevirtual.ca. http://www.virtualmuseum.ca/Exhibitions/Instruments/Francais/cmam_j_txt11a_fr.html.

Houweydî, Fahmy. 2007. Al-fatâwî al-gharîba: Man al-mas'ûlu anhâ? *Al-Sharq al-Awsat,* 7 January.

Howard-Hassman, Rhoda E. 2005. The second great transformation: Human rights leapfrogging in the era of globalization. *Human Rights Quarterly* 27: 1-40.

Hugon, Philippe, ed. 2003. *Les économies en développement à l'heure de la régionalisation.* Paris: Kharthala Éditions.

—. 2005. Intégrations régionales, normes et institutions. In Intégrations régionales dans les pays en développement région, special issue, *Région et Développement* 22: 5-18.

Hurbon, Laënnec. 2001. Pentecôtisme et transnationalisation dans la Caraïbe. In *La globalisation du religieux,* ed. Jean-Pierre Bastian, Françoise Champion, and Kathy Rousselet, 125-38. Paris: L'Harmattan.

Ibn Khaldûn. 1958. *The Muqaddimah: An introduction to history.* Trans. and ed. Franz Rosenthal. Bollingen Series 43. New York: Pantheon Books.

—. 1967. *Ibn Khaldun: Discours sur l'histoire universelle Al-Muqaddima.* Trans. into French by Vincent Monteil. Beirut: Thesaurus Sindbad.

—. 1969. *The Muqaddimah: An introduction to history.* Trans. Franz Rosenthal. Edited and abridged by N.J. Dawood. Princeton, NJ: Princeton University Press.

—. 2004. *Muqaddimat Ibn Khaldun.* Ed. Khalil Shihadah and Suhayl Zakkar. Beirut: Dar al-Fikr.

Ibn Rushd, Abu al-Walid Mohammed. 1966. *Averroes' commentary on Plato's Republic.* Translated by Erwin Isak Jakob Tosenthal. Cambridge: Cambridge University Press.

Jaffrin, Stéphane, and Bénédict de Saint-Laurent. 2005. *Les investissements directs étrangers (IDE) dans la région MEDA en 2004.* Notes et études ANIMA No. 15, janvier. http://www.animaweb.org/uploads/bases/document/Et15_MIPO-2004_VF.pdf.

Jayyusi, Salma Khadra, ed. 1987. *Modern Arabic poetry: An anthology.* New York: Columbia University Press.

Jobert, Bruno, and Bruno Theret. 1994. France: La conservation républicaine du néolibéralisme. In *Le tournant néolibéral en Europe,* ed. Bruno Jobert, 21-85. Paris: L'Harmattan.

Jung, Carl Gustav. 1988. *Dialectique du moi et de l'inconscient.* Paris: FolioEssai.

Kachru, Braj B. 1987. Englishization and contact linguistics. *World Englishes* 13 (2): 134-54.

Kanafani-Zahar, Aïda. 2000. Le sang, le porc et l'alcool dans un village multireligieux au Liban. In *Alimentation et pratiques de table en Méditerranée,* ed. Yassine Essid, 140-62. Paris: Maisonneuve et Larose.

Kardiner, Abram, and Ralph Linton. 1939. *The individual and his society.* New York: Columbia University Press.

Katsiaficas, George. 1999. Ibn Khaldun: A dialectical philosopher for the 21st century. *New Political Science* 21 (1): 45-57.

Kaufmann, Daniel. 2002. Governance matters. World Bank Policy Research Working Paper No. 2196, Washington, DC. http://www.worldbank.org/wbi/-governance.

Kébabdjian, G. 2004. Économie politique du régionalisme: Le cas euro-méditerranéen. *Revue Régions et Développement* 19: 151-84.

Kennedy, Chris J. 1985a. A brief survey of ESP in Tunisia. *English for Specific Purposes* 96: 5-6.

—. 1985b. The KELT ESP Project, Tunisia. *English for Specific Purposes* 96: 3-5.

Kennedy, Judith. 1985. The pioneer school for the teaching of sciences through English. *English for Specific Purposes* 96: 7-9.

Kepel, Gilles. 1985. Les oulémas, l'intelligentsia et les islamistes en Égypte: Système social, ordre transcendantal et ordre traduit. *Revue française de science politique* 35 (3): 424-45.

—. 2000. *Jihad: Expansion et déclin de l'islamisme*. Paris: Gallimard.

Khor, Martin. 1997. L'OMC au service des transnationales. *Le Monde diplomatique*, May: 15-17.

Kristiansen, Wendy. 2005. Visage féminin de l'islam. *Le Monde diplomatique*, September: 4-7.

Labica, George. 1968. *Politique et religion chez Ibn Khaldoun: Essai sur l'idéologie musulmane*. Alger: SNED.

Lacomba Vázquez, J. 2001. *El Islam inmigrado: Transformaciones y adaptaciones de las prácticas culturales y religiosas*. Madrid: MEC.

Laïdi, Zaki. 2002. *Le sacre du présent*. Paris: Flammarion.

Laval, Christian, and Louis Weber. 2003. Comme si l'école était une entreprise. *Le Monde diplomatique*, June: 6-7. http://www.monde-diplomatique.fr/2003/06/LAVAL/10135.

Lavergne, Marc. 2003. Fracture sociale et fragmentation spatiale dans un processus de métropolisation: Le cas d'Amman. *Insaniyat* 22: 95-113.

Lazare, Mosh, ed. 1990. *Yehudah Halevi, Book of the Kuzari*. Thundersley, UK: Labyrinthios.

Leclercq, Dieudonné, ed. 1998. *Pour une pédagogie universitaire de qualité*. Wavre, Belgium: Éditions Mardaga.

Lenski, Gerhard. 1994. Social taxonomies: Mapping the social universe. *Annual Review of Sociology* 20: 1-26.

Leonhardt Santini, Maud. 2006. *Paris, librairie arabe*. Paris: Parenthèses.

Léroi-Gourhan, André. 1973. *Milieu et techniques: Évolution et techniques*. Paris: Albin Michel.

Llamazares Ortega, Amparo, and Arturo Martínez Rodés. 2000. "La cebolla, un alimento sano y siempre presente." Government of Aragón: Surcos de Aragón, no. 66.

Lorente, Miguel. 2001. *La fuerza de la diferencia: La denominación de origen, un instrumento para el desarrollo*. Huesca: La Val de Onsera.

Lutrand, Marie-Claude. 2003. Les significations spirituelles du voile islamique. *Courrier International* 679, 6-12 November.

Mahfouz, Naguib. 1995. *Les fils de la Médina*. Paris: Sindbad-Actes Sud.

Mappa, Sophia, ed. 1995. *Développer par la démocratie? Injonctions occidentales et exigences planétaires*. Paris: Karthala.

Mason, Alane, Dedi Felman, and Samantha Schnee, eds. 2006. *Literature from the "Axis of Evil": Writing from Iran, Iraq, North Korea, and other enemy nations*. New York: New Press.

McArthur, Tom. 1997. The English languages. Paper presented at the TSAS Third International Conference, Sfax, Tunisia, 24-26 April.

McGrew, Anthony. 1997. *The transformation of democracy?* Cambridge: Open University.

Mermier, Frank. 2005. *Le livre et la ville: Beyrouth et l'édition arabe*. Paris: Actes Sud.

Metzger, Thérèse. 1975. The Alba Bible of Rabbi Moses Arragel. *Bulletin of the Institute of Jewish Studies* 3: 131-55.

Michalet, Charles Albert, and Jean Pierre Sereni. 2005. L'articulation gouvernance publique/privée au Maghreb et son impact sur l'investissement privé: Le cas de l'Algérie et de la Tunisie. Contribution prepared for the OECD Development Centre.

Milani, Carlos R.S. 2004. Les ONG dans la gouvernance mondiale. In *ONG et gouvernance dans le monde arabe*, ed. S. Ben Néfissa, N. Abd al-Fattah, S. Hanafi, and C. Milani, 29-47. Paris and Cairo: Karthala and Cedej (coll. Kalam).

Millán, Amado. 1997. Alrededor de la mesa: Aspectos normativos, rituales y simbólicos de la comensalía. In *La función simbólica de los ritos: Rituales y simbolismo en el Mediterráneo*, ed. F. Checa and P. Molina, 219-64. Barcelona: Icaria.

—. 2000a. Cultures alimentàries i globalitzaciò. In Transculturaciò, consum i alimentaciò, special issue, ed. A. Millán, *Revista d'Etnologia de Catalunya* 17: 72-81.

—. 2000b. Le scrupule alimentaire: Une approche socioculturelle. In *Alimentation et pratiques de table en Méditerranée*, ed. Yassine Essid, 123-38. Paris: Maisonneuve et Larose.

Mishra, Ramesh. 1999. *Globalization and the welfare state*. Northampton, MA: Edward Elgar Publishing.

Morrisson, Christian. 1996. *The political feasibility of adjustment*. Paris: OECD, Policy Brief No. 13.

Morvan, Yves. 1983. La politique industrielle française depuis la libération: Quarante années d'intervention et d'ambiguïtés. *Revue d'économie industrielle* 23: 19-35.

Mouaqit, Mohamed. 2004. Le mouvement des droits humains au Maroc. In *La société civile au Maroc*, ed. Maria-Angels Roque, 535-42. Paris: Publisud.

Mucchielli, Jean Louis. 1998. *Multinationales et mondialisation*. Paris: Seuil.

Naïr, Sami. 2003. *L'empire face à la diversité*. Paris: Hachette-littérature.

Narkiss, Bezalel. 1969. *Hebrew illuminated manuscripts*. Jerusalem/New York: Encyclopaedia Judaica/Macmillan.

Nassaux, Jean-Paul. 2005. L'ethnisme, projet d'autonomie sociale et individuelle de la mondialisation. *Pyramides, Les services publics et l'espace mondialisé* 9: 111-31.

Ndegwa, Stephen. 2002. Decentralization in Africa: A stocktaking survey. Africa Region Working Paper Series no 40, November. Available at http://www. worldbank.org/afr/wps/wp40.pdf (consulted 8 October 2008).

Next Page Foundation. 2005. *Annual Report*. Edited by Kevin Allen. http://www.npage.org/IMG/pdf/2005report-web.pdf.

Nicolas, Françoise. 1997. Mondialisation et régionalisation dans les pays en développement: Les deux faces de Janus. *Politique étrangère* 62 (2): 293-307.

Orelli, Luisa. 2002. Islam institutionnel égyptien et modernité: Aperçu du débat à travers les *Fatâwa* d'Al-Azhar et de *Dâr al-Iftâ'*. *Studia Islamica* 95: 109-33.

Orozco de la Torre, V. Olivia. 2006. Manifestaciones diversas del pensamiento económico en el mundo islámico medieval. In *Variaciones sobre la historia del pensamiento económico mediterráneo*, ed. Schwartz Pedro, 135-51. Almeria, Cajamar: Caja Rural Intermediterránea.

Pacios Lopez, Antonio. 1957. *La Disputa de Tortosa*. Madrid and Barcelona: Consejo Superior de Investigaciones Cientificas Institute Arias Montano.

Pastré, Olivier, and Jean-Marie Chevalier, eds. 2003. *5 + 5 L'ambition d'une association renforcée*. Les cahiers du Cercle des économistes, No. 4. http://www.lecercledeseconomistes.asso.fr/ (accessed 3 July 2008).

Payne, R.M., ed. 1983. *Language in Tunisia*. Tunis: IBLV Publications.

—. 1984. The Arabization quandary and Tunisian education. *Developments* 49 *AMIDEAST*: 10-11.

—. 1985. The training of English students at the Faculty of Letters, University of Tunis. *English for Specific Purposes* 96: 6-7.

Paz y Melia, A. 1922. *Biblia Antiguo Testamento traducida del hebreo al castellano por Rabi Mose Arragel de Guadalajarra (1422-1433?) y publicada por el Duque de Berwick y de Alba.* 2 vols. Madrid: Imprenta Artística.

Pécheul, Armel. 1999. La nation. In *Le libéralisme contre la mondialisation,* ed. ALCESTE, 52-67. Paris: L'oeil F.X. de Guibert.

Phillipson, Robert. 1992. *Linguistic imperialism.* Oxford: Oxford University Press.

Plihon, Dominique. 2003. *Le nouveau capitalisme.* Paris: Éditions La Découverte.

PNUD (Programme des Nations Unies pour le développement/United Nations Development Programme). 1992. *Rapport mondial sur le développement humain 1992.* Paris: Economica. http://hdr.undp.org/en/reports/global/hdr1992/chapters/french/.

—. 2005. *Rapport mondial sur le développement humain 2005.* http://hdr.undp.org/en/reports/global/hdr2005/chapters/french/.

Polanyi, Karl. 1957. *The great transformation.* Boston: Beacon Press.

—. 2001. *The great transformation: The political and economic origins of our time.* Preface and edited by Joseph E. Stiglitz. Boston: Beacon Press.

Pouillaude, Agnès. 1999. La bonne gouvernance, dernier né des modèles de développement: Aperçu de la Mauritanie. GED Working Paper 37, Université Montesquieu — Bordeaux IV. http://ged.u-bordeaux4.fr/ceddt37.pdf.

Poulain, Jean-Pierre. 2001. Les modèles alimentaires. In *Manger aujourd'hui: Attitudes, normes et pratiques,* ed. J.-P. Poulain, 13-29. Toulouse: Privat.

Prodi, Romano. 2002. L'Europe et la Méditerranée: Venons-en aux faits. Paper presented at Université catholique de Louvain-la-Neuve, Louvain-la-Neuve, 26 November. http://www.euromed-seminars.org.mt/archive/ministerial/EuroMed-time4action-fr-w.pdf.

Rabenoro, Irène, and Suzy Rajaonarivo. 1997. À l'aube du 21e siècle, quelle politique linguistique pour Madagascar? *Mots* 52 (1): 105-19.

Radio-Canada. 2005. Une fatwa lancée contre Ben Laden. *Nouvelles de RadioCanada.* http://www.radio-canada.ca/nouvelles/International/nouvelles/200503/10/010-oussama-esoagne.shtml.

Ramadan, Tariq. 2002. *Les Musulmans d'Occident et l'avenir de l'islam.* Paris: Sindbad-Actes Sud.

—. 2005. *Islam, le face à face des civilisations.* Tawhid Eds.

Regnault, Henri. 2003. *Libre-échange Nord-Sud et typologies des formes d'internationalisation des économies.* Séminaire EMMA-RINOS, Analyse comparatiste des processus d'intégration régionale Nord-Sud, Paris, 26-27 May, Maison des Sciences Économiques et CEPREMAP. http://web.univpau.fr/RECHERCHE/GDRI-EMMA/Rinos/SemParis/Regnault.pdf (consulted 11 July 2008).

—. 2004. Nord et Sud en Méditerranée: De la confrontation à la coopération, de la divergence à la convergence. *Régions et Développement* 19: 7-17.

Reich, Robert. 1991. *L'économie mondialisée.* Paris: Dunod.

Reinhardt, Klaus, and Horacio Santiago-Otero. 1986. *Biblioteca Biblica iberica medieval.* Madrid: Consejo Superior de Investigaciones Científicas.

Ricardo, David. 1995. *Des principes de l'économie politique et de l'impôt.* Paris: Flammarion.

Richards, Eddie. 1989. Developing a communication network. Paper presented at Seminar on Strategies for Developing ESP Projects in Francophone Africa, Tunis, 16 August.

Riffaat, Said. 2003. *Les islamistes: Qu'ont-ils fait de l'islam et de nous?* Cairo: Société Al Amal d'impression et d'édition.

Rivals, Éric. 2003. Où nous mène l'A.G.C.S.? *Site d'information sur l'A.G.C.S.* http://agcs.free.fr/agcst_fr.html (accessed 22 September 2008).

Robertson, Roland. 1997. Glocalization: Time-space and homogeneity-heterogeneity. In *Global modernities,* ed. M. Featherston, S. Lash, and R. Robertson, 25-44. London: Sage.

Rodríguez Díaz, Elena E. 1998. La manufactura del libro en la Castilla Cristiana: Artesanos judios y conversos (ss. XIII-XV). *Gazette du Livre médiéval* 33: 29-34.

Roque, Maria-Angels. 2004. Clés politiques et sociologiques de la société civile au Maroc. In *La société civile au Maroc,* ed. Maria-Angels Roque, 27-50. Paris: Publisud.

Roque, Maria-Angels, Myriam Catusse, Mohamed Mouaqit, and Omar Ouakrim, eds. 2004. *La société civile au Maroc: L'émergence de nouveaux acteurs de développement.* Paris: Publisud.

Roul, Guillaume. n.d. Chroniques — Arabo-Cuban [Hanine y Son Cubano]. *Mondomix.* http://hanine_y_son_cubano.mondomix.com/fr/chronique3799.htm.

Rucquoi, Adeline. 1993. *Histoire médiévale de la péninsule ibérique.* Paris: Seuil (collection Points histoire).

Ruel, Anne. 1991. L'invention de la Méditerranée. *Vingtième siècle, Revue d'histoire* 32: 7-14.

Saadé, Ignacio. 1966. La religión como factor de civilizacion. *Al-Andalus* 31: 155-83.

Sachwald, Frédérique. 2003. Du bon usage de la mondialisation. *Politique étrangère* 2: 2560-73.

Said, Edward. 1978. *Orientalism.* New York: Penguin.

Saint-Blancat, Chantal. 2001. Globalisation, réseaux et diasporas dans le champ religieux. In *La Globalisation du religieux,* ed. Jean-Pierre Bastian, Françoise Champion, and Kathy Rousselet, 75-86. Paris: L'Harmattan.

Scalambrieri, V. 2004. Democratic conditionality within the framework of the Euro-Mediterranean Partnerships. Jean Monnet Working Papers in Comparative and International Politics 55 (November), Université de Catania, Département de science politique. http://www.fscpo.unict.it/EuroMed/jmwp55.pdf.

Scholte, Jan Aart. 1997. Global capitalism and the state. *International Affairs* 73 (3): 427-52.

—. 2002. Société civile et gouvernance mondiale. In *Gouvernance mondiale,* 211-32. Paris: Conseil d'analyse économique.

Schonfield, Jeremy, ed. 1992. *La Biblia de Alba: An illustrated manuscript Bible in Castilian — The companion volume.* Madrid: Fundación Amigos de Sefarad.

Schwamm, Henri. 2003. *L'Europe dans le débat sur la mondialisation.* Geneva. http://www.ieug. ch/colloques/schwamm.pdf (no longer available).

Sed-Rajna, Gabrielle, and Sonia Fellous. *Les manuscrits hébreux enluminés des bibliothèques de France.* Leuven: Peeters, 1994.

Seddik, Youssef. 2007. *L'arrivant du soir: Cet islam de lumière qui peine à devenir.* Paris: l'Aube.

Séguin, Michel, Louis Maheu, and Jean-Guy Vaillancourt. 1995. Les nouveaux mouvements sociaux de l'environnement: Au coeur de changements politiques et culturels. *Journal of Canadian Studies* 30 (1): 102-14.

Sem Tob de Carrion. 1998. *Proverbios Morales.* Critical edition by Marcella Ciceri. Modène: Mucchi editore.

Seymour, Andy. 1994. English in Tunisia. *IATEFL Newsletter,* 123: 15-19.

Sghir Janjar, Mohamed. 2004. Associations de modernisation économique et de développement local. In *La société civile au Maroc,* ed. Maria-Angels Roque, 115-39. Paris: Publisud.

Shamsie, Yasmine. 2000. *Engaging with civil society: Lessons from the OAS, FTAA, and Summits of the Americas.* Ottawa: L'Institut Nord-Sud, January. http://www.iatp.org/tradeobservatory/ library.cfmrefID=24509 (accessed 26 September 2008).

Simmel, G. 1986. Sociología de la comida (1910). In *El individuo y la libertad: Ensayos de crítica de la cultura,* 263-70. Barcelona: Península.

Simon, Róbert. 2002. *Ibn Khaldun: History as science and the patrimonial empire.* Budapest: Akadémiai Kiadó.

Sinclair, Timothy J. 1994. Between state and market: Hegemony and institutions of collective action under conditions of international capital mobility. *Policy Sciences* 27: 447-66.

Siroën, Jean-Marc. 2004. *La régionalisation de l'économie mondiale*. Paris: La Découverte.

Smith, Adam. 1976 [1776]. *La richesse des nations*. Paris: Gallimard.

Sourdel, Janine, and Dominique Sourdel. 2004. *Dictionnaire historique de l'islam*. Paris: PUF.

Spickard, James V. 2001. Tribes and cities: Towards an Islamic sociology of religion. *Social Compass* 48 (1): 103-16.

Stiglitz, Joseph. 2002. *La grande désillusion*. Paris: Fayard.

Talib, Mohammad. 2005. Review of *The Epistemology of Ibn Khaldûn*, by Zaid Ahmad. *Journal of Islamic Studies* 16 (1): 70-72.

Tersigni, Simona. 2005. La pratique du hijab en France: Prescription, transmission horizontale et dissidence. In *La politisation du voile*, ed. Françoise Lorcerie, 37-51. Paris: L'Harmattan.

Thual, François. 2003. La mondialisation des religions, toujours recommencée? *Hérodote* 1 (108): 189-205.

Thuot, Jean-François. 1994. Déclin de l'État et formes postmodernes de la démocratie. *Revue québécoise de sciences politique* 26: 75-102.

Tillion, Germaine. 1966. *Le harem et les cousins*. Paris: Seuil.

Trigo, d'Aurora. 2003. Commerce intra-branche et intégration Nord-Sud. In *Intégration euro-méditerranéenne et stratégies économiques*, ed. Henri Regnault, 290-311. Paris: L'Harmattan.

Triki, Fathi. 1998. *La stratégie de l'identité*. Paris: Arcantères.

Tyan, Émile. 1965. Fatwa. *Encyclopédie de l'Islam*. Vol. 1. Leiden: E.J. Brill.

United Nations Development Programme. 2003. *Arab human development report 2003*. New York: UNDP. http://www.arab-hdr.org/publications/other/ahdr/ahdr2003e.pdf.

Vallet, Odon. 2003. *Les religions dans le monde*. Paris: Flammarion.

Wehr, Hans. 1994. *A dictionary of modern written Arabic (Arabic-English)*. New York: Ithaca.

[Werber, Eugene]. 1999. *The Sarajevo Haggadah*. Study by Eugene Werber. Sarajevo: Svetlost.

Willaime, Jean-Paul. 2001. Les recompositions internes au monde protestant: Protestantisme établi et protestantisme évangélique. In *La globalisation du religieux*, ed. Jean-Pierre Bastian, Françoise Champion, and Kathy Rousselet, 171-82. Paris: L'Harmattan.

Wong, Megan. 2007. World literature: Found in translation. *Christian Science Monitor*, 1 February. http://www.csmonitor.com/2007/0201/p13s02bogn.html (accessed 27 August 2008).

World Bank. 1998. *L'enseignement superieur tunisien: Enjeux et avenir*. Washington, DC: World Bank. http://www-wds.worldbank.org/external/default/WDSContentServer/WDSP/IB/2000/07/19/000009265_3980513111735/Rendered/PDF/multi_page.pdf.

—. 1999. *World Development Report 1998/1999: Knowledge for development*. New York: Oxford University Press. http://www-wds.worldbank.org/external/default/WDSContentServer/WDSP/IB/1998/11/17/000178830_98111703550058/Rendered/PDF/multiopage.pdf.

Yata, Fahd. 2004. L'explosion de la société civile ou le temps des manifestations. In *La société civile au Maroc*, ed. Maria-Angels Roque, 57-71. Paris: Publisud.

Yehudà Halevi. 1996. *El Cuzari, Edicion facsimil del Ms. 17812 (s. XV) de la Biblioteca Nacional*. Madrid: Biblioteca Nacional.

Yvars, Bernard. 2006. Convergences et divergences du processus d'intégration régionale du Mercosur. Working Papers in Economic and Social Integration, Chaire Jean Monnet en Intégration régionale comparée, Université de Bordeaux. http://integeco.u-bordeaux4.fr/art1.pdf.

Contributors

Mongi Bahloul teaches in the English Department in the Faculty of Letters and Humanities of Sfax.

Samouel Béji is a doctoral student in economics in Paris. His dissertation topic is financial development under globalization.

Houda Ben Hassen is a teaching assistant at the Higher Institute of Industrial Management of Sfax.

Almudena Hasan Bosque is a Spanish language teacher at the Instituto Cervantes in Beirut, Lebanon.

Lotfi Bouzaïane is a professor of higher learning in economics at the Faculty of Economic Sciences and Management at Tunis University.

Abdeljabbar Bsaies is a professor emeritus in the Faculty of Economic Sciences at Tunis University.

Faika Charfi is a professor in the Faculty of Economic Sciences and Management of Sfax.

William D. Coleman is director of the "Globalization and Autonomy" Major Collaborative Research Initiative and Chair in Globalization and Public Policy at the Balsillie School of International Affairs in Canada.

Hachmi Dhaoui is a psychiatrist and psychoanalyst. He is the founding chair of the Groupe tunisien d'études en psychologie analytique.

Yassine Essid is a historian, a professor in the Faculty of Humanities and Social Sciences of Tunis, and chair of the Groupe d'études et de recherches interdisciplinaires sur la Méditerranée (GERIM).

Sonia Fellous has a PhD in religious studies and is a research professor at Centre national de la recherche scientifique (CNRS), Institut de recherches et d'histoire des textes. She teaches at the École doctorale d'histoire des religions, Université de Paris IV Sorbonne, and at INALCO.

Amado A. Millán Fuertes is a professor of anthropology at the Universidad de Zaragoza / President of EIMAH (Equipo de Investigación Multidisciplinar en Alimentación Humana / Multidisciplinary Research Team in Human Food).

Nizard Jouini is a manager at the African Development Bank and a doctoral student in economics (France). His dissertation topic is liberalization of services.

Rulof Kerkhoff is a tutor in the Department of Anthropology at UNED Centro Asociado Catalayud.

Myriem Lakhoua is a musicologist, doctoral student at the École des hautes études en sciences sociales in Paris and, since 2006, a teaching assistant at the Institut Supérieur de Musique de Tunis.

Latifa Lakhdhar is a senior lecturer at the Faculty of Letters and Humanities, Sousse, Tunisia.

Jihen Malek is a teacher at the ISET de Siliana (Tunisia) and a doctoral student in economics (Tunis). Her dissertation topic is industrial policies.

Paula Durán Monfort is an anthropologist and researcher with the UNESCO Chair of Intercultural Dialogue in the Mediterranean in Universitat Rovira i Virgili and EIMAH (Equipo de Investigación Multidisiplinar en Alimentación Humana) in Universidad de Zaragoza.

Rim Ben Ayed Mouelhi is a professor at the Institut supérieur de comptabilité et d'administration des entreprises, Manouba University campus, Tunisia.

Olivia Orozco de la Torre has a PhD in history and civilizations from the European University Institute, Florence, Italy. She is currently coordinator of the Socioeconomic Programme of the Arab Centre in Madrid.

Fatma Sarraj is a manager at Siemens Tunisia and a doctoral student in economics (Tunis). Her dissertation topic is innovation networks.

François Zabbal is a philosopher born in Lebanon. He is a lecturer at the Institut du monde arabe des programmes de conférences et de colloques, and he has been editor-in-chief of the magazine *Qantara* since 1996. He has translated into French eight Arabic novels, including *Les seigneurs de la nuit,* by Salim Barakat, and *L'herbe de la nuit,* by Ibrahim al-Koni. He edits a series at Albin Michel, for which he translated from English *La cité vertueuse d'Alfarabi* by Muhsin Mahdi.

Sameh Zouari is an assistant teacher at the Institute of Advanced Business Studies of Sfax and is writing a dissertation on the issues and impact of liberalization of agricultural and agrofood trade between Tunisia and Europe.

Index

Printed and bound in Canada by Friesens

Set in Syntax and Bembo by Artegraphica Design Co. Ltd.

Text design: George Kirkpatrick

Copy editor: Lesley Erickson

Inexer: Annette Lorek